The Management of Change and Conflict

Selected Readings

Edited by John M. Thomas
and Warren G. Bennis

Penguin Books

Penguin Books Ltd, Harmondsworth,
Middlesex, England
Penguin Books Inc, 7110 Ambassador Road,
Baltimore, Md 21207, USA
Penguin Books Australia Ltd,
Ringwood, Victoria, Australia

First published 1972
This selection copyright © Penguin Books Ltd, 1972
Introduction and notes copyright © Penguin Books Ltd, 1972

Made and printed in Great Britain by
Richard Clay (The Chaucer Press) Ltd,
Bungay, Suffolk
Set in Monotype Times

David Imberg

Penguin Education

The Management of Change and Conflict

Edited by John M. Thomas
and Warren G. Bennis

Penguin Modern Management Readings

General Editor

D. S. Pugh

Contents

Introduction*

The prominence of our subject has been well expressed by Richard Kostelanetz (1968): 'Change is the metaphysic of our age' (p. xiii). Its dramatic impact has been summarized by Bennis (1970a) as follows:

I asked a colleague, who is a scientist, if he could figure out some broad, very general estimates of how much we have changed in certain dimensions. He came up with the following: In the last century, he told me, we have increased our speed of communication by a factor of 10^7, speed of travel by 10^2, our speed of data-handling by 10^6, our ability to control diseases by 10^2. These changes came over the last 100 years. Did anyone suppose that human relations around the world would not be affected to the very roots by such changes? (p. 5).

For the contemporary manager change has become the *Zeitgeist*; its acceleration and growing complexity weigh heavily on the structure, interpersonal dynamics and effectiveness of his organization. As a consequence, the major catch phrases of the day include 'planned organizational change', 'change agentry', and 'organization development'. A major search is underway for ways – new structures and managerial principles – to 'institutionalize organizational flexibility'.

This book is addressed to the problem of managing change in organizations. And because we strongly believe that the effective management of change demands recognition of the interdependence of planned change and conflict, sections have been included which are devoted to the problem of organizational conflict. The purpose of this introduction is not to review principles and strategies in these areas – these are well covered, particularly by the selections in Parts Four to Six. Our goal, rather, is to provide a context for these readings by commenting more generally on the nature of contemporary change and its impact on the organization.

We also stress the importance of understanding what it is that

*We wish to thank our colleague Rolf P. Lynton for his helpful suggestions and Gloria Aniebo and Susan Snyder for their invaluable clerical assistance.

governs a particular orientation to organizational change and conflict – the role of 'paradigms' in influencing strategies for managing these problems. From the perspective of this book, for example, a basic paradigm would be the set of assumptions held about the role of conflict in efforts at planned change. And finally, this introduction discusses an important corollary to the management of change: what we refer to as 'the management of intelligence' – the problem of utilizing knowledge and of orchestrating the specialization and expertise required for coping with the complexity of change thrust upon the organization.

The impact of change on the organization

Clearly, change will have an increasingly profound impact upon the nature of power and authority in the organization. Specialization, for example, has had and will continue to have dramatic effects on the nature of the superior–subordinate relationship.[1] Rational–legal authority has in large measure given way, under the weight of technological complexity, to an authority based upon expertise. The unfortunate consequence of this has been described by Victor Thompson (1963) as follows:

There is a growing gap between the right to decide, which is authority, and the power to do, which is specialized ability. This gap is growing because technological change, with resulting increase in specialization, occurs at a faster rate than the change in cultural definitions of hierarchical roles. . . . the growing imbalance between the rights of authority positions, on the one hand, and the abilities and skills needed in a technological age, on the other, generates tensions and insecurities in the system of authority. Attempts to reduce such insecurity often take the form of behavior patterns which are dysfunctional from the point of view of the organization, although functional enough from that of the insecure official. From the standpoint of the organization such

1. Wilbert Moore (1967) has identified three major sources of specialization as a phenomenon of change in American society:

(a) Population growth and increasing density, providing opportunities for specialization and virtually assuring it.

(b) The rapid growth of knowledge and of rational technique, so that any individual can command only a small portion of the total stock.

(c) The rapid expansion of options in both products and practices, permitting discretionary choices and novel combinations by eclectic mixture (p. 2).

It is the second of these sources, the knowledge revolution, which is of major concern in this essay.

behavior is pathological, and in our analysis we shall refer to it as bureaupathic behavior (pp. 6, 23–4).

According to Dubin (1965) one of the most significant trends in technological change is 'a fundamental shift in industry from the management of people to the management of things' (p. 47). Certainly computer technology and the widespread utilization of 'systems' in organizations are 'things' whose purpose is to rationalize the flow of information and decision-making. It is important for the manager of change to be able to assess their impact on the use of power and authority in his organization.

One effect of introducing computer and systems technology can be the adoption of what Robert Boguslaw (1965) has termed a 'formalist' approach. By this he means that the exercise of power is, in effect, 'screened' by the prevailing technology and tends to become heavily formalized, standardized and aimed at serving the new system at all costs. This single, uniform set of values of keeping the technology going is deceptively attractive. And since these values must be maintained, the primary purpose of authority becomes to check deviance and eliminate any conflict which is perceived to threaten this equilibrium. In Boguslaw's words 'technology-screened power' operates as follows:

The specification of future and current system-states within this orientation characteristically requires an insistence upon a uniformity of perspective, a standardization of language and a consensus of values that is characteristic of highly authoritarian social structures. Non-conforming perspectives, language, and values can be and, indeed, must be excluded as system elements (p. 186).

From another perspective, change is now frequently identified with 'post-industrialism' – the growing dominance of theoretical knowledge and organized intelligence. Brzezinski (1970) prefers the label 'technetronic society': one which is shaped culturally, psychologically, socially and economically by the impact of technology and electronics – particularly in the area of computers and communications (p. 9) (see also Bell, 1967). The impact of these developments means that power will accrue to those organizations (and positions within organizations) which can develop access to and control of the knowledge and information needed for complex problem-solving. The manager's problem in attempting to adapt to this change has been well stated by Donald Michael (1967), the futurist and social planner:

Accumulating evidence from research about management technology indicates that open and free exchange of information throughout the organization is necessary for high production and morale. Power in industrial, university, and government bureaucracies has in part been determined by who has privileged access to information. Certainly this cannot be the case in the future as information becomes more critical to the conduct of society. What is to be the resolution in view of conventional political and bureaucratic processes? (p. 891).

New forms of organizational conflict are destined to emerge as the information explosion continues. An essential task in managing this knowledge revolution will be to invent ways of replacing outmoded 'conventional political and bureaucratic processes' which are, in large measure, the potential source of these conflicts, and at the same time constrain the impulse to over-conformity inherent in the new systems of technologies.

In addition to its impact on the nature of power and authority, change (defined as technological and material advance) appears to be spawning a new ethos of individualism. Schaar (1970) refers to this as '. . . growth of the special modern form of individual self-consciousness as consciousness of separation . . . modern man has determined to live without collective ideals and disciplines and thus without obedience to and reliance upon the authorities that embody, defend, and replenish those ideals' (p. 65).[2] The specialization of the knowledge revolution, the 'use of the meritocratic state' – these dimensions of change are all congruent with an ethic of individualism. Yet, the problem of managing change is also one of managing interdependence and creating settings where this can flourish. Here, then, is a major dilemma for the manager: how to handle an increase in specialization and values centered on self-expression, while at the same time the growth of complex problems demanding the opposite of these forces: interdependence and collaboration. Max Ways (1970), *Fortune*'s astute monitor of social change, has stated the issue this way in a recent article:

2. For a brilliant analysis of this theme, see Slater (1970).

To summarize this summary tone of the American scene, all the main disturbances and anxieties result from the acceleration of trends that are encompassed by two super-trends: (1) that toward a deepening individuality, a wider diversity and more freedom: (2) that toward the increasing interdependence of individuals, organizations, and nations (p. 126).

Strategies of planned organizational change need to be developed within a framework that includes an awareness of the major 'exogenous' forces of social–cultural–political change confronting the organization. The contemporary manager, concerned with managing change and conflict in his organization, can profit from a knowledge of such new concepts as 'post-industrialism' and 'futures research'.[3] And in acquiring this knowledge he cannot afford the illusion of total mastery over change which many technocratic approaches seem to imply; nor can he afford that brand of fatalism which can cause us to give up attempting to implement the 'planning for change' ethos necessary for our organizations. We need to recognize when our idiosyncratic ways of coping with change, although comfortable, are no longer viable and have come to serve ends other than effective adaptation. At the very least we need to appreciate the paradoxical nature of the very notion of planning for change as reflected for example, in Eric Trist's concept of the planner's dilemma.

... the contemporary environment ... is taking on the quality of a turbulent field. ... The planner's dilemma ... may be summarized as follows: the greater the degree of change, the greater the need for planning – otherwise precedents of the past could guide the future; but the greater the degree of uncertainty, the greater the likelihood that plans right today will be wrong tomorrow (quoted in Schmidt, 1970, p. 29).

3. The relevance of futures research, or what is variously referred to as 'futuristics' and 'futurology', for organization planning, has not been well defined. This is a potentially useful area to integrate into the theory and practice of organizational change because of its emphasis on examining developments which will occur in the socio-economic and political environment of the organization. Futures research is distant – twenty to thirty years – is often concerned with macro changes and is also aimed at understanding the systemic consequences of present policies. The best sources are Bell (ed.) (1968), for a general introduction; McHale (1970), for a comprehensive review of the field; and the *Daedalus* issue entitled *Perspectives on Business*, Winter, 1969, for general conjectures and predictions about the future of the business corporation and its environment.

The role of 'paradigms' in organizational change and conflict

There are no universally applicable guideposts which show the way in coping with change and the conflict which invariably accompanies it. Perhaps the closest thing to such a prescription would be that the management of change is above all a function of the way we think about and conceive this problem. We need to make an important distinction between the specific strategies ultimately applied to the problem of change and the governing framework, the 'controlling imagination', which influences and guides the choice of these strategies.

The concept of a 'paradigm' is useful for communicating this perspective, as developed by Thomas Kuhn (1969) in his seminal book *The Structure of Scientific Revolutions*. According to Kuhn, a paradigm has both a subjective meaning and one which is essentially sociological (p. 175). The latter refers to the guidelines and rules of operations which govern approaches to problems and practice as a professional. In the former sense, a paradigm '... stands for the entire constellation of beliefs, values, techniques and so on shared by the members of a given community'. Both these meanings are relevant for understanding how unique orientations toward the management of change evolve.

The concept of a paradigm can be defined, for our purposes, as that dimension of management ideology which informs the posture an organization assumes with respect to change and conflict. A paradigm emerges from the constellation of beliefs and the assumptions which individuals in the organization, particularly key decision-makers, share about the nature of their organization and its environment.

A rather pervasive example of a paradigm of planned organizational change in recent years has been that variously known as the 'human relations' or power-equalization model. Simon (1967) has offered a hypothesis about its origins, advocating the general thesis that developments in administrative theory are often the consequence of change in the social, political and cultural environment of the organization. While generally supportive of the contribution of 'the human relations approach', Simon raises an intriguing question: 'How far is the effectiveness of modern human relations due to a waning of the acceptance of authoritarian behavior and a shift toward less authoritarian personality structures in the general populace?' (p. 89). The question, in turn, raises a hypothesis about the source of resistance to change in organizations: when, in fact, an organizational paradigm reflects a dominant cultural theme, then efforts to change it will be met with considerable resistance. The effective management of change implies having an awareness of the origins of the paradigm presently governing the organization.

Examples abound of the significance of managerial assumptions and the ease with which they can evolve into self-fulfilling prophesies.[4] One of the most revealing is Tannenbaum's study of the nature of the distribution of influence in the organization, an area which is the focus of many efforts at planned organizational change.

Tannenbaum (1968) has shown that a common assumption that the total amount of influence in the organization is fixed is not necessarily true. This assumption, though, means that efforts to change the distribution of influence in the hierarchy are governed by a 'paradigm' which states that if lower levels are given more influence, then by definition this must entail a loss in influence higher up. Tannenbaum suggests that organizations may differ in terms of 'their total amount of control as well as in the relative amount of control exercised by the respective hierarchical echelons' (p. 12).

There are several important concepts which lend more precision to the definition of a paradigm. One is Kenneth Boulding's (1956) idea of *the image*, the subjective content of knowledge. Boulding (1964) makes the important point that we draw from our images of the world inferences about the future (p. 40). Thus, his concept helps us to understand the possible origin of resistance to change, as well as of other modes of adaptation: such conflicts logically arise because of a conflict between the expectations we have about the future and both the goals and reality of change

4. What we have in mind here is similar to the late Douglas McGregor's concept of the managerial 'cosmology', the manager's view of reality (see McGregor, 1967). It is the case that the most lasting import of his famous theory dichotomy is that these should be viewed as assumptions, as part of the managerial 'cosmology', rather than as good or bad or hard or soft, or even distinct styles of supervision.

thrust upon us. Adaptation, therefore, can be facilitated by developing a greater awareness of and a capacity to change images.

A conceptualization similar to Boulding's is Vickers's (1967) 'appreciative system'. This idea applied to an analysis of the policy-making process in organizations is as follows:

Appreciation manifests itself in the exercise through time of mutually related judgements of reality and value. Such judgements disclose what can best be described as a set of readinesses to distinguish some aspects of the situation rather than others and to classify and value these in this way rather than in that.

Vickers intimates that there is more to the management of change than simply establishing new directions, and setting new goals. There is a more basic process which involves changing the appreciative system which governs how the organization and its environment are perceived and judged. An important application of Vickers' concept to the development of a theory and method of changing organizations is provided by the Clark and Krone selection in Part Four.

An important part of the definition of a paradigm as we have been applying this concept, are assumptions characteristically made about the process of future change rather than specific content. Wilbert Moore has demonstrated the influence of these kinds of assumptions in a discussion of the applied role of sociology in the developing nations and what he terms *teleology* and *teleonomy*. These two concepts define two very different key assumptions which can operate at the organizational as well as the societal level in attempts to effect change. *Teleology*, according to Moore, is an orientation which 'involves the identification and implementation of future goals', or what we might refer to as the planned or proactive stance toward change. *Teleonomy*, on the other hand, is an assumption about change which 'involves the "inevitable" future and making preparatory adaptations to it.'

Economic planners in Latin America may assume, for example, that a certain level of population growth is inevitable (teleonomy) and set goals of growth in per capita income accordingly (teleology). Population planners or foreign experts, in contrast, may not assume a teleonomic rate of change in population and may select this as the area in which to concentrate goal-setting and attempt change. As this example demonstrates, the assumptions we make about change – its inevitability, pessimism *v.* optimism, its sources, its acceleration, the image of the future which it conjures – all influence the manager's views and choices about strategic leverages for changing.

Finally, we can say that the metaphors which define the manager's concept of his organization – in a sense the caricature of it he has evolved – are important contributors to the paradigm governing his approach to the management of change. One of Schon's (1963) major points, in his analysis of the innovation process, is that innovation and change occur through the development of new metaphors as concepts used to explain and visualize situations are 'displaced' to a new situation.[5]

The significance of organizational metaphors is revealed, for example, in an opinion voiced by a strong critic of Clark Kerr's university administration to the effect that his real problem (Kerr was formerly the Chancellor of the University of California at Berkeley) was conceiving of the university as a system of 'parking lots' rather than as a 'community of scholars'. (Such a remark, of course, is equally revealing of the way its author conceives of such organizations.)

Scott Greer (1969) has recently offered the proposition that the guiding metaphors in social science have included 'the meteorological, the game, the machine, and the organism' (p. 143). In this analysis, he emphasizes the importance of being guided by a metaphor appropriate to the problem at hand, and that most often we do not self-consciously select a metaphor but rather

5. Warren Bennis, in his paper in Part One, makes the point that the adaptiveness of organizations depends upon finding a correct organizational metaphor, in particular one which might transcend the anachronisms of the metaphor of 'bureaucracy'.
Melvin Lasky (1970) has recently traced the historical and literary origins of perhaps the dominant metaphor of change – revolution. He concludes: 'The tentacular hold of the metaphor of revolution over the imagination of modern man raises far-reaching questions about its deep mythic character. ... Surely it is tantalizing that no other word for radical social change – rebellion, uprising, overturn – has so captivated, so dominated the modern vocabulary' (p. 41).

'take them for granted' and adopt those given by conventions of thought and various disciplines. Professor Greer also points out that each of the four metaphors which he feels have guided theory development in social science handle the problem of change in different ways. For example, in the metaphor of the social machine, change is viewed as 'a matter of either attrition and breakdown, or conscious human tinkering with design and detail; in the organic metaphor it is much less consciously produced and systematically effected' (p. 148).

The role of metaphors in guiding our approaches to change raises several issues. Among the most imperative are: what organizational metaphors are most appropriate now for meeting the challenge posed by the main currents of change; for coping with the revolution in values confronting society? Not an inaccurate summary of this revolution would be that it takes the form of questioning the appropriateness of a particular metaphor which has historically governed the evolution of Western civilization – that of *growth*.[6] The problem according to many prophets of the new values is that technology and organization have always been evaluated in terms of their contribution to this metaphor. In contrast, there now seems to be an emergent and deepening pressure to, as Slater (1970) puts it, 'evaluate the worth of an industrial firm not in terms of the money made or the number of widgets manufactured or sold, or how distended the organization has become, but in terms of how much pleasure or satisfaction has been given to people' (p. 129).

In summary, the important point about paradigms is that when a problem of planned change is confronted, an existing 'set of implicit theories' will be evoked. Schon (1963) has discussed the problem of innovation in terms of how established concepts become relevant for defining new situations, and he makes the following observation: 'Any situation for which we attempt to develop new theories already has theory-structure of a sort' (p. 71). Such 'theory-structures' can become the genesis of our strategies for managing change rather than any new rational assessment of the situation; they often generate the solutions ultimately selected. Although there is an appreciation of this process in most theories of planned change, a key assumption of

6. For an historical analysis of its pervasive influence, see Nisbet (1969).

this introduction is that too rarely are our 'implicit theories of changing' informed by an adequate understanding of the major forces for change in the environment of the organization.

Paradigms in use: the problem of managing conflict

One strategy of conflict management which seems to confront basic assumptions about the relationship of conflict with change has been termed 'the absorption of protest' by Ruth Leeds (1968). This paradigm allows an organization to offset the potentially destructive effects of dissent by admitting the protest group as a sub-unit of the organization. In this way the protest group attains legitimation in exchange for its acceptance of the legitimacy of the larger system. Other key dimensions of the 'absorption of protest' paradigm are:

1. A reliance on the top to recognize the potential for the protesting 'enclave' to contribute to organization goals. To be effective, this paradigm requires a lessening of 'trained incapacity', a widening of 'perspectivistic orientation' as one goes up the hierarchy of the organization. Or in Leeds' words: 'With its broader, more substantive, perspective the top is more amenable to innovation than the middle hierarchy, especially when faced with internal weakness or external challenge' (p. 204).

2. Accessibility of the protest group to the top: a communication channel has to be established as a vehicle for the protest enclave to gain visibility for its program. Here we have a specific instance of how a more restrictive paradigm of conflict management could suppress the useful potential in a dissenting group. If the manager conceives of such a development only as an instance of interpersonal tension, or intergroup conflict, he may adopt a strategy of conflict resolution which could be detrimental to organizational innovation. Put another way, if meaningful change is to occur it may, in fact, mean that a particular group or faction will 'lose', and another 'win' in terms of their respective images of what the future should be. Strategies which speak of 'problem-solving' or consensus, and attempt to deny the reality of 'win–lose' conditions with respect to change, are somewhat limited in this sense.

3. A model of the situation which can help determine the implications of the protest for the organization's central policies. This includes two images: the impact the organization would prefer the protest to have as against what it will allow; and similarly, the impact the protest group feels it should have as against what it is willing to accept. Within the framework of these four parameters, negotiation occurs between the protest group and the organization aimed at defining the ultimate consequences of the issue of dissent.

Bargaining occurs in this paradigm not over the legitimacy of dissent itself, but over the amount of impact dissent is to have. The situation might usefully be interpreted as conflict over the amount of change which is to take place rather than simply inter-group tension. The distinction is subtle; however, management's definition of the situation has much to do with the strategies ultimately adopted. And those strategies, in turn, have much to do with the extent to which conflict can be creatively utilized in the development of meaningful change.

The *absorption of protest* concept provides a structural way of realizing the positive potential of dissent while yet accommodating the organization's essential goals and policies. It is a paradigm for managing conflict which recognizes the interdependency between conflict and change. Other paradigms for handling protest within the organization do not recognize this possibility and can be invidious. An excellent example is what Robert Thomson (1968) has termed *the domestication of dissent*. This dynamic, which Thomson has applied to an analysis of White House policy-making on Vietnam, is also a way of absorbing nonconformity, but with the result of nullifying its impact on policy and change.

Thomson describes this paradigm as one where the desires of dissenters to 'stay on board' and the conscience of non-dissenters coagulate to create a predictable 'house' protest. His description of George Ball, the former Under-Secretary of State, graphically portrays this paradigm in action: 'Once Mr Ball began to express doubts, he was warmly institutionalized: he was encouraged to become the inhouse devil's advocate on Vietnam' (p. 49).[7]

As Hirschman (1969) has conceived it in a recent essay, an

organization can be more or less sensitive to either the threat of individuals leaving it (exit) or a steady expression of internal dissatisfaction directed at authority (voice). When an organization is in need of change because of a growing atrophy in its policy-formation capacity, *exit* and *voice* are the strategies of protest which are aroused in some of its members – individuals dissent by leaving, or they remain and voice protest internally. The 'domestication of dissent' syndrome is one where voice has become so institutionalized that real change might be better served by leaving the organization. The conflict between dissenters and authority might have to culminate in 'exit' if the cause of protest, the new course of action, is not being attended to. As the example cited by Thomson and Reedy shows, 'voice' as a paradigm of protest can be made powerless. The predictability of the conflicting point of view is easily rationalized so long as the impulse to remain a member of the team is the overriding consideration, so long as there is little inclination to invoke the 'exit' option.

Important diagnostic questions need to be asked about organizations in need of change and renewal. And perhaps the most significant of these is how internal dissent demanding change is implicitly managed. What is the operative paradigm in these situations: *the absorption of protest or the domestication of dissent*?

7. George Reedy (1971) corroborates this example in a recent symposium on *The Presidency:* 'During President Johnson's Administration I watched George Ball play the role of devil's advocate with respect to foreign policy. The Cabinet would meet and there would be an overwhelming report from Robert McNamara, another overwhelming report from Dean Rusk, another overwhelming report from McGeorge Bundy. Then five minutes would be set aside for George Ball to deliver his dissent, and, because they expected him to dissent, they automatically discounted whatever he said. This strengthened them in their own convictions because the Cabinet members could quite honestly say: "We heard both sides of this issue discussed." Well they heard it with wax in their ears. I think that the moment you appoint an official devil's advocate you solidify the position he is arguing against' (pp. 12–13).

The importance of a situational perspective

An effective paradigm incorporates what might be termed a 'situational' or 'contingency' framework, a point of view reflected in much of the current theoretical and empirical work in organization theory. There is a primary emphasis upon diagnosis and the assumption that it is self-defeating to adopt a 'universally' applicable set of principles and guidelines for effecting change or managing conflict. The major contributions to the development of this paradigm have been the essay by Bennis (1961) on leadership style and authority; Vroom's (1960) study demonstrating that effective supervision was contingent on subordinate personality; Schein's (1965) conceptualization of 'complex man' as a basis for assumptions about individual motivation in the organization; Woodward's (1965) demonstration that organization structure is a function of technology; Fiedler's (1967) 'contingency theory of leadership', relating group effectiveness to task, leader–member interaction, power and leadership style; and Lawrence and Lorsch's (1967) studies of the influence of the organization's environment on the differentiation and integration of its functional units.

The area of power in organizations is one where a contingency paradigm has been relatively lacking in the design of strategies for managing change and conflict. In many theories of organization development, assumptions about the relationship of power to change and conflict appear at best ambivalent, at worst deficient. These approaches have traditionally made assumptions about the importance of power-equalization, trust and, at some level, commonality of goals. But the capacity to conceive change and conflict politically, that is, in terms of the dynamics of power, is essential to the effective management of these issues. And the nature of contemporary change – from the revolution in values characterized by rampant individualism and self expression to an increasing technological specialization to, in general, more and more pluralism – is such that assumptions about common goals and purposes, even though desirable, may be no longer tenable.

The analysis of organizational conflict by March and Simon (1958) is a significant example of the importance of a political perspective. They categorize conflict strategies into 'bargaining' and 'analytic' processes; bargaining approaches are appropriate when 'disagreement over goals is taken as fixed', whereas analytic processes require an assumption that objectives are shared or 'that disagreement over sub-goals can be mediated by references to common goals'. Bargaining is often not a part of the conflict paradigms in many normative theories of planned organization change. Their 'guiding assumptions' are inclined to be limited and non-situational, often based upon the universality of trust formation, 'problem-solving', consensus, and openness.[8] These perspectives need to be supplemented with a capacity to conceive problems in terms of the realities of partisanship and the use of power.

The contemporary organization must necessarily adapt to change by constantly monitoring the relevance and legitimacy of its present goals; and change almost invariably disturbs the power equilibrium in the organization by calling goals into question, unsettling present formulas for distributing resources, and shaking

8. Bennis makes the point in his paper in Part One that consensus and trust strategies evolved from face-to-face conflict situations where they were most likely to be effective. Change has moved the plane of confrontation away from what he terms 'micro' situations to more 'macro-power' issues.

Also, we are not advocating in this discussion that every conflict situation where common goals cannot be assumed is what Schelling (1960) calls a condition of 'pure conflict' of the zero-sum type. A valid perspective, and one given considerable credibility through applied behavioral science, is that many zero-sum situations are self-fulfilling prophecies and with effort (third party intervention, for example), this 'definition of the situation' can be changed.

Paul Lawrence's fifteen-year retrospective commentary on his *Harvard Business Review* classic, 'How to deal with resistance to change', also makes a case for the political perspective. In discussing the current utility of human relations and participative approaches he notes in 1970: 'I am more aware than in 1954 of the limits of such approaches. They do not always enable management to prevent situations from developing in which some individuals win while others lose.

'The values lost as skills become obsolete cannot always be replaced. The company's earnings may go up but the percentage payouts from even an enlarged "pie" have to be recalculated, and then the relative rewards shift. In these situations enlightened problem solving will not completely displace old-fashioned bargaining, and better communication will only clarify the hard core realities' (p. 196).

the status structure. If the direction of change is towards greater goal disparity where a bargaining, political perspective on these conflicts would be appropriate, March and Simon (1958) have shown why 'analytic' paradigms persist:

Bargaining almost necessarily places strains on the status and power systems in the organization . . . furthermore, *bargaining acknowledges and legitimizes heterogeneity of goals in the organization* . . . Because of these consequences of bargaining . . . we predict that almost all disputes in the organization will be defined as problems in analysis, . . . that such reactions will persist even when they appear to be inappropriate, that *there will be a greater explicit emphasis on common goals where they do not exist than where they do, and that bargaining* (*when it occurs*) *will frequently be concealed within an analytic framework* (p. 131; our emphases).

Still another theme of contemporary change is relevant to the March and Simon argument. The important interface problems for organizations are shifting with the pace of technological change away from the internal, intra-organizational to organization–environment and inter-organizational issues. Kahn *et al.* have found, for example, that role conflict and job tension are high for individuals in the organization occupying such 'boundary' or 'interface' positions. March and Simon (1958) raise the possibility that some tension may arise as organizations which have assiduously cultivated an 'analytic' paradigm for the management of internal conflict now find themselves facing an increasingly complex set of relationships with other organizations which require skills associated with a 'bargaining' paradigm. In their view: '. . . there will generally be more pressure toward the use of analytic techniques within the organization than in relations between organizations', and 'the literature on inter-organizational conflict has been particularly concerned with the resolution of conflict through bargaining processes – with who gets what' (p. 131).

This hypothesis at least illustrates the importance of a situational perspective and the realization that the management of conflict should accommodate bargaining *and* analytic assumptions. The organization confronts both internal and external problems of change. And its capacity to respond effectively to the conflict which such problems create can be highly dependent upon its flexibility in adopting bargaining and analytic paradigms, and sorting out their appropriateness for situations of *inter*-organizational and *intra*-organizational conflict.

The management of intelligence

Change is producing certain effects which necessitate adaptation on the part of the organization. In a broad sense, the following can be stated, all related to the post-industrial knowledge and values revolutions:

1. Change is increasing the complexity of the relationship between the organization and its environment.

2. Change is increasing the problem of maintaining internal organizational solidarity, of coordination; values and goals are becoming more diverse, more pluralistic and conflicting.

3. Change is producing a greater impulse toward rationality in organization decision-making and operations.

As Wilensky (1967, p. 38) has recently pointed out, each of these impacts increases considerably the amount of resources and energy which the organization must expend on the intelligence function.

As a consequence, the problem of managing change can usefully be viewed as the problem of 'managing intelligence'; and this in turn, has unique forms of organizational conflict associated with it. The importance of this issue was noted earlier in our discussion of the effects of change on the nature of power and authority in the organization. Knowledge and information increasingly determine the base of power in the organization as we enter an age of post-industrialism. The conflicts include the following:

1. The specialization and expertise evolving from the knowledge revolution mean potential conflicts in developing the interdisciplinary ethos required for complex problem-solving; a related problem has been posed by Bell (1969) in his prognosis of the effects of a post-industrial society: 'Conflicts will arise between men trained in the new intellectual technology versus the politicians' (p. 52).

2. More important, perhaps, is the conflict emerging between the

prominent value changes in society and the knowledge revolution.

The values revolution has several dimensions: a rejection of rationality, of the 'evils' of science and technology, of the metaphor of progress; demands, in particular, from newer members that their organizations begin to pursue a broader range of goals appropriate to social problems; and even a kind of metaphysical anguish because knowledge is no longer believable as an inevitable creator of harmony. As John Schaar (1970) puts it, this is a root cause of the crisis of legitimization facing society: 'The social and political world becomes " unfrozen ", as it were, moveable by skill and power, for it is seen that there is no necessity in any given arrangement of things.'

The following discussion is based upon the assumption that an effective paradigm for the management of change is one which is oriented to the 'management of intelligence'. And while Wilensky (1967) defines organizational intelligence primarily in an informational sense – 'the problem of gathering, processing, interpreting and communicating the technical and political information needed in the decision-making process' (p. 3) – for our purposes, this concept will also include the important 'process' of knowledge utilization in the organization. A noted planning theorist commented recently that 'it may now be a fatal flaw if we are indeed into a new epoch with our basic institutions structured to respond to crisis ("management by exception") rather than to anticipate what is coming' (see Ewald, 1970, p. 32). A prescription for correcting this incongruity certainly demands comprehensive planning, but above all an ability on the part of the organization to utilize the knowledge and intelligence which, if we accept the concept of post-industrialism, is now the hallmark of change.

The management of intelligence requires the collection and utilization of new knowledge required for decision-making and planned change. The problem is one of design, of developing a metaphor of the organization as an information processing system. The criterion of performance is similar to that defined by Galbraith (1969): '. . . the information processing capacity of an organization must be equal to the information processing requirement of the task' (p. 11).[9] A review of the literature reveals a number of principles which should govern our practice with respect to the intelligence problem.

First, planned change requires that major questions be asked and resolved which transcend the problem of obtaining information about changes in the environment of the organization. Stafford Beer (1970) has stated the issue as follows:

... the problem of information management is now a problem of filtering and refining a massive overload – for all of us, whether citizens, firms, institutions or governments. We might well say that it is a problem not so much of data acquisition as of right storage; not so much of storage as of fast retrieval; not so much of retrieval as of proper selection; not so much of selection as of identifying wants; not so much of knowing wants as of recognizing needs ... (p. 46).

The 'intelligence problem' for effecting change, then, is a complex chain and has to include the assembly of information and knowledge about several 'ultimate' issues. How do we know 'wants' and then recognize 'needs'? Clearly, we need a form of 'meta' intelligence to guide us in selecting intelligence about the changing environment.

Second, it is important to underscore a point made earlier – a major change facing the organization is the rapidity with which the possession of information means power in the organization (see Michael, 1967; Forrester, 1965). It should be emphasized that information affects power in the organization in two ways: (a) by creating new sources of power since control of information means influence; and (b) conversely, by threatening existing power. Broadly speaking, the use of more intelligence means that some organizational roles will become more rationalized, and as Michel Crozier (1968) has observed with respect to the French bureaucracy:

... each individual, each group and category within an organization, will always struggle to prevent the rationalization and maintain the

9. Galbraith makes the point that the information processing requirements of an organizational design are a function of three variables: (a) the degree of uncertainty concerning the task; (b) the number of elements – department, specialities, etc. – relevant to decision-making; and (c) the degree of interdependence among the elements necessary for decision-making.

unpredictability of their own task and function. Their power, the influence they can wield, depend, as we have demonstrated, on the amount of discretion and finally, on the uncertainty they have to face (p. 360).

The capacity to keep intelligence and rationality from having an impact on one's role – maintaining uncertainty – can itself be an important source of power in the organization.

A third issue in managing intelligence concerns the type of information obtained for the purpose of decision-making and planned change. In his seminal *The Nerves of Government*, Karl Deutsch (1963) makes the point that any organization, political party or government requires what he terms 'an internal intelligence function' enabling it to obtain a continual flow of accurate information about itself (p. 159). Yet, most organizations do not systematically gather this information, let alone utilize it for the planning of change.

In beginning this process, the manager should be cognizant of the important distinction made by Katz and Kahn (1966, p. 159) between *operational feedback*, *operational research* and *systemic research*. Operational feedback refers to information processes which in most organizations are a routine function – number of units turned out, cost data, descriptive information serving the need for general control of operations. Operational research is more explanatory than descriptive, but is confined to gathering intelligence and applying knowledge to the improvement of the output, the product, of the organization. It is oriented specifically to in-depth studies and the re-design of the *technology* of the system. Systemic research, on the other hand, seeks to gather intelligence about the organization as a social system and as an entity in interaction with a rapidly changing environment. In the words of Katz and Kahn:

Systemic research, like operational research, seeks new information, but its target is the functioning of the total system in relation to its changing environment. . . . Where operational research concentrates upon improving technical aspects of production, systemic research explores the organizational changes which technical improvement would produce, including both the intended and the usually unanticipated consequences of the technical change (p. 251).

An effective paradigm for the management of change requires above all a capacity for systemic research aimed at diagnosis of change in the institutional setting of the organization. Howard McMahon, President of Arthur D. Little, has referred recently to the coming need for corporate managers 'to submit to social as well as fiscal audits'. He feels these will emerge 'as corporations become convinced that accountability to their employees, customers, and the community at large is as crucial to corporate survival as profits'.[10] The point is that intelligence about the nature of the organization as a social system should be combined with two other types of diagnosis if effective planned change is to be realized: (a) intelligence about the general, probable nature of change; and (b) continued monitoring of the precise relationship of the organization with its environment.

Fourth, in addition to the problem of how to develop 'systemic' intelligence, it is critical to have some awareness of the assumptions which influence the utilization or non-utilization of knowledge: how intelligence is or is not converted into innovation for the organization.[11] Charles Frankel (1968) has recently given us an important framework for analysing these assumptions. He makes the point that any effort to translate social theory into social action, where we are concerned with the organization as the social unit, depends upon assumptions about the importance of an ideal goal, an ultimate objective (Platonism); upon our ability to be relatively predictable – have valid theories – about human nature and social phenomena (conservatism); upon the extent to which the context, historical evolution and immutable laws of social evolution constrains attempts at social invention (historicism); and, finally, upon whether change is best launched in a simplified way without grand theories or abstract ideals – beginning 'where the pain is actually felt' rather than 'with a blueprint of *what ought to be*' (piece-meal social engineering) (p. 15).

Each of these four sets of assumptions – in our terminology 'paradigms' which govern the choices made available in planned change – has its pluses and minuses. An effective paradigm would be one which could integrate what is valuable in each. Frankel's

10. *New York Times*, Sunday, February 14, 1971.
11. For an overview and generalized model of the utilization process, see Havelock and Benne (1967).

remarks about the functions of the four are revealing in this respect. On Platonism:

The Platonic view has exercised its appeal because it appears to state what must be stated if social action deserves to be called rational. It states what the action is all about. It states an ultimate objective (p. 8.).

On conservatism:

It points to certain fundamental facts about the relation of theory to practice. The first of these facts is a psychological fact about human beings; we are all more traditional then we know. To make changes we begin, inevitably, with where we are and what we have been; and where we are and what we have been have a more important influence than anything else on where we can go. Proposals for social change that do not take this fact into account are bound to lead to disappointment or self-deception (p. 11).

On historicism:

To translate theory into action we need more . . . than general theories about human nature or society and more than close empirical knowledge of limited ranges of facts. We need to be aware of the more important dynamics of change and the probable evolution of controlling institutions and social attitudes. Without such awareness, social theory remains just theory and social inventiveness becomes an exercise in gimmickry (p. 14).

On piece-meal social engineering:

Born out of opposition to other philosophies of politics it is not Utopian – as Platonism is; it does not distrust rational human efforts to rearrange inherited social institutions – as conservatism does; and it does not assume – as does Marxism – that all problems are of a single piece and that one key unlocks them all (p. 15).

If the synthesizing of these diverse points is too difficult, an organization or individual manager can profit from using Frankel's typology to assess which paradigm – Platonism, conservatism, historicism, or piece-meal engineering – is *de facto* the dominant influence in guiding planned change. With this framework one might hypothesize, for example, that the field of organization development has been governed primarily by the 'piece-meal social engineering' model. A basic assumption of this essay is that the management of change could profit from greater use of a paradigm similar to Frankel's 'historicism', particularly if this is also coupled with what we might term a 'futures' paradigm derived from the legitimate new and promising work in this field (see McHale, 1970 and Bell, 1968).

We have to this point been concerned with that dimension of the 'management of intelligence' related to the way the organization utilizes knowledge and information. We now turn to the 'people' dimension – the problem of managing the specialists who provide the knowledge utilized in the planning and implementation of change.

The essence of this dilemma and its potential for generating organizational conflict is well stated in these observations by Bennis (1970b) and Thompson (1967) respectively:

Like C. P. Snow, I feel that there is a growing separation of two isolated cultures. However, I speak not of the chasm between scientist and humanist, but of that between men with knowledge who lack power and men with power who lack knowledge (p. 39).

When ideologies deny legitimation to laymen, but the realities of interdependence require that laymen be incorporated in the dominant coalition, conflict is likely (p. 139).

Change demands that we develop an all-important, yet elusive, interdisciplinary ethos. And this is less a problem in structural design, and more a very complex issue in group dynamics – organizing intellectuals, experts and professionals who, because of their training often have little inclination to grasp a systems approach to tasks. In addition, this aspect of the management of intelligence also involves the complex interpersonal dynamics between the expert and manager, or policy maker.[12]

Galbraith (1967) mentions one implication of this problem in discussing the nature of motivation in what he terms the corporate technostructure: 'Specialized knowledge and its coordination have now, as we have seen, become the decisive factor in economic success. This requires that men work in groups. And

12. See Churchman and Schainblatt (1966) for an excellent analytic framework for this problem.

power passes to these groups' (p. 141). The motivation of specialists derives from an overarching identification with a body of knowledge and a methodology which may not be compatible with the need for the organization to change goals and reorder priorities. Moreover, the motivational structure of experts can lapse into an identification with means, with technique, rather than with ends. Alvin Gouldner (1961) once coined the term 'Hamletic strategy' to refer to a related phenomenon – the tendency of 'engineering' approaches in planned change to be obsessively concerned with data-gathering, methodology and analysis, in contrast to action.[13]

The impact of change on the organization manifests itself in terms of (a) more differentiation and specialization of function and role within the organization; and (b) the increasing salience and complexity of *inter*-organizational relationships – the 'organization-set' (see Evan, 1967). Since our specific concern at this point is the problem of managing specialists and what constitutes effective interaction between the expert and the policy-maker, it is important to trace the origins of this issue in these two themes. An organization's way of relating to its 'organization-set' – its exchanges with other organizations in its environment – influences the form of differentiation (division of tasks) within the organization between experts and policy-makers.

An example of this interaction is provided in the study by Litwak and Hylton (1962) of the inter-organizational dynamics of the Community Chest. The authors of this study point out that a focal, coordinating organization such as the Chest has both a need to cooperate with related organizations (agencies), and a need to preserve its autonomy and ability to engage in conflict when such behaviour is required (see Gouldner, 1961). Mechanisms need to be instituted to maintain the latter, and what emerges from this interorganizational requirement is a differentiation of function between professional experts and 'lay' policy-

13. In a fascinating description of the culture of bureaucracy in Washington, Taylor Branch (1970) recently quoted an official in HEW as follows: 'Everyone feels frustrated, telling himself that if they had a little more information, then they could really do something. So everyone wants to "get a handle on something" or find "a few salient facts with wide typicality", or "get a new scope" on inputs and outputs . . .' (p. 14).

makers in the Community Chest. This process is spelled out in the following comment of Litwak and Hylton (1962):

Another possible procedure for maintaining legitimate areas of conflict is to have a division of labor *within* the co-ordinating agency, with one group dealing with areas of co-operation and the other with areas of conflict and autonomy. Thus the budget committee of the community chest is frequently dominated by lay people who exercise considerable control over fund raising and allocation. Problems of fund allocations frequently lead to questions about the respective merits of various services, however, and the non-professional members may lean heavily on their staff experts. The professional members are frequently educated to accept the legitimacy of multiple and competing forms of service and act as a barrier to demands for merger *or premature resolution of conflict* (p. 414) [our italics – Eds.].

Interestingly then, the need to preserve conflict with its environment can lead the organization to adopt a unique structural arrangement between its experts and managers. And if this relationship is not maintained – if conflict ensues because of a breakdown in this differentiation – considerable autonomy may be lost by the organization – at least in situations similar to that examined by the Litwak and Hylton case. In this example the importance of our second dimension of the management of intelligence, managing experts and their linkages with others in the organization, is highlighted because of its potential impact on maintaining the integrity of existing *inter*-organizational relationships.

Robert Wood (1970) has observed the growing tendency of professionals in public bureaucracies, in particular those at lower levels, to confuse policy making with professional parochialism. This, combined with a lack of comprehensive strategy at the top – the tendency to become mired down with excessive details, rather than provide overall policy guidance – can cause near disaster for the invention and implementation of new alternatives to social problems. Wood's observations are instructive:

Today, the danger is not so much that administration policy will be carried out grudgingly as that it will be carried out excessively. As a disposition to handle operational detail grows at the top of the executive branch and a disposition to dabble in policy-making infects the lower ranks, the uncertainty of bureaucratic performance increases (p. 47).

Often policy is created almost accidentally at the operational level as a by-product of occupational creativity, since *the decision-maker's preoccupation can be with his profession's values, not program objectives* (p. 48) [our italics – Eds.].

The new spirit of policy activism combined with the old tradition of occupational provincialism is a disaster for effective government (p. 48).

A similar perspective has been provided by Kissinger (1969) in his analysis of the use of experts in governmental decision-making. He notes that 'one of the characteristics of a society based on specialization is the enormous work load of its top personnel' (p. 157). One effect can be an unhealthy dependence by the top on subordinate definitions of problems.

When the conditions spelled out by Wood and Kissinger define an organization's policy-making and planned change paradigm, severe pathologies in carrying out these efforts develop. The problem is a failure at the top to grasp what it means to manage specialists. Above all, this increasingly important dimension of the management of intelligence should not be looked at merely as the problem of providing administrative support for experts. The responsibility for setting new goals, for planning change, cannot be carried out effectively without some responsibility assumed by the top in establishing the knowledge utilization strategy through which new policy alternatives should arise.

Obviously, this does not mean that the effective manager of change must be a twentieth-century da Vinci; the complexity of the knowledge revolution precludes this. What is required to prevent Victor Thompson's condition of 'bureaupathology' and those analysed by Wood and Kissinger, is a major involvement in defining the criteria and overall philosophy necessary to guide the organization's management of intelligence. In industrial organizations, in particular, this has come to be known as developing a corporate strategy.[14] This means establishing such a paradigm collaboratively with specialists, which can serve as a framework for systematically integrating their efforts. Without this, as Kissinger states, 'The specialization of functions turns into a caricature when decision-making and the pursuit of

14. An innovative consulting philosophy based upon this concept has been developed by *The Boston Consulting Group*, Boston, Mass.

knowledge on which it is based are treated as completely separate activities, by either executives or intellectuals' (p. 168).

Robert Lane (1966) has argued that we live in an increasingly 'knowledgeable society', and that new intelligence more or less in and of itself serves as a major pressure for change: '. . . knowledge – discovered, organized and communicated by professional men – creates a pressure for policy change with a force all its own. Knowledge (and what is regarded as knowledge) is pressure even without pressure groups, and without reference to an articulated forensic ideology' (p. 661). But the question of utilization must not go unanswered and involves more than the design of an appropriate information processing system, or a leadership style which allows knowledge to be 'discovered, organized and communicated by professional men'. For these conditions to emerge, a particular set of attitudes and assumptions about the relationship of knowledge to practice, about the role of intelligence for change is required by top management. To conclude this discussion, we can do no better than quote Wilensky's (1967) excellent study of the role of intelligence in organizational decision-making:

Some gains in the quality of intelligence are possible from a reorganization of the intelligence function, but . . . much of an organization's defense against information pathologies lies . . . *in the top executive's attitude toward knowledge* – a product of his own education and orientation, his exposure to independent sources, his capacity to break through the wall of conventional wisdom (p. 174; our emphasis [Ed.]).

Conclusions

What we can discern about the nature of change and its likely impact on corporations says something about the deficiencies of many contemporary approaches to planned organizational change. In general, these have tended to be primarily oriented to the internal dynamics of the organization, aimed at contributing to the established goals of economic and organizational growth, and relatively unconcerned with affected constituencies other than the formal members of the organization.

Yet the nature of change is such that there are increasing pressures in the socio-political-cultural environment of the corporation for new forms of planned change which will make the corporation more responsive to external interest groups. Moreover, even when we consider the long, and for the most part vital, history of efforts to provide greater participation and democracy within the organization, it appears that we may now be entering an era when more fundamental issues in the internal government of organizations need to be confronted. As far as the US is concerned, Professor Robert Dahl has recently argued:

One of the unheralded miracles of American business is that during a period when many traditional systems of authority are passionately contested – in government, law enforcement, prisons, churches, education, and the military, for some examples – the internal government of the large corporation seems to have escaped all serious challenge.[15]

The signs of this challenge are now inherent in the revolution in values recently discussed by such authors as Philip Slater in his *The Pursuit of Loneliness* and Charles Reich in *The Greening of America*. The message in this for those of us involved in the field of organization development is that our paradigms of planned change need to be broadened to account for the goals and concerns of outside interest groups and to incorporate models of management which are more innovative and far-reaching in their definition of who governs the corporation. Without such an effort, which we believe is based upon a realistic 'image' of the forces of change now present in the environment, the contemporary organization will no doubt be forced to change in ways it will find odious.

The design of this volume

The Readings in Parts One and Two reflect key assumptions in the design of this volume.

1. The management of planned change and organizational conflict should be informed by greater awareness and understanding of the major social, political and cultural 'revolutions' of the day and their probable 'futures'. The selections in Part One are designed with this purpose in mind. It is our hope they will whet the appetite of students of management for further reading in

15. 'Citizens of the corporation', *New York Times*, Wednesday, March 17 1971.

these areas. In the introduction to Part One we mention a number of additional works.

2. The management of change and conflict should be informed by 'images' and models of organization developed by relevant and current perspectives in organization theory. Several new contributions are represented by the readings in Part Two. These include a conceptualization of the organization as an open system where the nature of its environmental transactions is the critical dimension; an analysis of the problem of adapting an organization to become more pluralistic, thus enabling it to pursue multiple new goals; and a critique of the much-discussed matrix overlay form of organization structure for managing change.

The remaining selections in the volume in Parts Three to Six are organized into (a) more theoretical discussions of issues and concepts in organizational change and conflict, and (b) 'theories of practice': methodologies and strategies for managing these problems.

References

BEER, S. (1970), 'Managing modern complexity', in *The Management of Information and Knowledge*, US Government Printing Office.

BELL, D. (1967), 'Note on the post-industrial society', *The Public Interest*, no. 6, pp. 24–35.

BELL, D. (ed.) (1968), *Towards the Year 2000: Work in Progress*, Daedalus Library, Houghton Mifflin.

BELL, D. (1969), 'Review of an MIT Alumni Seminar', in *Technology Review*, February.

BENNIS, W. G. (1961), 'A revisionist theory of leadership', *Harvard Business Review*, Jan.–Feb.

BENNIS, W. G. (1970a), 'An era of change: the consequences', *MRI Quarterly*, Fall.

BENNIS, W. G. (1970b), 'The failure and promise of the social sciences', *Technology Review*, Oct./Nov.

BOGUSLAW, R. (1965), *The New Utopians*, Prentice-Hall.

BOULDING, K. (1956), *The Image*, University of Michigan Press.

BOULDING, K. (1964), *The Meaning of the 20th Century*, Harper Colophon.

BRANCH, T. (1970), 'We're all working for the Penn Central', *Washington Monthly*, November.

BRZEZINSKI, Z. (1970), *Between Two Ages: America in the Technocratic Era*, Viking Press.

CHURCHMAN, C. W., and SCHAINBLATT, A. H. (1966), 'The manager and the researcher: a dialectic of implementation', *Management Science*, vol. 12, no. 1.

CROZIER, M. (1968), 'Bureaucratic organizations and the evolution of industrial society', in A. Etzioni (ed.), *A Sociological Reader on Complex Organizations*, Holt, Rinehart & Winston.

DEUTSCH, K. (1963), *The Nerves of Government*, Free Press.

DUBIN, R. (1965), 'Supervision and productivity: empirical findings and theoretical situations', in R. Dubin (ed.), *Leadership and Productivity*, Chandler Publishing Co.

EVAN, W. (1967), 'The organization-set', in J. D. Thompson (ed.), *Organizational Design*, University of Pittsburgh Press.

EWALD, W. (1970), 'A third force to deal with change', *Center Magazine*, vol. 3, no. 6.

FIEDLER, F. (1967), *A Contingency Theory of Leadership*, McGraw-Hill.

FORRESTER, J. (1965), 'A new corporate design', *Industrial Management Review*, vol. 17, no. 1, pp. 5–18.

FRANKEL, C. (1968), 'The relation of theory to practice', in H. Stein (ed.), *Social Theory and Social Invention*, Case-Western Reserve Press.

GALBRAITH, J. K. (1967), *The New Industrial State*, Houghton Mifflin.

GALBRAITH, J. K. (1969), 'Organization design: an information processing view', *Sloan School of Management Working Paper*, no. 425–69.

GOULDNER, A. (1961), 'Engineering and clinical approaches to consulting', in W. G. Bennis, K. Benne and R. Chin (eds.), *The Planning of Change*, Holt, Rinehart & Winston, pp. 643–52.

GREER, S. (1969), *The Logic of Social Inquiry*, Aldine.

HAVELOCK, R., and BENNE, K. (1967), 'An exploratory study of knowledge utilization', in G. Watson (ed.), *Concepts for Social Change*, NTL Publications, pp. 47–70.

HIRSCHMAN, A. (1969), *Exit, Voice and Loyalty*, Harvard University Press.

KATZ, D., and KAHN, R. L. (1966), *The Social Psychology of Organizations*, Wiley.

KISSINGER, H. A. (1969), 'The policymaker and the intellectual', in T. E. Cronin and S. D. Greenberg (eds.), *The Presidential Advisory System*, Harper & Row.

KOSTELANETZ, R. (1968), *Beyond Left and Right: Radical Thought For Our Time*, William Morrow & Co.

KUHN, T. (1969), *The Structure of Scientific Revolutions*, University of Chicago Press.

LANE, R. (1966), 'The decline of politics and ideology in a knowledgeable society', *American Sociological Review*, October.

LASKY, M. (1970), 'The birth of a metaphor', *Encounter*, March.

LAWRENCE, P. (1970), 'How to deal with resistance to change', in G. Dalton, P. Lawrence and L. Greiner (eds.), *Organizational Change and Development*, Dorsey Press.

LAWRENCE, P., and LORSCH, J. W. 1967), *Organization and Environment*, Harvard University Press.

LEEDS, R. (1968), 'The absorption of protest', in W. G. Bennis, K. Benne and R. Chin (eds.), *The Planning of Change*, Holt, Rinehart & Winston.

LITWAK, E., and HYLTON, L. F. (1962), 'Interorganizational analysis: a hypothesis on coordinating agencies', *Administrative Science Quarterly*, vol. 6, no. 4, pp. 395–420.

MARCH, J., and SIMON, H. (1958), *Organizations*, Wiley.

McGREGOR, D. (1967), *The Professional Manager*, McGraw-Hill.

McHALE, J. (1970), 'Typological survey of futures research', *NIMH*.

MICHAEL, D. (1967), 'Social engineering and the future environment', *American Psychologist*, vol. 22, November.

MOORE, W. (1970), 'Changes in American social structure', *Denver Law Review*, vol. 44, Fall.

NISBET, R. (1969), *Social Change and History*, Oxford University Press.

REEDY, G. (1971), 'Symposium on the Presidency', *Center Magazine*, vol. 4, no. 1.

REICH, C. (1970), *The Greening of America*, Allen Lane the Penguin Press.

SCHAAR, J. (1970), 'Reflections on authority', *New American Review*, no. 8.

SCHEIN, E. H. (1965), *Organizational Psychology*, Prentice-Hall.

SCHELLING, T. (1960), *The Strategy of Conflict*, Harvard University Press.

SCHMIDT, W. H. (1970), *Organizational Frontiers and Human Values*, Wadsworth Publishing Co.

SCHON, D. (1963), *Invention and the Evolution of Ideas*, Tavistock.

SIMON, H. (1967), 'The changing theory and changing practice of public administration', in I. de S. Pool (ed.), *Contemporary Political Science*, McGraw-Hill.

SLATER, P. (1970), *The Pursuit of Loneliness*, Beacon Press.

TANNENBAUM, A. (1968), *Control in Organizations*, McGraw-Hill.

THOMPSON, J. (1967), *Organizations in Action*, McGraw-Hill.

THOMPSON, V. (1963), *Modern Organization*, Alfred Knopf.

THOMSON, R. (1968), 'How could Vietnam happen?', *Atlantic Monthly*, October, pp. 47–53.

VICKERS, G. (1967), *The Art of Judgement*, Basic Books.

VROOM, V. (1960), *Some Personality Determinants of the Effects of Participation*, Prentice-Hall.

WAYS, M. (1970), 'Finding the American direction', *Fortune*, vol. 82, no. 4.

WILENSKY, H. (1967), *Organizational Intelligence*, Basic Books.

WOOD, R. (1970), 'When government works', *The Public Interest*, Winter, no. 18, pp. 39–51.

WOODWARD, J. (1965), *Industrial Organization: Theory and Practice*, Oxford University Press.

Part One
The Future Context of Organizational Change and Conflict

The Readings in this opening section address an important issue in the management of change and conflict: what kinds of societal changes are occurring, creating in their wake new forms of conflict and requiring adaptation on the part of the organization. Prominent among these are the following:

1. The continued acceleration of what Kahn (1969) terms 'manipulative rationality'; namely, further decline in the sacred in favor of the secular, more pragmatism, the rise of 'future oriented thinking' and the improvement of tools for this purpose, the increasing application of rationality to social, political and cultural problems, the decreasing importance of primary occupations, and so on. In general, an acceleration of those trends which have become associated with 'post-industrialism'.

2. In the US, and perhaps other more industrially developed nations, three 'societies' in one are emerging, according to Brzezinski (1970) – a group of professionals embodying the ideals of the knowledge revolution (the institutionalization of technological change by the developers of manipulative rationality); a force of blue- and white-collar workers now beginning to enjoy the fruits of relative affluence and leisure, but who fiercely eschew any emergent 'new hedonism'; and a continued group of as yet *pre*-industrial minorities – urban immigrants who are 'desirous' of getting into and getting a share of the system of materialism.

3. The rise of what Reich (1970) has termed 'Consciousness III' – a system of values and a life-style which is normative, ideological, utopian, visceral, humanistic, communal,

sometimes hedonistic and transcendental, opposed to what is viewed as a dominant societal drift toward the technocratic rationality of post-industrialism and, at this point in time, mostly centered in the youth. This trend is also characterized by certain shifts in cultural values identified by Eric Trist and discussed in Bennis' paper in this section: from 'achievement' to 'self-actualization', from 'self-control' to 'self-expression' from 'full employment' to 'full lives'.

4. According to a recent General Electric study, 'Changes in value systems will be the major determinant of social, political and economic developments in the domestic scene' (Wilson, 1970, p. 7). Among the specific value shifts foreseen are the following:

(a) Organization ⟶ individual. Organizations will be accepted or rejected according to the emphasis they place on the rights of the individual.

(b) Uniformity (conformity) ⟶ pluralism.

(c) Independence ⟶ interdependence. There will be an awareness of the need for cooperation and inter-disciplinary approaches.

(d) Future ⟶ immediacy. One of the major tensions of the future may result from a growing demand for instant solutions, for immediate gratification.

(e) Moral absolutes ⟶ situation ethics.

Individual systems of values and beliefs will become more prominent; and such change can be the harbinger of new kinds of societal conflict.

A comprehensive and thoughtful assessment of the revolutionary forces shaping society is provided in Reading 1, 'The Nature of Our Changing Society', by Harman. In keeping with our emphasis on the importance of paradigms for organizing change, he provides a framework within which the reader can begin to, in the author's words, 'construct his own dynamically changing view of alternative futures'.

In Reading 2, Bennis identifies several organizational dilemmas resulting from these revolutionary forces: a crisis of legitimacy – created in the main by a 'new pluralism' of goals and demands for localized power and control; the emergence of what he terms macro problems: those involving the growing complexity of constituencies in organizations and situations where collaboration and consensus become increasingly improbable and imperfect modes of conflict management; of an exponential increase in the 'scale, diversity, and formal relations' involving the manager, creating for him a 'hydra-headed' role set, interacting with many organizations and which, consequently, cannot be governed by any one style of leadership.

Katz and Georgopolous (Reading 3) discuss the impact of several changes on the organization which they conceive as an open system defined by key functional subsystems: production, maintenance, and adaptation, etc. In addition to proposing certain structural modifications by which the organization may more effectively manage change, their paper raises a central issue: above all else, we require a creative and active involvement by organizational leaders in formulating, communicating and implementing those values which can provide ideological guidance in times of chaotic change.

References

BRZEZINSKI, Z. (1970), *Between Two Ages: America in the Technocratic Era*, Viking Press.
KAHN, H. (1969), 'Forces for change: some long-range perspectives on current decisions', *Hudson Institute*, HI–1370–BN/1/1.
REICH, C. (1970), *The Greening of America*, Allen Lane the Penguin Press.
WILSON, I. (1970), 'How our values are changing', *Futurist*, February.

1 W. Harman

The Nature of Our Changing Society

Excerpt from W. Harman, 'The nature of our changing society',
Stanford Research Institute, 1969, unpublished paper.

Apparent long-term trends

As Kahn and Weiner (1967) note, a 'basic, long-term, multifold
trend' may be observed which provides a useful baseline against
which to contrast alternatives. More or less general agreement is
found among forecasters with regard to the components of this
trend summarized below.

Economic–political

World-wide industrialization and modernization. The preponderant
trend in the sense of forming a background context for all else in
the political and economic realms is undoubtedly what Robert
Heilbroner (1963) terms 'The Great Ascent', the industrialization
and modernization of the largely tropical belt of underdeveloped
areas.

The necessity of a shift from a parochial to a 'one world' view
of 'Spaceship Earth' hardly needs defense. Frequent reminding
comes from awareness that through present world communications networks repercussions of local events are rapidly felt and
reacted to around the world. Ecological problems are world
problems. Production/distribution and communication/trans-
portation systems are essentially global. They require, and are
dependent upon, the resource range of the entire planet and, more
importantly, upon the global interchange of research, development, and technical and managerial expertise. Most significantly
of all, perhaps, there are no 'local' political and economic problems any more. Political events in remote lands, famines or other
catastrophes in underdeveloped countries, all have direct and
immediate impact on the technologically developed world.

On this one-world stage the dominant event is the Great
Ascent. 'The process of economic development . . . visible

throughout the newly awakened areas . . . is a worldwide struggle to escape from the poverty and misery, and not less from the neglect and anonymity, which have heretofore constituted "life" to the vast majority of human beings. It is not mere rhetoric to speak of this attempted Great Ascent as the first real act of world history. Certainly in size and scope it towers over any previous enterprise of man. . . . (It) is not merely a struggle against poverty. The process which we call economic development is also, and in the long run primarily, a process through which the social, political and economic institutions of the future are being shaped for the great majority of mankind. On the outcome of this enormous act will depend the character of the civilization of the world for many generations to come, not only in the poor and struggling nations, but in the rich and privileged ones as well' (Heilbroner, 1963, p. 9). The economic development of the world is likely to be marked by profound 'revolutions of rising expectations', disharmony and social discontent; the almost inevitable gaps between expectations and accomplishments may well breed political authoritarianism and economic collectivism; the process will almost surely not be accomplished smoothly and according to plan. The educational jump from a tradition-bound peasant society to a modern industrial one is immense. Strong infusions of knowledge as well as capital will be required if the underdeveloped world is to succeed in this ambitious attempt.

Institutionalization of change. Emergent change, not homeostasis, is the order of the day. The trend is toward institutionalization of the process of research-development-innovation-dissemination, and toward the development of organizational forms adapted to promoting change.

Emergence of a 'knowledge society'. Drucker (1969) describes this development in detail. The emerging society is based upon knowledge as the central capital. Educational and 'intellectual' institutions play a key role (Bell, 1967). Demand grows for skilled, semi-professional and professional laborers, and diminishes for unskilled, unknowledgeable labor. Some writers have speculated about the future problem of increased leisure as a consequence of the cybernated society. More likely is the prospect of forty-hour (and up) weeks for the 'knowledge workers' and unemployment for the untrained. There will be an expanding fraction of the populace involved in education, and an expanding fraction of the national income going to education. There will be an increasing involvement of education with, and functional relationship to, other social institutions.

Scientific–technological

Accumulation of scientific and technological knowledge. The one forecast upon which practically all analysts agree is that of an increasing level of applied scientific knowledge, and an increasing degree of cybernation. Kahn and Weiner (1967) list a hundred likely technical innovations, and Chase (1968) describes the society which may result.

Increasing lag of technological solutions behind technology-created problems. Examples abound. Increasing industrialization creates problems of resource depletion, fouling of the environment, waste disposal, technological unemployment, which show no sign of doing anything but increase. Medical advances are largely responsible for dramatic rates of population growth and consequent overpopulation and food supply problems. Advances in weapons of mass destruction and their delivery systems have brought us to the threshold of an internecine conflict which resembles some of the nightmares of yesterday's science fiction writers.

Robert Heilbroner (1960) in *The Future as History* points out that the 'new forces' generating problems in the nation today are essentially extensions of three main currents of American historical development, namely rampant scientific and technological development, extension of opportunities to the underprivileged, and increasing social control over private economic life. Those same currents are likely to continue, and so are the problems.

Social–ecological

Increasing problems of ecological balance, environmental deterioration, population concentration, and food supply. There is no indication that any of these problems will do other than get worse in the years immediately ahead. A drastic shift in values to supplement regulatory action seems necessary to reverse trends toward increasing ecological imbalance, increasing pollution of air, water and soil, increasing nuclear and agrichemical contamination. We hear brave talk of approaches to population and food problems through new methods of contraception, through floating cities and undersea communities, through increased yield by crop breeding, and farming the oceans and coastal deserts. Most projections indicate that these measures will only ease the problems somewhat.

Increasing affluence, with increasing self-consciousness of the under-class. The world-wide trend toward increasing per capita income will continue, with a more rapid rise in the industrialized countries, thus increasing the gap between have and havenot groups. Both in this nation, and around the world, increasing pressure to redress the imbalance can be expected from the have-nots.

Growth of a 'knowledge elite'. Trends toward increasing bureaucratization and toward knowledge as power combine in the development of a meritocratic, 'knowledge power elite'.

Increasing interdependence of social and political institutions. Partly in response to these world problems we can expect a continuation of the trend toward limited-purpose international organizations and corporations (together with attempts – probably unsuccessful – to move further in the direction of a strong United Nations) and toward recognition, in institutional forms and practices, of the interlocking nature of economics, technological development, education, health and social order.

Within the nation the trends toward greater urbanization and industrialization will continue, and with them the increasing level of associated problems – urban decay, technological unemployment, poverty, crime, accumulating waste products. This too makes for movement toward increasing social control, increasing pluralism of institutional power (with ethnic, economic, and age minority groups insisting on representation), and increasing meshing of the activities of local, state and federal government agencies, and private business and nonprofit institutions. Detailed central control will tend to be replaced by generalized central control with local decision making on the specifics of carrying out broad policies.

Cultural–psychological

Increasing proportion of growth-motivated persons. Past trends of increasing affluence, increasing level of education, and changing child-rearing patterns combine to indicate that an increasing fraction of the population will be, in Maslow's terms, 'growth-motivated' rather than 'deficiency-motivated'. This is showing itself in signs of changing values in the direction of higher valuation of the feeling and subjective side of life, of self realization, of meaning and significance in work. There is more questioning of traditional work values, and a tendency to blur the distinctions between work, leisure and education.

Increasing stress-producing forces on the individual. These include continuing international and domestic tensions, fear and hostility in the cities, rapid obsolescence of job skills, increasing complexity of the individual's network of interpersonal relations, continued instability and change in life patterns.

Two contrasting forecasts

We are tempted to say, of the decades immediately ahead, paraphrasing Charles Dickens as he opens *A Tale of Two Cities*, 'it will be the best of times, it will be the worst of times, it will be the spring of hope, it will be the winter of despair'. Within the melange of trend forecasts we have just examined are to be found a broad range of portrayals. At one extreme are descriptions of the utopian benefits of technology relieving man once and for all of concern over supply of human wants, unlimited leisure and universal education for constructive use of it, and democratic freedom and equality such as only a high technology-affluent society can provide. At the other extreme we find dire predictions of uncontrollable fouling of the planet, reduced privacy and political significance of the individual, and widespread overpopulation, poverty, famine, and civil disorder. What sort of order can we bring out of this divergent prophesying?

At the everpresent risk of oversimplifying to the point of distortion, let us compare two composite forecasts for, say, the last decade of the century (see Figure 1). I will term them the 'second-phase industrial' society and the 'person-centered' society. The former is the sort of description which might emerge from a weighted summation of the multifarious trend projections, Delphi forecasts, and brave-new-world predictions which abound in technical and popular literature. (It is similar, in its basic concept of extrapolation of present trends, to 'The Most Probable World' of Chase (1968).) The 'person-centered' society is a composite picture based on a group of writers and analysts who assume (or hope) that a rapid change to some kind of 'post-economic' institutionalized values will take place. This group includes John Kenneth Galbraith, Michael Harrington, Erich Fromm, John Rader Platt, Kenneth Boulding, Robert Theobald, Abraham Maslow.

These are not presented, even by their proponents, on an equal basis. The first assumes a relatively continuous transition from the 'first-phase' industrial society which lasted from the Industrial Revolution to the present, to the 'second-phase' computerized, cybernated state. Implicit is the further assumption that such trends as the expanding economy and the advancing technology have, so to speak, a life of their own. Once set in motion their own dynamic carries them forward. Thus it is appropriate to project them ahead and ask such questions as, 'What effect will increased knowledge in bio-engineering have on human values?' To be sure, the advance of technological achievement will bring with it new social problems such as the industrial pollution, poisoning by agrichemicals, encroachment on privacy, traffic congestion, and threat of nuclear destruction which are our present heritage. But these, in turn, will be 'solved' by still higher technology.

The second forecast, the 'person-centered' society, assumes by contrast a significant discontinuity with past trends. Its proponents tend to view our present 'time of troubles' as a transition period to a state radically different from the present, both in institutional forms and in institutionalized values. The level of technological development would be comparable with (or somewhat lower than) that in the first forecast, but the uses to which technology would be put might differ significantly. The value

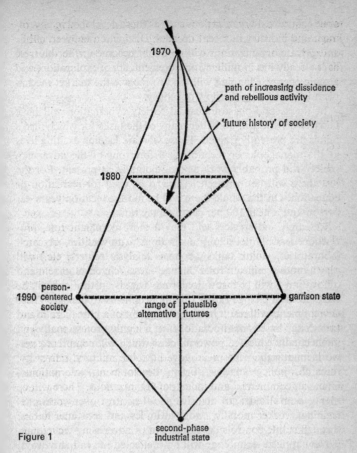

path of increasing dissidence
and rebellious activity

'future history' of society

1970

1980

1990 person-centered society

range of | plausible
alternative | futures

garrison state

second-phase
industrial state

Figure 1

shift would be in the direction of a more 'person-centered' culture. Critics of this forecast would say it is unrealistic; critics of the first would say it is undesirable, if not self-destructing.

The 'second-phase' industrial society

In both of these forecasts we can assume that certain trends and developments are here to stay, at least for the near future. One is a high and increasing level of technology and of cybernation. Second is the carrying on of most purposeful activities by large-scale centralized organizations such as those developed in government and industry in recent decades. Distinction between public and private organizations will no doubt become further blurred, as it already has in military procurement, space exploration, and atomic energy. Planning will tend to replace the market mechanism in controlling the flow of money.

In the second-phase industrial society cybernation will have taken over, and will do better many of the tasks for which men's minds are presently trained. Those who are leading exciting lives at the managerial or technological forefront of the advancing society will probably work as long hours as at present. For the rest there will be increased leisure to be used for recreation or education. On the whole there will be more education years per person and a near 100 per cent literacy rate.

Research and services will play a more dominant role, production less. 'Intellectual institutions' (universities, research laboratories, 'think tanks', systems analysis centers, etc.) will play a more significant role. Change – research, development and innovation – will be institutionalized. That is, institutions will be facilitators of change rather than impediments to change. These developments will result in the enlargement of a bureaucratic and knowledge-based 'meritocratic' elite, a highly professionally and intellectually educated powerful class which will comprise a network linking the widespread governmental, military, university, research, policy analysis, urban development, international, financial, commercial and industrial organizations. There will be highly centralized and intensive social control over vocational training, worker mobility, work attitudes and consumer habits, through subtle controls developed out of advertising techniques.

New applied technology will have affected life in many ways. New types of household devices, many based on small computers and elaborated communication services, will be available, not only transforming the life of the housewife, but also allowing education and various forms of business to be carried on in the home. Through cybernation and genetic management of plants and animals, the agricultural industry will be made many times more productive in terms of use of land and labor. Desert lands will be reclaimed through desalinated water. Nuclear power and fuel cells will provide ample energy for all demands. Automated factories will produce practically all consumer goods, with variety programmed in to satisfy customers. New transportation systems will have more people traveling further, faster. The housing industry will indeed have become an industry, producing new types of improved housing with mass production economy, yet with aesthetic and functional variety.

There will be variety in cities too – specialized forms (scientific city, university city, festival and ceremonial cities, recreation city, experimental cities) and planned communities. There will be experimentation with alternatives to the main patterns of living (precursors being communes, bohemian urban communities, new sexual arrangements and substitutes for marriage, etc.). Schools as we have known them will virtually disappear. Education will take place via combined systems of machines and human assistants, located in homes, neighborhood centers, specialized learning centers, museums, industrial and business locations.

Along with these advantages there will be some problems. Because of the lag in modernization of underdeveloped countries, there will be an even greater gap between rich nations and poor nations. International organizations of various sorts will somehow have managed to contain the nuclear threat, and will have made great strides in fostering economic development of poor nations, but there will still be international strife and the economy will continue to be semi-militarized. Fed by the dynamic character of science–technology, and unchecked by failure to find any satisfactory alternative to technological approaches to international problems, the arms race will have continued to escalate.

There will be internal tension too. Although some progress will have been made on the poverty problem, the white–nonwhite conflict will continue, and the alienated young of the sixties will be raising another generation, also alienated. But the law enforcement agencies will have regained the initiative, violence and counter-violence will be under control, and the conflict will mainly take the form of rather widespread subterranean resentments.

It will be interesting to speculate on the nature of this dissenting view. The dissenters will be, on the whole, at a higher level of material well-being than in the sixties, and better educated. We can imagine their criticism of the basic contradictions in the society as follows: The operative goals of the society are continuing expansion of output (goods and services), a companion increase in consumption, technological advance, efficient use of resources to these ends, and the public images that sustain all these. Individual lives are to be spent in the service of these goals, human wants and state policies are to be managed in accordance with the needs of the industrial system, education is adapted to them, conventional morality amounts to the disciplines required by the system. The necessity to close the gap between rich and poor nations is recognized, yet it is uneconomical to trade freely with them or to invest heavily in their balanced economic development. The need is recognized to abolish the slums, poverty, racism, and to provide adequate education and equal opportunity to minority poor, yet it is uneconomical for private capital to do this, and effective government action is opposed by threatened lower-middle- and working-class whites. Humans need contact with nature and beauty, but it is uneconomical to design a humane urban environment, to provide moneys for parks, aesthetics, history or civility. The channels of mass communication offer a great potentiality for public enlightenment, yet they are used mainly as sales and propaganda distributors for business and government interests. Somehow the social system is not serving the interests of the individuals who make it up, and nothing short of a radical change in the operative values within it can alter this.

The 'person-centered' society

In the other forecast of the 'humanized technological' society, it is precisely these operative values which have changed. The goals of the society include economic growth to human ends, control over social problems to the end of bettering the opportunity of individuals to progress toward their own supremely human goals of self fulfillment, and achievement of knowledge and aesthetic advance. The industrial system is subservient to, and responsible to, the larger purposes of the society. The overarching goal is the cultivation and enrichment of all human beings, in all their diversity, complexity and profundity.

In the forecasts which describe this society, each individual will be provided with enough resources and in such a way as to enable him to live in dignity. The basis of the economics will be the proposition that each free man has the right to a full life, which includes useful, rewarding work and self development. This will not be done solely by welfare payments or guaranteed income maintenance. In part, at least, it will be accomplished by an extension of the principle of free goods and services from those already provided – elementary education, library services, fire and police protection, inoculations, lunch milk for children, etc. – to include others, such as re-education for a new occupation, food and nutrition staples, urban transportation, etc. In the 'knowing society' (Drucker, 1969), education will be as central to the economy as mass production has been in the past. Thus education is a valid occupation, entitling the educatee to subsistence as well as learning opportunity. A diversity of educational paths will be available, and men will not be judged on the basis of a single uniform academic standard. (Competitive grading will assume much less significance.) Similarly, the society will provide a diversity of ways in which a person can win the esteem of others. In other words, economic failure or academic failure will not be equated with failure as an individual.

Mumford (1965) has analysed the basic attitude shifts that would have to accompany conversion to the 'person-centered' society. There are, he says, 'serious reasons for reconsidering the whole picture of both human and technical development on which the present organization of Western society is based. . . . The deliberate expression and fulfillment of human potentialities requires a quite different approach from that bent solely on the control of natural forces. . . . Instead of liberation *from* work being the chief contribution of mechanization and automation, liberation *for* work, for educative, mind-forming work, self-rewarding even on the lowest physiological level, may become the most salutary contribution of a life-centered technology.'

The society will be a planned society, but planned in such a way as to deepen, not diminish, the freedom of the individual. Opportunity will be provided for real participation in planning by those for whom the planning is done. Management structures will be such that power flows both ways.

The technological level will be high, as in the 'second-phase industrial' forecast, but the priorities for technology development will be influenced by human and global needs. The problems of the ghetto and the underdeveloped societies will not have been completely eliminated, but their attack will have had high priority. As a consequence of this, and of the perceived goals of the society, international tensions will have lowered and internal alienation will have decreased markedly. The military establishments of the industrialized nations will have moved a long way toward a cooperative international policing role. Internally, new standards will govern the recruitment and training of officials responsible for maintaining justice and order, and the image of the police will be one of fairness and justice to all, regardless of skin color, economic condition, or type of haircut and beard.

Education will center on developing self-learning habits and skills, problem-solving and decision-making abilities, personal style, sound valuing capabilities, capability of continuous self-renewal, and self understanding. Education will be much more equated with life, and the distinction between formal and informal education will have become blurred. Education will be much more a lifetime activity. The significant distinctions will not be work *v.* education or work *v.* leisure, but work-education-leisure *v.* 'killing time'.

Hutchins (1968) describes 'the learning society' as 'one that, in addition to offering part-time adult education to every man and woman at every stage of grown-up life, had succeeded in transforming its values in such a way that learning, fulfillment, becoming human, had become its aims and *all its institutions were directed to this end*. This is what the Athenians did. . . . They made their society one designed to bring all its members to the fullest development of their highest powers. . . . In Athens, education was not a segregated activity, conducted for certain hours, in certain places, at a certain time of life. It was the aim of the society. . . . The Athenian was educated by the culture, by Paideia.'

The Athenian education was made possible by slavery, which was the necessary provider of leisure. But 'machines can do for every modern man what slavery did for the fortunate few in Athens. The vision of a learning society . . . can be realized. . . . Whether it does or not depends upon the transformation of values.'

But values in turn are based on a picture of the nature of man, his potentialities, and the possibilities for their manifestation. That is to say, the choice between the two alternative futures we have described is also in a sense choice between two images of man.

Beliefs and values in transition

We have argued that not only are values in transition, not only does advancing technology have an impact on values (and, more fundamentally, values have an influence on what technology comes into application), but also that a choice among significantly different alternative futures is implicitly a choice among belief-and-value systems (Baier and Rescher, 1969).

Let us compare summary descriptions of four belief-and-value positions which are interacting at the present time to generate the future. They are:

1. US middle class (traditional).

2. 'New' values (proposed by humanistic-psychology writers and 'forerunner' youth).

3. Behavioral science.

4. American origin (implicit in founding documents and Western political tradition).

US middle-class traditional beliefs and values

We mean by this title the beliefs and values which have dominated US industrial society and which the new youth tend to reject, at least in part. It is difficult to be explicit, since the values of the middle class are changing and have clearly departed considerably from what they were in the 1930s, both in the direction of diversity and pluralism, and in an overall shift toward the 'new' values described below. This brief summary describes, at any rate, a representative position.

Beliefs. Implicit in this belief-and-value system is that, while religious beliefs are good to have as a basis for morality, the values derived from the Judaeo–Christian tradition will stand by themselves on a pragmatic basis. Hence there tends to be little emphasis on specific religious beliefs or metaphysical premises as a source of values – atheists, agnostics, Christians and Jews are expected to have more or less the same values. Thus, without being tied to a particular cosmology, there tends to be a generalized belief (a) in the perfectability of man and his ability to better his position through his own efforts; (b) in material progress as the meaning of social progress; and (c) in humanitarianism and a moral orientation to the world.

Individual-rights values. A high value is attached to the right to individual pursuit of economic security and happiness, to personal liberty (freedom, privacy and property rights), to equality of opportunity and justice, and to essential respect as a human being.

Life-setting values. The orderly society is valued, with well-defined social roles and rules for transition, commonly held domestic and civic virtues, pleasantness of environment. Meaning in life centers largely around success and achievement in terms of money, property, power and status. For these, one is willing to sacrifice present pleasures and postpone gratification to the future. Self discipline, hard work, and efficiency and productivity are honored; the emotional life should be well regulated and rationalized.

Personal characteristics. The following personal characteristics are valued: industry, integrity, dependability, self-sufficiency, control of inner feelings, moderation, rationality, orderliness, regularity, conformity, cleanliness, responsibility, loyalty to family and firm, patriotism – Apollonian style, action as contrasted with contemplation, youthfulness.

'New' values

These are the beliefs and values of the humanistic and existential psychologists (Erich Fromm, Abraham Maslow, Carl Rogers, Rollo May, etc.) and the youth culture labeled 'forerunner youth' by *Fortune* magazine in a recent survey (January, 1969). The position is much more explicit than the previous one in what it affirms about man.

Beliefs. Basic premises include the affirmation that fundamental to all else in human experience is awareness, and that through his awareness of himself and of his relations to others and to the universe, man can discover values which are wholesome in terms of promoting his growth toward the most fully human state and his actualization of his highest potentialities. Man responds to a hierarchy of perceived needs, but ultimately his basic dynamic is toward growth and becoming.

Individual-rights values. The highest value is attached to the individual's right to the pursuit of self fulfillment, to personal liberty, to equality of opportunity and justice, and to essential respect as a human being. These are considered to be not just pragmatically desirable, but rather to follow directly from the affirmation of the essential validity of inner experience and from the collective subjective experience of the race.

Life-setting values. Meaning in life centers around the discovery and actualization of one's highest potentialities, the pursuit of self fulfillment. The desirable environment is one which promotes growth and fosters inner freedom. This implies that it is truthfully responsive and ultimately supportive, as the therapist is to his client. Beauty and deep personal relationships are highly valued.

Personal characteristics. The following personal characteristics are valued: openness, authenticity, integrity, sensitivity, aliveness, self-honesty, balance between or transcendence of opposites, i.e. reason/emotion, Apollonian/Dionysian, work/play, self/not-self (Maslow, 1967).

Behavioral science

There is, of course, no single viewpoint which faithfully represents the views of behavioral scientists as they apply their knowledge to matters of social policy and social values. One could perhaps think of some kind of center-of-gravity viewpoint. The attempt is important because the behavioral-science viewpoint is influential, and because it represents the background of so many of those who wrestle with social policy questions. A reasonable approach would seem to be to examine writings of behavioral scientists relating to social problems, and the textbooks from which behavioral science is taught. The latter particularly are strongly influenced in their implicit premises by the behaviorist tradition in psychology and by Freudian psychoanalytic theory.

Beliefs. The basic premises include the assertion that human behavior can best be understood as an interaction among more or less stable characteristics of the individual and the immediate situational context. The individual characteristics – personality pattern, values, goals, etc. – arise in turn from the historical interaction between physiological needs and instinctual energies and desires on the one hand, and environment – particularly early-childhood – on the other. Socially acceptable behavior is arrived at through socialization (conditioning) processes.

The behavioral-science position tends to be reductionist, especially regarding such 'higher values' as freedom, justice, love, cooperation, reason, courage, free will, truth, beauty and goodness, self fulfillment, and responsibility, regarding them as sublimations of instinctual drives or as more straightforward cultural conditionings. Thus the basic value position is one of moral relativism.

Individual-rights values. Such rights as the individual pursuit of happiness, personal liberty, and equality of opportunity seem good ones for a society to have on a rational, pragmatic basis. However, altruistic behavior is basically at variance with man's instinctual (aggressive, territorial, etc.) nature, and it has to be instilled by the culture.

Life-setting values. Likewise, such values as social order, justice, social consciousness, democracy, humanitarianism, public service, morality, achievement, etc., are perpetuated by the culture because of their usefulness, but they have no deeper transcendental roots. Because of the implicit deterministic assumption, values such as freedom and democracy, which imply that the individual ultimately has free will and is responsible for his actions, are not only cultural invention, but illusion.

Personal characteristics. Various personal characteristics may be valued, particularly scientific objectivity, intelligence, impassivity

– however, with the realization that the choice to value these is itself illusory in its freedom, since these tastes must have been culturally imposed somewhere along the way.

American origin

In the speeches and writings of the men who were present at the founding of this nation are to be discerned the basic premises and central values of the Western political tradition and the specifically American additions.

Beliefs. The most important basic premises underlying the nation's founding are that the universe has a physical and moral order, that Natural Law is discoverable by man, and that man intrinsically strives toward the understanding of the natural order and toward the perfection of his nature. 'Unerring order and universal harmony reigning throughout the whole . . . God is the power of first cause, nature is the law, and matter is the subject acted upon' (Thomas Paine). Social order is to be derived from man's universal nature. The history of man is a progression in time toward a definite, supremely meaningful end, in which human fulfillment is achieved. Man's purpose in history is to seek individual realization and social and political justice. Man has the free will to accept or reject natural purpose and natural law.

Individual-rights values. Supreme rights are those to life, liberty, and the pursuit of self fulfillment; to equality before the law and equality of opportunity; and to freedom with regard to spiritual beliefs and the rituals and life patterns in which those are expressed.

Life-setting values. Among the specific life-setting values commanding high allegiance here are:
(a) The mission of America to bring a new order into the world.
(b) The prime function of society being to serve the individual's rational and purposeful perspectives and acts.
(c) A binding, just, adaptive system of common and constitutional law.
(d) The supremacy of the General Will (what people ought to want in the light of the ethic of the Western political tradition and

of their own rational, individual and social interests) over temporary popular desire.

(e) The right and duty to resist when government does not fulfill its responsibilities to the individual and becomes tyrannical and destructive.

(f) Equal opportunity, special privilege for none.

(g) Education: 'Enlighten the people generally, and oppression of mind and body will vanish like evil spirits at the dawn of day' (T. Jefferson).

(h) Harmonious and successful human relations, spiritual salvation, reason, tolerance, freedom, justice, cooperation, persuasion rather than force, individual responsibility, enlightened self interest.

Personal characteristics. The following personal characteristics are highly valued: integrity, responsibility, rationality, industry, self-sufficiency, fairness, spirituality, patriotism, humanitarianism, idealism.

With these summaries of four belief-and-value systems before us we have a useful way of looking at some contemporary issues. The traditional middle-class premises are congenial to the 'second-phase industrial' kind of future. The 'person-centered society', on the other hand, would require a shift of dominant values in the direction of the 'new', humanistic-psychology and forerunner-youth basic premises. Changes in basic premises are not easily brought about; there is little indication that deliberate attempts to change basic premises and value positions, through conventional educational processes, are very successful. On the other hand the 'new' values appear to have a strength in today's culture which would hardly have been anticipated even a half decade ago.

Formal education positions have been strongly affected by the behavioral-science premises in recent decades. These premises are more in line with, and supportive of, the traditional middle-class values.

Interestingly enough, the 'new' beliefs and values turn out to be remarkably similar to those which form the ideological basis for the nation, as is indicated by the criticisms of disaffected youth that the Establishment is false to its declared values.

Manifest revolutionary forces

There is little need to make the case that recent years have brought a rapid growth of disruptive forces, increasing level of overt and violent white–nonwhite conflict, and increasing alienation of youth and minority groups from the 'military–industrial–education complex' and national aims and policies. Educational institutions have found themselves furnishing a stage for much of the enactment of this drama. We have seen campus demonstrations escalate from sit-ins to forcible seizure, and then to armed seizure, and responses move from debate to bayonets, teargas and mass arrests. There seems no reason to assume that events in the months to come will not move further in the same direction.

On the contrary, we may confidently expect that educational institutions will continue, by virtue of their central position in a high-technology society, to be at the center of the fray. Thus it will be useful to consider a framework for viewing the significance of contemporary revolutionary forces. This conceptualization will attempt the sort of fitting of superficially unrelated events into an overall pattern which can be seen with sureness only in historical retrospect. Thus its 'fit' cannot be demonstrated – the test is how well it seems to accommodate further developments. We may hope that this framework will help us see better the relationship to alternative futures of present responses to revolutionary forces.

The overall situation regarding civil unrest, dissidence and violence is obviously complex. At the level of manifest phenomena it has many aspects – student rebellions, ghetto riots, minority group threats, organized movements for violence and assassination, rising sentiment against the Vietnam war, deteriorating national image at home and abroad, attacks on the 'military–industrial–education complex', concern over inadequate response to such social problems as the rapidly deteriorating physical environment and forthcoming mass starvation abroad, demands for participatory democracy, to mention a few. At the more fundamental level of the social structure, present institutions and institutionalized roles, and present forms of power distribution, are being assailed. At what is in some sense a still deeper level the operational values and goals of the power structure are being challenged. Under particular attack are obsession with technocratic–economic values and depersonalizing aspects of computerized bureaucracy. Some of these phenomena are worldwide. The underlying causes are clearly multi-faceted.

Among the multiple causes put forth to explain various of these phenomena and their appearance in history at this particular time are such hypotheses as:

(a) Disillusionment with liberal promises and programs.
(b) Natural youth rebellion.
(c) Permissive child-rearing patterns.
(d) Neo-Marxist revolutionary movement.
(e) Activities of foreign subversive agents and internal revolutionaries.
(f) Moral reaction against the Vietnam war.
(g) Rising expectations among have-not groups.
(h) Disillusionment with widespread competitiveness, inequity, and hypocrisy.
(i) Revolution for the thrill of it.
(j) Rebellion against impersonality and 'students as commodities' attitudes in universities.
(k) The continuing fight for civil rights.
(l) The demand for student participation in educational decisions.
(m) The draft.
(n) More average years of formal education and, hence, extended period of 'youth' with its own, separate youth culture.
(o) Underlying anxiety over the threat of nuclear annihilation.
(p) Bewildering rapidity of change in the knowledge–technology explosion.

And yet such partial explanations do not appear to do justice to the facts. Various evidences suggest that instead of coincident but relatively unrelated phenomena, we are in actuality dealing with a complex of highly interrelated phenomena – so interrelated that it may be profitable to view it as one intricate underlying phenomenon, of which the specific events are manifestations. Such an interpretation is suggested by the fact that the student revolutions are worldwide. Specific issues in Paris, Mexico City, Tokyo, Morningside Heights, Berkeley, San Francisco, and Montreal differ widely – yet youth unrest appears to be almost a universal phenomenon. Student radicals may be seen in labor picket lines and union members participate in student demonstrations; militant leaders have indicated that their targets will include industrial corporations and nonprofit think-tanks.

A crisis is also often an opportunity. If, when a unified view is taken of contemporary revolutionary phenomena, constructive as well as destructive forces can be observed to be present; this is most important to understand. As Noam Chomsky (1969) recently observed, 'There now exist opportunities for change that are not very likely to recur.' Perhaps the greatest danger in the present situation is that, in reacting to crush the destructive threat to the social order represented by coercive force and deliberate violence, we may unwittingly repress a constructive force for change in the direction of fuller realization of the most basic goals of the nation and of Western political tradition.

Two components of revolutionary force

The two main issues implicit in the revolutionary activity are:

1. A demand for emancipation on the part of various subjugated or underprivileged groups.

2. A demand for societal and moral reform on the part of persons, mainly privileged youth, who are not subjugated or impoverished in any ordinary sense.

These need to be viewed somewhat separately because, while satisfaction of the second demand tends to imply satisfaction of the first, the reverse is not true. The revolutionary fervor associated with the first issue could probably be reduced by offering economic gains and limited shared power, but the force of the second might still remain.

The first issue is a demand, by groups who feel subjugated, for emancipation, for potency in the society, for an effective voice in decisions affecting their individual destinies, for the right to feel a sense of self-worth, for equal opportunity in a system that does not deprive them of meaningful participation because they are black, or students, or poor, or 'culturally deprived'. Among such groups are:

Black	Homosexuals, sexual deviates
Third World	Marijuana smokers
Students	Draft-age youth
Teachers	Psychedelic drug advocates
Labor	Free-love advocates
Women	Opponents of the Vietnam war
Consumers	Welfare recipients and poverty groups

These various groups do not have identical aims, of course. Nevertheless they frequently find adequate common cause in collaboration. (We do not mean to blur over the very real differences either – success has not crowned attempts to marry black, student and labor groups.) They vary considerably in the extent to which their claims for emancipation are recognized by, and trouble the conscience of, the dominant majority.

The second issue is a demand for person-centered values, and for institutional reform to that end, and a challenging of the values and the power of the 'military–industrial–education complex'.

In terms of values, this force represents a rejection of what we earlier described as traditional middle-class values, and espousal of what we called the 'new' values. This group tends to see our national policy as token reform at home and counter-revolutionary imperialism abroad, and to find this immoral and bankrupt. They point to a demonstrated inability of the present power structure to create a viable international order, to cope with environmental problems, to correct institutionalized and legitimated inequities, and to construct a high-technology society which does not at the same time affront and humiliate the human spirit.

Analysis of revolutionary forces

We propose to discuss contemporary revolutionary forces and their significance in the context of the diagram of Figure 2. The attempt here is to indicate various possible states of mind with regard to felt need for action, and to note transitions that seem to have taken place as reflected in past events. With the aid of this framework we will then attempt to say something about the alternative future courses which events might take. We can only hope that the inevitable shortcomings of such a deliberately oversimplified model will be outweighed by the conceptual power contributed.

The general picture Figure 2 attempts to convey is that the current situation of widespread civil dissidence involves numerous actors who hold various attitudes regarding desirable action, mainly regarding subjugated or underprivileged groups in the society or societal and moral reform. As a result of his experiences a person may shift from one such state to another. Alternative policies may affect the probabilities of such shifts in different ways, and thus may contribute to the bringing about of alternative futures.

As we examine the dynamics of this situation with the aid of Figure 2, some interesting aspects of the overall picture will emerge.

O. No special action called for. The box at the top of the diagram represents the main body of the population, out of which the primary actors in the revolutionary drama are drawn. It comprises a wide range of positions along the dimension inert-unconcerned to active-concerned, and also along the dimension liberal to conservative. The characterizing basic premise is that no unusual actions are called for, progressive social change is taking place at a safe and appropriate rate, and normal political institutions and processes are adequate for the accomplishment of desirable change.

A. Accelerate social change. Box A represents the state of having recognized the perpetuation in the society of serious inequities and inhumanities and, assuming that declared intentions are genuine and legitimated political actions are adequate to the needs, having concluded that acceleration of social change is required.

Actions connected with civil-rights issues involving persons with these premises included the rise of civil-rights activity following Brown *v.* Board of Education (1954) from the Montgomery bus boycott (1955), forced integration of schools (1956 on),

Southern lunch-counter sit-ins (1961), Civil Rights Act (1965). Persons of this attitude-state were involved in the poverty issue in, for example, the Poor People's March (1968), the Economic Opportunity Act and the beginning of Community Action Pro-

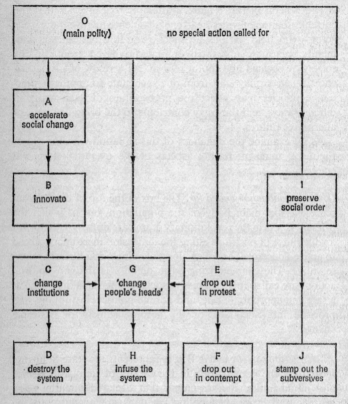

Figure 2 State diagram of premises regarding contemporary revolutionary forces

grams (1964), the Elementary and Secondary Education Act and other portions of the War on Poverty (1965). Clearly the actors in these cases included both members of the economically and socially underprivileged minorities and persons for whom the demand for societal and moral reform was a more idealistic one.

Student reactions to the Vietnam war, the draft, 'non-relevance' in higher education, etc., began mildly in the early sixties (remember the apathetic fifties?), gained momentum rapidly in 1964, and in a sense culminated in the youth-for-McCarthy campaign of 1968.

B. Innovate. State B in the diagram represents the position that speeding up of processes underway is not adequate to the need, and innovation is required. Many students and minority leaders came to this position as a consequence of disillusionment over the failures of type A responses. These engendered loss of faith in the adequacy of normal political processes, and questioning of the genuineness of intentions, and led to the conviction that new types of political actions would be necessary to awaken moral sensibilities and to generate adequate response to the problems.

Among the significant 'tests' of the system were the HUAC demonstration in San Francisco (1961), the Mississippi summer project and MFDP at the Democratic Convention (1964), the Mississippi anti-fear march and the shooting of James Meredith (1966), and the stop-the-draft demonstrations of 1967, particularly at the Oakland Induction Center and the Pentagon. Innovative political actions included the formation of SDS (with its initial emphasis on working with Congress) (1962), Free Speech Movement (1964), initiation of experimental colleges and free universities (1966) and NSA-sponsored tutorials for minority-group students (1963), first forms of Black Power (1966).

C. Change institutions. State B turned out for many to be a transition state, leading to the conviction that present forms of institutionalized power are intrinsically inadequate to deal with the massive social problems of the day, and thus that the solution to social ills must come through radical change of institutional forms. Since awareness of this inadequacy is obscured by the ability of the Establishment to enculturate and to co-opt, it follows that confrontations and other radicalizing activities are necessary to bring about this awareness.

A subsidiary premise is that groups in power seldom share that power willingly. Hence a group perceiving itself to be without legitimated power must fall back on coercion and at least the threat of violence to effect social change.

Among events involving persons of this persuasion were the emergence (around 1967), as major confrontation-instigating agencies, of SDS, Black Student Unions, Black Panther Party; major student–police confrontations on campuses (1967-9) and student strikes (1968); 'street people' and police clashes over 'people's park' issue in Berkeley (1969); urban ghetto riots (1965-8). Again both the economically underprivileged and the disaffected privileged were involved, with goals significantly different. (In terms of Maslow's need–concern levels, both deficiency-motivated and growth-motivated persons are involved, but their inner dynamics are different and at certain stages or on some issues they may part company.)

The groups holding this radical premise comprise a wide range along the dimension of willingness to escalate. This depends upon the nature and severity of suppressive forces applied. The overall radical strategy has been made clear in the statements of radical leaders, and is simple enough in its logic. It is to continue to apply force, moving toward methods that are more and more economical of resources (in terms of losing fewer men to jail, hospital and morgue) and more and more difficult to suppress. Thus the canonical sequence moves from mass demonstrations, strikes and riots, through sabotage, terrorizing, and urban guerilla warfare, to the weapon of last resort – selective assassination. The extremist end of this sequence corresponds to state D, the real political revolutionary. But many of the students, particularly, seem to be moving from this premise to state G, the 'psychological revolutionary'. And we see some signs that severe repressive measures combined with little evidence of solid social change can lead many of this group to retreat into apathetic resentment, discouragement, and smoldering hate for the whole system.

D. Destroy the system. The basic premise represented here is that the whole system is evil and has to be torn down. Whereas some persons of persuasions C and G feel that the threat of 'destroying the system' is necessary therapy to jolt people into awareness, this group means it. This point of view is represented by the positions of the Progressive Labor Party, various Marxist, Castroist and Maoist groups, and extremist anarchist nongroups. It is patently true that the overall revolutionary Movement is not solely Communist-inspired in its origins; to exaggerate the contribution of subversive exogenous agents is as serious an error as to assume that they are not present at all. However, it is equally true that elements of the Movement are closely allied to the International Radical Left.

E. Drop out in protest. Another branch of the revolutionary-state diagram, stemming from the basic premise of the possibility of expanded consciousness, became nationally significant with the foundation by Timothy Leary of the International Foundation for Internal Freedom (IFIF) in 1963, promulgating the ethic 'Turn on, tune in, drop out'. This led to the hippie phenomenon; widespread interest in Eastern philosophical religions and meditative practices; psychedelic light shows, rock music and lyrics (with rock radio stations as a worldwide communication network carrying the revolutionary message); black-market drugs and the psychedelic movement in the name of 'religious freedom'; hippie dropouts, love and flower power, sexual freedom, and the establishment of communes.

F. Drop out in contempt. Of group E some, with their new-found 'expanded awareness', took a good look at what man was doing to man in the social system, and moved from a position of 'drop out in protest' to one of 'drop out in contempt'. With this are often associated libertinism and unrepressed sensuality, flaunted hedonism, and general rejection of work, discipline and conventional social amenities. Although this group have removed themselves from the field of action, they are of concern both because of the loss of human resources they represent, and because they tend to become associated with drug abuse and related crime.

G. 'Change people's heads'. Not all of the 'turned-on' generation, however, view the dropout as the desired permanent state. Rather, it became for some more like the 'withdrawal and return' of Toynbee and Jung. These persons tended to 're-enter' with a new political awareness, joining forces (state G) with some of the political activists who were 'turning on' to the conviction that 'the real revolution is not in the ghetto or on the campus, but in people's heads' – that without this, institutional reform alone will not bring about necessary changes.

Here they find common cause with another group which sometimes refer to themselves as the 'human potential movement' (represented by the dotted line in the diagram). If one wanted to pick a date for the beginnings of this component, the initiation of the Esalen Institute programs in 1961 would be as suitable as any. From these Big Sur beginnings the movement has grown to include well over a hundred 'growth centers' and free-university programs, and thousands of psychotherapists, sensitivity training and psycho-drama group leaders, sensory awareness teachers, yoga teachers, and assorted gurus.

Thus the basic premise associated with this state is that necessary social change will come about only through widespread person-changing. To this end they have developed and use a 'person-changing technology' as indicated in Table 1. Emphasis is on a dual awareness (a) of the higher-consciousness nature of man and of the bankruptcy of the scientific–technocratic and behaviorist views of man, and (b) of institutionalized inequity and inhumanity in the social system. The techniques near the top of the list in Table 1 tend to aim more at expanded self-awareness, and those near the bottom at heightened social awareness.

H. Infuse the system. The number in this state is small but apparently growing. The basic premises are similar to G, with the additional premise that the way to get radical change is to carry on a 'subtle revolution' – to dress and act conventionally, to infuse the system, to be 'in the world but not of it'.

I. Preserve social order. The rapid rise of revolutionary thought and action in the last decade, particularly among the nonwhite and the youth, has caused a considerable fraction of the polity to conclude that special action is called for to preserve the social order – in particular, that the existence of states D and F constitute a serious social problem, and that the extent of the phenomenon indicates the need for some sort of counter-response from the system.

J. Stamp out the subversives. Some who may once have held similar opinions to I have moved on to the premise that all of these revolutionary views from B through H are subversive, anti-American, and must be stamped out. The right-extremist groups are exemplars of this position.

This rather extended analysis of revolutionary forces, and of what might at first glance seem to be but one of many indicators of future trends, has seemed justified because it is here that the

Table 1

Elements of 'person-changing technology'	Typical outcomes
Meditation Yoga Psychedelic drugs Hypnosis, auto-hypnosis Psychosynthesis	Awareness of spiritual dimensions, of transcendental self, of the 'hypnotic' or 'encapsulated' nature of ordinary life
Sensory awareness	Sensitivity to feelings and emotions, beauty
Self-awareness exercises Psychotherapies Group therapy Sensitivity training Encounter groups Gestalt therapy Psychodrama	Sensitivity to human closeness, self-honesty, realization that there is nothing to hide Spontaneous response to experience, self-expression, individual autonomy, emotional freedom
Group nudity, marathons Radicalizing confrontations	Removal of guilt and fear stemming from early training regarding morality and sin
Synanon games New Theater (ridicule of establishment, crudity and nudity, audience encounter) Underground press Forceful disruption of normal social processes	Ego-reducing experience, awareness of ego-defense nature of social institutions and customs
Deliberate provocation of 'instructive encounter' such as police confrontation, black–white confrontation, etc.	Perception of oppressive nature of social institutions

forces shaping the future are focused. The issue in the revolutionary activity *is* the future. If the insurrectionist forces are seen by the populace and its elected representatives essentially as lawbreakers attempting to gain by coercion that which should properly be obtained by legitimate process, the tendency will simply be to suppress. If the demands for reform are persistent, and if a large dissident fraction of the polity consider them legitimate, this could lead us a long way toward a garrison-state kind of future in which a partially armed militant minority (consisting possibly of elements of militant blacks, other nonwhite groups, far-left labor, and idealist youth) is held in check by the overwhelming power of the military state.

Another possible sequence of future events is a period of disruptive violence followed by a restructuring of social institutions to accommodate a new power balance. This would be a course of events somewhat similar to that of the labor movement of fifty years ago. The 'establishment' (management and owners in that case) perceives the demand for sharing of power as illegitimate and threatening. They make attempts at token sharing that delay confrontation, but in the end fail to satisfy the developing radical consciousness. The 'outs' increasingly resort to force and violence, and the 'ins' continue to counter with limited force. It becomes apparent that the rising tide of expectations and demands is not going to go away. Furthermore, the 'outs' have the power to disrupt and incapacitate industries, social institutions, and social processes in general to any degree they deem necessary as long as their numbers remain significantly large – and the repressive force limited. Thus they win on their demands for shared power, the alternative being massive repression, which is unacceptable to the populace. Social inventions (unions, collective bargaining techniques) are worked out to implement the new power balance. A consensus emerges that the new shared-power arrangement is workable and even seems more in line with our declared national and cultural values than was the previous arrangement.

One version of this latter 'future history' would be characterized by the 'buying off' of students by granting student power, and of minority groups by providing a measure of equality and security, thus thwarting or postponing the threatening revolution for drastically revised operational values and reconstitution of social structures. That is to say, the major changes demanded by the revolutionary forces might be relinquished if enough secondary prizes were offered. This might leave the social, political and economic structure of the nation relatively unchanged – at least temporarily.

On the other hand, a point of view more or less represented by state G in Figure 2 might ascend to dominance. In brief, this is the position in which the present revolutionary agitation is in direct line of descent from the American Revolution – where the central aims were to secure for the individual (a) representation in the making of decisions which affect his destiny, and (b) freedom to pursue self fulfillment in ways that do not result in others being deprived of the same right – and also from the social-reform component of the labor movement. In this view the revolutionary forces tend to be seen as essentially an accompaniment to a drastic evolutionary jump which society, and perhaps man himself, are attempting to make. If indeed this interpretation comes to dominate, then national policies will tend to utilize the opportunity provided by the militant pressure to accelerate progress toward the basic goals implicit in the founding of the nation, while continuing the necessary suppression of violence and of infringement of others' rights. A development which makes this course of history fairly likely is discussed in the next section.

In concluding this brief discussion of the significance of contemporary revolutionary forces let us say again that this has particular relevance to the problem of educational policy and the future, not only because it gives us some clues as to the kind of future we may have to design education for, but also because it faces us squarely with the question of what kind of future we want to design education to help bring about.

A possible underlying conceptual revolution

Political revolutionaries and struggles of subjugated groups to redress the power balance are not new in history. The 'psychological revolutionaries' we examined in the last section may seem more unique. But here and there in the literature on the future – in Platt (1966), Boulding (1964), Teilhard de Chardin (1969), Mumford (1956), Matson (1964), Becker (1969) – we find suggestions that something more rare in the history of man may be taking place, a major conceptual revolution.

In fact, one could argue that in the history of the Western world since Christianity rose to provide the first unified Western thought there has been only one such drastic shift in dominant basic premises – that associated with the Protestant Reformation. Max Weber and his followers in sociology have contended that when one examines the major changes in a society it is the whole socio-cultural system which changes, including institutionalized organizational forms, roles, norms, traditions, values and basic belief premises. Thus, related to the belief-and-value shift from the theological view of the Middle Ages to the Protestant ethic and economic view of the modern Western world were, it is claimed, such social changes as the rise of modern corporate capitalism, the industrial revolution, and the subsequent explosive ubiquitousness of technology.

There do seem to be superficial parallels, at least, between events of the past decade and those of the sixteenth century. That period, too, was one of multiple revolutions:

1. The Protestant revolt with its anabaptist groups so reminiscent of modern student protest groups.
2. The challenge of a new economics in the rise of capitalism.
3. Beginnings, with Copernicus, of the scientific revolution.
4. A revolutionary 'age of exploration and discovery'.
5. The commercial and price revolution – rearrangement of social classes and re-distribution of wealth; urban growth.
6. Redistribution of authority – political centralization and nationalism, replacing religious by secular authority.
7. Technological revolution (the printing press).

If indeed the contemporary manifold evidences of revolutionary ferment are related to a shifting in dominant belief-and-value assumptions within the culture, this may well be accompanied by as pervasive and varied changes in the society as accompanied the rise of the Protestant ethic.

Evidences of a basic-assumption shift

The evidence we shall examine briefly indicates, first of all, an increased tolerance in the popular culture for belief systems which tend in the metaphysical or transcendental direction, in contrast to the agnosticism and skeptical materialism of the post-First World War period, and secondly, an opening up of the basic presuppositions within science to allow conceptual models not limited by the positivistic premise.

Aldous Huxley (1945) was one of the modern writers to suggest that an age-old set of basic assumptions about the nature of man was showing new strength. We shall borrow his term, the *Perennial Philosophy*.

Philosophia Perennis – the phrase was coined by Leibniz; but the thing – the metaphysic that recognizes a divine Reality substantial to the world of things and lives and minds; the psychology that finds in the soul something similar to, or even identical with, divine Reality; the ethic that places man's final end in the knowledge of the imminent and transcendent Ground of all being – the thing is immemorial and Universal. Rudiments of the Perennial Philosophy may be found among the traditionary lore of primitive peoples in every region of the world, and in its fully developed forms it has a place in every one of the higher religions. A version of this Highest Common Factor in all preceding and subsequent theologies was first committed to writing more than twenty-five centuries ago, and since that time the inexhaustible theme has been treated again and again, from the standpoint of every religious tradition and in all the principal languages of Asia and Europe.

The basic proposition to the 'Perennial Philosophy' is an experiential one, that man can under certain conditions attain to a higher awareness, a 'cosmic consciousness', in which state he has immediate knowledge of a reality underlying the phenomenal world, in speaking of which it seems appropriate to use such words as infinite and eternal (Divine Ground, Brahman, Godhead, Clear Light of the Void). From this vantage point one's own growth and creativity, and one's participation in the evolutionary process, are seen to be under the ultimate direction of a higher center (Atman, the Self of Vedantic writings, the Oversoul). Ordinary perceptions of one's life and one's environment are likened to the perceptions of a hypnotic trance. Such phenomena as extra-sensory perception, precognition of future events, 'instant' diagnosis and healing, levitation and other psychokinetic events, etc., are only extraordinary, not *a priori* impossible.

The basic assumptions of positivistic science stand in relationship to the Perennial Philosophy much as Newtonian mechanics stands to relativistic physics – they are in no way invalidated for those aspects of human experience to which they are inappropriate, but comprise a special case, a more limited form. Similarly, the philosophies of materialism and idealism are to each other as the wave and particle theories of light and matter.

The Perennial Philosophy is not new to Western culture, of course. It has been present through the Rosicrucian and Freemasonry traditions. Its symbolism in the Great Seal of the United States, on the back of the one-dollar bill, is testimony to the role it played in the formation of this country. It appears in the Transcendentalism of Emerson, the Creative Evolution of Bergson, and the extensive writings of William James.

Whether one ascribes its recent popularity to increased intellectual openness and tolerance, or to anxiety brought on by the nuclear threat, indications abound that increasing numbers of persons seem to be taking these premises seriously. Book sales in religion, metaphysics, transcendental philosophy, Eastern religious philosophies, and parapsychology indicate increased interest in these related areas. Contemporary song lyrics, from the rock music of Dylan, Donovan, and the Beatles, to the recent 'Age of Aquarius', to the melodic 'On a Clear Day' ('rise and look around you, and you will see who you are') contain numerous subtle and not-so-subtle references to monistic viewpoints and to the role of psychedelic chemicals in initiation into the new culture ('Lucy in the Sky with Diamonds'). Metaphysically oriented churches, societies and study groups are much in evidence. Courses and lectures on Eastern religious philosophies are well attended in the Free Universities, at the sixty or more Esalen-type growth centers, university extension courses, adult education courses, etc.

A part of the negative reaction of the society to monistic and Eastern kinds of beliefs as they have appeared in the hippie culture, the drug scene and numerous cults, has been related to the fear that they would lead to quietism and withdrawal which would undermine the social structure. While it is true that this association has been characteristic in the Eastern world, there is in fact nothing in the Perennial Philosophy premises which is contrary to virile and active participation in economic and political affairs. Neither are these premises in any way contrary to a high-technology society; they only say something about the *ends* to which that technology would be put. The kinds of society which Erich Fromm talks about in *The Sane Society*, or John Galbraith in *The New Industrial State*, or Michael Harrington in *The Accidental Century* are all completely compatible with the Perennial Philosophy premises. Such a society would, with all its high technology, tend to be education- and growth-centered, somewhat along the lines of the Greek ideal as described in Werner Jaeger's *Paidea*.

Beginnings of a new science

Even more important than indications of a popular shift, which otherwise might appear to be a mere fad, are indications of a new science of subjective experience (or 'altered states of consciousness'). Scientists – that is, persons with recognized scientific training, on the staffs of research organizations and universities with high standards, and holding membership in recognized scientific associations – are manifesting more and more interest in developing a science of ordinary and extraordinary subjective experience. This is not completely new, of course. The phenomena of hypnosis have been studied in a scientific way, off and on, for at least a century and a half. Phenomenology has been a sometime influence in psychology. Freud's psychoanalysis and its offshoots have attempted to probe the unconscious processes.

Many of the pioneering works in this area assume the appropriateness of premises in the 'perennial philosophy' direction, e.g. F. W. H. Myers's *Human Personality and its Survival of Bodily Death*, Richard Bucke's *Cosmic Consciousness*, Pitirim Sorokin's *The Ways and Power of Love*, not to mention the writings of numerous Vedanta, Sufi and Zen scholars. Among modern psychotherapists whose works all fit into this same basic philosophical framework are C. G. Jung, Roberto Assagioli, and Hubert Benoit.

New scientific journals implicitly friendly to the 'perennial philosophy' premises include the *Journal of Transpersonal Psychology* and the *Journal for the Study of Consciousness*. At the popular level we have the new and glossy *Psychic*, a magazine 'devoted to every aspect of psychic phenomena and related topics'.

Research activity is currently significant in at least three approaches to 'altered states of consciousness' – feedback of EEG signals, psychedelic chemicals and classical (by which we mean sensory deprivation, yoga, auto-hypnosis, hypnosis, meditation, etc.). It should be noted that there are two recent and significant advances in this area. One is increased access to and control of altered states, making them more available for exploration. The other is the appearance of physiological correlates to altered states (EEG, EMG, GSR, REM, etc.). This latter is of extreme importance in a philosophy-of-science sense. The scientist of subjective experience is now much more in the position of the physicist studying an electron, or the astronomer studying a galaxy, in that he can say 'here is a phenomenon (dream, satori state, etc.) which defies strict definition, but which I can study through various correlates (alpha waves, rapid-eye-movement, verbal report, observable behavior, etc.)'. In effect it means that the barrier between objective 'public' data and subjective 'private' data is gone for good, and the legitimated boundaries for scientific scrutiny are thus extended.

Characteristics of the new science

The science of man's subjective experience is in its infancy. Even so, some of its foreshadowings are evident. With the classification of these questions into the realm of empirical inquiry, we can anticipate an acceleration of research in this area. As a consequence, there is new hope of consensus on issues – especially value issues – which have been at the root of conflict for centuries (just as earlier there came about consensus on the place of the Earth in the universe, and on the origin of man). The new science bids fair to incorporate the most penetrating insights of psychology, the humanities and religion. These developments will have profound impacts on goal priorities in society, on our concepts of education, on the further development and use of technology, and perhaps (as in the case of Copernican revolution) on the distribution of power among social institutions and interest groups.

Young and incomplete as the science of subjective experience is, it nevertheless already contains what may very well be extremely significant precursors of tomorrow's image of man's potentialities. Space does not permit documenting them here (see Harman, 1967); however, the following three propositions have accumulated an impressive amount of substantiating evidence:

1. The potentialities of the individual human being are far greater, in extent and diversity, than we ordinarily imagine them to be, and far greater than currently in-vogue models of man would lead us to think possible.

2. A far greater portion of significant human experience than we ordinarily feel or assume to be so is comprised of unconscious processes. This includes not only the sort of repressed memories and messages familiar to us through psychotherapy. It includes also 'the wisdom of the body' and those mysterious realms of experience we refer to with such words as 'intuition' and 'creativity'. Access to these unconscious processes is apparently facilitated by a wide variety of factors, including attention to feelings, emotions, inner attention, 'free association', hypnosis, sensory deprivation, hallucinogenic and psychedelic drugs, and others.

3. Included in these partly or largely unconscious processes are self expectations, internalized expectations of others, images of the self and limitations of the self, and images of the future, which play a predominant role in limiting or enhancing actualization of one's capacities. These tend to be self fulfilling. Much recent research has focused on the role of self expectations and expectations of others in affecting performance, and the improvement–performance level research findings are buttressing the intuitive wisdom that one of the most important characteristics of any society is its vision of itself and its future, what Boulding calls 'organizing images'. The validity of the self fulfilling prophecy and the self realizing image appears to grow steadily in confirmation.

Assuming that the evidence continues to mount, substantiating these propositions and supporting their extrapolation further in the direction they now point, this will have the most profound implications for the future.

Relation to revolutionary forces

The real significance of a science of subjective experience and 'altered states of consciousness' is that it is in this area that our individual and social values are experientially and historically rooted. This development amounts to bringing in a new means of obtaining concensus on value questions. Already in the field of clinical psychology several scientists are proposing to formulate through their researches 'a natural value system, a court of ultimate appeal for the determination of good and bad, of right and wrong' (Maslow); 'universal human value directions emerging from the experiencing of the human organism' (Rogers).

As previously noted, the student concern with 'awareness-expanding' and 'consciousness exploring' activities is intimately related to their own reformulated value convictions. These in turn lead to their demands for a person-centered, rather than scholarship-centered, education, and for a society adapted to transcendental (or at least humane) man rather than economic man.

The relationship to the political revolutionary forces is only slightly less apparent. The revolutionary press intersperses articles on Eastern philosophies, hip drug use, the human potential movement, transcendental meditation and Krishna consciousness, among the political discussions and the diatribes against various aspects of the social system. On the other hand, *Cosmos*, monthly newspaper of 'the occult, psychic phenomena, spiritualism, ESP, metaphysics, New Age philosophies, and allied subjects', publishes articles on the youth revolution, crisis in values, generation discrepancy, and social injustice. The farflung network of 'rock stations', broadcasting revolutionary messages in the lyrics of their songs and in their parodies of news programs, also carry interviews and lectures relating to religious, metaphysical, psychic and esoteric topics, and supply as a public service announcements of meetings and fund-raising campaigns of religious study groups, Subud, Scientology, Vedanta, and assorted similar organizations.

It is obviously too early to tell whether the shift in dominating values and the corresponding change in basic assumptions described above is taking place in a lasting way. If it does, we may expect to see changes as radical in the sociocultural system as when the belief system of the Middle Ages gave way to the Protestant ethic and capitalistic economics. If it does, that would tend to support the 'person-centered society' and the 'new values' and 'American origin' values discussed above.

Meta-issues of the future

Thus far we have examined manifest trends and counter-trends, and examined several aspects of the alternative futures among which we, as a society, are in the process of choosing. We have argued that in a fundamental sense, choosing the future involves choosing to have a set of beliefs and values be dominant. Because the current issues in the dissidence of youth and minority groups may be assumed to be indicators of choice points with which the society is faced, we examined these in some detail. Various bits of evidence pointed to the possibility of a conceptual revolution in process, and we looked at those.

We are now, at long last, ready to look at what we might be able to summarize out of all of this that is directly relevant to educational policy. The term 'choice point' was introduced in the preceding paragraph. This seems a useful concept for our purposes. By choice point is meant a point or period in time where the society as a whole makes a commitment of psychic, human, and economic resources in a particular direction. The associated decisions are multifold and are diffused in level (political, structural, value-belief), in time, and in space (some in Washington, some in other capitals, some in Wall Street, etc). Some are made with awareness; others may be made by default, or with relative unawareness of making any decision at all. The choice is not necessarily associated with a major decision of any one identifiable agency, but is rather an aggregate of decision made more or less simultaneously (in the long-term historical sense) by different elements of society. An example would be the choice to provide some sort of old age security, which reached its present form as a consequence of numerous state laws, federal acts, amendments, and a host of less identifiable decisions.

It will be seen that in these terms, we have argued in the preceding that the society is involved with such a choice point in moving either toward what we termed the 'second-phase industrial' society or the 'person-centered society'. It is obvious that no one in the White House or anywhere else actually makes such a decision. But in effect, through a multiplicity of decisions ranging from Congress and the Pentagon to the local school-board and industrial management, the choice is in process of being made. At one level a component decision may have to do with pollution of a local river, at another with the structure of regional government, at another with the values inculcated in the schoolroom. The form of future education will be much affected by which way this choice is eventually made. On the other hand, those involved in the nation's educational enterprise have the opportunity to affect this choice to some small extent. The beliefs and values of a society determine the kind of educational system it chooses to set up (and the technology it develops and applies, and a great many other things). On the other hand, what goes on in that educational system has some effect, at least, on what beliefs and values are either perpetuated or changed.

A component of this choice rests in the decision of how to handle the forces of political dissent and insurrection which exist particularly among our youth and minority groups, since the issues they thrust before us are in considerable measure these same issues. The possibility of a conceptual revolution, which we examined on p. 75, is also involved. We have seen that this is intimately involved with the youth revolt. It also appeared that the perennial-philosophy premises are compatible with the person-centered society, although not demanded by it.

Now let us look at the changes in society one more way before summarising how all of this relates to education. From the trends and alternative futures and revolutionary issues there emerge some meta-issues, or 'issues behind the issues'. We shall single out four. These may seem to be at the level of questions about the nature of the good life and the good society. And indeed they are. But they are also implicit in such questions as what shall we do about local control of schools, drug use in high schools, student rebellion over school rules, sensitivity training, Black Studies programs, the role of vocational education, quality of ghetto schools, new career ladders for minority-group teacher candidates, and person-centered curriculum. More than that. The diffused choice the society as a whole makes on these meta-issues will determine in considerable measure what the schools will be allowed to do on the more specific issues.

Thus, far from being theoretical and impractical, these meta-issues are the important ones to keep our eyes on. We select four as being among the most crucial. We shall label them as four crises, using the word in its root meaning, as a turning point, although not all would see them as meriting the emergency connotation which is often associated with that word. They are, then a crisis in human image, a crisis in authority, a crisis in economic values and a crisis in pluralism.

The crisis in human image

We have already noted, in discussing the possible conceptual revolution, that a conflict exists between the basic premises of a democracy, that man is, by virtue of his transcendental nature, endowed with reason, will, and a valid sense of value, and the reductionistic, deterministic, physicalistic premises of the behavioural-science socio-political theory our universities give the budding sociologists and political scientists going into public life.

The young social scientist receives a background in a sociology which has shifted its emphasis from the earlier semi-philosophical 'humanities' approach to an emphasis on techniques and empirical studies, with the implication that man is a creature of his drives, habits, and social roles, in whose behavior reason and choice play no decisive part. In the courses he is offered in psychology this is likely to be made even more explicit, with consciousness considered to be an epiphenomenal or at least inconsequential accompaniment to behavior governed by external stimuli and instinctive urges. His political science tends to focus on the processes by which public policies are made, and to be relatively little concerned with their contents. Amid the measurement of attitudes, population movements, organizational trends and political behavior, and the modeling of society and governments, little attention is given to the historic questions relating to man, his condition and his destiny.

On the other hand, the concept of a transcendental, choosing ultimately responsible self is essential to the entire theory of democratic government. It underlies the assumption that the criminal is responsible for his act (while recognizing in providing rehabilitation opportunities that his antisocial traits may have their roots in environmental conditioning). It is basic to the assumption in the judicial process that the judge can meaningfully make a normative judgment. Matson (1964) has given a particularly cogent analysis of the consequences of overemphasizing the objective perspective in political affairs (as contrasted with a complementary relationship between objective and humane perspectives).

Drucker (1939) was one of those who early rose to sound the demise of the image of Economic Man:

'The belief in the desirability and in the necessity of the sovereignty and autonomy of the economic sphere is disappearing; and with the belief, the reality. . . . It is the characteristic feature of our times that no new concept lies ready under the surface to take the place of Economic Man.' As we earlier noted, such a new image may be emerging now.

Mendel (1969) speaks of the youth rejection of the Economic Man image as

the Great Refusal against that pitiful caricature of man created by five centuries of urban, technological, and scientific progress – *homo economicus*. The essential accusation of the Great Refusal is directed against the subordination of human experience to the economic processes of the consumer society and its increasingly more absurd products, to the aggressive militarism that at least in our case has become so tightly interwoven with this society, and to the gigantic, impersonal organizations through which it all functions.

The ramifications of this conflict go much further than has been indicated so far. The kind of educational system and educational goals a society sets up, the way it handles the problem of poverty, the priorities given to aesthetic considerations, the extent to which it considers its citizens need for easy access to communion with nature, the uses of leisure it fosters – all these aspects and many more are affected by the image of man held by the society. In our times a potent emerging force pushes for a change in the image, in the direction of transcendent man, but thus far the power is on the side of reductionists.

The crisis in authority

If the issue of the image of man is crucial but unobtrusive, the issue of authority is immediately and obviously before us. We have witnessed in recent decades the hastening erosion of the authority of the parent, the teacher, the scholar, the church, the law, the state. Today's youth deeply question the meaning of the nation's policies and apparent aims. We need only to remind ourselves of the change, within a generation or two, of the connotations of the military uniform, the American flag on foreign soil, the policeman's badge, the draft card, patriotism.

This issue is, essentially, the issue of the balance between authority based on power and authority based upon voluntarily given respect. The central fact of our day is that a significant fraction of the population, largely black and youth, have concluded that established authority on national and local levels is illegitimate – that is, it does not adequately represent their interest, and it is not based on trust, nor on a general concensus.

Varied is the speculation as to how this erosion of legitimacy of authority came about. Flacks (1969) analyses the possible origins or correlates; his list plus a few others from other sources includes:

1. Widespread decline of commitment to 'middle-class values' and the capitalist ethic, while political and institutional elites continue to represent themselves in traditional ways.

2. Rapid growth of a sector of the middle class whose status depends on high education rather than property, and who tend to be critical of traditional capitalism and skeptical about the sanctity and benevolence of established authority.

3. Child rearing by that group, and by significant minority cultures, to have doubts about established authority.

4. Extension of education, leading to increased feelings of competence, self esteem, and sense of efficacy and potency, which in turn emphasizes self awareness rather than socialization as a suitable guide to behavior,

5. Transformation of the American family in the directions of greater equality, encouragement of self-expression and autonomous behavior, and fewer parental demands for self-discipline.

6. The Prohibition experience in particular, and sumptuary laws in general, with accompanying widespread disregard of such laws.

7. Stringent punitive laws regulating marijuana usage, while such usage is considered by a rapidly increasing minority (adults as well as youth, teachers as well as students) to be a more desirable substitute for the cocktail (a repetition of the Prohibition era).

8. Increased distrust by Negroes arising from liberal promises which they view as unkept, and experiences which repeatedly reinforce their conviction that the system is biased against them.

9. Harassment of blacks and hippies by police.

10. Reaction to the unpopular draft and 'immoral' Vietnam war.

11. Specific incidents of dishonesty (e.g. 1959 television quiz show scandals, Eisenhower denial of U-2 capture).

12. Lowering of faith in integrity of scholars and scientists (because of university involvement in military research, 'quantification' and 'dehumanization' of the social sciences, misinformation regarding marijuana and LSD).

Flacks provides several generalizations about the problem of maintenance of the legitimacy of the authority structure:
Individuals tend to attribute legitimacy to authority when the exercise of that authority is perceived as beneficial to groups, individuals or values to which that individual is committed. Legitimacy tends to be eroded if members of minority subcultures experience a persistent pattern of inequity, or if groups perceive significant discrepancies between their goals and those of the larger society.

1. Attribution of legitimacy is a function of trust, which in turn depends upon such matters as the objectivity of the authorities in mediating conflicts, the implementation of equality before the law, the openness of the political system to dissenting views, the trustworthiness of statements made by national leaders, and the degree to which officially espoused policies are actually implemented.

2. Individuals tend to attribute legitimacy to authority if they perceive a generalized concensus supporting legitimacy.

3. A person's sense of competence, potency, efficacy, is related to his response to different kinds of authority. Persons with a low

sense of competence will tolerate authoritarian power; for those with high competence the legitimacy of authority depends on the degree to which they have access to the decision-making process, or believe that their judgements are taken seriously by their superiors, or have the freedom to shape their own situation without reference to higher authority.

These considerations suggest that the restoration of the image of America as provider of moral leadership and as advancer of civilization, and the development of a sense of legitimacy of established authority, is perhaps the most urgent educational task of our day. It is a task not just for the schools, but for the law enforcement agencies, for political leadership, and for the polity as a whole.

The crisis in economic values

We have discussed this earlier so it requires only brief mention here. The essential issue is the extent to which values which are non-economic, at least in the strict sense, shall be a part of our operational (as contrasted with declared) values. The issue is central to resolution of the revolutionary forces. It becomes specific in spelling out the goals for program budgeting, or listing the benefits in a cost/benefit analysis, or evaluating achievement of educational objectives, or deciding what kinds of educational experiences shall be offered out of public funding, or planning for continuing education. If one is persuaded that education has any effect at all in changing values, the issue becomes a crucial one for the schools – what values shall be fostered?

The crisis in pluralism

A simple society can have a single culture; a complex modern civilization such as the United States cannot. The question is not whether we shall have a multi-modal culture with a variety of behavior patterns and norms in different socio-economic, educational, religious and ethnic groups. Rather, it is whether we shall have mutual hostility and exploitation of weaker groups by stronger ones, or whether we shall have between diverse groups mutual respect and cooperation.

As Lawrence Frank wrote in a recent essay entitled 'Psychology and the social order': 'A social order which tolerates such wide-ranging pluralism of norms must seek unity through diversity. This means recognizing and cultivating differences while simultaneously enlisting people's loyalty and allegiance to a core of conduct and relationships. Only education and persuasion, not force, can build a social concensus out of these massive and varied elements. . . . Social change and improvement must come through the concert of a population composed of individual personalities. . . . Instead of relying chiefly upon legislation, as in the past, we (must) begin to think how each person may become self-consciously aware of his role as a participant in his social order.'

The issue of pluralism with respect to subcultures arises in the educational world most directly over such specific questions as Black Studies programs and community control of schools.

References

ALI, T. (ed.) (1969), *The New Revolutionaries: A Handbook of the International Radical Left*, William Morrow.

BAIER, K., and RESCHER, N. (1969), *Values and the Future*, Free Press.

BECKER, E. (1969a), *Beyond Alienation: A Philosophy of Education for the Crisis of Democracy*, George Braziller.

BECKER, E. (1969b), *The Structure of Evil: An Essay on the Unification of the Science of Man*, George Braziller.

BELL, D. (1967), 'Notes on the post-industrial society', *The Public Interest*, nos. 6 and 7, Winter and Spring.

BENNIS, W. G., and SLATER, P. E. (1968), *The Temporary Society*, Harper & Row.

BOULDING, K. (1964), *The Meaning of the 20th Century: The Great Transition*, Harper & Row.

BOULDING, K. E. (1969), 'The emerging superculture', in K. Baier and H. Rescher (eds.), *Values and the Future*, Free Press.

BRZEZINSKI, Z. (1967), 'The American transition', *New Republic*, vol. 157, no. 26, December 23.

CALDER, N. (ed.) (1965), *The World in 1984*, Penguin Books, two volumes.

CAREY, J. T. (1969), *The College Drug Scene*, Prentice-Hall.

CHASE, S. (1968), *The Most Probable World*, Harper & Row.

CHOMSKY, N. (1969), *American Power and the New Mandarins*, Pantheon.

CONANT, J. B. (1964), *Shaping Educational Policy*, McGraw-Hill.

CREMIN, L. A. (1965), *The Genius of American Education*, Vintage Books.

CURTIS, R., and HOGAN, E. (1969), *Perils of the Peaceful Atom*, Doubleday.

DRUCKER, P. (1939), *The End of Economic Man*, John Day.

DRUCKER, P. (1969), *The Age of Discontinuity*, Harper & Row.

ELLUL, J. (1967), *The Technological Society*, Alfred A. Knopf.

EMERY, F. E. (1967), 'The next 30 years: concepts, methods and anticipations', *Human Relations*, vol. 20, no. 3, pp. 199–238.

ETZIONI, A. (1968), *The Active Society. A Theory of Societal and Political Processes*, Free Press.

EURICH, A. C. (ed.) (1968), *Campus 1980: The Shape of the Future in American Higher Education*, Delacorte Press.

EWALD, W. R. (ed.) (1967), *Environment for Man: The Next 50 Years*, Indiana University Press.

EWALD, W. R. (ed.) (1968a), *Environment and Policy: The Next 50 Years*, Indiana University Press.

EWALD, W. R. (ed.) (1968b), *Environment and Change: The Next 50 Years*, Indiana University Press.

FERKISS, V. C. (1969), *Technological Man: The Myth and the Reality*, George Braziller.

FLACKS, R. E. (1969), 'Protest or conform: some social psychological perspectives on legitimacy', *Journal of Applied Social Science*, vol. 5, no. 2, pp. 127–50.

GABOR, D. (1963), *Inventing the Future*, Secker and Warburg; Penguin Books, 1964.

GALBRAITH, J. K. (1967), *New Industrial State*, Houghton Mifflin.

GALBRAITH, J. K. (1969), *The Affluent Society*, Houghton Mifflin.

GLAZER, N. (1969), 'For white and black, community control is the issue', *New York Times Magazine*, April 27.

GOODMAN, P. (1956), *Growing Up Absurd*, Vintage Books.

GOODMAN, P. (1962), *Compulsory Mis-Education and the Community of Scholars*, Vintage Books.

GREEN, T. (1968), *Work, Leisure and the American Schools*, Random House.

HARMAN, W. (1967), 'Belief systems, scientific findings and educational policy', E.P.R.C. Research Note no. 6747–4, *Stanford Research Institute*, November.

HARRINGTON, M. (1966), *The Accidental Century*, Penguin Books (Pelican series).

HEILBRONER, R. L. (1960), *The Future as History*, Grove Press.

HELMER, O. (1965), *Social Technology*, Delphi Predictions, Rand Corporation (P-3063), February.

HIRSCH, W. (1967), *Inventing Education for the Future*, Chandler.

HUTCHINS, R. M. (1968), *The Learning Society*, Praeger.

HUXLEY, A. (1945), *The Perennial Philosophy*, Harper & Brothers.

JACOBS, P., and LANDAU, S. (1966), *The New Radicals*, Vintage Books.

JENCKS, C., and RIESMAN, D. (1968), *The Academic Revolution*, Doubleday.

JOHANSEN, W. (n.d.), *Education and Technology in the 21st Century*, proceedings of a symposium directed by W. Johansen, Chairman of San Francisco State College's School of Creative Arts; published as a class project; paperback.

JUNGK, R., and GALTUNG, Y. (eds.) (1968), *Mankind 2000*, Norwegian Universities Press.

KAHN, H., and WEINER, A. J. (1967), *The Year 2000: A Framework for Speculation on the Next 33 Years*, Macmillan.

KENISTON, K. (1967), 'The sources of student dissent', *Journal of Social Issues*, June, vol. 23, pp. 108–37.

KENISTON, K. (1968), *Young Radicals*, Harcourt, Brace & World.

KENISTON, K. (1969), 'You have to grow up in Scarsdale to know how bad things really are', *New York Times Magazine*, April 27.

KENNAN, G. F. (1968), *Democracy and the Student Left*, Little, Brown & Co.

KERBER, A., and SMITH, W. (1962), *Educational Issues in a Changing Society*, Wayne State University Press.

KIMBALL, S. T., and MCCLELLAN, J. E. (1962), *Education and the New America*, Vintage Press.

LEONARD, G. B. (1968), *Education and Ecstasy*, Delacorte Press.

LIEBERMAN, M. (1960), *The Future of Public Education*, Phoenix Books.

LIPSET, S. M. (1963), *The First New Nation*, Basic Books.

MACK, R. (1967), *Transforming America: Patterns of Social Change*, Random House.

MASLOW, A. H. (1961), 'Eupsychia – the good society', *Journal of Humanistic Psychology*, vol. 1, pp. 1–11.

MASLOW, A. H. (1967), 'A theory of metamotivation: the biological rooting of the value-life', *Journal of Humanistic Psychology*, Fall, pp. 93–127; reproduced in A. J. Sutich and M. A. Vich, *Readings in Humanistic Psychology*, Free Press.

MATSON, F. W. (1964), *The Broken Image: Man, Science and Society*, George Braziller.

MAYHEW, L. B. (1967), *Higher Education in the Revolutionary Decades*, McCutchan Publishing Company.

MCDERMOTT, J. (1969), 'Technology; the opiate of the intellectuals', *New York Review of Books*, July 31, pp. 25–35.

MCEVOY, J., and MILLER, A. (1969), *Black Power and Student Rebellion*, Wadsworth.

MCLUHAN, M., and LEONARD, G. B. (1967), 'The future of education: the class of 1989', *Look*, vol. 31, no. 4, February 21.

MENDEL, A. P. (1969), 'Robots and rebels', *New Republic*, January 11, p. 16.

MICHAEL, D. N. (1968), *The Unprepared Society*, Basic Books.

MORPHET, E. L., and RYAN, C. O. (1967 and 1968), *Designing Education for the Future*, vols. 1–4, Citation Press; vol. 1: *Prospective Changes in Society by 1980;* vol. 2: *Implications for Education of Prospective Changes in Society;* vol. 3: *Planning and Effecting Needed Changes in Education;* vol. 4: *Cooperative Planning for Education in 1980*.

MUMFORD, L. (1956), *The Transformation of Man*, Harper & Brothers.

MUMFORD, L. (1965), 'Technics and the nature of man', *Nature*, December 4, pp. 923–8.

National Industrial Conference Board's Experimental Forecast for 1968, *NICE Report*.

NOWLIS, H. H. (1969), *Drugs on the College Campus*, Anchor Books.

OPPENHEIMER, M. (1969), *The Urban Guerrilla*, Quadrangle Books.

PINES, M. (1966), *Revolution in Learning: The Years from Birth to Six*, Harper & Row.

PLATT, J. R. (1966), *The Step to Man*, Wiley.

POLAK, F. L. (1961), *The Image of the Future*, Leyden, A. W. Sijthoff.

PREHODA, R. W. (1967), *Designing the Future*, Chilton Book Co.

RESCHER, N. (1967), *Value Considerations in the Public Policy Issues of the Year 2000*, RAND.

SANFORD, N., and KATZ, J. (1969), *Search for Relevance*, pamphlet.

SPENDER, S. (1969), *The Year of the Young Rebels*, Random House.

TAYLOR, H. (1969), *Students Without Teachers: The Crisis in the University*, McGraw-Hill.

Technology and the American Economy (1966), vol. 1, February, Report of the National Commission of Technology, Automation and Economic Progress.

TEILHARD DE CHARDIN, P. (1964), *The Future of Man*, Harper & Row; Fontana Books, 1964.

TEILHARD DE CHARDIN, P. (1969), 'The future of the humanities', *Daedalus*, Summer.

THEOBALD, R. (1962), *The Challenge of Abundance*, New American Library.

THEOBALD, R. (1968), *An Alternative Future for America*, Swallow Press.

THEOBALD, R. (ed.) (1969), *Social Policies for America in the Seventies: Nine Divergent Views*, Doubleday Anchor Books.

'Toward the year 2000: work in progress' *Daedalus*, Summer, 1967.

Toward the year 2018 (1968), published for the Foreign Policy Association by Cowles Education Corporation.

TRIST, E. (1968), 'Urban North America: the challenge of the next 30 years', unpublished paper delivered to the Annual Meeting and Conference of the Town Planning Institute of Canada, June.

WARE, C., PANIKKAR, K. M., and ROMEIN, J. M. (1966), *The 20th Century*, vol. 6 of *History of Mankind: Cultural and Scientific Development*, Harper & Row, prepared under the auspices of UNESCO.

WASKOW, A. I. (1969), *Notes from 1999*, New American Library.

YOUNG, M. (1958), *The Rise of the Meritocracy, 1870–2033*, Thames and Hudson; Penguin Books, 1961, 1967.

2 W. G. Bennis

A Funny Thing Happened on the Way to the Future

From W. G. Bennis, 'A funny thing happened on the way to the future', *American Psychologist*, 1970, vol. 25, no. 7, pp. 595–608.

Analysis of the 'future', or, more precisely, inventing relevant futures, has become in recent years as respectable for the scientist as the shaman. Inspired by Bertrand de Jouvenal, Daniel Bell, Olaf Helmer, and others, there seems to be growing evidence and recognition for the need of a legitimate base of operations for the 'futurologist'. Writing in a recent issue of the *Antioch Review*, groping for a definition of the future, I wrote:

For me, the 'future' is a portmanteau word. It embraces several notions. It is an exercise of the imagination which allows us to compete with and try to outwit future events. Controlling the anticipated future is, in addition, a social invention that legitimizes the process of forward planning. There is no other way I know of to resist the 'tyranny of blind forces' than by looking facts in the face (as we experience them in the present) and extrapolating to the future – nor is there any other sure way to detect compromise. Most importantly, the future is a conscious dream, a set of imaginative hypotheses groping toward whatever vivid utopias lie at the heart of our consciousness. 'In dreams begin responsibilities,' said Yeats, and it is to our future responsibilities as educators, researchers and practitioners that these dreams are dedicated (Bennis, 1968, p. 227).

Most students of the future would argue with that definition, claiming that it is 'poetic' or possibly even 'prescientific'. The argument has validity, I believe, though it is difficult to define 'futurology', let alone distinguish between and among terms such as 'inventing relevant futures', scenarios, forecasts, self-fulfilling prophecies, predictions, goals, normative theories, evolutionary hypotheses, prescriptions, and so on. Philosophers and sociologists, for example, are still arguing over whether Weber's theory of bureaucracy was in fact a theory, a poignant and scholarly admonition, an evolutionary hypothesis, or a descriptive statement.

However difficult it may be to identify a truly scientific study of the future, most scholars would agree that it should include a number of objectives:

1. It should provide a survey of possible futures in terms of a spectrum of major potential alternatives.

2. It should ascribe to the occurrence of these alternatives some estimates of relative *a priori* probabilities.

3. It should, for given basic policics, identify preferred alternatives.

4. It should identify those decisions which are subject to control, as well as those developments which are not, whose occurrence would be likely to have a major effect on the probabilities of these alternatives (Helmer, 1969).

With these objectives only dimly in mind, I wrote a paper on the future of organizations (five years ago to the day that this paper was delivered to the American Political Science Association) which was called 'Organizational developments and the fate of bureaucracy' (Bennis, 1964). Essentially, it was based on an evolutionary hypothesis which asserted that every age develops a form of organization most appropriate to its genius. I then went on to forecast certain changes in a 'postbureaucratic world' and how these changes would affect the structure and environment of human organizations, their leadership and motivational patterns, and their cultural and ecological values. A number of things have occurred since that first excursion into the future in September 1964 which are worth mentioning at this point, for they have served to reorient and revise substantially some of the earlier forecasts.

Perhaps only a Homer or Herodotus, or a first-rate folk-rock composer, could capture the tumult and tragedy of the five years since that paper was written and measure their impact on our lives. The bitter agony of Vietnam, the convulsive stirrings of black America, the assassinations, the bloody streets of Chicago have all left their marks. What appears is a panorama that goes in and out of focus as it is transmitted through the mass media and as it is expressed through the new, less familiar media, the strikes, injunctions, disruptions, bombings, occupations, the heart attacks of the old, and the heartaches of the young. Strolling in late August 1969 through my own campus, lush, quiet and sensual, I was almost lulled into thinking that nothing fundamental has happened to America in the past five years. Only the residual graffiti from last spring's demonstrations ('Keep the Pigs Out!' 'Be Realistic – Demand the Impossible!'), hanging all but unnoticed in the student union, remind us that something has – though what it is, as the song says, 'ain't exactly clear'. One continually wonders if what has happened is unique and new ('Are we in France, 1788?' as one student asked), whether what is happening at the universities will spread to other, possibly less fragile institutions, and, finally, whether the university is simply the anvil upon which the awesome problems of our entire society are being hammered out. No one really knows. Despite the proliferation of analyses attributing campus unrest to everything from Oedipal conflicts (the most comforting explanation) to the failure of the Protestant Ethic, the crises continue relentlessly.

In his *Report to Greco*, Nikos Kazantzakis tells us of an ancient Chinese imprecation: 'I curse you; may you live in an important age.' Thus, we are all damned, encumbered and burdened, as well as charmed, exhilarated and fascinated by this curse.

In the rueful words of Bob Dylan:

Come writers and critics
Who prophesy with your pen
And keep your eyes wide
The chance won't come again.
And don't speak too soon
For the wheel's still in spin
And there's no tellin' who
That it's namin'
For the loser now
Will be later to win
For the times are a-changin'.

Reactions to our spastic times vary. There are at least seven definable types:

1. First and most serious of all are the *militants*, composed for the most part of impotent and dependent populations who have been

victimized and infantilized, and who see no way out but to mutilate and destroy the system which has decimated its group identity and pride. Excluded populations rarely define their price for belated inclusion in intellectual terms, which confuses and terrifies the incumbents who take participation for granted.

2. The *apocalyptics*, who with verbal ferocity burn everything in sight. So, in *Supergrow*, Benjamin DeMott (1969) assumes the persona of a future historian and casts a saddened eye on everyone from the Beatles to James Baldwin, from the *Berkeley Barb* to Alfred Kazin, while contemplating the age of megaweapons. DeMott writes: 'By the end of the sixties the entire articulate Anglo-American community . . . was transformed into a monster-chorus of damnation dealers, its single voice pitched ever at hysterical level, its prime aim to transform every form of discourse into a blast.' These voices are hot as flamethrowers, searing all that get in their way and usually fired from a vantage point several terrain features away.

3. The *regressors*, who see their world disintegrating and engage in fruitless exercises in nostalgia, keening the present and weeping for a past: orderly, humane, free, civilized and non-existent. Someone recently recommended that the university insulate itself from outside pollutants – I suppose he meant students and the community – and set up, medieval Oxford style, a chantry for scholars which he warmly referred to as a 'speculatorium'.

4. There are the *retreaters*, apathetic, withdrawn, inwardly emigrating and outwardly drugged, avoiding all environments except, at most, a communal 'roll your own' or a weekend bash at Esalen, longing for a 'peak experience', instant nirvana, hoping to beat out reality and consequence.

5. The *historians*, who are always capable of lulling us to sleep by returning to a virtuous past, demonstrating that the 'good old days' were either far better or worse. 'The good old days, the good old days,' said a Negro comedienne of the 1930s, 'I was there; where were they?' I learned recently, for example, that the university, as a quiet place devoted to the pursuit of learning and unaffected by the turbulence of the outside world, is of comparatively recent date, that the experience of the medieval university made the turbulence of recent years seem like a spring

zephyr. It was pointed out that a student at the University of Prague cut the throat of a Friar Bishop and was merely expelled, an expedient that may have had something to do with the fact that in dealing with student morals, university officials were constrained to write in Latin.

6. The *technocrats*, who plow heroically ahead, embracing the future and in the process usually forgetting to turn around to see if anybody is following or listening, cutting through waves of ideology like agile surfers.

7. And, finally, the rest of us, 'we happy few', the *liberal-democratic reformers*, optimists believing in the perfectibility of man and his institutions, waiting for a solid scientific victory over ideology and irrationality, accepting the inevitability of technology and humanism without thoroughly examining *that* relationship as we do all others, and reckoning that the only way to preserve a democratic and scientific humanism is through inspiriting our institutions with continuous, incremental reform.

The 1964 paper I mentioned earlier was written within the liberal–democratic framework, and it contained many of the inherent problems and advantages of that perspective. The main strategy of this paper and its focus of convenience are to review briefly the main points of that paper, to indicate its shortcomings and lacunae in light of five years' experience (not the least of which has been serving as an administrator in a large, complex public bureaucracy), and then proceed to develop some new perspectives relevant to the future of public bureaucracies. I might add, parenthetically, that I feel far less certainty and closure at this time than I did five years ago. The importance of inventing relevant futures and directions is never more crucial than in a revolutionary period, exactly and paradoxically at the point in time when the radical transition blurs the shape and direction of the present. This is the dilemma of our time and most certainly the dilemma of this paper.

The future: 1964 version

Bureaucracy, I argued, was an elegant social invention, ingeniously capable of organizing and coordinating the productive processes of the Industrial Revolution, but hopelessly out-of-joint with contemporary realities. There would be new shapes, patterns and models emerging which promised drastic changes in the conduct of the organization and of managerial practices in general. In the next twenty-five to fifty years, I argued, we should witness and participate in the end of bureaucracy as we know it and the rise of the new social systems better suited to twentieth-century demands of industrialization.

This argument was based on a number of factors:

1. The exponential growth of science, the growth of intellectual technology, and the growth of research and development activities.

2. The growing confluence between men of knowledge and men of power or, as I put it then, 'a growing affinity between those who make history and those who write it' (Bennis, 1964).

3. A fundamental change in the basic philosophy which underlies managerial behavior, reflected most of all in the following three areas: (a) a new concept of man, based on increased knowledge of his complex and shifting needs, which replaces the oversimplified, innocent push-button concept of man; (b) a new concept of power, based on collaboration and reason, which replaces a model of power based on coercion and fear; and (c) a new concept of organizational values, based on humanistic–democratic ideals, which replaces the depersonalized mechanistic value system of bureaucracy.

4. A turbulent environment which would hold relative uncertainty due to the increase of research and development activities. The environment would become increasingly differentiated, interdependent, and more salient to the organization. There would be greater interpenetration of the legal policy and economic features of an oligopolistic and government–business-controlled economy. Three main features of the environment would be interdependence rather than competition, turbulence rather than a steady, predictable state, and large rather than small enterprises.

5. A population characterized by a younger, more mobile, and better educated work force.

These conditions, I believed, would lead to some significant changes. The increased level of education and rate of mobility would bring about certain changes in values held toward work. People would tend to (a) be more rational, be intellectually committed, and rely more heavily on forms of social influence which correspond to their value system; (b) be more 'other-directed' and rely on their temporary neighbors and workmates for companionships, in other words, have relationships, not relatives; and (c) require more involvement, participation and autonomy in their work.

As far as organizational structure goes, given the population characteristics and features of environmental turbulence, the social structure in organizations of the future would take on some unique characteristics. I will quote from the original paper.

First of all, the key word will be temporary: organizations will become adaptive, rapidly changing temporary systems. Second, they will be organized around problems-to-be-solved. Third, these problems will be solved by relative groups of strangers who represent a diverse set of professional skills. Fourth, given the requirements of coordinating the various projects, articulating points or 'linking pin' personnel will be necessary who can speak the diverse languages of research and who can relay and mediate between various project groups. Fifth, the groups will be conducted on organic rather than on mechanical lines; they will emerge and adapt to the problems, and leadership and influence will fall to those who seem most able to solve the problems rather than to programmed role expectations. People will be differentiated, not according to rank or roles, but according to skills and training.

Adaptive, temporary systems of diverse specialists solving problems, coordinated organically via articulating points, will gradually replace the theory and practice of bureaucracy. Though no catchy phrase comes to mind, it might be called an organic-adaptive structure.

(As an aside: what will happen to the rest of society, to the manual laborers, to the poorly educated, to those who desire to work in conditions of dependency, and so forth? Many such jobs will disappear; automatic jobs will be automated. However, there will be a corresponding growth in the service-type of occupation, such as organizations like the Peace Corps and AID. There will also be jobs, now being seeded, to aid in the enormous challenge of coordinating activities between groups and organizations. For certainly, consortia of various kinds are growing in number and scope and they will require careful attention. In times of change, where there is a wide discrepancy between cultures and generations, an increase in industrialization, and especially urbanization, society becomes the client for skills in human resources. Let us hypothesize that approximately 40 per cent of the population would be involved in jobs of this nature, 40 per cent in technological jobs, making an organic-adaptive majority with, say, a 20 per cent bureaucratic minority) (Bennis, 1964).

Toward the end of the paper, I wrote that

The need for instinctual renunciation decreases as man achieves rational mastery over nature. In short, organizations of the future will require fewer restrictions and repressive techniques because of the legitimization of play and fantasy, accelerated through the rise of science and intellectual achievements (Bennis, 1964).

To summarize the changes in emphasis of social patterns in the 'postbureaucratic world' I was then describing (using Trist's 1968 framework), the following paradigm may be useful:

From	Toward
Cultural values	
Achievement	Self-actualization
Self-control	Self-expression
Independence	Interdependence
Endurance of stress	Capacity for joy
Full employment	Full lives
Organizational values	
Mechanistic forms	Organic forms
Competitive relations	Collaborative relations
Separate objectives	Linked objectives
Own resources regarded as owned absolutely	Own resources regarded also as society's resources

I hope I have summarized the paper without boring you in the process. One thing is clear; looking backward, re-examining one's own work five years later is a useful exercise. Aside from the protracted decathexis from the original ideas, new experiences and other emergent factors all help to provide a new perspective which casts some doubt on a number of assumptions, only half implied in the earlier statement. For example:

1. The organizations I had in mind then were of a single class: instrumental, large-scale, science-based, international bureau-

cracies, operating under rapid growth conditions. Service industries and public bureaucracies, as well as nonsalaried employees,
were excluded from analysis.

2. Practically no attention was paid to the boundary transactions
of the firm or to interinstitutional linkages.

3. The management of conflict was emphasized, while the strategy
of conflict was ignored.

4. Power of all types was underplayed, while the role of the leader
as facilitator – 'linking pin' – using an 'agricultural model' of
nurturance and climate building was stressed. Put in Gamson's
(1968) terms, I utilized a domesticated version of power, emphasizing the process by which the authorities attempt to achieve
collective goals and to maintain legitimacy and compliance with
their decisions, rather than the perspective of 'potential partisans', which involves diversity of interest groups attempting to
influence the choices of authorities.

5. A theory of change was implied, based on gentle nudges from
the environment coupled with a truth–love strategy; that is, with
sufficient trust and collaboration along with valid data, organizations would progress monotonically along a democratic con-
tinuum.

In short, the organizations of the future I envisaged would
most certainly be, along with a Bach Chorale and Chartres
Cathedral, the epiphany to Western civilization.

The striking thing about truth and love is that whereas I once
held them up as the answer to our institution's predicaments, they
have now become the problem. And, to make matters worse, the
world I envisaged as emergent in 1964 becomes, not necessarily
inaccurate, but overwhelmingly problematical. It might be useful
to review some of the main organizational dilemmas before going
any further, both as a check on the previous forecast, as well as a
preface to some new and tentative ideas about contemporary
human organizations.

Some new dilemmas
The problem of legitimacy

The key difference between the Berkeley riots of 1964 and the
Columbia crisis of May 1969 is that in the pre-Columbian case

the major impetus for unrest stemmed from the perceived abuse or misuse of authority ('Do not bend, fold, or mutilate'), whereas the later protest denied the legitimacy of authority. The breakdown of legitimacy in our country has many reasons and explanations, not the least of which is the increasing difficulty of converting political questions into technical–managerial ones. Or, put differently, questions of legitimacy arise whenever 'expert power' becomes ineffective. Thus, black militants, drug users, draft resisters, student protestors, and liberated women all deny the legitimacy of those authorities who are not black, drug experienced, pacifists, students, or women.

The university is in an excruciating predicament with respect to the breakdown of legitimacy. Questions about admissions, grades, curriculum and police involvement – even questions concerning rejection of journal articles – stand the chance of being converted into political–legal issues. This jeopardizes the use of universalistic–achievement criteria, upon which the very moral imperatives of our institutions are based. The problem is related, of course, to the inclusion of those minority groups in our society which have been excluded from participation in American life and tend to define their goals in particularistic and political terms.

Kelman (1969) cites three major reasons for the crisis in legitimacy: (a) serious failings of the system in living up to its basic values and in maintaining a proper relationship between means and ends, (b) decreasing trust in leadership, and (c) dispositions of our current youth. On this last point, Flacks (1969)

suggests the existence of an increasingly distinct 'humanist' subculture in the middle class, consisting primarily of highly educated and urbanized families, based in professional occupations, who encourage humanist orientations in their offspring as well as questioning attitudes to traditional middle class values and to arbitrary authority and conventional politics. . . . Although this humanist subculture represents a small minority of the population, many of its attributes are more widely distributed, and the great increase in the number of college graduates suggests that the ranks of this subculture will rapidly grow.

In short, as the gap between shared and new moralities and authoritative norms, i.e. the law, widens, questions of legitimacy inevitably arise.

Populist versus elite functions?

Can American institutions continue to fulfill the possibly incompatible goals of their elitist and populist functions? Again, the American university is an example of this dilemma, for the same institution tries to balance both its autonomous-elite function of disinterested inquiry and criticism and an increasingly service-populist-oriented function. This has been accomplished by insulating the elite (autonomous) functions of liberal education, basic research, and scholarship from the direct impact of the larger society, whose demands for vocational training, certification, service and the like are reflected and met in the popular functions of the university. As Trow (1969) puts it:

These insulations take various forms of a division of labor within the university. There is a division of labor between departments, as for example, between a department of English or Classics, and a department of Education. There is a division of labor in the relatively unselective universities between the undergraduate and graduate schools, the former given over largely to mass higher education in the service of social mobility and occupational placement, entertainment, and custodial care, while the graduate departments in the same institutions are often able to maintain a climate in which scholarship and scientific research can be done to the highest standards. There is a familiar division of labor, though far from clear-cut, between graduate departments and professional schools. Among the faculty there is a division of labor, within many departments, between scientists and consultants, scholars and journalists, teachers and entertainers. More dangerously, there is a division of labor between regular faculty and a variety of fringe or marginal teachers – teaching assistants, visitors and lecturers – who in some schools carry a disproportionate load of the mass teaching. Within the administration there is a division of labor between the Dean of Faculty and Graduate Dean, and the Dean of Students. And among students there is a marked separation between the 'collegiate' and 'vocational' subcultures, on the one hand, and academically or intellectually oriented subcultures on the other (p. 2).

To a certain extent, the genius of American higher education is that it *has* fulfilled both of these functions, to the wonder of all, and especially to observers from European universities. But with the enormous expansion of American universities, proportional strains are being placed on their insulating mechanisms.

Interdependence or complicity in the environment

The environment I talked about in 1964, its interdependence and turbulence, is flourishing today. But my optimism must now be tempered, for what appeared then to be a 'correlation of fates' turns out to have blocked the view of some serious problems. The university is a good example of this tension.

The relationship between the university and its environment has never been defined in more than an overly abstract way. For some, the university is a citadel, aloof, occasionally lobbing in on society the shells of social criticism. Both the radical left and the conservative right seem to agree on this model, maintaining that to yield to the claims of society will fragment and ultimately destroy the university. Others, for different reasons, prefer a somewhat similar model, that of the 'speculatorium', where scholars, protected by garden walls, meditate away from society's pollutants. Still others envisage the university as an 'agent of change', a catalytic institution capable of revolutionizing the nation's organizations and professions. In fact, a recent socio-logical study listed almost fifty viable goals for the university (Gross, 1968) (a reflection of our ambivalence and confusions as much as anything), and university catalogs usually list them all.

The role of the university in society might be easier to define if it were not for one unpalatable fact. Though it is not usually recognized, the truth is that the university is not self-supporting. The amount available for our educational expenditures (including funds necessary to support autonomous functions) relates directly to the valuation of the university by the general community. The extent to which the university's men, ideas and research are valued is commensurate with the amount of economic support it receives (Parsons, 1968). This has always been true. During the Great Awakening, universities educated ministers; during the agricultural and industrial revolutions, the land-grant colleges and engineering schools flourished; during the rise of the service professions, the universities set up schools of social welfare, nursing, public health, and so on. And during the past thirty years or so, the universities have been increasingly geared to educate individuals to man the Galbraithean 'technostructure'.

Thus, the charge of 'complicity' of the universities with the power structure is both valid and absurd; without this alleged complicity, there would be no universities, or only terribly poor ones. In the late 1960s, the same attack comes from the New Left. The paradox can be blinding, and often leads to one of two pseudosolutions, total involvement or total withdrawal – pseudosolutions familiar enough on other fronts, for example, in foreign policy.

If I am right that the university must be valued by society in order to be supported, the question is not should the university be involved with society, but what should be the *quality* of this involvement and *with whom*? For years, there has been tacit acceptance of the idea that the university must supply industry, the professions, defense, and the technostructure with the brains necessary to carry on their work. Now there are emerging constituencies, new dependent populations, new problems, many without technical solutions, that are demanding that attention of the university. We are being called upon to direct our limited and already scattered resources to newly defined areas of concern – the quality of life, the shape and nature of our human institutions, the staggering problems of the city, legislative processes, and the management of human resources. Will it be possible for the modern university to involve itself with these problems and at the same time avoid the politicization that will threaten its autonomous functions? One thing is clear, we will never find answers to these problems if we allow rational thought to be replaced by a search for villains. To blame the establishment, or Wall Street, or the New Left for our problems is lazy, thoughtless and frivolous. It would be comforting if we *could* isolate and personalize the problems facing the university, but we cannot.

The last two dilemmas that I have just mentioned, elitist *versus* populist strains vying within a single institution and the shifting, uncertain symbiosis between university and society, contain many of the unclear problems we face today, and I suspect that they account for much of the existential groaning we hear in practically all of our institutions, not just the university.

The search for the correct metaphor

Metaphors have tremendous power to establish new social realities, to give life and meaning to what was formerly perceived only dimly and imprecisely. What *did* students experience before Erikson's 'identity crisis'? Greer (1969) wrote recently:

[But] much of our individual experience is symbolized in vague and unstandardized ways. There is, as we say, no word for it. One of the great contributions of creative scientists and artists is to make communicable what was previously moot, to sense new meanings possible in the emerging nature of human experience, giving them a form which makes communication possible. The phrase-maker is not to be despised, he may be creating the grounds for new social reality. (On the other hand, he may merely be repackaging an old product.) (p. 46).

Most of us have internalized a metaphor about organizational life, however crude that model or vivid that utopia is – or how conscious or unconscious – which governs our perceptions of our social systems. How these metaphors evolve is not clear, although I do not think Freud was far off the mark with his focus on the family, the military, and the church as the germinating institutions.

Reviewing organizational metaphors somewhat biographically, I find that my first collegiate experience, at Antioch College, emphasized a 'community democracy' metaphor, obviously valid for a small, town-meeting type of political life. In strong contrast to this was the Massachusetts Institute of Technology, which employed the metaphor (not consciously, of course) of 'The Club', controlled tacitly and quite democratically, but without the formal governing apparatus of political democracies, by an 'old-boy network', composed of the senior tenured faculty and administration. The State University of New York at Buffalo comes close, in my view, to a 'labor-relations' metaphor, where conflicts and decisions are negotiated through a series of interest groups bargaining as partisans. There are many other usable metaphors: Clark Kerr's 'City', Mark Hopkins's 'student and teacher on opposite ends of a log', 'General Systems Analysis', 'Therapeutic Community', 'Scientific Management', and my own 'temporary systems', and so on, that compete with the pure form of bureaucracy, but few of them seem singularly equipped to cope with the current problems facing large-scale institutions.

Macrosystems versus microsystems

One of the crude discoveries painfully learned during the course of recent administrative experience in a large public bureaucracy turns on the discontinuities between microsystems and macrosystems. For quite a while, I have had more than a passing *theoretical* interest in this problem, which undoubtedly many of you share, but my interest now, due to a sometimes eroding despair, has gone well beyond the purely theoretical problems involved.

My own intellectual 'upbringing', to use an old-fashioned term, was steeped in the Lewinian tradition of small-group behavior, processes of social influence, and 'action-research'. This is not terribly exceptional, I suppose, for a social psychologist. In fact, I suppose that the major methodological and theoretical influences in the social sciences for the last two decades have concentrated on more microscopic, 'manageable' topics. Also, it is not easy to define precisely where a microsocial science begins or where a macrosocial science ends. Formally, I suppose, microsystems consist of roles and actors, while macrosystems have as their constituent parts other subsystems, subcultures, and parts of society. In any case, my intellectual heritage has resulted in an erratic batting average in transferring concepts from microsystems into the macrosystem of a university.

An example of this dilemma can be seen in a letter Leonard Duhl wrote in response to an article by Carl Rogers which stressed an increased concern with human relationships as a necessary prerequisite for managing society's institutions. Duhl (1969) wrote:

Though I agree with [Rogers] heartily, I have some very strong questions about whether, indeed, this kind of future is in the cards for us. I raise this primarily because out of my experiences working in the US Department of Housing and Urban Development and out of experiences working in and with cities, it is clear that in the basic decision making that takes place, the values Dr Rogers and I hold so dear have an extremely low priority. Indeed, the old-fashioned concerns with power, prestige, money and profit so far outdistance the concerns for human warmth and love and concern that many people consider the latter extremely irrelevant in the basic decision making. Sadly, it is my feeling that they will continue to do so.

The following examples from my own recent experience tend to confirm Duhl's gloomy outlook.

The theory of consensus falters under those conditions where competing groups bring to the conference table vested interests based on group membership, what Mannhein referred to as 'perspectivistic orientation'. Where goals are competitive and group (or subsystem) oriented, despite the fact that a consensus might rationally create a new situation where all parties may benefit – that is, move closer to the Paretian optimal frontier – a negotiated position may be the only practical solution. There was a time when I believed that consensus was a valid operating procedure. I no longer think this is realistic, given the scale and diversity of organizations. In fact, I have come to think that the quest for consensus, except for some microsystems where it may be feasible, is a misplaced nostalgia for a folk society as chimerical, incidentally, as the American search for 'identity'.

The collaborative relationship between superiors and subordinates falters as well under those conditions where 'subordinates' – if that word is appropriate – are *delegates* of certain subsystems. Under this condition, collaboration may be perceived by constituents as a threat because of perceived cooption or encroachment on their formal, legal rights.

Or, to take another example, in the area of leadership, my colleagues at the State University of New York at Buffalo, Hollander and Julian (1969), have written for *Psychological Bulletin* one of the most thoughtful and penetrating articles on the leadership process. In one of their own studies (Julian & Hollander, 1966), reported in this article, they found that aside from the significance of task competence, the 'leader's interest in group members and interest in group activity' were significantly related to the group acceptance of the leader. Yet, in macropower situations, the leader is almost always involved in boundary exchanges with salient interorganizational activities which inescapably reduce, not necessarily interest in group members or activities, but the amount of interaction he can maintain with group members. This may have more the overtones of a rationalization than an explanation, but I know of few organizations where the top leadership's commitment to internal programs and needs fully meets constituent expectations.

In short, interorganizational role set of the leader, the scale, diversity and formal relations that ensue in a pluralistic system place heavy burdens on those managers and leaders who expect an easy transferability between the cozy *gemütlichkeit* of a Theory Y orientation and the realities of macropower.

Current sources for the adoption or rejection of democratic ideals

I wrote (Bennis, 1966b), not long ago, that

While more research will help us understand the conditions under which democratic and other forms of governance will be adopted, the issue will never be fully resolved. ... I. A. Richards once said that 'language has succeeded until recently in hiding from us almost all things we talk about.' This is singularly true when men start to talk of complex and wondrous things like democracy and the like.[1] For these are issues anchored in an existential core of personality (p. 35).

Today I am even more confused about the presence or absence of conditions which could lead to more democratic functioning. Somedays I wake up feeling 'nasty, brutish, and short', and, other times, feeling benign, generous, and short. This may be true of the general population, for the national mood is erratic, labile, depending on repression or anarchy for the 'short' solution to long problems.

Let us consider Lane's (1962) 'democraticness scale', consisting of five items: (a) willingness or reluctance to deny the franchise to the 'ignorant or careless'; (b) patience or impatience with the delays and confusions of democratic processes; (c) willingness or reluctance to give absolute authority to a single leader in times of threat; (d) where democratic forms are followed, degree of emphasis (and often disguised approval) of underlying oligarchical methods; (e) belief that the future of democracy in the United States is reasonably secure.

Unfortunately, there has been relatively little research on the 'democratic personality', which makes it risky to forecast whether conditions today will facilitate or detract from its effective functioning. On the one hand, there is interesting evidence that would lead one to forecast an increased commitment to democratic ideals. Earlier I mentioned Flacks's (1969) work on the 'transformation of the American middle-class family', which

1. See Sartori (1957). 'No wonder, therefore, that the more "democracy" has become to be a universally accepted honorific term, the more it has undergone verbal stretching and has become the loosest label of its kind' (p. 112).

would involve increased equality between husband and wife, declining distinctiveness of sex roles in the family, increased opportunity for self-expression on the part of the children, fewer parental demands for self-discipline, and more parental support for autonomous behavior on the part of the children. In addition, the increase in educated persons, whose status is less dependent on property, will likely increase the investment of individuals in having autonomy and a voice in decision making.

On the other hand, it is not difficult to detect some formidable threats to the democratic process which make me extremely apprehensive about an optimistic prediction. Two are basically psychological, one derived from some previous assumptions about the environment, the other derived from some recent personal experience. The third is a venerable structural weakness which at this time takes on a new urgency.

1. Given the turbulent and dynamic texture of the environment, we can observe a growing uncertainty about the deepest human concerns: jobs, neighborhoods, regulation of social norms, life styles, child rearing, law and order; in short, the only basic questions, according to Tolstoy, that interest human beings are How to live? and What to live for? The ambiguities and changes in American life that occupy discussion in university seminars and annual meetings and policy debates in Washington, and that form the backbone of contemporary popular psychology and sociology, become increasingly the conditions of trauma and frustration in the lower middle class. Suddenly the rules are changing – all the rules.

A clashy dissensus of values is already clearly foreshadowed that will tax to the utmost two of the previously mentioned democraticness scale items: 'impatience or patience with the delays and confusions of democratic processes' and the 'belief that the future of democracy in the United States is reasonably secure'.

The inability to tolerate ambiguity and the consequent frustration plus the mood of dissensus may lead to the emergence of a proliferation of 'minisocieties' and relatively impermeable subcultures, from George Wallace's blue-collar strongholds to rigidly circumscribed communal ventures. Because of their rejection of incremental reform and the establishment, and their impatience with bureaucratic-pragmatic leadership, their movements and leadership will likely resemble a 'revolutionary-charismatic' style (Kissinger, 1966).

2. The personal observation has to do with experience over the past two years as an academic administrator, experience obtained during a particularly spastic period for all of us in the academy.[2] I can report that we, at Buffalo, have been trying to express our governance through a thorough and complete democratic process, with as much participation as anyone can bear. There are many difficulties in building this process, as all of you are undoubtedly aware: the tensions between collegiality and the bureaucratic–pragmatic style of administrators, the difficulty in arousing faculty and students to participate, etc. I might add, parenthetically, that Buffalo, as is true of many state universities, had long cherished a tradition of strong faculty autonomy and academic control. Our intention was to facilitate this direction, as well as encourage more student participation.

When trouble erupted last spring, I was disturbed to discover – to the surprise of many of my colleagues, particularly historians and political scientists – that the democratic process we were building seemed so fragile and certainly weakened in comparison to the aphrodisia of direct action, mass meetings, and frankly autocratic maneuverings. The quiet workings of the bureaucratic-democratic style seemed bland, too complex and prismatic for easy comprehension, and even banal, contrasted to the headiness of the disruptions. Even those of us who were attempting to infuse and reinforce democratic functioning found ourselves caught up in the excitement and chilling risks involved.

Erich Fromm (1941) said it all, I reflected later on, in his *Escape from Freedom*, but what was missing for me in his formulation was the psychic equivalent for democratic participants.

During this same period, I came across a paper by Argyris (1969) which reinforced my doubts about the psychological

2. I am reminded here of Edward Holyoke's remark, written over 200 years ago on the basis of his personal experience: 'If any man wishes to be humbled or mortified, let him become President of Harvard College.'

attractiveness of democracy. Using a thirty-six-category group observational system on nearly thirty groups, in 400 separate meetings, amounting to almost 46,000 behavioral units, he found that only six of the thirty-six categories were used over 75 per cent of the time, and these six were 'task' items such as 'gives information, asks for information', etc. Almost 60 per cent of the groups showed no affect or interpersonal feelings at all, and 24 per cent expressed only 1 per cent affect or feelings. These groups represented a wide cross-section of bureaucratic organizations, research and development labs, universities, and service and business industries.

Argyris's data, along with my own personal experience, have made me wonder if democratic functioning can ever develop the deep emotional commitments and satisfactions that other forms of governance evoke, as for example, revolutionary-charismatic or ideological movements? The question which I leave with you at this time is not the one from the original paper ('Is democracy inevitable?'), but, 'Is democracy sexy?'

3. The structural weakness in present-day democracy, using that term in the broadest possible political sense, is the 200-year-old idea first popularized by Adam Smith (1776) in *The Wealth of Nations*. This was 'the idea that an individual who intends only his own gain is led by an invisible hand to promote the public interest.' The American Revolution brought about a deep concern for the constitutional guarantees of personal rights and a passionate interest in individuals' emotions and growth, but without a concomitant concern for the community.

In a recent issue of *Science*, Hardin (1968), the biologist, discusses this in an important article, 'The tragedy of the commons'. Herdsmen who keep their cattle on the commons ask themselves: 'What is the utility to me of adding one more animal to my herd?' (p. 1244). Being rational, each herdsman seeks to maximize his gain. It becomes clear that by adding even one animal, as he receives all the proceeds from the sale of the additional increment, the positive utility is nearly $+1$, whereas the negative utility is only a fraction of -1 because the effects of overgrazing are shared by all herdsmen. Thus, 'the rational herdsman concludes that the only sensible course for him to pursue is to add another animal to his herd. And another, and another . . .' (p. 1244) until 'Each man is locked into a system that compels him to increase his herd without limit. . . . Ruin is the destination toward which all men rush. . . . Freedom in a commons brings ruin to all' (p. 1244).

A recent, less elegant example along these lines occurred at my own campus where there is a rather strong commitment against institutional racism. A recent form this commitment has taken is the admission of at least double the number of black students ever before admitted. However, more disadvantaged students could have been accepted if the students had chosen to vote for 'tripling' in the dormitories. It was voted down overwhelmingly, and it was interesting to observe the editor of the student newspaper supporting increased admission for black students and at the same time opposing tripling.

The democratic process as we know it, expressed through majority vote, contains many built-in guarantees for individual freedom without equivalent mechanisms for the 'public interest', as Gans's (1969) recent article in the Sunday Magazine section of *The New York Times* argues.

A character in Balchin's (1949) *A Sort of Traitors* expresses this structural problem with some force:

You think that people want democracy and justice and peace. You're right. They do. But what you forget is that they want them on their own terms. And their own terms don't add up. They want decency and justice without interference with their liberty to do as they like.

These are the dilemmas as I see them now: the threat to legitimacy of authority, the tensions between populist and elitist functions and interdependence and complicity in the environment, the need for fresh metaphors, the discontinuities between microsystems and macrosystems, and the baffling competition between forces that support and those that suppress the adoption of democratic ideology. All together, they curb my optimism and blur the vision, but most certainly force a new perspective upon us.

A new perspective
These profound changes lead me to suggest that any forecast one makes about trends in human institutions must take into account the following:

1. The need for fundamental reform in the purpose and organization of our institutions to enable them to adapt responsively in an exponentially changing social, cutural, political and economic environment.

2. The need to develop such institutions on a human scale which permit the individual to retain his identity and integrity in a society increasingly characterized by massive, urban, highly centralized governmental, business, educational, mass media, and other institutions.

3. The significant movement of young persons who are posing basic challenges to existing values and institutions and who are attempting to create radical new life styles in an attempt to preserve individual identity or to opt out of society.

4. The increasing demands placed upon all American institutions to participate more actively in social, cultural and political programs designed to improve the quality of American life.

5. The accelerating technical changes which require the development of a scientific humanism: a world view of the social and humanistic implications of such changes.

6. The necessity of a world movement to bring man into better harmony with his physical environment.

7. The need for change toward a sensitive and flexible planning capability on the part of the management of major institutions.

8. The rising demand for social and political justice and freedom, particularly from the American black community and other deprived sectors of society.

9. The compelling need for world order which gives greater attention to the maintenance of peace without violence between nations, groups or individuals.

A new forecast for public bureaucracy

The imponderables are youth, and tradition, and change. Where these predicaments, dilemmas and second thoughts take us, I am not exactly sure. However, by way of a summary and conclusion – and at the risk of another five-year backlash – there are a number of trends and emphases worth considering.

*The organization's response to the environment will continue
to be the crucial determinant for its effectiveness*

Economists and political scientists have been telling us this for
years, but only recently have sociologists and social psychologists,
like Terreberry (1968), Emery and Trist (1965), Levine and White
(1961), Litwak and Hylton (1962), and Evan (1966), done so. To
quote Benson Snyder,[3] concerning a recent trip to California universities:

There is another consequence of this limited response to rapid change.
The climate of society becomes suffused and distrait, positions ossified,
and one hears expressions of helplessness increase, like dinosaurs on
the plains of mud. Each in his own way frantically puts on more weight
and thinks this form of strength will serve him. He doesn't know he
has lost touch until the mud reaches the level of his eyes.

Three derivatives of this protean environment can be anticipated. First, we will witness new ecological strategies that are
capable of anticipating crisis instead of responding to crisis, that
require participation instead of consent, that confront conflict
instead of dampening conflict, that include comprehensive
measures instead of specific measures, and that include a long
planning horizon instead of a short planning horizon.

Second, we will identify new roles for linking and correlating
interorganizational transactions – 'interstitial men'.

Third, and most problematical, I anticipate an erratic environment where various organizations coexist at different stages of
evolution. Rather than neat, linear and uniform evolutionary
developments, I expect that we will see both more centralization
(in large-scale instrumental bureaucracies) and more decentralization (in delivery of health, education and welfare services); both
the increase of bureaucratic-pragmatic and of revolutionary-
charismatic leadership; both the increase in size and centralization of many municipal and governmental units and the proliferation of self-contained minisocieties,[4] from the

3. B. Snyder, personal communication, 1969.
4. Sometimes it is difficult to distinguish the reform groups from the
reaction groups, except that the affluent, particularly the young, uncom-
mitted affluent, have already begun to invent and manage environments,
cutting across class and ethnic lines, that reflect unique life styles. And these
begin and end as rapidly as boutiques on Madison Avenue, which in many

'status-spheres' that Tom Wolfe writes about like Ken Kesey's 'electric kool-aid acid-heads' and the pump-house gang of La Jolla surfers to various citizen groups. Ethnic groups organize to 'get theirs', and so do the police, firemen, small property owners, and 'mothers fighting sex education and bussing', and so on.

Large-scale public and private bureaucracies will become more vulnerable than ever before to the infusion of legislative and judicial organs

These probably will become formalized, much like the Inspector General's office in the Army. In one day's issue of a recent *New York Times*, three front-page stories featured: (a) the 'young Turks' within the State Department who are planning to ask the Department to recognize the Foreign Service Association as the exclusive agent with which the Department would bargain on a wide scale of personal matters, (b) antipoverty lawyers within the Office of Equal Opportunity who have organized for a greater voice in setting policy, and (c) the informal caucus of civil rights lawyers in the Justice Department to draft a protest against what they consider a recent softening of enforcement of the civil rights law.

I have always been fascinated by Harold Lasswell's famous analogy between the Freudian trinity of personality and the tripartite division of the federal government. Most bureaucracies today contain only one formal mechanism, that is, the executive or ego functions. The legislative (id) and the judicial (superego) have long been underrepresented; this will likely change.[5]

---

ways they resemble, rather than the massive, more familiar conglomerates of yesteryear.

5. The labor unions have been relatively unsuccessful in organizing either top levels of management or professionals. They have failed to do so, in my view, because they have operated at the lowest level of the Maslow hierarchy of needs, economic, physiological, safety, failing to understand the inducements of most professionals: achievement, recognition, intrinsic quality of work and professional development. Ironically, this has provided more 'due process' and, in some cases, more legitimate participation to nonsalaried employees than to higher level personnel. It is no coincidence that the cutting edge of last year's French revolution, in addition to the students, were middle-class professional employees and technicians.

According to William Evan (1966), the lack of 'due process' for the high-ranking managerial and professional personnel has led to or reinforced the 'organization man'.

There will be more legitimization for 'leave-taking' and shorter tenure at the highest levels of leadership

One aspect of 'temporary systems' that was underplayed in my 1964 paper was the human cost of task efficiency. Recently, James Reston observed that the reason it is difficult to find good men for the most responsible jobs in government is that the good men have burnt out, or as my old infantry company commander once said, 'In this company, the good guys get killed.' Perhaps this creates the appearance of the Peter Principle, that is, that people advance to the level of their greatest incompetence. What is more likely is that people get burnt out, psychologically killed. Many industries are now experimenting with variations on sabbaticals for their executives, and I think it is about time that universities woke up to the fact that a seven-year period, for a legalized moratorium, is simply out of joint with the recurring need for self- and professional renewal.[6]

It may also be that leaders with shorter time horizons will be more effective in the same way that interregnum Popes have proven to be the most competent.

New organizational roles will develop, emphasizing different loci and commitments of colleaguiality

Aside from consultants and external advisory groups, organizations tend to arrogate the full working time and commitments of their memberships. One works for Ford, or the Department of Health, Education and Welfare, or Macy's, or Yale. Moonlighting is permitted, sometimes reluctantly, but there is usually no doubt about the primary organization or where there might be a possible 'conflict of interest'. This idea of the mono-organizational commitment will likely erode in the future where more and more people will create pluralistic commitments to a number of organizations.

To use my own university as an example once again, we have

6. At Buffalo, we have tried to develop a policy whereby all administrators would hold an academic appointment as well as an administrative post. They would be expected to return to their academic calling after no longer than five, possibly ten, years. The response to this formulation was less than positive, and I suspect that the basic reason for its unpopularity was the psychological blow to the self-concept which equates role-leaving (without manifest promotion) to failure.

set up one new experimental department which includes three different kinds of professors, different in terms of their relatedness and loci to the department. There is a core group of faculty with full-time membership in the department. There is an associated faculty with part-time commitments to the department, but whose appointment is in another department. And finally, there is a 'network faculty', who spend varying periods of time in the department, but whose principal affiliation is with another university or organization. Similar plans are now being drawn up for students.

Similarly, a number of people have talked about 'invisible colleges' of true colleagues, located throughout the world, who convene on special occasions, but who communicate mainly by telephone, the mail, and during hasty meetings at airports. I would wager that these 'floating crap-games' will increase, and that we will see at least three distinct sets of roles emerge within organizations: those that are *pivotal* and more or less permanent; those that are *relevant*, but not necessarily permanent; and those that are *peripheral*. A person who is pivotal and permanent to one organization may have a variety of relevant and peripheral roles in others.

There are many reasons for this development. First and most obvious is the fact that we live in a jet age where air travel is cheap and very accessible. (A good friend of mine living in Boston commutes daily to New York City for his analytic hour and manages to get back to his office by about 10.30 a.m.) Second, the scarcity of talent and the number of institutions 'on the make' will very likely lead more of the top talent to start dividing their time among a number of institutions. Third, the genuine motivational satisfaction gained from working within a variety of comparable institutions seems to be important, not for all, but among an increasingly growing fraction of the general population.

We must educate our leaders in at least two competencies: (a) to cope efficiently, imaginatively, and perceptively with information overload. Marxist power was property. Today, power is based on control of relevant information. (b) As Michael (1968) says in his *The Unprepared Society*: 'We must educate for empathy, compassion, trust, nonexploitiveness, nonmanipulativeness, for self-growth and self-esteem, for tolerance of ambiguity, for acknowledgement of error, for patience, for suffering.'

Without effective competence, and the strength that comes with it, it is difficult to see how the leader can confront the important ethical and political decisions without succumbing to compromise or to 'petite Eichmannism'.

We will observe in America a society which has experienced the consequences of unpreparedness and which has become more sanguine about the effects of planning – more planning not to restrict choice or prohibit serendipity, but to structure possibilities and practical visions.

Whether or not these forecasts are desirable, assuming their validity for the moment, really depends on one's status, values and normative biases. One man's agony is another's ecstasy. It does appear as if we will have to reckon with a number of contradictory and confusing tendencies, however, which can quickly be summarized:

1. More self- and social consciousness with respect to the governance of public bureaucracies.

2. More participation in this governance by the clients who are served, as well as those doing the service, including lower levels of the hierarchy.

3. More formal, quasi-legal processes of conflict resolution.

4. More direct confrontations when negotiation and bargaining processes fail.

5. More attention to moral–ethical issues relative to technical efficiency imperatives.

6. More rapid turnover and varying relationships within institutions.

I think it would be appropriate if I concluded this paper with a quote from the earlier 1964 paper which still seems valid and especially pertinent in light of the new perspectives gained over the past five years. I was writing about the educational requirements necessary for coping with a turbulent environment (Bennis, 1964):

Our educational system should (1) help us to identify with the adaptive process without fear of losing our identity, (2) increase tolerance of ambiguity without fear of losing intellectual mastery, (3) increase our ability to collaborate without fear of losing our individuality, and (4) develop a willingness to participate in social evolution while recognizing implacable forces. In short, we need an educational system that can help make a virtue out of contingency rather than one which induces hesitancy or its reckless companion, expedience.

References

ARGYRIS, C. (1969), 'The incompleteness of social-psychological theory: examples from small group, cognitive consistency, and attribution research', *American Psychologist*, vol. 24, pp. 893–908.

BALCHIN, N. (1949), *A Sort of Traitors*, Collins.

BENNIS, W. G. (1964), 'Organizational developments and the fate of bureaucracy', paper presented at the annual meeting of the American Psychological Association, Los Angeles, 4 September.

BENNIS, W. G. (1966a), 'Organizational developments and the fate of bureaucracy', *Industrial Management Review*, vol. 7, pp. 41–55.

BENNIS, W. G. (1966b), 'When democracy works', *Trans-action*, vol. 3, p. 35.

BENNIS, W. G. (1968), 'Future of the social sciences', *Antioch Review*, vol. 28, p. 227.

DEMOTT, B. (1969), *Supergrow*, Dutton.

DUHL, L. (1969), Letter to the editor, *Journal of Applied Behavioral Science*, vol. 5, pp. 279–80.

EMERY, F. E., and TRIST, E. L. (1965), 'The causal texture of organizational environments', *Human Relations*, vol. 18, pp. 1–10.

EVAN, W. M. (1966), 'The organization-set: toward a theory of interorganizational relationships', in J. D. Thompson (ed.), *Approaches to Organizational Design*, University of Pittsburgh Press.

FLACKS, R. (1969), 'Protest or conform: some social psychological perspectives on legitimacy', *Journal of Applied Behavioral Science*, vol. 5, pp. 127–50.

FROMM, E. (1941), *Escape from Freedom*, Farrer & Rinehart.

GAMSON, W. A. (1968), *Power and Discontent*, Dorsey Press.

GANS, H. J. (1969), 'We won't end the urban crisis until we end majority rule', *New York Times Magazine*, no. 119, 3 August, section 6.

GREER, S. (1969), *The Logic of Social Inquiry*, Aldine.

GROSS, E. (1968), 'Universities as organizations: a research approach', *American Sociological Review*, vol. 33, pp. 518–44.

HARDIN, G. (1968), 'The tragedy of the commons', *Science*, vol. 162, pp. 1243–8.

HELMER, O. (1969), 'Political analysis of the future', paper presented at the annual meeting of the American Political Science Association, New York, 4 September.

HOLLANDER, E. P., and JULIAN, J. W. (1969), 'Contemporary trends in the analysis of leadership processes', *Psychological Bulletin*, vol. 71, pp. 387–97.

JULIAN, J. W., and HOLLANDER, E. P. (1966), 'A study of some role dimensions of leader–follower relations', (Tech. Rep. No. 3, Office of Naval Research Contract No. 4679) State University of New York at Buffalo, Department of Psychology, April.

KELMAN, H. C. (1969), 'In search of new bases for legitimacy: some social psychological dimensions of the black power and student movements', paper presented at the Richard M. Elliott Lecture, University of Michigan, 21 April.

KISSINGER, H. A. (1966), 'Domestic structures and foreign policy', *Daedalus*, vol. 96, pp. 503–29.

KORTON, F. F., COOK, S. W., and LACEY, J. I. (eds.) (1970), *Psychology and the Problems of Society*, American Psychological Association.

LANE, R. E. (1962), *Political Ideology*, Free Press.

LEVINE, S., and WHITE, P. E. (1961), 'Exchange as a conceptual framework for the study of interorganizational relationships', *Administrative Science Quarterly*, vol. 6, pp. 583–601.

LITWAK, E., and HYLTON, L. (1962), 'Interorganizational analysis: a hypothesis on coordinating agencies', *Administrative Science Quarterly*, vol. 6, pp. 395–420.

MICHAEL, D. (1968), *The Unprepared Society*, Basic Books.

PARSONS, T. (1968), 'The academic system: a sociologist's view', *Public Interest*, vol. 13, pp. 179–97.

SARTORI, G. (1957), 'Democracy', in E. R. A. Seligman (ed.), *Encyclopedia of Social Sciences*, Macmillan.

TERREBERRY, S. (1968), 'The evolution of organizational environments', *Administrative Science Quarterly*, vol. 12, pp. 590–613.

TRIST, E. (1968), *The Relation of Welfare and Development in the Transition to Post-Industrialism*, Western Management Science Institute, University of California.

TROW, M. (1969), 'Urban problems and university problems', paper presented at the 24th All-University Conference, University of California at Riverside, 23–25 March.

3 D. Katz and B. Georgopoulos

Organizations in a Changing World

D. Katz and B. Georgopoulos, 'Organizations in a changing world', *Journal of Applied Behavioral Science*, vol. 7, 1971, no. 3.

Our nation has been aptly characterized as an organizational society. Most of our working hours are spent in one organizational context or another. If the dominant institution of the feudal period was the church, of the early period of nationalism the political state, the dominant structure of our time is the organization. Even among those in revolt the old union line still works: 'organize the guys'.

But organization forms today are under challenge and without creative modification may face difficulties in survival. On the one hand, they are growing in size and complexity, with criss-crossing relationships with other systems and with increasing problems of coordination. The traditional answer in organization structure is on the technical side, more computerized programs for feedback and coordination, more specialization of function, more centralization of control. On the other hand, the social and psychological changes in the culture are increasingly at odds with the technological solution of more and more of the same.

Before exploring this conflict and its implication in greater detail, let us examine the structure and functions of organizations as open social systems. We can distinguish among the sub-systems which comprise the larger structure. The production sub-system is concerned with the basic type of work that gets done, with the throughput, the modification of inputs which result in products or services. Attached to the productive sub-system are the supportive services of procurement of supplies, material and resources, and the disposal of the outputs.

The maintenance or social sub-system is concerned not with maintenance of physical plant but with the social structure, so that the identity of the system in relation to its basic objectives is preserved. People not only have to be attracted to the system and remain in it for some period of time, but they have to function in roles which are essential to the mission of the organization. The maintenance sub-system is concerned with rewards and sanctions, with system norms and values. In short, its function has to do with the psychological cement that holds the structure together, with the integration of the individual into the system. The channeling of collective effort in reliable and predictable pathways is the basis of organizational structure.

The managerial sub-system cuts across all other sub-systems as a mechanism of control, coordination and decision-making. To meet environmental changes both with respect to inputs and receptivity for outputs and to handle system strains, the managerial system develops an adaptive sub-system of staff people as in the case of research, development and planning operations.

Let us look at the maintenance function more closely. Over time it requires more than sheer police power and coercive sanctions. It depends upon some degree of integration or involvement of people in terms of their own needs. Values, norms and roles tie people into the system at different psychological levels and in different ways.

Values provide the deepest basis of commitment in their rational and moral statement of the goals of a group or system. To the extent that these values are accepted by individuals as their own beliefs, we speak of the internalization of group goals. The degree of internalization will vary among the members of any group, but it is important for all organizations to have some hard core of people dedicated to its mission both for accomplishment of many types of tasks and as models for others. Such value commitment can come about through self selection into the system of those possessing beliefs congruent with its goals, through socialization in the general society or in the organization, through participation in the rewards and decision-making of the group. The internalization of group goals is facilitated by the perception of progress toward these objectives. Such progress is interpreted as an empirical validation of values.

Normative involvement refers to the acceptance of system requirements about specific forms of behavior. These requirements are seen as legitimate because rules are perceived as necessary and because in general the rules are equitable. A particular demand by a particular officer may be seen as unjust, but in general there is acceptance of the need for directives from those in positions of authority, provided that they have attained their positions properly and that they stay within their areas of jurisdiction in the exercise of their authority. The rules of the game can be improved, but they are universalistic and do not permit particularistic favoritism or discrimination.

At the level of *role behavior* people make the system function because of their interdependence with others, the rewards for performing their roles, and the socio-emotional satisfactions from being part of a role-interdependent group. Not all role performance provides expressive gratifications, however, and hence other rewards such as monetary incentives, as well as group accomplishment and socio-emotional satisfactions can be linked to adequate behavior in the given role. In most large organizations extrinsic rewards of pay, good working conditions, etc., are relied on heavily.

It is apparent that these three levels of involvement are not necessarily intrinsically related. The values of a particular organization may have little to do with many of the roles in the system, and the norms of legitimacy are not necessarily specific to organizational values. A research organization may furnish a nice fit between values, norms and roles for its research workers but a poor fit for its supportive personnel. Few organizations, however, can rely on value commitment to hold their people, and hence they maximize other conditions and rewards to compete with other systems. The development of universalistic norms has provided great mobility for people in an expanding economic society, and has contributed to its growth, but at the expense of value commitment.

In a well integrated system, however, there is some relationship between these levels such that they are mutually reinforcing. In an ideal hospital, even the attendant can be affected by the values of saving lives and improving health, can perceive the normative requirements as necessary and fair and can derive satisfaction from his role, particularly if he is made part of a therapy team. Values can contribute to the strength of the normative system in providing a broader framework of justifiable beliefs about the rightness of given norms. Thus they can be seen not only as equitable rules but as embodiments of justice and of equality. The strength of maintenance forces lies in the many mechanisms for supporting the role structure and for some degree of mutual reinforcement.

Four major changes have occurred in our society which challenge both the production and social sub-systems of organizations: (1) a break, at first gradual and now pronounced, with traditional authority and the growth of democratic ideology; (2) economic growth and affluence; (3) the resultant changes in needs and motive patterns; and (4) the accelerated rate of change. These changes are significant for organizations, since as open systems they are in continuing interaction with their environment both with respect to production inputs of material resources and social inputs from the culture and from the larger social structure.

The break with the older pattern of authority

This has eroded some of the formerly dependable maintenance processes. Bureaucratic systems had long profited from the socialization practices of traditional society, in which values and legitimacy had a moral basis of an absolutistic character. It was morally wrong to reject in word or deed the traditional teachings about American institutions. It was wrong to seek change other than through established channels. Not everyone, of course, lived up to the precepts, but those who deviated generally felt guilty about their misconduct. If they did not, they were considered to be psychopaths. Organizations had the advantage that there was a degree of built-in conformity to their norms and in some cases to their values because of the general socialization in the society about agreed-on standards. This consensus, moreover, made nonconformity a matter of conscience. There was an all-or-none quality about virtue, honesty and justice and these values were not seen as relativistic or empirical generalizations.

The very growth of bureaucratic systems helped to demolish absolutistic values of a moral character. As conscious attempts to organize collective enterprises, organizations were guided by rational objectives and empirical feedback. Pragmatism replaced tradition. Results and accomplishment were the criteria rather than internal moral principle. Furthermore, the normative system shifted, as Weber noted, from traditional authority to rational authority. Rules and laws were the instruments of men to achieve their purposes and lacked any transcendental quality. They could be changed at will as situations and needs changed or they became ineffective. Having undercut the traditional basis of authority, the bureaucratic system can no longer rely upon the older moral commitment to its directives.

The growth of organizations affected the larger society and its socialization practices and in turn was affected by it. The training of children in a rational and democratic framework further increased a non-traditional orientation to values and norms.

The decline of traditional authority has been accompanied by the growth of the democratic ethic and democratic practices. The source of power has been shifting from the heads of hierarchies to the larger electorate. This process can be observed in the political system where restrictions have been removed on suffrage. Non-property owners, women, and now blacks are eligible to vote. Indirect mechanisms of control from above are changing as in the political conventions of major parties. But democratic ideas of governance have extended into other institutions as well.

Economic growth and affluence

The tremendous technological advances which have increased the productivity of the nation need no documentation. We are already using the phrase 'post-industrial society' to characterize our era. This development raises questions about the basic functions of colleges and universities. Havighurst has pointed out that in the past two functions have been dominant: the *opportunity function* and the *production function*. Education was a means of social mobility, the opportunity function. On the production side, education provided the training for professional, technical and industrial roles in the society. Today, however, when we are over the economic hump, these two functions are less important and a third function comes to the fore: the consumption function. 'Education as a consumption good is something people want to enjoy, rather than to use as a means of greater economic production.' This means not only greater attention to the arts, but also greater concern with education as it relates to living here and now.

One reason why the demands of black students are often easier to deal with in spite of the rhetoric is that they are directed in good part to the opportunity and production functions. These are understandable issues in our established ways of operating. Demands on the consumption side present new problems. For the blacks, however, there is the complexity of sometimes attempting to achieve all three objectives at the same time.

Resultant changes in motive patterns

Economic affluence and the decline in traditional authority are related to a shift in motive patterns in our society. Maslow developed the notion years ago of a hierarchy of motives ranging from biological needs, through security, love and belongingness, to ego needs of self-esteem, self-development and self-realization. His thesis was that the motives at the bottom of the hierarchy were imperative in their demands and made the higher level motives relatively ineffectual. Once these lower level needs are assured satisfaction, however, the higher level needs take over and become all-important.

Maslow's thesis has abundant support among the young people in an educational system. They are less concerned with traditional economic careers than was once the case. A recent study reported only 14 per cent of the graduates of a leading university planning business careers, compared with 39 per cent five years earlier and 70 per cent in 1928.

The content analysis of children's readers by de Charms and Moeller shows that a great rise in achievement themes occurred in the last part of the nineteenth century, but a great decline in this emphasis occurred in recent decades.

The decline in the older motive patterns has one direct consequence for all organizations, including educational institutions. Extrinsic rewards such as pay, job security, fringe benefits and conditions of work are no longer as attractive. Younger people are demanding intrinsic job satisfactions as well. As students, they are less likely to accept the notion of deferring gratifications in the interests of some distant career.

The forms which newly aroused ego motives take can vary, but at present there are a number of patterns familiar to all of us. First there is the emphasis upon self-determination or self-expression, or doing one's thing. Second is the demand for self-development and self-actualization, making the most of one's own talents and abilities. Third is the unleashing of power drives. The hippies represent the first emphasis of self-expression, the SDS leaders the emphasis upon power. Fourth is the outcome of the other three, a blanket rejection of established values – a revolutionary attack upon the existing system as exploitive and repressive of the needs of individuals.

With the need for self-expression goes the ideology of the importance of spontaneity, of the wholeness of human experience, the reliance upon emotions, and the attack upon the fragmentation, the depersonalization and the restrictions of present social forms. It contributes to the anti-intellectualism of the student movement and is reminiscent of the romanticism of an older period in which Wordsworth spoke of the intellect as that false secondary power which multiplies delusions. Rationality is regarded as rationalization.

The accelerated rate of change

Not only are we witnessing significant shifts in the economic and value patterns of society, but they are happening at a very fast rate. There has probably always been some conflict between the older and younger generations, but in the past there has been more time to socialize children into older patterns and the patterns were of longer duration. History becomes less relevant for predicting change. It is difficult to know what the generation now entering high school will be like when they enter college.

All organizations face a period of trouble and turmoil because of these changes, which affect all three levels of integration in social systems. Some of the basic values of the social system are under fire, such as representative democracy of the traditional, complex type, the belief in private property, conventional morality, the importance of work and of economic achievement, the good life as the conventional enjoyment of the products of mass culture.

The norms legitimized by societal values of orderly procedures, of conformity to existing rules until they are changed by socially sanctioned procedures are also brought into question. The rebels emphasize not law and order but justice, and justice as they happen to see it. It is interesting that President Nixon, the spokesman for the establishment, modified his plea for law and order by stressing law, order and justice. The challenge to the norms of any system is especially serious, since it is genuinely revolutionary or anarchistic in implication, whether voiced by official revolutionaries or reformers. If the legitimate channels for change are abandoned and the resort is to direct action, then people are going outside the system. If enough do, the system collapses.

At the level of role integration there is also real difficulty. As has already been noted, extrinsic rewards have lost some of their importance in our affluent society. Moreover, the usual set of roles in an organization segmentalize individuals. A role is only partially inclusive of personality at most levels of the organization. This fractionation runs counter to the needs for wholeness and for self-expression.

In linking the changed patterns of many of the younger generation to societal changes, we want to emphasize that it is an error to simplify the problem as a younger–older generation conflict. It is broader and deeper than that and many of the developing trends predate the present student generation. In fact, the revolt started with people now in their sixties, if not earlier. We were the ones to attack the inequities of bureaucratic society, the ones to raise children in democratic practices and to think for themselves. The older generations furnished the ideology of the present student movements. Try to find any ideology in these movements which is not a bastardized version of old revolutionary doctrines. We started the rebellion and now we are astonished to find that we are the establishment.

This is one reason why organizations have been so vulnerable to attack. Older citizens do not rally to their support because they feel the rebels are in good part right. Or else why should we so often hear it stated, 'We agree with your objectives but we don't like your tactics'?

The problem of adaptation

The dynamic nature of our society makes imperative greater attention to processes of adaptation. In the past, industrial organizations, because of their dependence upon a market, have developed adaptive sub-systems of planning, research and development. The major emphasis has been, however, upon production inputs, upon product development, upon finding new markets and exploiting old ones, upon technology in improving their productive system. Only minor attention has been placed upon social inputs, upon restructuring the organization to meet the psychological needs of members. For organizations to survive and perform their functions effectively in the future, some sizeable proportion of their resources will have to be committed to enlarging their adaptive sub-systems to deal with new social inputs. Social effectiveness will have to be added to productive efficiency as an important objective.

Without an adequate adaptive sub-system to modify and filter new inputs leading to planned change, two things can happen. The new potential inputs can be summarily rejected. The organizational structure becomes rigid and the problems are postponed and often intensified. The other possibility with no adaptive mechanism is that the inputs slip into the system and are incorporated in undigested fashion. There is erosion of basic values and the system loses its identity. It does not acquire a formal death certificate but for practical purposes it has been replaced. If a university were to accept research inputs uncritically for the defense department, it could end up as a branch of the military and not as an institution for advancing science. Sometimes in organizations the first response of blanket rejection and rigidity cannot be maintained over time, and the opposed reaction of wholesale acceptance of any demands follows. For example, a university may show rigidity to suggested reforms and then, as pressure mounts, capitulate completely without critical evaluation of the suggested changes. To complicate matters, both rigidity and uncritical incorporation can occur in different parts of the same organization.

Most organizations suffer from a lack of adequate adaptive structures concerned with their maintenance sub-systems. We would like to indicate some of the lines of inquiry which adaptive sub-systems should follow and some directions in restructuring organizations which seem consistent with the present state of knowledge in the field. The views of our critics from the left are at times helpful, though not original, in pointing up vulnerable aspects of bureaucratic structures, but they are singularly lacking in constructive suggestions for reform. Some of them, of course, are not interested in reform, but are committed to destruction of the system. In short, they make no attempt to come to grips with the problems of the one and the many, with the fact that the individual doing his thing may interfere with other individuals doing their things. Anarchy may have its philosophic appeal, but it cannot be practised in crowded settings where millions of people live in constant interdependence.

The young dissenters have focused upon some fundamental weaknesses in organizational structure which have been recognized before, but which become more critical in that the younger generation no longer finds them acceptable. In the first place, there is a growing dissatisfaction with the fragmentation of life in an organization, with the difficulties of being a whole personality and of finding personal satisfactions in relating to others in impersonal role relationships. The major point is that many organization arrangements and procedures in our society cut the individual into segments in his various role responsibilities. This is especially true once we leave the more satisfying roles for the elite groups at the top of the structure. In this process we move toward a disintegrated personality. Once his wholeness and unity are violated, he may become alienated or seek personality expression outside his role responsibilities. Then we attempt artificial devices such as mass leisure pursuits of sports, movies and television, and of company programs of recreation, or even human relations training for supervisors to remedy the weaknesses in the system. But this is the organizational fallacy *par excellence*. Once we have destroyed the integrated individual, we no longer have the unified pieces to provide a truly integrated system. It is not like making an automobile out of pieces of steel, rubber and other materials. One cannot have a truly integrated social system if the human pieces are not themselves integrated. It is not possible to have a moral society made up of immoral men.

The second major criticism concerns the exploitive character of bureaucratic structures, namely that the rewards of the system, both intrinsic and extrinsic, go disproportionately to the upper hierarchical levels and that the objectives of organizations are distorted toward the immediate interests of the elite and away from desirable social goals of the many.

One important line of structural reform which can be significant with respect to these weaknesses is the fuller extension of democratic principles to the operation of organizations. Many writers on organizations fail to address themselves to this problem in structural terms, but talk about improvement of interpersonal relations, sensitivity training and consultative practices. The extreme left is also not concerned with democratic reform. Nonetheless, we believe that much can be done in organizational settings through democratic restructuring to improve their social effectiveness, i.e. their psychological returns to their members.

Two issues must be faced in the extension of democratic principles to organizational functioning. One is direct versus indirect or representative democracy. The second is the appropriate area of decision making for various subgroups in different types of complex systems.

Representative democracy has been under fire because it can be elaborated through complex mechanisms to distort the wishes of the electorate and give top decision makers great power. Such abuses do not negate its potential virtues. What is critical here is the imposition of hierarchical levels in the form of a pyramid similar to the administrative structure, for example, in the older practice in some states of the elected state legislators in turn electing senators. The general rule of never allowing more than two levels, that of the electorate and that of their duly chosen representatives, is gaining recognition in political organizations and can be applied to other organizations as well. It insures more responsible and more responsive decision making.

Direct democracy of the town-meeting sort is a cumbersome and ineffective mechanism for many purposes, once the electorate is numbered in hundreds and thousands. In many of our universities we still persist, however, in town meetings of a faculty of over a thousand. It is small wonder that such meetings get stalemated on details and often fail to come to grips with the central issue. Representative assemblies of a smaller number of democratically elected delegates would be a more effective mechanism for decision making.

Direct democracy, however, is still a necessary part of the

picture. In the first place, the full electorate should have the opportunity to veto major policy changes suggested by their elected leaders. In the second place, direct democracy can be more adequately utilized in smaller units of the system. Within a university, for example, there is a greater role for direct democracy at the departmental level than at the university level. We still have a long way to go to achieve the goal, however. The great advantage of direct democracy within the smaller unit is that it ties the individual into his own group on matters of direct concern to him, and thus permits the possibilities of tying him into the larger system of representative democracy. If he is not integrated through participation in his own group, then he is more likely to be apathetic toward or alienated from the larger structure. Democracy, like charity, begins at home, and in most organizations home is the functional group where the individual spends most of his time.

To take an esoteric example of this model of combining direct and indirect democracy, we can consider the kibbutzim of Israel. These utopian communities are remarkable in that they have survived, even prospered, for sixty years under the most difficult circumstances. Each kibbutz is a community with a great deal of autonomy, run by direct democracy, with town meetings, with direct election of all decision-making officers including the farm manager and with rotation of such officers. In addition, however, the individual kibbutz belongs to a larger movement which can include forty or fifty similar communities. The larger movement operates training centers, banking facilities and other services which the individual community could not afford. The management of the movement is handled through representative democracy. The sense of community achieved in the small kibbutz contributes to the integration of the individual into the larger system. Remote as this example is from the size and complexity of the American scene, it is of some interest in that the 220 communities of the kibbutz federation involving 200,000 people have no problems of violence, delinquency, crime or unemployment. Psychotic breakdown is an unusual event and crime a rare occurrence. Farm productivity is higher than the productivity of private farms in Israel.

A model of this sort, combining direct and representative

democracy, has obvious limitations in its application to large scale organizations which restrict areas of decision making in many ways. In the first place, a complex system tends to reduce the decision-making powers of any component group. Even the president of a university will feel that his margin for decision making is within a fairly narrow band of possibilities. And the individual member will feel even less room for meaningful participation for determining policy. In the second place, the administrative agency of a public institution has to operate within the legislation of a representative democracy in which it has had little say. In the third place, activities that have to be thoroughly coordinated on a rigorous time schedule, as in the military or space program, heavily restrict the areas of decision making for component groups.

Nevertheless, we do not take full advantage of the opportunities available within these limitations, nor do we examine the nature of these restrictions to see to what extent they can be made less rigid. Though coordination by experts may be necessary after a policy decision, there is still room for the involvement of people in making that decision. Though legislation determines objectives, there is often considerable leeway in how these directives can be implemented. Though size and complexity limit the amount of decision making possible for any one group, matters that are not of significance to the overall system may loom large for individuals in their own work setting. For example, we are constantly expanding the plant in many organizations with new buildings and new construction. Yet the people who have to use these facilities are frequently not consulted about them with respect to their own needs and the uses to which the buildings will be put. There are instances of windowless structures dictated by considerations of economy and standardization from above which turn out to be frightfully inefficient. We need to analyse the assumptions about coordination and centralization as demanding decisions only from top echelons.

The facts are that centralization *de jure* often leads to decentralization in practice. We need to be more critical of the whole centralization concept to see where tight controls are really necessary and are genuinely effective. Even with centralized controls in large organizations, it is sometimes true that the right hand does not know what the left hand is doing. Hence the criterion should not be some abstract concept of centralization, but objective data about how it operates in practice.

Moreover, we need to distinguish among the types of organizations and their objectives. In some organizations there is a necessary coordination of all effort so that there is a convergence of activities upon one outcome, as in the space program getting men on the moon. But many organizations do not have single products which require such convergence of the energies of all members of the system. In a university, for example, where we are concerned with training people and extending knowledge, there is a great variety of outcomes and hence much more freedom and degrees of autonomy within the total system. The traditional model of organizational structure deriving from the military and industry is not necessarily the appropriate model for all organizations, nor even for all aspects of industry or the military. For example, the concept of job enlargement and job enrichment has been pretty much limited to a single role. There are, however, serious limits beyond which we cannot go with a single job. What is possible, though, is group responsibility for a meaningful cycle of work. It has been demonstrated by the Tavistock researchers that a cohesive group can be created about a task objective. With some reduction in specialized roles within the group, some rotation of roles, removal of status differences and responsibility given to the group to get the job done, the results in such widely separated industries as a calico mill in India and a coal mine in Great Britain have been spectacular in the improvement of productivity and morale. The findings are particularly important because they give us new leverage on an old problem. Many jobs in themselves are routine and without challenge. Overall they add up to something significant in the way of performance. If they are not rigorously delimited and assigned to particular people, they can be given to a group with the group itself assuming responsibility for the outcome. Thus the advantages of collective accomplishment become not the ideal of top management, but the objective and psychological reality for group members.

Another structural reform to make roles more meaningful has to do with organizational divisions based upon process specialization. Supportive activities are often separated off from production activities, as when we set apart people performing a service, such as personnel recruitment or typing services, in a bureau or section of their own. We organize on the basis of process rather than purpose, to use a distinction made by Aristotle. Then we proceed to institutionalize the separation by removing the given service unit from its production counterpart physically and psychologically. The service people may in fact never have direct personal contact with production people. This separation may be particularly damaging to the morale of various service units, since the major production functions enjoy the greater prestige and often the more rewarding types of work. It is difficult for the girls in a typing pool to identify with their task or with organizational objectives when they have no meaningful relationship to them. Moreover, the service unit split off from major functions develops a compensatory defensive posture which often interferes with the effective functioning of the larger system.

The type of restructuring that needs to be considered is the creation of teams and groups for accomplishing an objective in which service people have primary membership in the production unit and secondary membership in a service unit, and sometimes the secondary membership can be dispensed with.

We may need more sub-groups than we now have because people can identify more readily with one another and with the group task in small settings than in large. What is important, however, is that the sub-groups are broadly enough designed with respect to an objective so that people with different skills can cooperate with one another and identify with the group goal. Groups should be small but their task responsibility large. This runs counter to the traditional way of organizing for turning out automobiles, but it may be more appropriate for many types of organizations not mass-producing a physical product.

In general, the changes we have been discussing all point toward a looser role system with broader role definitions, more flexibility and openness of sub-system boundaries, with group responsibility for task objectives. Admittedly, this may add to the noise in the system, but some of what appears to be noise from the point of view of the formal chart-maker may be meaningful activity directed toward important goals. It should also be remembered that in supposedly tight structures the empirical system may be at variance with the formal chart, with real noise that goes undetected because the formal channels do not code it.

We have left to the last the most difficult problem of all: the system values which can bind the individual to the organization and furnish the ideology to justify its norms and requirements. Values are seldom static and our dynamic period with its accelerated changes has seen fundamental challenges to the older belief structure. The task for the adaptive processes of an organization is one of the creative adaptation of central values to changing inputs. Such adaptation means the preservation of the basic nature of the system with modifications which clarify issues but do not destroy the system.

The great need of our time is a reformulation of social values. Organizational leaders should play a much more vigorous role as the responsible agents of the adaptive mechanisms in their social structures. In many instances they have given much time and energy to the adaptive function, but generally in terms of mediation, negotiation and compromise in crisis situations. Negotiation and compromise are important, but they are far from a complete answer. Compromise without consideration of principle can merely lead to a new round of demands. Various factions within and without an organization interpret concessions and compromises as an invitation to mobilize their forces for a new offensive. Politics has been called the art of compromise, but if we rely wholly upon this process we leave everything to power and power-driven individuals. The conceptualization of values and the enunciation of basic principles should not be left to the extremists on either the left or the right. Organizational leadership has a challenge in meeting the rhetoric of the dissidents with a compelling statement of principles and an implementation of them in practice. Many people today are eager for such a formulation of values. When Senator McCarthy took a clear position on foreign policy, the popular response was of such a magnitude as to confound political analysts.

In the past we have been a pragmatic nation, and leaders as well as followers have tended to shy away from ideological discussion. And some of this pragmatic emphasis is to be found in the present demands for relevance and in the anti-intellectualism of the new left. Nonetheless, values and principles which transcend the single case, the single individual, the single faction are critical to the maintenance of social order. The facts are that there are many assumptions, as well as practices of a moral character in a contemporary society, which need re-emphasis and reformulation. Without attempting to catalog them, may we cite a few examples?

In the first place, research and observation show that the norm of reciprocity, of cooperation, of mutual helpfulness, runs wide and deep. Organizations could not exist without many uncounted acts of cooperation which we take for granted. If people merely operated on a basis of role prescription, organizations would run poorly. And role prescriptions also take account of mutual inter-dependence. Berkowitz has shown experimentally that people will respond to others who need their help. Studies of citizenship orientation show that individuals see themselves as good citizens not if they are flag wavers, but if they are cooperative and helpful toward their fellows. We cite this basic value of mutual helpfulness because we lose sight of it in the self-oriented push of some protestors.

In the second place, justice and fairness are not outmoded values. The underdog elicits sympathy partly because there is an assumption he has not been fairly treated. In fact, justice and fairness are the ideological weapons of the dissenters, but they have no monopoly on them. It is important to emphasize the importance of justice and fairness in the operation of an organization and to introduce reforms where inequity is the practice.

In the third place, social responsibility or involvement in matters of more than local concern has a potential that remains to be developed. It is no longer acceptable to brag about one's non-participation in political affairs. It is apparently less difficult to recruit candidates for public office than was once the case. There seems to be more concern about national decisions which the little people were once content to leave to the authorities. Again, the new left has taken advantage of this broadened conception of political and social responsibility to urge direct action by students on all types of issues. But again the doctrine of social concern can be formulated to make people more aware of the social consequences of their actions. This social concern, which transcends the individual's own self-oriented needs, is reflected in the positive esteem achieved by leaders who show humanitarian values. Part of Robert Kennedy's popular appeal was the conviction that he was concerned, that he cared about the fate of others.

All of these values are related to, if not an integral part of, the democratic ethic which is still our basic creed. We have already noted the development of democratic practices in our political system and their extension to other social institutions. The democratic doctrine is invoked by the left in its attack upon the establishment but not in its own operations and program. With this group the use of democratic phrases seems to be more of a tactic than an ideological commitment. As the right mobilizes, there is some revival of reactionary beliefs. With the increasing polarization, the middle of the spectrum could profit greatly from a reformulation of the democratic creed by those who believe that democracy is not an outmoded concept in spite of inadequacies in its application. Organization reform needs such a value base both as a set of social principles and as guidelines for action.

Part Two
New Perspectives from Organization Theory and Practice

In a recent list of seventy probable events for 1980 and beyond, George Steiner (1970) states: 'In the business world, there will be an important shift in emphasis from concentration on production to strategy in relating the business to its environment.' Our ability to conceptualize the organization–environment relationship has been considerably enhanced by those theories and researchers who have applied systems theory to organizations. Terreberry's 'The evolution of organizational environments' (Reading 4) is an example of this perspective. This paper cites evidence for the growing interdependence of organizations and discusses the proposition that organizational change is increasingly externally induced.

The necessity for viewing the problem of change in terms of the organization–environment system is one issue; however, an important problem in organization design, necessitated by change in the environment, is the invention of means to enable organizations simultaneously to pursue a variety of major goals. Robert Bolt's paper (Reading 5) is of both theoretical and practical interest on this crucial issue. He demonstrates the importance for organizations to innovate explicitly in order to be able to satisfy multiple values. To illustrate programmatically, he analyses the experience of his own firm in implementing planned efforts to become 'a multi-valued institution'.

In their book, *The Temporary Society*, Bennis and Slater (1968) described several major social, technological and cultural forces which have made the Weberian pyramidal organization, with its image of stability and permanence, somewhat anachronistic for coping with the complexity and uncertainty of change. As an alternative, a number of organizations have begun to experiment with a structural innovation often referred to as the 'matrix' or 'overlay' system. The essential purpose of these innovations is to provide for temporary project teams drawn from more permanent departments so that interdisciplinary efforts can be concentrated on problems which 'cut across' functions. These new theories of organizational design are aimed at developing structures which can, in effect, enable the organization to 'institutionalize flexibility'.

Reading 6 by Chris Argyris argues that while such structural innovations are basically valid for working on problems of great complexity, the manner in which they are implemented is critical to their ultimate effectiveness. In particular, the 'matrix organization' is a response to change which creates unique individual tension and intergroup conflict for the organization. The Argyris article is an illustration of the importance of adopting a paradigm of action which can account for the inevitable linkage between planned change and organizational conflict – conflict which, in point of fact, is not always simply 'resistance to change'.

References

BENNIS, W. G., and SLATER, P. (1968), *The Temporary Society*, Harper.

STEINER, G. (1970), 'Seventy probable major domestic, non-military trends and events in 1980 and beyond', in W. A. Schmidt (ed.), *Organizational Functions and Human Values*, Wadsworth Publishing Co.

4 S. Terreberry

The Evolution of Organizational Environments

S. Terreberry, 'The evolution of organizational environments',
Administrative Science Quarterly, March 1968, vol. 12, no. 4 pp. 590–613.

Darwin published *The Origin of Species by Means of Natural Selection* in 1859. Modern genetics has vastly altered our understanding of the variance upon which natural selection operates. But there has been no conceptual breakthrough in understanding *environmental* evolution which, alone, shapes the direction of change. Even today most theorists of change still focus on *internal* interdependencies of systems – biological, psychological or social – although the external environments of these systems are changing more rapidly than ever before.

Introduction

Von Bertalanffy (1956) was the first to reveal fully the importance of a system being open or closed to the environment in distinguishing living from inanimate systems. Although von Bertalanffy's formulation makes it possible to deal with a system's exchange processes in a new perspective, it does not deal at all with those processes in the environment *itself* that are among the determining conditions of exchange.

Emery and Trist (1965) have argued the need for one additional concept, 'the causal texture of the environment'. Writing in the context of formal organizations, they offer the following general proposition:

That a comprehensive understanding of organizational behavior requires some knowledge of each member of the following set, where L indicates some potentially lawful connection, and the suffix 1 refers to the organization and the suffix 2 to the environment:

L_{11} L_{12}
L_{21} L_{22}

L_{11} here refers to processes within the organization – the area of internal interdependencies; L_{12} and L_{21} to exchanges between the organization and its environment – the area of transactional interdependencies, from either direction; and L_{22} to processes through which parts of the environment become related to each other – i.e. its causal texture – the area of interdependencies that belong within the environment itself (p. 22).

We have reproduced the above paragraph in its entirety because, in the balance of this paper, we will use Emery and Trist's symbols (i.e. L_{11}, L_{21}, L_{12}, *and* L_{22}) to denote intra-system, input, output, and extra-system interdependencies, respectively. Our purpose in doing so is to avoid the misleading connotations of conventional terminology.

Purpose

The theses here are: (a) that contemporary changes in organizational environments are such as to increase the ratio of externally induced change to internally induced change; and (b) that *other* formal organizations are, increasingly, the important components in the environment of any focal organization. Furthermore, the evolution of environments is accompanied – among viable systems – by an increase in the system's ability to learn and to perform according to changing contingencies in its environment. An integrative framework is outlined for the concurrent analysis of an organization, its transactions with environmental units, and interdependencies among those units. Lastly, two hypotheses are presented, one about organizational *change* and the other about organizational *adaptability*; and some problems in any empirical test of these hypotheses are discussed.[1]

Concepts of organizational environments

In Emery and Trist's terms, L_{22} relations, i.e. interdependencies within the environment itself, comprise the 'causal texture' of the field. This causal texture of the environment is treated as a quasi-independent domain, since the environment cannot be con-

1. I am particularly grateful to Kenneth Boulding for inspiration and to Eugene Litwak, Rosemary Sarri and Robert Vinter for helpful criticisms. A Special Research Fellowship from the National Institutes of Health has supported my doctoral studies and, therefore, has made possible the development of this paper.

ceptualized except with respect to some focal organization. The components of the environment are identified in terms of that system's actual and *potential* transactional interdependencies, both input (L_{21}) and output (L_{12}).

Emery and Trist postulate four 'ideal types' of environment, which can be ordered according to the degree of *system connectedness* that exists among the components of the environment (L_{22}). The first of these is a 'placid, randomized' environment: goods and bads are relatively unchanging in themselves and are randomly distributed, e.g. the environments of an amoeba, a human foetus, a nomadic tribe. The second is a 'placid, clustered' environment: goods and bads are relatively unchanging in themselves but clustered, e.g. the environments of plants that are subjected to the cycle of seasons, of human infants, of extractive industries. The third ideal type is 'disturbed-reactive' environment and constitutes a significant qualitative change over simpler types of environments: an environment characterized by similar systems in the field. The extinction of dinosaurs can be traced to the emergence of more complex environments on the biological level. Human beings, beyond infancy, live in disturbed-reactive environments in relation to one another. The theory of oligopoly in economics is a theory of this type of environment.[2]

These three types of environment have been identified and described in the literature of biology, economics and mathematics.[3] 'The fourth type, however, is new, at least to us, and is the one that for some time we have been endeavouring to identify' (Emery and Trist, 1965, p. 24). This fourth ideal type of environment is called a 'turbulent field'. Dynamic processes 'arise from the *field itself*' and not merely from the interactions of components; the actions of component organizations and linked

2. The concepts of ideal types of environment, and one of the examples in this paragraph, are from Emery and Trist (1965, pp. 24–6).

3. The following illustrations are taken from Emery and Trist (1965). For random-placid environment see Simon (1957, p. 137); Ashby (1960, sec. 15/4; the mathematical concept of random field; and the economic concept of classical market).

For random-clustered environment see Tolman and Brunswick (1935); Ashby (1960, sec. 15/8; and the economic concept of imperfect competition).

For disturbed-reactive environment see Ashby (1960, sec. 7; the concept of 'imbrication' from Chein (1943); and the concept of oligopoly).

sets of them 'are both persistent and strong enough to induce autochthonous processes in the environment' (p. 26).

An alternate description of a turbulent field is that the accelerating rate and complexity of interactive effects exceeds the component systems' capacities for prediction and, hence, control of the compounding consequences of their actions.

Turbulence is characterized by complexity as well as rapidity of change in causal interconnections in the environment. Emery and Trist illustrate the transition from a disturbed-reactive to a turbulent-field environment for a company that had maintained a steady 65 per cent of the market for its main product – a canned vegetable – over many years. At the end of the Second World War, the firm made an enormous investment in a new automated factory that was set up exclusively for the traditional product and technology. At the same time post-war controls on steel strip and tin were removed, so that cheaper cans were available; surplus crops were more cheaply obtained by importers; diversity increased in available products, including substitutes for the staple; the quick-freeze technology was developed; home buyers became more affluent; supermarkets emerged and placed bulk orders with small firms for retail under supermarket names. These changes in technology, international trade, and affluence of buyers gradually interacted (L_{22}) and ultimately had a pronounced effect on the company: its market dwindled rapidly. 'The changed texture of the environment was not recognized by an able but traditional management until it was too late' (Emery and Trist, 1965, p. 24).

Sociological, social psychological, and business management theorists often still treat formal organizations as closed systems. In recent years, however, this perspective seems to be changing. Etzioni (1960) asserts that inter-organizational relations need intensive empirical study. Blau and Scott (1962, pp. 194–221) present a rich but unconceptualized discussion of the 'social context of organizational life'. Parsons (1960, pp. 63–4) distinguishes three distinct levels of organizational responsibility and control: technical, managerial and institutional. His categories can be construed to parallel the intra-organizational, i.e. technical or L_{11}, the inter-organizational, i.e. managerial or L_{21} and L_{12}, and the extra-organizational levels of analysis, i.e. the institutional or L_{22} areas. Perhaps in the normal developmental course of a science, intra-system analysis necessarily precedes the inter-system focus. On the other hand, increasing attention to inter-organizational relations may reflect a real change in the phenom-enon being studied. The first question to consider is whether there is evidence that the environments of formal organizations are evolving toward turbulent-field conditions.

Evidence for turbulence

Ohlin (1958, p. 63) argues that the sheer rapidity of social change today requires greater organizational adaptability. Hood (1962, p. 73) points to the increasing complexity, as well as the accelerat-ing rate of change, in organizational environments. In business circles there is growing conviction that the future is unpredictable. Drucker (1964, pp. 6–8) and Gardner (1963, p. 107) both assert that the kind and extent of present-day change precludes pre-diction of the future. Increasingly, the rational strategies of planned-innovation and long-range planning are being under-mined by unpredictable changes. McNulty (1962) found no association between organization adaptation and the introduction of purposeful change in a study of thirty companies in fast-growing markets. He suggests that built-in flexibility may be more efficient than the explicit reorganization implicit in the quasi-rational model. (*Dun's Review* 1963, p. 42, questions the effective-ness of long-range planning in the light of frequent failures, and suggests that error may be attributable to forecasting the future by extrapolation of a noncomparable past.) The conclusion is that the rapidity and complexity of change may increasingly preclude effective long-range planning. These examples clearly suggest the emergence of a change in the environment that is suggestive of turbulence.

Some writers with this open-system perspective derive implica-tions for inter-organizational relations from this changing environment. Blau and Scott (1962, p. 217) argue that the success of a firm increasingly depends upon its ability to establish sym-biotic relations with other organizations, in which extensive advantageous exchange takes place. Adler (1966) proposes 'sym-biotic marketing'. Dill (1958) found that the task environments of two Norwegian firms comprised four major sectors: *customers*, including both distributors and users; *suppliers* of materials, labor, capital, equipment, and work space; *competitors* for both markets and resources; and *regulatory groups*, including governmental agencies, unions and interfirm associations. Not only does Dill's list include many more components than are accommodated by present theories, but all components are themselves evolving into formal organizations. In his recent book, Thompson (1967, pp. 27–8) discusses 'task environments', which comprise the units with which an organization has input and output transactions (L_{21} and L_{12}), and postulates two dimensions of such environments: homogeneous–heterogeneous, and stable–dynamic. When the task environment is *both* heterogeneous and dynamic, i.e. probably turbulent, he expects an organization's boundary-spanning units to be functionally differentiated to correspond to segments of the task environment and each to operate on a decentralized basis to monitor and plan responses to fluctuations in its sector of the task environment. He does not focus on other organizations as components of the environment, but he provides a novel perspective on structural implications (L_{11}) for organizations in turbulent fields.

Selznick's (1949) work on TVA appears to be the first organizational case study to emphasize transactional interdependencies. The next study was Ridgway's (1957) study of manufacturer-dealer relationships. Within the following few years the study by Dill (1958) and others by Levine and White (1961), Litwak and Hylton (1962), and Elling and Halebsky (1961) appeared, and in recent years, the publication of such studies has accelerated.

The following are examples from two volumes of the *Administrative Science Quarterly* alone. Rubington (1965) argues that structural changes in organizations that seek to change the behavior of 'prisoners, drug addicts, juvenile delinquents, parolees, alcoholics [are] . . . the result of a social movement whose own organizational history has yet to be written'. Rosengren (1964) reports a similar phenomenon in the mental health field whose origin he finds hard to explain: 'In any event, a more symbiotic relationship has come to characterize the relations between the [mental] hospitals and other agencies, professions, and establishments in the community.' He ascribes changes in organizational goals and technology to this inter-organizational evolution. In the field of education, Clark (1965) outlines the increasing influence of private foundations, national associations, and divisions of the federal government. He, too, is not clear as to how these changes have come about, but he traces numerous changes in the behavior of educational organizations to inter-organizational influences. Maniha and Perrow (1965) analyse the origins and development of a city youth commission. The agency had little reason to be formed, no goals to guide it, and was staffed by people who sought a minimal, no-action role in the community. By virtue of its existence and broad province, however, it was seized upon as a valuable weapon by other organizations for the pursuit of their own goals. 'But in this very process it became an organization with a mission of its own, in spite of itself.'

Since uncertainty is the dominant characteristic of turbulent fields, it is not surprising that emphasis in recent literature is away from algorithmic and toward heuristic problem-solving models (Taylor, 1965); that optimizing models are giving way to satisficing models (March and Simon, 1958); and that rational decision making is replaced by 'disjointed incrementalism' (Braybrooke and Lindblom, 1963). These trends reflect *not* the ignorance of the authors of earlier models, but a change in the causal texture of organizational environments and, therefore, of appropriate strategies for coping with the environment. Cyert and March (1963) state that 'so long as the environment of the firm is unstable – and predictably unstable – the heart of the theory [of the firm] must be the process of short-run adaptive reactions' (p. 100).

In summary, both the theoretical and case study literature on organizations suggests that these systems are increasingly finding themselves in environments where the complexity and rapidity of change in external interconnectedness (L_{22}) gives rise to increasingly unpredictable change in their transactional interdependencies (L_{21} and L_{12}). This seems to be good evidence for the emergence of turbulence in the environments of many formal organizations.

Inter-organizational environment
Evidence for increasing dependence on environment

Elsewhere the author has argued that Emery and Trist's concepts can be extended to *all* living systems; furthermore, that this evolutionary process gives rise to conditions – biological, psychological and social – in which the rate of evolution of environments exceeds the rate of evolution of component systems (Terreberry, 1967, pp. 1–37).

In the short run, the openness of a living system to its environment enables it to take in ingredients from the environment for conversion into energy or information that allows it to maintain a steady state and, hence, to violate the dismal second law of thermodynamics, i.e. of entropy. In the long run, 'the characteristic of living systems which most clearly distinguishes them from the nonliving is their property of progressing by the process which is called evolution from less to more complex states of organization' (Pringle, 1956, p. 90). It then follows that to the extent that the environment of some living system X is comprised *of other living systems*, the environment of X is *itself* evolving from less to more complex states of organization. A major corollary is that the evolution of environments is characterized by an increase in the ratio of externally induced change over internally induced change in a system's transactional interdependencies (L_{21} and L_{12}).

For illustration, let us assume that at some given time, each system in some set of interdependent systems is equally likely to experience an internal (L_{11}) change that is functional for survival, i.e. improves its L_{21} or L_{12} transactions. The greater the number of other systems in that set, the greater the probability that some system other than X will experience that change. Since we posit interdependence among members of the set, X's viability over time depends upon X's capacity (L_{11}) for adaptation to environmentally induced (L_{22}) changes in its transactive position, or else upon control over these external relations.

In the case of formal organizations, disturbed-reactive or oligopolistic environments require some form of accommodation between like but competitive organizations whose fates are negatively correlated to some degree. A change in the transactional position of one system in an oligopolistic set, whether for better or worse, automatically affects the transactional position of all other members of the set, and in the opposite direction, i.e. for worse or better, as the case may be.[4] On the other hand, turbulent environments require relationships between dissimilar organizations whose fates are independent or, perhaps, positively correlated.[5] A testable hypothesis that derives from the formal argument is that the evolution of environments is accompanied, in viable systems, by an increase in ability to learn and to perform according to changing contingencies in the environment.

The evolution of organizational environments is characterized by a change in the important constituents of the environment. The earliest formal organizations to appear in the United States, e.g. in agriculture, retail trade, construction, mining (see Stinchcombe, 1965, p. 156) operated largely under placid-clustered conditions. Important inputs, such as natural resources and labor, as well as consumers, comprised an environment in which strategies of optimal location and distinctive competence were critical organizational responses (Emery and Trist, 1965, p. 29). Two important attributes of placid-clustered environments are: (a) the environment is itself *not* formally organized; and (b) transactions are largely initiated and controlled by the organization, i.e. L_{12}.

Later developments, such as transport technology and derivative overlap in loss of strength gradients, and communication and automation technologies that increased economies of scale, gave rise to disturbed-reactive (oligopolistic) conditions in which similar formal organizations become the important actors in an organization's field. They are responsive to its acts (L_{12}) *and* it must be responsive to theirs (L_{21}). The critical organizational response now involves complex operations, requiring sequential choices based on the calculated actions of others, and counteractions (Emery and Trist, 1965, pp. 25–6).

When the environment becomes turbulent, however, its constituents are a multitude of other formal organizations. Increasingly, an organization's markets consist of other organizations; suppliers of material, labor and capital are increasingly organ-

4. Assuming a non-expanding economy, in the ideal instance.

5. Emery and Trist argue that fates, here, are positively correlated. This author agrees if an expanding economy is assumed.

ized, and regulatory groups are more numerous and powerful. The critical response of organizations under these conditions will be discussed later. It should be noted that *real* environments are often mixtures of these ideal types.

The evolution from placid-clustered environments to turbulent environments[6] can be summarized as a process in which formal organizations evolve: (a) *from* the status of systems within environments not formally organized; (b) *through* intermediate phases, e.g. Weberian bureaucracy; and (c) *to* the status of sub-systems of a larger social system.

Clark Kerr (1963) traces this evolution for the university in the United States. In modern industrial societies, this evolutionary process has resulted in the replacement of individuals and informal groups by organizations as *actors* in the social system. Functions that were once the sole responsibility of families and communities are increasingly allocated to formal organizations; child-rearing, work, recreation, education, health, and so on. Events which were long a matter of chance are increasingly subject to organizational control, such as population growth, business cycles, and even the weather. One wonders whether Durkheim, if he could observe the current scene, might speculate that the evolution from 'mechanical solidarity' to 'organic solidarity' is now occurring on the *organizational level*, where the common values of organizations in oligopolies are replaced by functional interdependencies among specialized organizations (see Durkheim, 1947).

Inter-organizational analysis

It was noted that survival in disturbed-reactive environments depends upon the ability of the organization to anticipate and counteract the behavior of similar systems. The analysis of inter-organizational behavior, therefore, becomes meaningful only in these and more complex environments. The interdependence of organizations, or any kind of living systems, at less complex environmental levels is more appropriately studied by means of ecological, competitive market, or other similar models.

The only systematic conceptual approach to inter-organiza-

6. The author does not agree with Emery and Trist, that *formal* (as distinct from social) organization will emerge in placid-random environments.

tional analysis has been the theory of oligopoly in economics. This theory clearly addresses only disturbed-reactive environments. Many economists admit that the theory, which assumes maximization of profit and perfect knowledge, is increasingly at odds with empirical evidence that organizational behavior is characterized by satisficing and bounded rationality. Boulding (1965) comments that 'it is surprisingly hard to make a really intelligent conflict move in the economic area simply because of the complexity of the system and the enormous importance of side effects and dynamic effects' (p. 189). A fairly comprehensive search of the literature has revealed only four conceptual frameworks for the analysis of inter-organizational relations outside the field of economics. These are briefly reviewed, particular attention being given to assumptions about organization environments, and to the utility of these assumptions in the analysis of inter-organizational relations in turbulent fields.

William Evan (1966) has introduced the concept of 'organization-set', after Merton's 'role-set' (pp. 177–80). Relations between a focal organization and members of its organization-set are mediated by the role-sets of boundary personnel. 'Relations' are conceived as the flow of information, products or services, and personnel (pp. 175–6). Presumably, monetary, and legal, and other transactions can be accommodated in the conceptual system. In general, Evan offers a conceptual tool for identifying transactions at a given time. He makes no explicit assumptions about the nature of environmental dynamics, nor does he imply that they are changing. The relative neglect of inter-organizational relations, which he finds surprising, is ascribed instead to the traditional intra-organizational focus, which derives from Weber, Taylor and Barnard. His concepts, however, go considerably beyond those of conventional organization and economic theory, e.g. comparative versus reference organizations and overlap in goals and values. If a temporal dimension were added to Evan's conceptual scheme, then it would be a very useful tool for describing the 'structural' aspects of transactional interdependencies (L_{21} and L_{12} relations) in turbulent fields.

Another approach is taken by Levine and White (1961, p. 586) who focus specifically on relations among community health and welfare agencies. This local set of organizations 'may be seen as a system with individual organizations or system parts varying in the kinds and frequencies of their relationships with one another'. The authors admit that interdependence exists among these local parts only to the extent that relevant resources are not available from *outside* the local region, which lies beyond their conceptual domain. Nor do we find here any suggestion of turbulence in these local environments. If such local sets of agencies are increasingly interdependent with other components of the local community and with organizations outside the locality, as the evidence suggests, then the utility of Levine and White's approach is both limited and shrinking.

Litwak and Hylton (1962) provide a third perspective. They too are concerned with health and welfare organizations, but their major emphasis is on coordination. The degree of interdependence among organizations is a major variable; low interdependence leads to *no* coordination and high interdependence leads to merger, therefore they deal only with conditions of moderate interdependence. The type of coordinating mechanism that emerges under conditions of moderate interdependence is hypothesized to result from the interaction of three trichotomized variables: the *number* of interdependent organizations; the degree of their *awareness* of their interdependence; and the extent of *standardization* in their transactions. The attractive feature of the Litwak and Hylton scheme is the possibility it offers of making different predictions for a great variety of environments. Their model also seems to have predictive power beyond the class of organizations to which they specifically address themselves. If environments are becoming turbulent, however, then increasingly fewer of the model's cells (a $3 \times 3 \times 3$ space) are relevant. In the one-cell turbulent corner of their model, where a large number of organizations have low awareness of their complex and unstandardized interdependence, 'there is little chance of coordination' (p. 417), according to Litwak and Hylton (1962). If the level of awareness of interdependence increases, the model predicts that some process of arbitration will emerge. Thus the model anticipates the inter-organizational implications of turbulent fields, but tells us little about the emerging processes that will enable organizations to adapt to turbulence.

The fourth conceptual framework available in the literature is by Thompson and McEwen (1958). They emphasize the inter-dependence of organizations with the larger society and discuss the consequences that this has for goal setting. 'Because the setting of goals is essentially a problem of defining desired relationships between an organization and its environment, change in either requires review and perhaps alteration of goals' (p. 23). They do not argue that such changes are more frequent today, but they do assert that reappraisal of goals is 'a more constant problem in an unstable environment than in a stable one', and also 'more difficult as the "product" of the enterprise becomes less tangible' (p. 24).

Thompson and McEwen outline four organizational strategies for dealing with the environment. One is competition; the other three are subtypes of a cooperative strategy: bargaining, co-optation, and coalition. These cooperative strategies all require direct interaction among organizations and this, they argue, increases the environment's potential control over the focal organization (p. 27). In bargaining, to the extent that the second party's support is necessary, that party is in a position to exercise a veto over the final choice of alternative goals, and thus takes part in the decision. The cooptation strategy makes still further inroads into the goal-setting process. From the standpoint of society, however, co-optation, by providing overlapping memberships, is an important social device for increasing the likelihood that organizations related to each other in complicated ways will in fact find compatible goals. Cooptation thus aids in the integration of heterogeneous parts of a complex social system. Coalition refers to a combination of two or more organizations for a common purpose and is viewed by these authors as the ultimate form of environmental conditioning of organization goals (Thompson and McEwen, 1958, pp. 25–8).

The conceptual approaches of Levine and White and of Litwak and Hylton therefore appear to be designed for non-turbulent conditions. Indeed, it may well be that coordination *per se*, in the static sense usually implied by that term, is dysfunctional for adaptation to turbulent fields. (This criticism has often been leveled at local 'councils of social agencies'; see Morris and Randall, 1965, Harris, 1964, and Wilensky and Lebeaux, 1958, especially pp. 263–5). On the other hand, Evan's concept of organization-set seems useful for describing static aspects of inter-organizational relations in either disturbed-reactive *or* turbulent-field environments. Its application in longitudinal rather than static studies might yield data on the relationship between structural aspects of transactional relations and organizational adaptability. Lastly, Thompson and McEwen make a unique contribution by distinguishing different *kinds* of inter-organizational relations.

As an aside, note that Evan's extension of the role-set concept to organizations suggests still further analogies, which may be heuristically useful. A role is a set of acts prescribed for the occupant of some position. The role accrues to the position; its occupants are interchangeable. If formal organizations are treated as social actors, then one can conceive of organizations as occupants of positions in the larger social system. Each organization has one or more roles in its behavioral repertoire (these are more commonly called functions or goals). The organization occupants of these social positions, however, are also interchangeable.

Integrative framework
Model

It is assumed that the foregoing arguments are valid: (a) that organizational environments are increasingly turbulent; (b) that organizations are increasingly less autonomous; and (c) that other formal organizations are increasingly important components of organizational environments. Some conceptual perspective is now needed, which will make it possible to view any formal organization, its transactional interdependencies, and the environment itself within a common conceptual framework. The intent of this section is to outline the beginnings of such a framework.

A formal organization is a system primarily oriented to the attainment of a specific goal, which constitutes an output of the system and which is an input for some other system (Parsons, 1962, p. 33). Needless to say, the output of any living system is dependent upon input into it. Figure 1 schematically illustrates the skeletal structure of a living system. The input and output regions are partially permeable with respect to the environment, which is the region outside the system boundary. Arrows coming into a system represent input and arrows going out of a system represent output. In Figure 2, rectangles represent formal organizations and circles represent individuals and *non*formal social organizations. Figure 2 represents the *statics* of a system X and its turbulent environment. Three-dimensional illustration

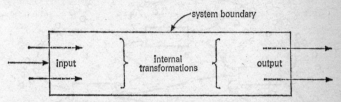

Figure 1 Structure of living systems such as a formal organization

would be necessary to show the *dynamics* of a turbulent environment schematically. Assume that a third, temporal dimension is imposed on Figure 2 and that this reveals an increasing number of elements and an increasing rate and complexity of change in their interdependencies over time. To do full justice to the concept of turbulence, we should add other sets of elements even in Figure 2 above, although these are not yet linked to X's set. A notion that is integral to Emery and Trist's conception of turbulence is that changes outside of X's set, and hence difficult for X to predict and impossible for X to control, will have impact on X's transactional interdependencies in the future. The addition of just one link at some future time may not affect the super-system but may constitute a system break for X.

This schematization shows only one-way directionality and is meant to depict energic inputs, e.g. personnel and material, and output, e.g. product. The organization provides something in exchange for the inputs it receives, of course, and this is usually informational in nature – money, most commonly. Similarly the organization receives money for its product from those systems for whom its product is an input. Nor does our framework distinguish different kinds of inputs, although the analysis of inter-organizational exchange requires this kind of taxonomic device. It seems important to distinguish energic inputs and outputs from informational ones. Energic inputs include machinery, personnel, clientele in the case of service organizations, electric power, and so on. Informational inputs are not well conceptualized although there is no doubt of their increasing importance in environments which are more complex and changeable. Special divisions of organizations and whole firms devoted to information collecting,

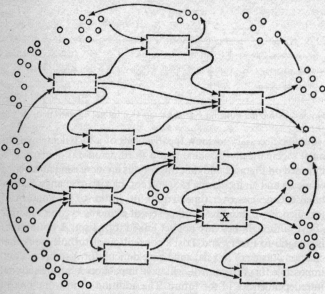

Figure 2 Illustration of system *X* in turbulent environment

processing and distributing are also rapidly proliferating, e.g. research organizations, accounting firms, the Central Intelligence Agency.

An input called 'legitimacy' is popular in sociological circles but highly resistant to empirical specification. The view taken here is that legitimacy is mediated by the exchange of other resources. Thus the willingness of firm *A* to contribute capital to *X*, and of agency *B* to refer personnel to *X* and firm *C* to buy *X*'s product testifies to the legitimacy of *X*. This 'willingness' on the part of organizations *A*, *B* and *C*, however, can best be understood in terms of informational exchange. For example, *A* provides *X* with capital on the basis of *A*'s information about the market for X's product. Or B refuses to refer skilled workmen to X since B has information on X's discriminatory employment practices and also knows of consequences to itself from elsewhere if it is party to X's practice. Technology is also sometimes treated as an input to organizations. We use the term, however, to refer to the complex set of interactions among inputs which takes place in the internal region shown in Figure 1. It is technology which transforms the inputs of the system into the output of the system. Transportation and communication technologies, however, are of a uniquely different order; the former constitutes an energic and the latter an informational transcendence of space–time that enabled the evolution of the more complex environments (L_{22}) which concern us here. Automation and computer technologies are roughly equivalent, i.e. energic and informational, respectively, but on an intra-organizational (L_{11}) level.

Our attention to 'legitimacy' and 'technology' was tangential to our main theme, to which we now return. Our simplistic approach to an integrative framework for the study of organizations (L_{11}), their transactional interdependencies (L_{21} and L_{12}) and the connectedness within their environments (L_{22}), gives the following conceptual ingredients: (a) units that are mainly formal organizations, and (b) relationships between them that are the directed flow (Cartwright, 1959) of (c) energy and information. The enormous and increasing importance of informational transaction has not been matched by conceptual developments in organization theory. The importance of information is frequently cited in a general way, however, especially in the context of organizational change or innovation. Dill (1962) has made a cogent argument on the need for more attention to this dimension.

The importance of communication for organizational change has been stressed by Ohlin (1958, p. 63), March and Simon (1958, pp. 173–83), Benne (1962, p. 232), Lippitt (1958, p. 52), and others. Diversity of informational input has been used to explain the creativity of individuals as well as of social systems (see, e.g. Allport, 1955, p. 76, Ogburn and Nimkoff, 1964, pp. 662–70). The importance of boundary positions as primary sources of innovative inputs from the environment has been stressed by March and Simon (1958, pp. 165–8, 189) and by Kahn *et al.* (1964, pp. 101–26). James Miller (1955, p. 530) hypothesizes that up to a maximum, which no living system has yet reached, the more energy a system devotes to information processing (as opposed to productive and maintenance activity), the more likely the system is to survive.

Evolution on the biological level is accompanied by improvement in the ability of systems to discover and perform according to contingencies in their environments. The random walk which suffices in a placid-randomized environment must be replaced by stochastic processes under placid-clustered conditions, and by cybernetic processes in disturbed-reactive fields. Among biological/psychological systems, only man appears to have the capacity for the purposeful behavior that may permit adaptation to or control of turbulent environments. There is some question, of course, as to whether man actually *has* the capacity to cope with the turbulence that he has introduced into the environment.

Analogous concepts are equally applicable to the evolution of social systems in general and to formal organizations in particular. The capacity of *any* system for adapting to changing contingencies in its environment is inversely related to its dependence upon instinct, habit or tradition. Adaptability exists, by definition, to the extent that a system (L_{11}) can survive externally induced (L_{22}) change in its transactional interdependencies (L_{21} and L_{12}); therefore viability equals adaptability.

Hypotheses

Hypothesis 1. Organizational change is largely externally induced.

Any particular change may be adaptive or maladaptive, and it may be one of these in the short run and the other in the long run. There is *no* systematic empirical evidence on the relative influence of internal versus environmental antecedents to organizational change. The empirical task here is to identify organizational changes, and the internal or external origins of each change.

It is crucial to distinguish change on the organizational level from the multitude of changes that may occur in or among subsystems, only some of which give rise to change on the system level. Many social psychologists, for example, study change in individuals and groups *within* organizations, but with no reference to variables of organizational level. Likert's (1961) book is one noteworthy exception. The important point is that change on the organizational level is analytically distinct from change on other levels.

Organizational change means any change in the kind or quantity of output. Ideally, output is treated as a function of inputs and of transfer functions, i.e. intra-organizational change is inferred from change in input–output relations. Haberstroth (1965) illustrates the use of these general system concepts in the organization context. An excellent discussion of the efficiency and effectiveness of organizations, in an open-systems framework, is given in Katz and Kahn (1966, especially pp. 149–70).

However, the input–output functions in diversified industries and the outputs of many service organizations are resistant to objective specification and measurement. An empirical test of this hypothesis, with presently available tools, may have to settle for some set of input and internal change that seems to be reasonably antecedent to output change.

The identification of the origin of change is also beset by difficulties. An input change may indeed have external antecedents, but external events may also be responses to some prior internal change in the focal organization. And internal change may be internally generated, but it may also be the result of an informational input from external sources. Novel informational inputs, as well as novel communication channels, often derive from change in personnel inputs. Increasingly, organizations seek personnel who bring specialized information rather than 'manpower' to the organization. The presence of first, second and higher order causation poses a problem for any empirical test of this hypothesis.

Hypothesis 2. System adaptability, e.g. organizational, is a function of ability to learn and to perform according to changing environmental contingencies.

Adaptability exists, by definition, to the extent that a system can survive externally induced change in its transactional interdependencies in the long run. Diversity in a system's input (L_{21}) and output (L_{12}) interdependencies will increase adaptability. The recent and rapid diversification in major industries illustrates this strategy. Flexible structure (L_{11}, e.g. decentralized decision making) will facilitate adaptation. Beyond this, however, adaptability would seem to be largely a function of a system's perceptual and information-processing capacities.[7] The following variables appear crucial: (a) *advance information* of impending externally induced (L_{22}) change in L_{21} or L_{12} transactions; (b) *active search* for, and activation of, more advantageous input and output transactions; and (c) *available memory store* (L_{11}) of interchangeable input and output components in the environment.

Advance information and active search might be empirically handled with Evan's concept of the role-sets of boundary personnel, along with notions of channel efficiency. For example, overlapping memberships, e.g. on boards, would constitute a particularly efficient channel. Likewise, direct communication between members of separate organizations, while less effective than overlapping memberships, would be a more efficient channel between agencies A and B than instances where their messages must be mediated by a third agency, C. Efficiency of inter-organizational communication channels should be positively associated with access to advance information, and be facilitative of search, for example. The members of an organization's informational set may become increasingly differentiated from its energic set. Communication channels to research and marketing firms, universities, governmental agencies and other important information producing and distributing agencies would be expected to increase long-run viability. The third variable, memory store, is probably a function of the efficiency of past and present informational channels, but it involves internal (L_{11}) information processing as well.

Lastly, *any* internal change that improves an organization's transactional advantage, e.g. improved technology, will also be conducive to adaptability. Since organizational innovation is more often imitation than invention (Levitt, 1966), these changes are usually also the product of informational input and can be handled within the same integrative framework.

7. Igor Ansoff (1965, p. 162) speaks of the 'wide-open windows of perception' required of tomorrow's firms, and offers a perspective on the future that is fully compatible with that presented here.

Summary

The lag between evolution in the real world and evolution in theorists' ability to comprehend it is vast, but hopefully shrinking. It was only a little over one hundred years ago that Darwin identified natural selection as the mechanism of evolutionary process. Despite Darwin's enduring insight, theorists of change, including biologists, have continued to focus largely on internal aspects of systems.

It is our thesis that the selective advantage of one intra- or inter-organizational configuration over another cannot be assessed apart from an understanding of the dynamics of the environment itself. It is the environment which exerts selective pressure. 'Survival of the fittest' is a function of the fitness of the environment. The dinosaurs *were* impressive creatures, in their day.

References

ADLER, L. (1966), 'Symbiotic marketing', *Harvard Business Review*, vol. 44, November, pp. 59–71.

ALLPORT, F. H. (1955), *Theories of Perception and the Concept of Structure*, Wiley.

ANSOFF, I. (1965), 'The firm of the future', *Harvard Business Review*, vol. 43, September.

ASHBY, W. R. (1960), *Design for a Brain*, Chapman & Hall, 2nd edn.

BENNE, K. D. (1962), 'Deliberate changing as the facilitation of growth', in W. G. Bennis *et al.* (eds.), *The Planning of Change*, Holt, Rinehart & Winston.

BLAU, P. M., and SCOTT, R. (1962), *Formal Organizations*, Chandler.

BOULDING, K. E. (1965), 'The economies of human conflict', in E. B. McNeil (ed.), *The Nature of Human Conflict*, Prentice-Hall.

BRAYBROOKE, D., and LINDBLOM, C. E. (1963), *A Strategy of Decision*, Free Press.

CARTWRIGHT, D. (1959), 'The potential contribution of graph theory to organization theory', in M. Haire (ed.), *Modern Organization Theory*, Wiley, pp. 254–71.

CHEIN, I. (1943), 'Personality and typology', *Journal of Social Psychology*, vol. 18, pp. 89–101.

CLARK, B. R. (1965), 'Inter-organizational patterns in education', *Administrative Science Quarterly*, vol. 10, pp. 224–37.

CYERT, R. M., and MARCH, J. G. (1953), *A Behavioral Theory of the Firm*, Prentice-Hall.

DILL, W. R. (1958), 'Environment as an influence on managerial autonomy', *Administrative Science Quarterly*, vol. 2, pp. 409–43.

DILL, W. R. (1962), 'The impact of environment on organizational development', in S. Mailick and E. H. von Ness (eds.), *Concepts and Issues in Administrative Behavior*, Prentice-Hall, pp. 94–109.

DRUCKER, P. F. (1964), 'The big power of little ideas', *Harvard Business Review*, vol. 42, May.

DURKHEIM, E. (1947), *The Division of Labor in Society*, Free Press; translated by G. Simpson.

ELLING, R. H., and HALEBSKY, S. (1961), 'Organizational differentiation and support: a conceptual framework', *Administrative Science Quarterly*, vol. 6, pp. 185–209.

EMERY, F. E., and TRIST E. L. (1965), 'The causal texture of organizational environments', *Human Relations*, vol. 18, pp. 21–31.

ETZIONI, A. (1960), 'New directions in the study of organizations and society', *Social Research*, vol. 27, pp. 223–8.

EVAN, W. M. (1966), 'The organization-set: toward a theory of inter-organizational relations', in J. D. Thompson (ed.), *Approaches to Organizational Design*, University of Pittsburgh Press.

GARDNER, J. W. (1963), *Self-Renewal*, Harper & Row.

HABERSTROTH, C. J. (1965), 'Organization design and systems analysis', in J. G. March (ed.), *Handbook of Organizations*, Rand-McNally, pp. 1171–1211.

HARRIS, W. (1964), 'A modern council point of view', *Social Work*, vol. 9, pp. 34–41.

HOOD, R. C. (1962), 'Business organization as a class-product of its purposes and of its environment', in M. Haire (ed.), *Organizational Theory in Industrial Practice*, Wiley.

KAHN, R. L., *et al.* (1964), *Organizational Stress*, Wiley.

KATZ, D., and KAHN, R. L. (1966), *The Social Psychology of Organizations*, Wiley.

KERR, C. (1963), *The Uses of the University*, Harper Torchbooks.

LEVINE, S., and WHITE, P. E. (1961), 'Exchange as a conceptual framework for the study of inter-organizational relationships', *Administrative Science Quarterly*, vol. 5, pp. 583–601.

LEVITT, T. (1966), 'Innovative imitation', *Harvard Business Review*, vol. 44, September, pp. 63–70.

LIKERT, R. (1961), *New Patterns of Management*, McGraw-Hill.

LIPPITT, R. (1958), *The Dynamics of Planned Change*, Harcourt, Brace & World.

LITWAK, E., and HYLTON, L. (1962), 'Inter-organizational analysis: a hypothesis on coordinating agencies', *Administrative Science Quarterly*, vol. 6, pp. 395–420.

MANIHA, J., and PERROW, C. (1965), 'The reluctant organization and the aggressive environment', *Administrative Science Quarterly*, vol. 10, pp. 238–57.

MARCH, J. G., and SIMON, H. A. (1958), *Organizations*, Wiley.

MCNULTY, J. E. (1962), 'Organizational change in growing enterprises', *Administrative Science Quarterly*, vol. 7, pp. 1–21.

MILLER, J. G. (1955), 'Toward a general theory for the behavioral sciences', *American Psychologist*, vol. 10, no. 9, pp. 513–31.

MORRIS, R., and RANDALL, O. A. (1965), 'Planning and organization of community services for the elderly', *Social Work*, vol. 10, pp. 96–103.

OGBURN, W. F., and NIMKOFF, M. F. (1964), *Sociology*, Houghton Mifflin, 2nd edn.

OHLIN, L. E. (1958), 'Conformity in American society', *Social Work*, vol. 3, p. 63.

PARSONS, T. (1960), *Structure and Process in Modern Societies*, Free Press.

PARSONS, T. (1962), 'Suggestions for a sociological approach to the theory of organizations', in A. Etzioni (ed.), *Complex Organizations*, Holt, Rinehart & Winston.

PRINGLE, J. W. S. (1956), 'On the parallel being learning and evolution' *General Systems*, vol. 1, p. 90.

RIDGWAY, V. F. (1957), 'Administration of manufacturer–dealer systems', *Administrative Science Quarterly*, vol. 2, pp. 464–83.

ROSENGREN, W. R. (1964), 'Communication, organization and conduct in the "therapeutic milieu"', *Administrative Science Quarterly*, vol. 9, pp. 70–90.

RUBINGTON, E. (1965), 'Organizational strain and key roles', *Administrative Science Quarterly*, vol. 9, pp. 350–69.

SELZNICK, P. (1949), *TVA and the Grass Roots*, University of California.

SIMON, H. A. (1957), *Models of Man*, Wiley.

STINCHCOMBE, A. L. (1965), 'Social structure and organizations', in J. G. March (ed.), *Handbook of Organizations*, Rand-McNally.

TAYLOR, D. W. (1965), 'Decision making and problem solving', in J. G. March (ed.), *Handbook of Organizations*, Rand-McNally, pp. 48–82.

TERREBERRY, S. (1967), 'The evolution of environments', mimeographed course paper.

THOMPSON, J. D. (1967), *Organizations in Action*, McGraw-Hill.

THOMPSON, J. D., and MCEWEN, W. J. (1958), 'Organizational goals and environment', *American Sociological Review*, vol. 23, pp. 23–31.

TOLMAN, E. C., and BRUNSWICK, E. (1935), 'The organism and the causal texture of the environment', *Psychological Review*, vol. 42, pp. 43–72.

VON BERTALANFFY, L. (1956), 'General system theory', *General Systems*, vol. 1, pp. 1–10.

WILENSKY, L., and LEBEAUX, C. N. (1958), *Industrial Society and Social Welfare*, Russell Sage Foundation.

5 R. Bolt

Organizations that Serve Several Values

From R. Bolt, 'Organizations that serve several values', *Innovation*,
1969, no. 6.

Money, yes. You need it to use. And you have to make it if you
are a for-profit corporation. But today, whatever the form of your
organization – public or private corporation, university, or
government agency – as an innovating institution you have to
cope with a multiplicity of values that go beyond money alone.

What's more, you often have to put equal importance on two
or more values at the same time. This means, unless you already
are far out, that you will have to change not only the way you do
things but even the fundamental value structure of your organization itself.

In the past, society changed slowly enough and technology was
simple enough to let you innovate in an orderly, single-track
fashion. For example, a private corporation could pretty much
guide its course just in terms of return on capital invested.

Today, the accelerating pace of both society and technology
produces a cascade of overlapping opportunities and aspirations.
The research staff, with its intellectual values, and the society,
with its desire for a better life, want to see the innovation cycle
completed more rapidly in fulfillment of their own goals, which
they regard as at least as important as monetary return. Managing the innovative process has become a problem of sensitivity
balancing the several value scales involved.

To innovate requires capabilities of many kinds:

1. Intellectual capabilities, strongly centered in science and technology, to create new solutions and new ways of doing things.

2. Sociological capabilities, to identify social problems and provide leadership in carrying out the sociological change induction
involved.

3. Financial capabilities, whether provided through private investment or public funding, to support the work of innovating throughout the chain of events from research and invention to implementation and adoption of the innovation.

The following are equally needed, but cut across the three named above.

4. Managerial capabilities.

5. Political capabilities. These are the ones that guide and oversee the entire innovative process, and that represent and serve society in achieving the difficult end of changing itself.

Each set of capabilities carries with it a set of values. These include intellectual values and closely associated self values of the creative persons that innovate, social values, and financial values as perceived by the individual and collective investors in the innovation.

If you don't really serve social values, with timeliness and relevance, your would-be innovations won't go. If you ignore the personal and intellectual values of achievement and scientific truth, your creative staff will go – elsewhere. If you don't pay attention to the economic viability of your attempts to innovate, you'll find your activities constrained if you are a not-for-profit, university, or government agency, and as a private organization you'll risk eventual bankruptcy.

No matter how well you serve any one or two of these sets of values, if you ignore, let alone violate, the others you are not likely to survive as a successfully innovating organization.

The more complex and the larger in scale the innovation, the greater will be the extent to which the several capabilities must be brought to bear, and, consequently, the stronger will be the impact of the corresponding values in carrying out major innovations, whether they are technological or social. For example, the political process of debate among representatives of competing values will show itself as an inescapable activity that must be dealt with in conjunction with the managerial process.

Although in some cases a single organization can carry out the entire innovative process, more often this process involves many organizations of different kinds. As I shall discuss later, the future may see two trends, one in which individual organizations broaden themselves adequately to handle the entire innovation alone, and one in which several organizations join together to perform one particular innovation and then disband their joint venture.

But whether the innovating institution is a single organization or a joint venture, that institution will undergo changes produced by the very process of innovation in which it is engaged. The changes will involve adjustments to the different values held by the management, the staff, and the environment in which they operate.

Further, as I see it, this process of institutional change in time will produce a new kind of institution that has adapted itself specifically to innovate successfully. The essential characteristic of this new innovating institution will be *the simultaneous satisfying of two or more values that are taken to be of equal importance.* This property is different in kind from that of the traditional social institutions that say, when the chips are down, above all else we will satisfy value *x*. Of course value *x* might be return on investment or scientific truth or something else, depending on the particular institution.

It's a lot harder to manage an organization that serves not just a single, overriding purpose, such as profitability, but rather, serves several different values that often equally affect the ultimate decisions to be made.

I know how hard it is because I have come to realize and appreciate the multiple values in my own organization and its operating environment. Several times we have made changes in our organization, a private company, to adjust the fits among components motivated by different sets of values.

Our enterprise, Bolt, Beranek and Newman Inc., is twenty years old now and we find ourselves serving many more values than when we started out as partners consulting in the field of acoustics and noise control. Some of us were full-time faculty members at MIT, and in our consulting practice the intellectual values of understanding and truth in the scientific sense were similar to the value scales of a university.

As is usual with consultants, more jobs began to come to us as our work became known. In those early years, practically the only concept that governed our organization was that we were an affiliation of independent professional consultants sharing problems, ideas, facilities, and costs. What counted most to us was becoming pre-eminent in our specialties by doing the very best scientific job so people would want us to be their consultants and do research for them. Obviously there is one difference here from the university scale of value – the partners own part of the action and share the financial risk as well as the potential monetary returns.

When we incorporated about ten years later we carried over the idea of partnership, reflecting it in the ownership of stock, which then was all held internally. While a large fraction of the professional staff and some of the support staff now have some stock ownership of our company, there is an important segment of ownership that came in when we went public in 1961. Presumably these outside owners were motivated by investment reasons, seeking capital growth or, someday, dividends. The second value structure – financial success – was entering in more strongly and causing us to be concerned about variations in profitability, even though our sales were increasing steadily at a rate of 20–25 per cent per year.

We began to see the conflict between the two value structures and wondered how to achieve a better balance between them. From one experience we had about five years after BBN was formed, it seemed perfectly simple to increase financial returns by exploiting industrial services or products spawned by our fundamental professional activities in consulting and research. We had been called upon to find a way to take the high-intensity noise out of aircraft engine test cells. Our solution, which we patented, worked so well that we built another corporation to produce it and market it under the name of Soundstream.

Perhaps this early financial success spoiled us into believing we knew all about how to innovate. As it turned out, we had merely been fortunate in having all the ingredients for the innovation there to be brought together: we understood the problem, we knew how to solve it, and we could fit an economically viable product into a marketplace we knew well.

But there was something important which we didn't understand so well when we tried later, with varying degrees of success, to develop other industrial products and services: we were still doing things basically to satisfy our value scale of intellectual curiosity without fulfilling the co-equal values that govern survival and profitability in an industrial and production environment.

In retrospect, there were several factors that are related to our successes and failures.

There was simply a statistical factor, which I learned more about in the course of conversation with the chairman of the board of one of the largest corporations. His company has a very distinguished research facility and I was asking him how he made decisions on which ideas coming out of the lab were going to be carried into production. He replied that his basic rule was extraordinarily simple: 'The likelihood of an idea becoming a success is about one in twenty.'

We had been expecting that twenty out of twenty ideas coming out of our lab could be exploited industrially – just because we thought they were bright ideas. Now we've found through the years that if we accept more than about one in twenty, we're trying to make products that just don't work, either because the product isn't right or the market isn't right. If we turn down more than one in twenty, we're missing good opportunities.

That ratio isn't a magic number – it has to come out of an organization's own experience. But if you apply approximately those numbers, it's easy to see that they impose an automatic limit on the growth rate of industrial products and services – particularly if the ideas on which they are based depend on what comes out of a research group geared to a value scale that doesn't regard economic viability in the marketplace as co-equal with its own truth scale.

Of course we could pick an area for a product or a service and ask our research group to design things to sell in that area. But then we would completely change the concept of our professional services business (later I'll come to our industrial business), for we would be asking our research people to put economic viability ahead of their value scale – research for the sake of its own intellectual merit. Let me make the distinction here that there are many companies, ones with large and excellent research organizations, in which the ultimate decision on research activity is scaled to the profitability of the product or service area they support, and not to the value of the research in and of itself. Such companies tend to remain single-valued organizations.

But we were happy with our existing motivations and environment in the professional services business. We didn't want to lose them, and we had shown that it could run profitably all by itself even though its rate of growth was limited by the availability of high-quality professionals who understood the fields in which we specialized.

Could we swing a business based on industrial products and services on the same hinge and have it run profitably by itself, too, but somehow successfully combine both kinds of businesses, to their mutual benefit, within the same organization? If so, the question of which value scale predominates would become irrelevant.

Back in the 1930s, Burnham's well-known book, *The Managerial Revolution*, said that the manager who understands the technology holds the reins. I find it hardly as simple as that today.

For one thing, the people who often seem to hold the reins are the ones who best understand the technology of the new and fast growing fields – whether these people are the managers or not.

As it works out in physics, for example, or in the computer field, such people often have a greater fidelity to their own interests and talents than to the organization that employs them. Advancing a field rather than an organization often comes first to them.

If a manager knows how to channel such motivational goals to serve his corporate objectives also, his organization gains; if he doesn't, his best people may leave to regroup themselves. The computer field alone is full of brand-new small companies – splintered from more staid organizations – which have sold innovative ideas to the very organizations that originally harbored the talent.

Perhaps the larger organizations are slowly beginning to recognize this. At a recent meeting of SHARE, an IBM user's group, some of the brightest computer systems people there wore full hippie regalia. Evidently their nonconformity was tolerated by the major companies that employed them because such talents were so essential to their work – but the point is that such nonconformity these days often is simply an expression of a different set of values.

Because values are measured by human beings, not physical instruments, the performance of an innovating organization is really judged through a process of debate among competing groups representing the several values involved.

This is why I believe the managing process will become more like the political process, in which a diversity of goals and values must be reconciled before a decision can be reached. I do not mean the proverbial corporate politics of power struggle as taught, and often exaggerated, in the case studies of business schools, although such power politics will not vanish as long as man is man. Rather, I mean the open, constructive process of debate among groups representing or personally promoting alternative values and policies.

Is this management or anarchy?

Take this initial reaction of a newcomer to a renowned innovating organization: 'I was shocked and disturbed . . . but I soon was carried into a stream of interests in which questions of orderliness in corporate policy and administration no longer seemed important. Subsequently I have come to regard this anarchy as the strength if not the substance of the organization . . . a degree of intellectual freedom which is so unique that it seems like anarchy in terms of my earlier experience. . . .'

Where is this atmosphere of apparent near-anarchy? The RAND Corporation.

While you may contend that RAND Corporation is unique, it exemplifies one variety of a new kind of multivalued innovating institution now taking shape.

Here I am using the words multivalued institution in a general sense to mean a societal arrangement established to serve two or more values, co-equally, at the same time.

If these values are, in fact, different and all are requiring attention of management, it might be useful to think of each value as being represented by its own particular kind of capital and currency. Already the term, intellectual capital, is being used to talk about collected knowledge and problem-solving skills. Of course, intellectual currency is by no means a simple, linear sum – its qualitative aspect is paramount. But we do indeed use intellectual currency in innovating. In a similar vein perhaps we will come to use social capital and the currency of good-will – rapport with the social group for whom we innovate.

To innovate successfully today in such areas as, say, urban technology or environmental pollution, requires many kinds of 'capital' and 'currency'. Some organizations may contribute mainly financial capital, or the currency of good will and understanding with the social community affected by the innovation. At least one of the organizations involved should be able to contribute strong managerial capital to managing the total environment for innovation.

So several such organizations together could form a joint venture, in the usual sense of the term, each putting in its particular kind of capital resource. These days such ventures seem to be infrequent, merely temporary alliances for the purposes of winning and performing contracts, though I see them as intermediate stages in the development of multivalued organizations. Few members of such team ventures yet view their participation as a step toward institutionalizing this approach to innovation; they regard it only as a way of getting the present job done.

With a few interesting exceptions, most individual corporations or universities or research centers have been working only in a part of the innovation spectrum. Even when research and consulting organizations like RAND, or Arthur D. Little, or Stanford Research Institute contribute innovative ideas, usually some industrial company carries these through final development, production and marketing. In this way, the innovative cycle has been carried on by several organizations only loosely coupled together for convenience or expediency.

With the appearance of more complex problems of larger scale – better housing, networks of transportation, global communication – I see two trends: (a) toward tighter coupling of the partners in joint ventures; and (b) toward the emergence of multivalued single organizations. In the first trend, which we discussed, each of the organizations in the combine may back off after the innovative cycle is completed, perhaps to join quite different combinations to solve other kinds of problems.

In the second trend, a single organization will broaden itself, either by merger and acquisition or, by growing from within, in order to generate the full range of capabilities necessary to perform all aspects of the innovative cycle more effectively.

By a single organization I do not mean merely a collection of divisions or wholly-owned subsidiaries related only by a chart for purposes of accounting or accountability. Rather I mean an organization with components whose goals in research or consulting or education, in development or production or marketing, may be set by quite different values but whose interactions and contributions are managed in ways that become of mutual benefit to the induction of innovative change.

That is the direction in which Xerox, for example, seems to be going, gaining some special skills it wants by acquiring the companies that have them. Envisioning applications of its duplicating processes and ideas to the educational market, it merged Basic Systems into its organization to get the skills it needed in the technology of programmed learning. Xerox went on to acquire Ginn & Co., likely because Ginn really understands the sociology of schoolrooms – how to put together textbooks, how to bring together teaching experts from various fields as advisory committees for a series of texts, etc. This is a kind of social capital – one that enhances the acceptance of Xerox, via Ginn, in the educational community.

Naturally I can speak with some insight about such trends toward multivalued single organizations because of a similar direction in which our own company is moving. Earlier I said that we had grown to a point where we had two really distinctive kinds of businesses – professional services and industrial activities – which offered the potential of our single corporation involving itself in essentially all aspects of the innovative cycle. Here I shall talk specifically about mutual reinforcement of the two kinds of business in areas where our knowledge and understanding of computers, for example, can pay off.

We are working in artificial intelligence, computer communications, time-sharing, advanced systems, and education technology. Our income from these activities derives mainly from the time spent by a professional scientist or engineer doing consulting, or research and development, or teaching courses in continuing education.

But within the same parent organization we also produce computer peripherals and sell computer services. For these activities, we built separate development groups whose goals would be directed toward designing products services specifically for the marketplace. We make graphical input–output devices, advanced in technology but manufactured and marketed in accordance with industrial practice. We also sell computer services based on time-shared systems we have developed. So our industrial income derives from an inventory of products or services based on ideas sometimes germinated from our own research effort in professional services, sometimes from outside research, and sometimes from our own product development groups.

While we have been selling computer time-shared services for about four years, we are now deliberately sharpening our approach to specific markets related to other activities in the company. One of these is the architectural and building construction field where we understand the sociology of architectural practice.

In trying to develop computer services for this field we see a naturally useful linkage here to those special services we already supply in architectural technology – design services for rooms, theatres and office buildings, growing out of our original consulting in acoustics and noise control. Our people selling time-shared services to the architectural and building market can draw upon the market entree of our many consultants who are already serving the same field. Perhaps more significantly, by having so many people in our organization with architectural degrees and first-hand experience, we can enhance our capability to develop software application packages that really make sense to an architect.

In some cases, an organization like a large construction company or architectural engineering firm may want to acquire its own computers and needs help in developing the system configuration best suited to its special needs. Here our system development professional services and our architectural consultants could team up to help. Another activity, which we partly own and help to manage, Delos Computer Leasing Corporation, can even provide the computer system equipment. Thus we are prepared by development of such natural linkages to various parts of our organization, to carry out an entire innovative process.

How do we manage our company so that the values governing both sets of activities – professional and industrial – are understood and acceptable? In a way, this question serves to focus attention on one category of forces that I see shaping the innovating institution.

In the non-changing or slowly-changing society, each institution takes on a clear identity. Everyone inside and outside the institution knows what it is supposed to do. The corporate image becomes crystalized into a shorthand, an easy label. For example, the purpose of the private corporation is to return profit on investment. Everyone knows that the corporation will treat its employees well, and that the corporation will profess to serve, and often in fact will serve very well, a recognized social function. So why talk about the individual and social values?

In the fast-changing society, or more precisely, when the rate of innovation exceeds the rate of institutional response, the corporate image is blurred by the superposition of several different values at the same time. No single label suffices to satisfy all the people that the corporation is doing what it ought to do, because what it ought to do is many things and is changing. Therefore, it seems to me, the innovating institution is driven to make explicit the several values it is serving or is getting ready to serve. And these several values must receive equal consideration in the making of the ultimate decisions about resources and objectives.

There's an obvious financial value for any single organization in having the entire spectrum of capability for following through the innovative cycle; the owners enjoy the fruits of further expansion, diversification, and return on investment.

I have also seen another advantage as I observe the changes in our company: the various parts of a single organization can learn to work together, to communicate with one another, to help each other without having to re-learn these relationships with each new problem of innovation they take on in the future. A group specializing in sociological aspects will already know how to interact more effectively with the financially-oriented managers and with the research-oriented scientists. My point is that the single organization broadening itself to become more innovative may have a running start when it comes to tackling new problems.

As an interesting aside, I would ask if it is possible that some of our universities will move more in the direction of the expanding single organization than in the present direction of collaborating with local, state and federal agencies and not-for-profit institutions in helping to bring about innovation. Already we hear, especially among the students and younger professors, that the university should do more than just teach and do pure research; it should serve society by actually going out to solve the problems of the city, or the problems of transportation.

Indeed, I sense the reaction of engineering educators to this: many of them are quite willing to say there would be great educational value if the university went so far as to carry out a complete prototype of a new system, participating in its operation and management only until it could run itself. Innovation, as I am defining it, does not include the continued operation of something but certainly does go up to the point where society has adopted it.

There really isn't any set of rules by which a multi-valued innovating institution can be organized and managed successfully. But some helpful ideas come from observing the change processes that such organizations undergo.

Innovative organizations appear to evolve in stages. They can start in almost any way, just doing consulting, or just doing research, or just making and selling a product. As they start extending their capabilities for innovating, they have to build another *kind* of organization in which other sets of values start counting more heavily. Arthur D. Little, a consulting company, later started producing low temperature equipment. Information Research Associates (now Infoton) began with contract research for the Air Force, and now it also markets a product line of computer peripheral equipment.

My point is that in the process of generating innovative output, organizations unavoidably change themselves into multivalued institutions, with at least two or more major components each having different value structures, different kinds of people, a different environment and different management rules.

It is all too easy to run out and split off companies and say one kind of company is technically based and the other company is industrially based so the two don't hinge together. But that's not the only way to resolve a value conflict. If you work at it hard enough you can meld them together and then have continuing benefits from the several values served within one company.

Adjusting the fit among the several domains is a delicate management task. But any institution that learns to do it really well gains an opportunity for a kind of self-stimulating amplification of the innovation process. When several domains accept and understand the role each plays, they become supportive in essential ways.

The political process of which I spoke earlier brings with it serious questions concerning the efficiency of management. If debate goes on too long the organization may pay a prohibitive price in time used up or opportunity lost. Yet a debate cut too short may result in reluctant compliance or even costly revolt. I have not studied this problem systematically (it's an important topic for research in managerial style), but what I have seen suggests that such debate is more often cut too short than let run too long. Of course I am invoking a value judgement in relation to my theme, the emergence of the multivalued innovating institution. For the traditional corporation, the optimal debate would be shorter, and debate would practically vanish for the totally autocratic organization.

However, I am in no way implying that the multivalued innovating institution will eventually become a purely political institution. Whatever debate goes on must also be directed to questions of society's readiness to accept an innovation no matter how bright an idea seems, of understanding that marketplace, and of the economics of engineering for it.

If an institution is going to produce technological innovations successfully, and do so in a manner that satisfies the several values involved, including the monetary values, then it will retain some of the character of the private corporation.

Now let me turn to another management problem related to the characteristics of the kinds of people in an organization who may debate in favor of a value scale other than monetary. A person in a highly competent consulting field views himself as an independent professional. That image is valuable to him, to the market for his services, and can be valuable to his employer.

A subtle balance is involved. The client wants to view his consultant as giving his professional services independently, not just in the name of his organization. At the same time, the organization behind the consultant ensures his ability to draw on wider judgements and backing as needed.

Markets are often lost when such a man leaves. An organization ought to think very carefully about the nature of the business he has built throughout his quasi-independent status, for if it is important to the institution, then the particular kind of work the man does must be institutionalized. Otherwise, the organization has not ensured its ability – and fulfilled its ethical obligation – to continue to serve its clients even after the man leaves or retires.

In order for the organization to do this, it must have a certain commitment from the man. A delicate balance must be achieved between the man's independence and his level of responsibility to the organization, giving him the pride of accomplishment in building something that endures, that continues to bear his stamp after he has left. At the same time, he must understand why it is important to the corporation to honor the commitment to its market and clientele to provide the service.

When you are trying to attract a creative research man or consultant, if all you say is: 'Come with us and do your own thing in your own way,' then you are laying the ground for trouble down the road. Even the person who otherwise could have become a productive, happy member of your team may be turned into a person who, at least as long as he is in your organization, expects that you will do everything for him and that he need do nothing in return.

Sometimes the problem is that the corporation and the individual do not talk explicitly enough about this dual commitment. Such candid talk, right at the beginning, helps to produce a conducive environment in which the man easily becomes 'corporate house broken', not in the sense of the carbon-copy organization man, but in the sense of an independent spirit who effectively couples freedom with responsibility, who understands the dual commitment that he makes to the corporation and the corporation makes to him.

Such an environment also makes it easier for management to understand and even benefit from the apparently far-out ideas of the seeming radical. Sometimes you misinterpret the relation between his action and his value scale. Earlier this year, one of our brightest young scientists not only took an active part in a student–faculty protest movement but, I learned later, had been holding meetings with other scientists and engineers in the company to develop a position to be stated at the protest meeting.

He was widely quoted – or misquoted – in the newspapers. When we talked with him personally about this we found that he was most sincere in his goals and was trying to act responsibly. Essentially he was seeking ways in which present technical knowledge and capabilities could be turned to broader benefits for society than just support of defense establishment needs. So we encouraged his desire to find new outlets for our own capabilities within the potential marketplace for the kinds of innovative development he thought we ought to be doing according to his value scale. His consequent efforts hold promise of carrying us into new market areas of social need.

Another benefit often emerges from a mutual understanding of the dual commitment; it becomes easier to develop the optimal distance between a manager and the person who reports to him. Some managers simply stay too close. Others stay too close because they don't understand the values that govern what their people appear to be doing.

I like to define the optimal distance as one in which the supervisor can catch the really crucial mistakes soon enough to help fix them. However, within this framework, you help a man to grow faster because he has to make more decisions himself.

Still, there are people who prefer professional growth to managerial growth. Often a senior scientist is relieved that a bright young fellow who appreciates him is there to take all the administrative nuisances off his hands.

Recognizing that we are trying to manage multivalue scales, we have tried to be careful not to build a rigid hierarchy. Rather than develop highly formal reporting relationships, we have tried to organize our administration, marketing and management to complement and support the skills of our scientists. We have tried to distribute the business managers and marketing managers throughout our activities so they work side by side with the scientists as co equal professionals, though each is judged on performance by his own peers.

Advancement and professional recognition for the scientist means that some day he will be elected a Principal Scientist of our organization. The concept of a Principal Scientist is patterned after the distinguished university Professor and carries with it some similar privileges, such as a periodic sabbatical for professional enrichment. It also offers opportunity for a person to open up new areas of research and consulting that he finds interesting. He is an intellectual leader in the eyes of the organization, a position fully equal in stature to that of our corporate vice-presidents.

6 C. Argyris

Today's Problems with Tomorrow's Organizations

C. Argyris, 'Today's problems with tomorrow's organizations', *Journal of Management Studies*, 1967, vol. 4, no. 1, pp. 31–55.

There is a revolution brewing in the introduction of new organizational forms to complement or to replace the more traditional pyramidal form. I believe, on the basis of some recent research, that the new forms are basically sound. However, because of the methods used to introduce them and because of those used to maintain them, many of the unintended self-defeating consequences of the older structures are re-appearing.

Two major causes for this revolution are the new requirements for organizational survival in an increasingly competitive environment and the new administrative and information technology available to deal with complexity. Wallace (1963) summarizes these requirements as:

1. The technological revolution (complexity and variety of products, new materials and processes, and the effects of massive research).

2. Competition and the profit squeeze (saturated markets, inflation of wage and material costs, production efficiency).

3. The high cost of marketing.

4. The unpredictability of consumer demands (due to high discretionary income, wide range of choices available, and shifting tastes).

To make matters more difficult, the costs of new products are increasing while their life expectancy is decreasing.

Requirements of tomorrow's organizations

In order to meet these challenges, modern organizations need:

1. Much more creative planning.

2. The development of valid and useful knowledge about new products and new processes.

3. Increased concerted and cooperative action with internalized long-range commitment by all involved.

4. Increased understanding of criteria for effectiveness that meet the challenges of complexity.

These requirements, in turn, depend upon:

1. Continuous and open access between individuals and groups.

2. Free, reliable communication, where

3. Interdependence is the foundation for individual and departmental cohesiveness and

4. Trust, risk-taking, and helping each other is prevalent, so that

5. Conflict is identified and managed in such a way that the destructive win–lose stances with their accompanying polarization of views are minimized and effective problem-solving is maximized.

These conditions, in turn, require individuals who:

1. Do not fear stating their complete views.

2. Are capable of creating groups that maximize the unique contributions of each individual.

3. Value and seek to integrate their contributions into a creative total, final contribution.

4. Rather than needing to be individually rewarded for their contributions, thus

5. Finding the search for valid knowledge and the development of the best possible solution intrinsically satisfying.

Unfortunately these conditions are difficult to create. Elsewhere I have tried to show that the traditional pyramidal structure and managerial controls tend to place individuals and departments in constant interdepartmental warfare, where win-lose competition creates polarized stances that tend to get resolved by the superior making the decisions, thereby creating a dependence upon him. Also, there is a tendency toward conformity, mistrust, and lack of risk-taking among the peers that results in focusing upon individual survival, requiring the seeking out of the scarce rewards, identifying with successful ventures (be a hero), and being careful to avoid being blamed for or identified with a failure, thereby becoming a bum. All these adaptive behaviors tend to induce low interpersonal competence and can lead the organization, over the long run, to become rigid, sticky, less innovative, resulting in less than effective decisions with even less internal commitment to the decisions on the part of those involved.

Some people have experimented by structuring the organization in such a way that people representing the major functions (marketing, engineering, manufacturing and finance) are coerced to work together. Unfortunately, the pyramidal structure does not lend itself to such a strategy. As Wallace points out, the difficulty is that typically each function approaches the business problems inherent in the product from a somewhat different point of view: marketing wants a good product at a low price; production, a product that is easily produced; engineering, a product that outclasses – engineering wise – all other products, and so on. None of these stances tends to lead to the resolution of conflicting ideas into a decision that tends to integrate the best of each view.

The matrix organization

One of the most promising strategies to induce cooperation and integration of effort on crucial business problems is the development of project teams and the matrix organization. These administrative innovations were created initially to solve the complex problems of coordination and scheduling of large defense projects. They have been adapted and used by many other organizations because of their potential promise. The future role of the team approach and matrix organization is, in my opinion, an important one for administration.

A project team is created to solve a particular problem. It is composed of people representing all the relevant managerial functions, e.g. marketing, manufacturing, engineering and finance. Each member is given equal responsibility and power to solve the problem. The members are expected to work as a cohesive unit. Once the problem is solved, the team is given a new assignment or disbanded. If the problem is a recurring one, the team remains active. In many cases, especially in the defense programs, the project manager is given full authority and responsibility for the completion of the project including rewarding and penalizing the members of the team. An organization may have many teams. This results in an organization that looks like a matrix; hence the title of matrix organization.

Representatives of	Project 1	Project 2	Project 3
Manufacturing			
Engineering			
Marketing			
Finance			
	Team 1	Team 2	Team 3

How effective are the project teams and the matrix organizations? In order to begin to answer that question, I have been conducting some research in nine large organizations utilizing a matrix organization structure. In preliminary interviews the executives reported that the matrix organization and team approach made sense, but that they found them very difficult to put into actual practice. People still seemed to polarize issues, resisted exploring ideas thoroughly, mistrusted each other's behavior, focused on trying to protect one's own function, overemphasized simplified criteria of success, e.g. figures on sales, worked too much on day-to-day operations and short-term planning, engaged in the routine decisions rather than focus more on the long-range risky decisions, and emphasized survival more than the integration of effort into a truly accepted decision.

Others found fault with the team approach for not providing individuals with enough opportunity to get recognition in their own functional departments for their performance on the team. Still others insisted that individuals sought to be personally identified with a particular accomplishment; that it wasn't satisfying for them to know that their group (and not they) obtained the reward. Finally, some said that during their meetings the teams got bogged down in focusing on the negative, i.e. what had not been accomplished.

Why are these new administrative structures and strategies

having this trouble? I do *not* believe the concept of the matrix organization is inherently invalid. I believe the answer lies in the everyday *behavior styles that the managers have developed, in the past, to survive and to succeed within the traditional pyramidal organization*. The behavior styles needed for the effective use of the matrix organization are, I believe, very different. Also, the group dynamics that are effective in the pyramidal structure are different from those that will be effective in the matrix organization. Thus I do not agree that the comments above are 'natural' for all people. They are 'natural' for people living under the pyramidal concept. For example, groups *can* be created where individuals gain success from seeing integrated decisions; where recognition *does* come more from success and less from compliments from others, where overcoming barriers and correcting faults and failures are not perceived as negative.

A second important cause of the ineffectiveness of the matrix type organization lies in the very processes that have given it birth. Again, the difficulty has been that the birth processes used were more applicable to the pyramidal than to the matrix organization. In short, I am suggesting that a basic problem has been that a new form of organization has been introduced in such a way as to make difficulties inevitable and that the leadership styles that the executives use to administer the matrix organization, on the whole, compound the felony. In order to illustrate my point, I should like to take one of these nine studies and discuss it in some detail. The case that I have selected to discuss approximates the other eight. The variance among the cases was not high. More importantly, the establishment of a project and program approach had the most careful thought and analytical competence brought to bear on it by the top management. It is a study of a multi-million-dollar organization that decided to reorganize its *product planning* and *program review* activities into a team approach which resulted in a matrix organization. These two activities have been the ones most frequently organized into a matrix organization. The study lasted about one year. I interviewed all the top executives involved (twenty-five), asked them to complete questionnaires, and observed, taped, and analysed nearly thirty-five meetings of the teams, ranging from forty-five minutes to two-and-a-half hours in length.

Product planning and program reviews

The responsibility of product planning program reviews was to collect and integrate, and maintain up to date information of the progress of any given activity in the organization. Under this concept, the top men could go to one source to get complete information on the organization's present plans, progress against plans, and so on. The staff group had no authority to order any of the line executives. It was their task to analyse what the problems were and to get from the line executives their plans as to how they were to be solved. If the line executives were unable to agree then the problem was taken to the chief executive for his decision. In the manual of this company there existed a sentence which stated, '. . . the president retains the authority for final decisions and can ordinarily expect that his product planning staff will achieve the agreement of all other departments before plans are presented.' Still later, 'Product planning provides team leadership to a team made up of appropriate, fully responsible representatives of the (line) departments. The Product Planner as team leader encourages, challenges, and insists upon mature, complete and competent coverage by these representatives. Encouragement of better communication between departments is necessary and vital.'

The assumption behind this theory was that if objectives and critical paths to these objectives were defined clearly, people would tend to cooperate to achieve these objectives according to the best schedule that they could devise. However, in practice, the theory was difficult to apply. Why? Let us first take a look at the processes by which these new concepts were introduced.

The management strategy for implementing this new program was primarily one of pushing, persuading and ordering. The objective was to overcome the forces in the organization that were resisting change, thereby pushing the level of effectiveness upward. However, the way this was done added, unintentionally, to the resisting forces. For example, 76 per cent of the subordinates interpreted the processes of a small elite group planning the changes and then management unilaterally installing the activities by persuading the people to accept them, as implying that they (subordinates) had not been competent in the past and that they could not be trusted in making changes. These feelings were strengthened by the fact that the new activities required greater control over subordinates, more detailed planning, and more concrete commitments which could get the subordinate in trouble if he did not fulfill them. These activities of fear and mistrust still exist. For example:

Sometimes I wonder if the real impact of program reviews isn't to teach people that we don't trust them. I think that the top people have got to have faith in the people, and eliminate some of these constant and repetitive type of meetings, just to check being checked. I think we can get management to get themselves pretty well informed just through a nominal report type of thing, rather than all this paper work that we have.

The increasing lack of cooperation, hostility, resistance to meeting program plans, were recognized by the people responsible for the activities. They responded by making the controls even tighter. They asked for more detailed reports, for a wider distribution of minutes, and they used the minutes as evidence that agreements were arrived at that were binding. But again the impact was not completely what was expected. For example:

Do we need these complete minutes? We still have a number of people in the organization who feel that they have to document everything in terms of a letter or memo. To me this is an indication of fear.

The more trouble the programs got into the more paper work that we had to complete.

It was not long before the completion of the paper work became an end in itself. Seventy-one per cent of the middle managers reported that the maintenance of the product planning and program review paper flow became as crucial as accomplishing the line responsibility assigned to each group. For example:

I'm afraid that we program the most minute things and the more we program, the less work we get done. I have tried to get this across to the president, but have not been very successful.

One problem I find is the amount of paper work that this system generates. I dare say out of the five-day week it would take you three quarters of a day or a day of your week to just keep up with the paper work. All of the paper work you get does not affect you, but you have to go through it to find out what does and what does not.

In all honesty I think we waste too damn much time around here. These program reviews are especially costly in time. Why, one of the fellows the other day said that he received and sends out approximately fifty thousand pieces of paper a month.

The final quotation illustrates the next problem that arose. Since each individual had his regular job to accomplish in addition to his role of product planning and program reviews, the load became very heavy. *The executives increasingly felt overworked and overloaded with activities that were not leading to increased effectiveness (83 per cent).* For example:

I believe – held a scheduling type meeting, and they do call ordinary meetings, and then all the vice presidents call their people together for a meeting, so that one little meeting at the divisional level has a heck of a lot of man hours tied up into it for the background.

The number of jobs to be done. The sheer volume that has to be turned out. Sometimes you feel as though you are on a treadmill and you can't get off it because no matter what jobs you can see getting accomplished, there are so many more ahead of you that you know you are behind schedule, and it seems to drive you crazy at times. Everyone has the same feelings.

In spite of these difficulties the level of effectiveness eventually stabilized. But now the resisting forces became much stronger. Also the level of organizational pressure rose.

Most of the lower level managers reported that they did *not* like to be associated with the restraining activities, because they saw such alliances as an indication of disloyalty. I believe that one way to resolve these dissonant feelings about themselves was to strengthen their personal opinions about the negativeness of the program by finding faults with it and by knowingly (and unknowingly) acting so as to make it less effective.

Another mode of adaptation was to withdraw and let the upper levels become responsible for the successful administration of the program. (This is their baby – let them make it work.) At the same time much hostility could be released safely by constant joking about 'everything is programmed.' For example, girls were asked had they programmed their sex life; men were asked if they had defined the critical path to the men's toilet, etc.

These attitudes threatened the upper levels. They saw them as suggesting that the managers were not as loyal and committed as they should be. The executives reacted by involving the potential wrath of the president. (He really means business – let's climb on board.) Soon the president found himself in the position of being cited as the reason why the programs may not be questioned. Also, his immediate subordinates encouraged him to speak out forcefully on the importance of these functions. The president began to feel that he must defend the programs because if he did not, the restraining forces may begin to overcome the management pressure for change. For example:

Make no mistake about it, this is the president's baby. Have you ever tried to talk to him about it? He listens for a few minutes and then soon lets you know that he isn't going to tolerate much question.

No, we have pretty much consoled ourselves to the fact that the president is really behind this, and you might just as well forget it. You are entitled to a personal opinion, of course, but beyond that, you better not take any action.

The increasing number of control activities and the increasing feelings of pressure led the subordinates to feel that product planning and program reviews had become dominant in the organization. They unknowingly or knowingly placed less attention upon their original line function activities. This reaction increased the probability that failures would occur, which increased the pressures from the president and in turn his staff people, which infuriated the line managers, and the loop was closed. The top management forces tended to increase, the middle and lower management resistance also tended to increase (even though such action may have made them feel a sense of disloyalty), the tension and pressures increased, and the effectiveness of the program was at a lower level than was potentially possible.

To make the situation more difficult, the majority of the participants reported that, in addition to the process of introduction being a dissatisfying one, they also reported overall dissatisfaction with the way the programs were being carried out. For example, the meetings tended: to suppress individuality, polarize issues into win–lose stances, censor bad news to the top and immobilize the groups with unimportant issues.

Overall dissatisfaction with small group meetings

Dissatisfaction was found to exist with the product planning and program review meetings. The dissatisfactions increased as one went down the chain of command. Thus 64 per cent of the top executives and 83 per cent of the middle managers expressed dissatisfaction with the group meetings.

These committees are not the best way to administer an organization. We tend to make little problems into big ones and ignore the nasty ones. We also eat up a lot of time. People don't come in to really listen; they come in to win and fight not to lose.

I think the simple fact is even now there is probably less true acceptance of the product planning function than there was. And I think in truth there is quite fundamental and sincere nonacceptance of the role of planning in the function, not the general idea of –; I've talked to people about this quite a bit.

Why is that?

Because the fact remains that we do have a schedule, and someone is after them for their answer at that point. And I guess that's tough for most of us to accept. Maybe this game of having an objective and planning their work accordingly and say what you are going to do. Management is flexible, you're so right. They know we run a high risk here, and the top management never beat them over the back for this kind of stuff.

Suppressing individuality

The members reported that in practice, the groups functioned so that individuality was not optimized; conformity and non-risktaking predominated (71 per cent). Playing it relatively safe seemed to be a common activity. For example:

During a heated session about program reviews A accused B of being a coward for not standing up for his view. A replied 'Listen mister, when you have to live with these people as I do, then you can talk. If I really stuck to my views I'd be hated by everyone – and I'd come to hate myself'.

Yes, I think the choice that we have been asked to make between no decision and one not so good is a negative choice. Most of the time it is an eleventh-hour thing that they arrive at. You either can take it this way or you won't have it for another six months.

What prevents a person from sort of digging in and saying no, I don't want anything else?

Well, there is a lot of pressure. We've got commitments made to the management where we charge a certain amount of dollars for the dollars they have allowed us to invest in this business.

Polarizing issues

At the lower levels, there was a good deal more heated argument which caused the issues to be polarized and people felt that they were not being heard. This tended to lead to a decrease in the faith in the group's processes and, at the same time, increased the probability that people would tend to come to the meetings with prepared positions (83 per cent). For example:

We have a great deal of jockeying for position.

There are certain things that people are not willing to stick their necks out about. Particularly when it comes to a new program. When it comes to a new program everyone has preconceived positions, and they adhere to them.

I think at times people will take an extreme position one time, and another time be very compromising. To take the—committee as an example, there are occasions where they do not agree and they say, 'Too bad we couldn't agree, we'll set up a meeting at the next level'.

Censoring bad news to the top

Another major problem was that some of the more difficult issues developed at the lower levels were watered down by the time they were transmitted to the top. People had learned not to describe to their superiors the complete differences in views and the difficulties in discussing the issues in as strong terms as they experience them (71 per cent).

By the way, there is an awful lot of time spent at the lower level and people getting information ready to beat the people at the upper level. And I would say in all honesty that we don't give all the information to the people on top. If we do present them with all the problems it would probably bring this place to a screeching halt.

When you have an overly protected meeting the people upstairs don't really get the facts. For example, you soon learn that in a review you take all the things out that might be arbitrary or that might raise difficulties with somebody else.

Immobilizing the group with unimportant details

Still another frequently reported problem was the immobilization of the group with countless small decisions (63 per cent). Some department representatives brought everything to the meetings partially to make certain that the program review group took the responsibility for all activities. Other department representatives raised many issues when they were upset with the direction a particular decision was taking or when they wished to delay the making of a decision until further data could be obtained. For example:

Some people also don't mind flooding the committee with agenda items. And once there is an item on the agenda the board is committed to study it, whether it is important or not. I think it can be an awful expense of money and time.

If you looked at these minutes of our meetings, and you haven't attended any yet, of course, the number of topics we take up is fantastic and to the point where we feel that too many people aren't deciding at lower levels, and bucking it is up to us.

The members of a review group could postpone action or prevent themselves (and their department) from being held responsible for a decision by asking the group to make it. This was guaranteed to take time, since those in the group who did not specialize in that particular technical area had to be briefed.

To summarize, the product planning and program review committees were viewed as plagued with ineffectiveness and win–lose dynamics. An executive who kept a count of how people described these committees concluded that the two most frequent categorizations were 'Committee management at its worst' and 'Moscow delegates', i.e. delegates who couldn't make a contribution without checking with their department.

The same managers freely admitted that they could not see any resolution, 'any time you run a company by a committee, you'll always have trouble', or 'it's human nature for people to lie and fight when they believe they are being exposed.' Such pessimistic diagnoses will not lead to action for correcting the situation. On the contrary, such diagnoses probably provide ideal rationalization why 'things cannot be changed' and why they can go on feeling and behaving as they do.

As in the problems presented in the previous section, management's reaction was not to deal with the issues openly. More subtle and covertly controlling actions were typically taken. Meetings were scheduled with greater precision, presentations were made both with viewgraph and written script, and even more detailed minutes were taken. The hope was that with tighter outside controls, the groups would tend to operate more effectively. If we may judge from the comments reported above as well as from the observations, the group dynamics have not been altered – indeed, one could argue with some justification that the group defenses are becoming stronger. Thus we conclude again that although the members are aware that the relative ineffectiveness of the group is a crucial problem, they are not able to solve the problems. Moreover, most of the action taken actually helps to increase the members' feeling of being unduly controlled and mistrusted.

Why did the problems arise?

The explanations for problems like these are multiple and complicated. One way to begin to organize our thoughts is to view the problems as arising from a long causal chain of actions where one action causes several others, which in turn, breeds further actions, etc. I believe that at the beginning of this complicated causal chain lie the basic values or assumptions that executives have learned to hold about how to organize human effort effectively. These values, once internalized, act as commands to coerce the executives to behave in specific ways when they meet to solve problems.

Elsewhere I have shown that executives tend to hold three basic values about effective human relationships within organizations. They are:

1. Get the job done. We are here to manufacture shoes, that is our business, those are the important human relationships; if you have anything that can influence those human relationships, fine.

2. Be rational and logical and communicate clearly. Effectiveness *decreases* as behavior becomes more emotional. 'Gentlemen, let's get back to the facts,' is the classic conference table phrase, or in other words, if you want to be effective, be rational, be clear. If

you want to be ineffective, focus on the emotional and inter-personal.

3. People work best under carefully defined direction, authority and control, governed by appropriate rewards and penalties that emphasize rational behavior and achievement of the objective.

In Figure 1, I should like to illustrate what I believe may be one underlying causal chain causing the problems described above. Let us assume that an organization, at any given point in time, may be described as having a particular level of effectiveness; that there are forces pushing upward to increase the effectiveness, e.g. top management; and that, since the level is somewhat stable, there are forces pushing downward resisting or restraining the level from going higher.[1] A balance of forces exists.

Now, let us assume that management wants to increase the level of effectiveness (by developing new product planning and program review activities as in this case, or by any other change the reader wants to imagine). I am suggesting that the underlying *strategy* for, and the *processes of change* will tend to be greatly influenced by values the executives hold. For example:

1. Because of the emphasis on objectives and rationality, the executives will tend to assume that the way to get a new organizational activity accepted by the members of the organization is to show them clearly how it fits with the objectives of the organization and to explain rationally the advantages of the new activity over the old one. For example, 'we need tighter controls', 'effectiveness must be increased', 'I'm sure all of us want to manage in the best way available', 'we must always remain alert for new management innovations'. As seen by the subordinates, this means that management feels compelled to sell them a bill of goods; an implication that they resent. They see little need (if they are effective managers) for someone to tell them effectiveness should be increased, new concepts should be tried, etc. Indeed,

1. The model is taken from Kurt Lewin's (1947) concept of quasi-stationary equilibria. For the readers interested in organization theory, I mean to imply that people holding the three values above will always tend to create the problems originally depicted in Lewin's model. I am suggesting an explanation to Lewin's question as to why he found change activities in our society tended to take one form.

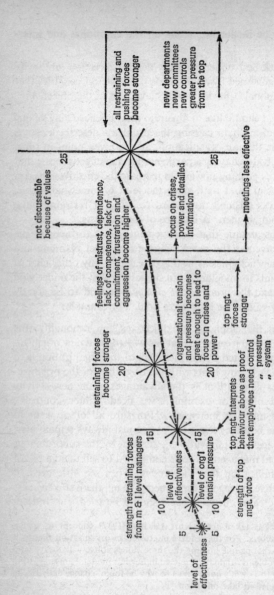

Figure 1 Causal chain in organizational human relations difficulties

many resent the implication that they are not doing this already.

In terms of our diagram, the strategy for change is to overcome the restraining forces by strengthening the pushing forces. This is done by management selling, pushing and ordering. As we can see, at the second set of forces in our diagram, the level of effectiveness does increase.

2. But the resisting forces are also increased. The resistance increases because of (a) the negative interpersonal impact the necessity to sell the program had upon the managers, (b) the mistrust and condemnation of the subordinates implied by the new program, (c) the inhibition of the questions and fears the subordinates wished to express *before* they were 'sold', (d) the feeling of being manipulated by the fact that the changes were kept a secret while they were being planned, and (e) the dependence and submissiveness caused by the unilateral management strategy.

3. As can be predicted from knowing that management is uncomfortable in discussing negative feelings openly, the restraining forces are not dealt with directly. The result, so far, is an increase in the level of effectiveness, an increase in resisting forces, and an increase in what we might call the gross organizational tension level.

4. Remaining true to their values, the top executives respond by creating new rational forces (a new sales pitch on the values of the program); bringing to bear new controls, and issuing new orders to overcome the resistance. This tends to coerce the subordinates to suppress their confusion, feelings of distrust and tension related to the new program, especially when interacting with the superiors. However, these feelings and tensions cannot be suppressed forever. They may erupt during the meetings that are part of the new change activities, thereby guaranteeing the ineffectiveness of these meetings.

5. The increased management pressure, the increase in controls through paper work, the overload of work, all act to increase the forces pushing the level of effectiveness upward. The mistrust, tension, ineffective meetings (in our case of product planning and program reviews), the willingness on the part of lower level management to make the top responsible for the change (this is their baby), become examples of how the restraining forces are

increased. The organizational tension also increases. This, in turn, stimulates management to develop new controls, check points, new courses to explain the importance of the program. These actions further increase the upward forces, which, in turn, increase the resisting forces, which in turn increase the organizational tension. The loop is now closed.

At some point the difficulties and tensions reach a breaking point among the members. The top executives usually sense this and typically call for a one or two day meeting away from home base 'to take out the kinks in the program'. In my experience most of these meetings were not very effective because the subordinates feared bringing out their real feelings and the true difficulties. One interesting sign that the true problems did not come out in these meetings was the degree to which the participants assigned the causes of their problems to conditions that were typical under the pyramidal organizational structure. For example, people may spend time trying to find out who was the *one* person responsible for decision making; they craved identification of their individual contribution; they competed in win–lose battles.

The difficulties with these meetings is illustrated in the example below. Three years after the reorganization plan went into effect developing a team approach, marketing and manufacturing were still having difficulties defining their roles and responsibilities. Manufacturing doubted that it needed marketing and *vice versa*. (If I included all the data we would see that engineering also had its doubts.) In reading the example, it is useful to note how many of the problems raised and the solutions suggested are typical of the traditional organizational climate and not those endemic of the matrix organization. Each group worried more about trying to show that it was truly 'the' most responsible. There was little attempt by the participants to help each other and to try to build a cohesive team where the whole was more important than any one part. Also, when personality issues were ever so gently brought out (toward the end), the leader changed the subject.

A. Just the same way that the R and D department resents it and marketing man says 'my technology manager' and he says 'my manufacturing team.'

D. You know I don't resent that at all because I talk about my marketing manager.

C. Some of us do. We're all getting over it, but at the beginning we all tended to be sensitive.

A. Rather than the marketing manager's decisions, isn't the direction of the company contingent upon the company's decisions for these market opportunities determine the direction in which our future lies?

B. I'd like to reply to that because strategy is knowing the customer. The big part of it is knowing what the hell your competition's in. If you don't know your competition, you don't really know what the hell to do and who helps you play the strategy defense. It's got to be manufacturing. They've got to know their competing existing technology. They're the people that tell you what dollars . . . they give you a good share of the judgements that you can apply to strategy.

D. An example to support your point is product X. This is a real good example because this is where the manufacturing team set, looked at all competitive economics, all known producers, all possible methods by which X could be produced, and came up with what we might call an equilibrium sales price. This is a price at which somebody could over the next ten years afford so this came out as an average sales price. Now that really established the basic strategy level, so we then compared all the methods by which we could apply ourselves to producing our requirements on this product and looked at the comparative economics of these and their performance in the in-use areas for all of the uses of the product. So all the market technology teams contributed to this area. But the prime mover in the whole thing and really the one who was developing the whole base for the decision was a manufacturing team who were drawing together all of these inputs on competitive products and competitive economics, long range planning, but the decision as it was arrived at was a completely composite decision in the different marketing areas where the products were going to be sold.

C. I don't have very much experience the way the other guys do, but I don't see how you can. There is no separation between our groups.

E. You fellows may not like this, but I really think that basically the company still sets the price beyond which profit can be made and it's the agents who are selling the goods from this company who still are responsible to maximize profit.

D. Well, what do you think this is? I can't see where we're in any conflict with manufacturing.

B. Like hell!

A. I think this is probably right and maybe this is because we don't agree with manufacturing's mandate. The whole group down there on the boondocks don't really understand what marketing's function is. That's why we're gathered around this table, to try to understand that. It's obvious that there are a lot of people that don't understand what marketing's function is because that's why we've got it on the agenda.

B. Well, maybe if we understand your point of view, maybe we can help you to understand us.

A. Manufacturing has to understand what every marketing group, how every marketing group understands their own job. If you're not going to be the same, then the manufacturing group has to understand how you understand your job and how everyone understands their job.

C. Let me ask this – maybe you can help clarify it. Suppose marketing technology's out of this thing and then just have the manufacturing team and the sales department. Could you operate on that basis? Do you need this marketing group?

A. It is a good question. The answer is probably no. We were almost doing this once before, before the reorganization, and obviously it wasn't working successfully. The thing we've got now is a good bit more successful.

B. This terminology really leaves me cold. What do you mean 'more successful'?

E. It's semantics, that's all.

B. The guys down at the boondocks now think that marketing should look at the sales department as a bunch of peddlers. These are the terms that are being thrown around.

D. I think this all helped. We understand each better, so what's the next topic? This is the thing that I want to avoid, that we bring personalities into this. It was nothing personal. It was simply a statement that you made that I was having trouble understanding.

B. Everybody's getting involved and yet the problem's not being solved. We talked about this last week. The manufacturing managers talked about this. All of us are talking and that's about all.

Some readers may wonder how typical this situation is. In my experience the confusion and conflict is quite typical. The meeting was more open than usual which permitted us to get a rich specimen of the conflict. By the way, I do hope that these observations will help top managements pause and question their belief that the best way to plan a reorganization is to appoint a top committee (with all the appropriate help) to develop a reorganization plan and then 'sell' it to the organization. The lower level managers soon hear about the meetings and see them as the first sign of mistrust. The reasons usually given for this strategy are that to get wider participation may upset people and make it more difficult to sell the new plan. In my experience people become doubly upset with the secrecy and the anxiety built up around the rumors related to the reorganization. The time necessary for getting the program truly accepted is easily doubled. (In some recent research with governmental bureaux the time is extended until the next reorganization.)

I also hope that these data will question the advice of some recent theorists who suggest that people's behavior can be changed by changing the organizational structure. If the data from these nine examples are valid, then we may conclude that their view is oversimplified. I would agree with them that changes in organizational structure do bring about intended changes in people's behavior. (In our figure the effectiveness level was increased.) However, they also bring about unintended behavioral changes; the restraining forces are strengthened and the organizational tension level is greatly increased. To my knowledge the proponents of this approach have never shown an example where by changing the organizational structure the restraining forces and tension levels were also not increased.

These results suggest that, in addition to organizational structural changes, one should also focus on altering the basic values of the executives so that they can develop change strategies that may minimize the unintended consequences. (One example will be discussed below.) Our approach is not to be viewed as taking sides in an argument of change in structure *v.* changes in people: our view is changes in structure *through* changes in people's values. Nor does the approach imply a blanket condemnation of the change strategy illustrated in Figure 1. Such a strategy may be necessary where, for whatever reason, people refuse to alter their values, to become fully involved in the change, to take on their share of creating the change. If there is a lack of time for the more involving change process, then one may use the more unilateral one depicted but may consider being quite open about the possible negative consequences and asking the people to help to reduce them.

A new philosophy of organizing and managing people

I should like, at the outset, to repeat my view that project teams and matrix organizations are fundamentally valid. I believe that they are the most effective organizational structures for decisions that are complex and risky, that require the integration of many different inputs, and that depend on the continuing, long-range commitment of everyone involved without the organization's being saddled with excess and unneeded structures. (Once the project is complete, the team can be disbanded or have a new project assigned to it.)

One of the most important first steps is to communicate to the people that the matrix organization is not a simple extension of the traditional pyramidal structure. The pyramidal structure acquires its form from the fact that as one goes up the administrative ladder (a) power and control increase, (b) the availability of information increases, (c) the degree of flexibility to act increases, (d) the scope of the decisions made and the responsibilities involved increase. Implicit in the matrix organization are almost opposite tendencies. For example, power and control are given to the individual and/or to the groups who have the technical skill to accomplish the task, no matter what their organizational level. Thus a team could be composed of five people representing all different levels of authority (on the traditional chart), who are equal. The group could be chaired by the individual with the least organizational authority. The individual or groups are given responsibility and authority to make decisions of the widest necessary scope.

If we may extrapolate to the probable matrix organization of the future, Forrester suggests that the organization will eventually eliminate the superior–subordinate relationship and substitute for it the individual self-discipline arising from self-interest created by a competitive market mechanism within the system. The individual would negotiate continuously changing relationships. Each individual would be a profit center whose objective would be to produce the most value for the least activity; who would have the freedom to terminate as well as to create new activity, who would have access to all the necessary information. The organization of the future would be rid of internal monopolies which is the usual status of most traditional departments.

Although I would agree with Forrester, I believe that the organizations of the future will be a combination of the old and the new forms of organization. I believe that the old forms are going to be more effective for the routine, non-innovative activity that requires little, if any, internal commitment by the participants. However, as the decisions become less routine, more innovative and require more commitment, the newer forms such as the matrix organizations will be more effective.

Leadership style and matrix organization

In addition to being able to differentiate clearly between the old and the new forms, the future executive must also be able to know the conditions under which he will use the different organizational forms. Moreover, he will need to become skillful in several different kinds of leadership styles, each of which is consistent with a particular form. For example, an authoritarian leadership style is more consistent with the traditional structure; a participative style with the link-pin organization defined by Likert and a style that develops risk-taking and trust for the matrix organization.

If recent research is valid, then the majority of executive leadership styles conform to the traditional pyramidal style. This is not surprising, since leadership styles and organizational design would naturally go together. The findings that did surprise us were (a) the degree to which the executives believed in leadership styles that were consonant with the matrix organization, and (b) the degree to which they were *unaware* that they were *not* behaving according to their ideals.

Another important first step therefore is to help executives become more aware of their actual leadership style. Unless they develop such awareness, they are not going to be able to unfreeze their old styles, develop new ones, and most importantly, switch from one style to another as the administrative situations and the organization structure used is changed. Unless the switching from one style to another can be clearly identified by the person and the receivers, confusion will result.

Another finding that surprised us about executive decision

making was how many executives focused on keeping people 'happy'. Indeed, the most frequently cited reason for not being open with another was the fear that it might upset the receiver (and thus upset the sender). The most frequently cited reason for not bringing two groups together who are locked in interdepartmental warfare was that it would simply 'involve personalities and nothing but harm could come of it'. Although the executives that we studied were happiness-oriented in their behavior, they were not in their attitudes. They believed in strong leadership that could call a spade a spade and let the chips fall where they may. Again according to the observations, the spades were called spades and the chips placed on the line, but in private settings where few could be witnesses, or by such deft and diplomatic processes that few people, including the targets, were aware of what was happening. I cannot refrain from adding that there seemed to be a strong correlation between those executives who were critical of the field of 'human relations' as one whose objective was to make people happy and the degree of their blindness to the fact that they tended to do the very same thing when they were actually leading.

The management of tension

Executives in the matrix organization will also need to learn, if I may be permitted to oversimplify, that there is productive and unproductive or crippling tension. The unproductive or crippling tension is tension that a person experiences but which he cannot control. The reason he cannot control the tension may be external (pressure from his superior) or internal (inability to control his own demands on himself, plus the accompanying feelings of impatience and guilt aimed at himself).

Productive tension is that tension which the individual can control and which comes from accepting new challenges, taking risks, expanding one's competencies, etc. These are the very qualities that are central to the matrix organization. Thus the executive of the future will have to learn how to define internal environments that challenge people, stretch their aspirations realistically, and help them face interpersonal reality. Some examples are financial controls that reward people for risk-taking; organizational situations that are optimally undermanned; incentive systems that reward excellence (not average performance), work that is designed to use people's complex abilities. To put this another way, we need to develop competence in manipulating the environment but not the people. (They should have the freedom and responsibility to choose if they will enter the new environment.)

The management of intergroup conflict

The matrix organization is composed of teams which in turn are populated by representatives of the traditional line functions. As we have seen, this leads to much intergroup conflict within the team as well as between teams.

Instead of trying to stamp out intergroup conflict as bad and disloyal, the executives need to learn how to manage it so that the constructive aspects are emphasized and the destructive aspects are de-emphasized. This means that the organization needs to put on the table for diagnosis the interdepartmental fires, the incidents of throwing the dead cat over into the other department's yard, the polarized competitive warfare where success is defined by the participants in terms of which side won rather than the contribution to the whole. The executives will have to learn how (a) to bring the groups together, (b) where each discusses and seeks, in private, to agree on its views and attitudes toward the other and toward self, (c) then the representatives of both groups talk together in the presence of the other group members, followed by (d) private discussion to establish the way they are perceived by others in order (e) to develop, through representatives, an understanding of the discrepancy between their and other's views.

The executive educational activities

Most organizations send their executives to university executive programs or to internal executive programs usually designed following the concept of the university. I do not want to get into philosophical discussions about the nature of university education at this point. I would like to point out, however, that *there may be a discrepancy between the characteristics of university education and the needs of the matrix organization.*

The university has typically assumed that learning (a) is for the individual, (b) occurs when it is given, (c) is tested by contrived examinations of the knowledge acquired, (d) need not be relevant to any immediate problem, (e) should be designed and controlled by the educator; it is the task of the educator to define the problems, develop ways to solve them and define the criteria for evaluation – who passes and who does not. The matrix organizations require education that (a) focuses on individuals in team systems and (b) it occurs where the problem is located, (c) is learned by the use of actual problems, and (d) is tested by the effectiveness of the actual results, and (e) is controlled by those participating in the problem (aided by the educator as a consultant).

Executive education in the matrix organization will focus on system effectiveness. This means that the central educational department will now become an organizational development activity. It will have systems as its clients. A small team of consultants will enter the system and develop a diagnosis of its human and technical effectiveness. These data will then be fed back to representatives at all levels of the system to generate, at the grass-roots level, action recommendations. A steering committee composed of representatives of the client system and the organizational development will then prepare a long-range educational program designed to increase the immediate as well as the long-range effectiveness of the system.

Classes may then be held at the plant location or at a central facility, depending upon the resources needed, the time available, the availability of the 'students', as well as the faculty. Teams and not disconnected individuals will study together for the majority of technical and management subjects. These teams will be actual working teams. This will place pressure on the faculty to develop learning that is valid for the real problems of the team and motivate the students to learn, since it is their problems upon which the education is focusing.

To put this another way, education will be for organizational and system diagnosis, renewal and effectiveness. It will be held with groups, subject material and faculty that are organic to the organization's problem. One of the dangers of this education is the possibility that it will focus on the trivial, short-range problems. The quality control in this area will depend partially on the diagnostic competence of the faculty. In defining the problem they can help the organization to get to the underlying and basic causes. The students can also help by being alert to the validity of the education that is being offered to them.

Some critics wonder if teams of people working together can be pulled away from work. The answer, in my experience, is affirmative. The fear, for example, that the company will be in trouble if the top team leaves for a week, has been quietly exploded in several cases. The explosions have been quiet lest, as one president put it, 'it was learned how well things ran while the top management was away'.

More importantly, this new type of education is central to the work of the system. Thus, the team is not being pulled away from work. Indeed, in many cases, it is pulled away *in order to work*. Systems, like cars, need to have their organizational hoods opened and the motor checked and tuned. Unless this maintenance work is done, the system will deteriorate as certainly as does an automobile.

Finally, the concern of being away physically from the location should be matched with the concern about the number of hours being consumed needlessly while at work. In the studies listed previously, I have found that as many as half the meetings and as much as three-quarters of the time spent at meetings are not productive and worse than unnecessary.

Organizational change

Anyone who has planned major organizational change knows (a) how difficult it is to foresee accurately all the major problems involved, (b) the enormous amount of time needed to iron out the kinks and get people to accept the change, (c) the apparent lack of internal commitment on the part of many to help make the plan work, manifested partly (d) by people at all levels resisting taking the initiative to make modifications that they see are necessary so that the new plan can work. In preparing this article, I reviewed my notes from thirty-two major re-organizations in large organizations in which I played some consulting and research role. I did not find one that could be labeled as fully completed and integrated three years after the change had been announced (and in many cases had gone through several revisions). That is, after three years there were still many people fighting, ignoring, questioning, resisting, blaming, the re-organization without feeling a strong obligation personally to correct the situation.

As I mentioned above, I believe the reasons for this long delay are embedded in the change strategy typically used by management. To refer to the figure, the basic strategy has been for the top management to take the responsibility to overcome and outguess the resistance to change. This strategy does tend to succeed because management works very hard, applies pressure, and if necessary knocks a few heads together (or eliminates some). However, as we have seen, the strategy creates resisting forces that are costly to the organization's effectiveness, to its long run viability and flexibility, as well as to the people at all levels.

Reducing the resisting forces

What would happen if management experimented with the strategy of reducing the restraining forces by involving, at least, the management employees at all levels in the diagnosis, design and execution of the change program? For example, in one organization a plan of re-organization was begun by getting all levels involved in diagnosing the present problems of the organization. Groups were formed (which met only twice for several hours each time) to diagnose the effectiveness of the present organization. These groups were initially composed of people from various functions but holding positions of about equal level. Each group brain-stormed as much as it desired to get out the problems. They were not asked to suggest solutions at this time because no one group would have a total picture of the organization, and therefore its recommendations could be incomplete and misleading, with the added danger of each group becoming attached to their suggestions. Finally, people tend to be hesitant about enumerating a problem if they are asked for solutions and do not have any.

The results of these diagnostic sessions were fed to a top level steering committee which contained representatives of all the major managerial levels. This committee had the diagnoses collated, analysed and developed into an integrated picture. Wherever they found holes and inconsistencies in the diagnoses they made a note of them. Eventually they had compiled a lengthy list of major questions to be answered before the overall diagnosis could be accepted as valid. These questions were fed to small task forces whose composition was specifically designed to be able to answer the questions. Thus, in this phase, the groups were composed of managerial personnel from many functions and levels who were relevant to the question being asked. These task forces were disbanded as soon as they provided the answers to the questions.

In the third phase, the steering committee tried to develop a new organizational structure. In achieving this objective the steering committee began, for the first time, to suggest arrangements of individuals and groups tasks that could be threatening to various interests. This led to the members becoming more involved, cautious and, at times, defensive. Members who, up to this point, had felt free to be objective were beginning to feel themselves slipping into the role of protecting the groups toward which they had the closest attachment.

At this point, the task force went to the education group and asked for a course in such subjects as how to deal with intergroup rivalries and issues, with emotionality in groups, and with hidden agendas. This course was quickly but carefully planned. The steering committee members reported that it was a great help to them. It was especially helpful in welding them into a more fully functioning, open confronting of issues and risk taking. They also reported that as the members' confidence and trust in their group increased, the more willing they were to invite, at the appropriate time, members of departments whose future roles were being discussed so that the problems could be discussed and solved jointly.

The fourth phase was the preparation of a final plan. It was fully discussed with the top executives, then discussed systematically with key representatives of all the departments. Alterations were invited and carefully considered. Two members of the steering committee were members of top management who had authority to represent the top in approving most changes.

During the fifth phase two kinds of data were collected. First a questionnaire was sent to all who had participated, asking them for any individual comments about the plan as well as any comments about the effectiveness of the process of change to date. This diagnosis uncovered, in several cases, new ideas to be considered as well as several suggestions to be re-examined because individuals felt that they had been pushed through by a small but powerful clique.

The final plan was then drawn up with a specific time table (which had been discussed and accepted by people below). The top management, with the help of the steering committee, then put the new organizational plan into action. These phases took nearly seventeen months. However, once the plan became policy (a) the resisting forces and the tensions were much lower than expected on the basis of previous experience, (b) wherever they existed there were organizational mechanisms already established and working to resolve them, (c) the internal commitment to the new policy was high ('It is ours, not theirs'), and thus (d) changes were made as they became necessary without much fanfare or difficulty.

One of the most important outcomes of this type of change strategy was that it provided a living educational experience for individuals and groups on how to work together; on how to develop internal commitment among the members of the organization, and how to reduce the unnecessary and destructive win-lose rivalries. Thus the change program became an opportunity for education at all levels. The result was that a new system had been created which could be used for future changes and to increase the capacity of the organization to learn.

Even with these results, I have encountered some managers who wonder if an organization can take this much time for changing organizational structure. In my experience, although time is a critical factor, it is a false issue. Time will be taken, whether management is aware of it or not, by people to ask all the questions, make all the politically necessary moves, develop all the protective devices, and create all the organizational escape hatches that they feel are necessary. The real issue is whether the time will be used constructively and effectively so that the organization can learn from its experiences, thereby increasing its competence in becoming a problem-solving system.

References

LEWIN, K. (1947), 'Frontiers in group dynamics', *Human Relations*, vol. 1, nos. 1 and 2, pp. 2–38.
WALLACE, W. L. (1963), 'The Winchester–Western Division concept of product planning', *Olin Mathieson Chemical Corporation*, January.

Part Three
Issues and Concepts in Organizational Change and Innovation

The Readings in this section reveal a number of important contingencies which should be considered before adopting a particular strategy of planned change. Wilson's propositions about the innovation process (Reading 9) demonstrate that those organizational characteristics favorable to the proposing of innovations may *not* be positively correlated with their adoption or implementation. His major hypothesis is that the adoption of innovations is contingent upon the diversity of the organization's task structure and incentive structure; the more pluralistic and diverse these two are, the more proposed innovations which are generated, and the less which actually become implemented.

This paper also raises important caveats about participation in decision making as a strategy for planned organizational change. Because of the nature of societal change, it is a fair bet that the incentive structure of organizations is becoming more complex (the rewards which appeal to different individuals are increasingly diverse). As a consequence the effect of participative decision making on performance is not only problemmatical; it is exceedingly difficult as well, to predict its utility for the management of change. Wilson's paper raises the possibility that a 'participative' paradigm may be most appropriate for the proposal of new innovations, while a political or bargaining model is required if proposals are to be implemented.

Planned organizational change – the deliberate design and implementation of a structural innovation, a new policy or goal, or a change in operating philosophy, climate and style – should be analysed within a framework which catalogues the major problems which may necessitate such an effort. Bennis (Reading 7) presents a comprehensive analysis of five such problem areas: (a) *integration* of the individual and the organization; (b) *social influence*, the problem of the organization's power equilibrium; (c) *collaboration*, conflicts due to increased specialization; (d) *adaptation*, responding to environmental change; and (e) *revitalization*, the problem of responding to evolutionary problems of growth and decay. Bennis provides a diagnostic map to assist the organization in answering the critical question: what problem should change be directed at? Planned change may well be synonymous with the management of conflict, for example, when the problem is that of *social influence* or *collaboration*.

The relationship of Whyte's paper (Reading 8) to the central themes of this volume is direct and obvious. He is concerned with what we have labeled 'paradigms' and the way they govern action with respect to change – specifically, with 'the organization models' which leaders carry around inside their heads and which constrain choices available in the design of new organizations. This paper discusses the applicability and relative merits of two widespread 'models': 'the community democracy model' and 'the bureaucratic model'. It is important to pay particular attention to the assumptions each of these models make, according to Whyte's analysis, about the nature and function of organizational conflict.

7 W. G. Bennis

Changing Organizations

W. G. Bennis, 'Changing organizations', *Journal of Applied Behavioral Science*, 1966, vol. 2, no. 3, pp. 247–63.

In every age there is a strain toward organizational forms which will encompass and exploit the technology of the time and express its spirit. It may be that the times in human history which we retrospectively identify as happy and renascent are those in which this tendency has been fulfilled and the organizational form appropriate to the genius of an era has been invented – or rediscovered. This paper identifies five 'core tasks' which any human organization has to cope with, and then goes on to describe some possibilities and adventures which may have to become realities if our organizations of the future are to catch up with the turbulent and uncertain demands of our technological society.

The idea of change

Not far from where the new Government Center is going up, in downtown Boston, a foreign visitor walked up to an American sailor and asked why the ships of his country were built to last for only a short time. According to the foreign tourist, 'The sailor answered without hesitation that the art of navigation is making such rapid progress that the finest ship would become obsolete if it lasted beyond a few years. In these words, which fell accidentally from an uneducated man, I began to recognize the general and systematic idea upon which your great people direct all their concerns.'

The foreign visitor was that shrewd observer of American morals and manners, Alexis de Tocqueville, and the year was 1835. He would not recognize Scollay Square today. But he caught the central theme of our country – its preoccupation, its *obsession* with change. One thing, however, *is* new since de

Tocqueville's time: the prevalence of newness, the changing scale and scope of change itself, so that, as Oppenheimer said, '... the world alters as we walk in it, so that the years of man's life measure not some small growth or rearrangement or moderation of what was learned in childhood, but a great upheaval.'

Numbers have a magic all their own, and it is instructive to review some of the most relevant ones. In 1789, when George Washington was inaugurated, American society comprised fewer than four million persons, of whom 750,000 were Negroes. Few persons lived in cities; New York, then the capital, had a population of 33,000. In all, 200,000 individuals lived in what were then defined as 'urban areas' – places with more than 2500 inhabitants. In the past ten years, Los Angeles has grown by 2,375,000, almost enough to people present-day Boston. In July, 1964, the population of the US was about 192 million. The US Census Bureau estimates that the population in 1975 will be between 226 and 235 million and that in 1980 it will be between 246 and 260 million. World population was over 3 billion in 1964. If fertility remains at present levels until 1975 and then begins to decline, the population of the world will reach 4 billion in 1977, 5 billion by about 1990.

In 1960, when President Kennedy was elected, more than half of all Americans alive were over thirty-three years of age and had received their formative experiences during the Great Depression, or earlier. By 1970, only ten years later, more than half of all Americans alive will be under twenty-five and will have been born after the Second World War. In one short decade the mid-age of the United States will have dropped by a full eight years – the sharpest such age drop recorded in history.

Observe the changes taking place in education. Thirty years ago only one out of every eight Americans at work had been to high school. Today four out of five attend high school. Thirty years ago 4 per cent or less of the population attended college. Now the figure is around 35 per cent, in cities about 50 per cent.

Consider one more example of social change. We are all aware of the momentum of the Scientific Revolution, whose magnitude and accelerating rate – to say nothing of its consequences – are truly staggering. By 1980 science will cut even a wider path, for in that year the government alone will spend close to $35 billion on research and development: $10 billion on arms and arms control, $7 billion on basic research, and $18 billion on vast civilian welfare programs and new technology.

'Everything nailed down is coming loose,' an historian said recently, and it does seem that no exaggeration, no hyperbole, no outrage can realistically appraise the extent and pace of modernization. Exaggerations come true in only a year or two. Nothing will remain in the next ten years – or there will be twice as much of it.

And it is to our credit that the pseudo-horror stories and futuristic fantasies about *accelerations* of the rate of change (the rate of obsolescence, scientific and technological unemployment) and the number of 'vanishing' stories (the vanishing salesman, the vanishing host, the vanishing adolescent, the vanishing village) – it is to our credit that these phenomenal changes have failed to deter our compulsive desire to invent, to overthrow, to upset inherited patterns and comfort in the security of the future.

No more facts and numbers are needed to make the point. We can *feel* it on the job, in the school, in the neighborhood, in our professions, in our everyday lives. Lyndon Johnson said recently, 'We want change. We want progress. We want it both at home and abroad – and we aim to get it!' I think he's got it.

Changing organizations

How will these accelerating changes in our society influence human organizations?

Let me begin by describing the dominant form of human organization employed throughout the industrial world. It is a unique and extremely durable social arrangement called 'bureaucracy', a social invention perfected during the Industrial Revolution to organize and direct the activities of the business firm. It is today the prevailing and supreme type of organization wherever people direct concerted effort toward the achievement of some goal. This holds for university systems, for hospitals, for large voluntary organizations, for governmental organizations.

Corsica, according to Gibbon, is much easier to deplore than to describe. The same holds true for bureaucracy. Basically, bureaucracy is a social invention which relies exclusively on the power to influence through rules, reason and the law. Max Weber, the German sociologist who developed the theory of bureaucracy around the turn of the century, once described bureaucracy as a social machine: 'Bureaucracy,' he wrote, 'is like a modern judge who is a vending machine into which the pleadings are inserted together with the fee and which then disgorges the judgement together with its reasons mechanically derived from the code.'

The bureaucratic 'machine model' Weber outlined was developed as a reaction against the personal subjugation, nepotism, cruelty, and capricious and subjective judgements which passed for managerial practices in the early days of the Industrial Revolution. The true hope for man, it was thought, lay in his ability to rationalize, to calculate, to use his head as well as his hands and heart. Bureaucracy emerged out of the need for more predictability, order and precision. It was an organization ideally suited to the values of Victorian Empire.

Most students of organizations would say that the anatomy of bureaucracy consists of the following 'organs': a division of labor based on functional specialization, a well-defined hierarchy of authority, a system of procedures and rules for dealing with all contingencies relating to work activities, impersonality of interpersonal relations, and promotion and selection based on technical competence. It is the pyramidal arrangement we see on most organizational charts.

Allow me to leap-frog to the conclusion of my paper now. It is my premise that the bureaucratic form of organization is out of joint with contemporary realities; that new shapes, patterns and models are emerging which promise drastic changes in the conduct of the corporation and of managerial practices in general. In the next twenty-five to fifty years we should witness, and participate in, the end of bureaucracy as we know it and the rise of new social systems better suited to twentieth-century demands of industrialization.

Reasons for organizational change

I see two main reasons for these changes in organizational life. One has been implied earlier in terms of changes taking place in society, most commonly referred to as the population and knowledge explosions. The other is more subtle and muted – perhaps less significant, but for me profoundly exciting. I have no easy name for it, nor is it easy to define. It has to do with man's historical quest for self-awareness, for using reason to achieve and stretch his potentialities and possibilities. I think that this deliberate self-analysis has spread to large and more complex social systems, to organizations. I think there has been a dramatic upsurge of this spirit of inquiry over the past two decades. At new depths and over a wider range of affairs, organizations are opening their operations up to self-inquiry and analysis. This really involves two parallel shifts in values and outlooks, between the men who make history and the men who make knowledge. One change is the scientist's realization of his affinity with men of affairs, and the other is the latter's receptivity and new-found respect for men of knowledge. I am calling this new development *organizational revitalization*. It is a complex social process which involves a deliberate and self-conscious examination of organizational behavior and a collaborative relationship between managers and scientists to improve performance.

This new form of collaboration may be taken for granted by many members of the Sloan School of Management. For myself, I have basked under t he light of Professor Douglas McGregor's foresight and I have simply come to regard reciprocity between the academician and the manager as inevitable and natural. But I can assure you that this development is unprecedented, that never before in history, in any society, has man, in his organizational context, so willingly searched, scrutinized, examined, inspected, or contemplated – for meaning, for purpose, for improvement.

I think this shift in outlook has taken a good deal of courage from both partners in this encounter. The manager has had to shake off old prejudices about 'eggheads' and long-hair intellectuals. More important, he has had to make himself and his organization vulnerable and receptive to external sources and to new, unexpected, even unwanted information – which all of you know is not such an easy thing to do. The academician has had to shed some of his natural hesitancies. Scholarly conservatism is admirable, I think, except to hide behind, and for a long time caution has been a defense against reality.

It might be useful to dwell on the role of academic man and his growing involvement with social action, using the field of management education as a case in point. Until recently, the field of business was disregarded by large portions of the American public, and it was unknown to or snubbed by the academic establishment. Management education and research were at best regarded there with dark suspicion, as if contact with the world of reality – particularly monetary reality – was equivalent to a dreadful form of pollution. In fact, academic man has historically taken one of two stances toward the Establishment, *any* Establishment – that of rebellious critic or of withdrawn snob. The former (the rebel) can be 'bought', but only in paperback books under such titles as: *The Power Elite, The Lonely Crowd, The Organization Man, The Hidden Persuaders, The Tyranny of Testing, Mass Leisure, The Exurbanites, The Death and Life of Great American Cities, The American Way of Death, Compulsory Mis-Education, The Status Seekers, Growing Up Absurd, The Paper Economy, Silent Spring, The Child Worshippers, The Affluent Society, The Depleted Society.* On the basis of these titles and reports of their brisk sales, I am thinking of writing one called *Masochism in Modern America,* practically a guaranteed success.

The withdrawn stance can be observed in some of our American universities, but less so these days. It is still the prevailing attitude in many European universities. There, the university seems intent to preserve the monastic ethos of its medieval origins, offering a false but lulling security to its inmates and sapping the curriculum of virility and relevance. Max Beerbohm's whimsical and idyllic fantasy of Oxford, *Zuleika Dobson,* dramatizes this: 'It is this mild, miasmal air, not less than the grey beauty and the gravity of the buildings that has helped Oxford to produce, and foster, eternally, her peculiar race of artist-scholars, scholar-artists. . . . The buildings and their traditions keep astir in his mind whatsoever is gracious; the climate enfolding and enfeebling him, lulling him, keeps him careless of the sharp, harsh exigent realities of the outer world. These realities may be seen by him. . . . But they cannot fire him. Oxford is too damp for that.'

'Adorable dreamer,' said Matthew Arnold, in his valedictory to Oxford, 'whose heart has been so romantic! who has given thyself so prodigally, given thyself to sides and to heroes not mine, only never to the Philistine! . . . what teacher could ever so save us from that bondage to which we are all prone . . . the bondage of what binds us all, the narrow, the mundane, the merely practical.'

The intellectual and the manager have only recently come out of hiding and recognized the enormous possibilities of joint ventures. Remember that the idea of the professional school is new; this is true even in the case of the venerable threesome – law, medicine and engineering – to say nothing of such recent upstarts as business and public administration. It is as new as the institutionalization of science, and even today, this change is not greeted with unmixed joy. Colin Clark, the economist, writing in a recent *Encounter*, referred to the 'dreadful suggestion that Oxford ought to have a business school.'

It is probably true that we in the United States have had a more pragmatic attitude toward knowledge than anyone else. Many observers have been impressed with the disdain European intellectuals seem to show for practical matters. Even in Russia, where one would least expect it, there is little interest in the 'merely useful'. Harrison Salisbury, the *New York Times*'s Soviet expert, was struck during his recent travels by the almost total absence of liaison between research and practical application. He saw only one great agricultural experimental station on the American model. In that case, professors were working in the fields. They told Salisbury, 'People call us Americans.'

There may not be many American professors working in the fields, but they can be found, when not waiting in airports, almost everywhere else: in factories, in government, in less advanced countries, more recently in backward areas of our own country, in mental hospitals, in the State Department, in educational systems, and in practically all the institutional crevices Ph.D. recipients can worm their way into. They are advising, counseling, researching, recruiting, interpreting, developing, consulting, training, and working for the widest variety of clients imaginable. This is not to say that the deep ambivalence which some Americans hold toward the intellectual has disappeared, but it does indicate that academic man has become more committed to action, in greater numbers, with more diligence, and with higher aspirations than at any other time in history.

Indeed, Fritz Machlup, the economist, has coined a new economic category called the 'knowledge industry', which, he claims, accounts for 29 per cent of the gross national product. And Clark Kerr, the President of the University of California, said not too long ago, 'What the railroads did for the second half of the last century and the automobile did for the first half of this century may be done for the second half of this century by the knowledge industry: that is, to serve as the focal point of national growth. And the university is at the center of the knowledge process.'

Changes in managerial philosophy

Now let us turn to the main theme and put the foregoing remarks about the reciprocity between action and knowledge into the perspective of changing organizations. Consider some of the relatively recent research and theory concerning the human side of enterprise which have made such a solid impact on management thinking and particularly upon the moral imperatives which guide managerial action. I shall be deliberately sweeping in summarizing these changes as much to hide my surprise as to cover a lot of ground quickly. (I can be personal about this. I remember observing Professor McGregor's class some seven years ago, when he first presented his new theories, and I remember the sharp antagonism his Theory X and Theory Y analysis then provoked. Today, I believe most of you would take these ideas as generally self-evident.)

It seems to me that we have seen over the past decade a fundamental change in the basic philosophy which underlies managerial behavior, reflected most of all in the following three areas:

1. A new concept of *man*, based on increased knowledge of his complex and shifting needs, which replaces the oversimplified, innocent push-button idea of man.

2. A new concept of *power*, based on collaboration and reason, which replaces a model of power based on coercion and fear.

3. A new concept of *organizational values*, based on humanistic–democratic ideals, which replaces the depersonalized mechanistic value system of bureaucracy.

Please do not misunderstand. The last thing I want to do is overstate the case. I do not mean that these transformations of man, power and organizational values are fully accepted or even understood, to say nothing of implemented, in day-to-day affairs. These changes may be light-years away from actual adoption. I do mean that they have gained wide intellectual acceptance in enlightened management quarters, that they have caused a tremendous amount of rethinking and search behavior on the part of many organizations, and that they have been used as a basis for policy formulation by many large-scale organizations.

I have tried to summarize all the changes affecting organizations, resulting both from the behavioral sciences and from trends in our society, in the chart of human problems confronting contemporary organizations. These problems (or predicaments) emerge basically from twentieth-century changes, primarily the growth of science and education, the separation of power from property and the correlated emergence of the professional manager, and other kinds of changes which I will get to in a minute. The bureaucratic mechanism, so capable of coordinating men and power in a stable society of routine tasks, cannot cope with contemporary realities. The chart shows five major categories, which I visualize as the core tasks confronting the manager in coordinating the human side of enterprise:

1. The problem of integration grows out of our 'consensual society', where personal attachments play a great part, where the individual is appreciated, in which there is concern for his well-being – not just in a veterinary–hygiene sense but as a moral, integrated personality.

2. The problem of social influence is essentially the problem of power, and leadership studies and practices reveal not only an ethical component but an *effectiveness* component: people tend to work more efficiently and with more commitment when they have a part in determining their own fates and have a stake in problem solving.

3. The problem of collaboration grows out of the same social processes of conflict, stereotyping, and centrifugal forces which inhere in and divide nations and communities. They also employ the same furtive, often fruitless, always crippling mechanisms of conflict resolution: avoidance or suppression, annihilation of the weaker party by the stronger, sterile compromises, and unstable

Table 1 **Human problems confronting contemporary organizations**

	Problem	Bureaucratic solutions	New twentieth-century conditions
Integration	The problem of how to integrate individual needs and management goals	No solution because of no problem. Individual vastly over-simplified, regarded as passive instrument or disregarded	Emergence of human sciences and understanding of man's complexity. Rising aspirations. Humanistic–democratic ethos
Social Influence	The problem of the distribution of power and sources of power and authority	An explicit reliance on legal–rational power but an implicit usage of coercive power. In any case, a confused, ambiguous, shifting complex of competence, coercion, and legal code	Separation of management from ownership. Rise of trade unions and general education. Negative and unintended effects of authoritarian rule
Collaboration	The problem of managing and resolving conflicts	The 'rule of hierarchy' to resolve conflicts between ranks and the 'rule of coordination' to resolve conflict between horizontal groups. 'Loyalty'	Specialization and professionalization and increased need for interdependence. Leadership too complex for one-man rule or omniscience
Adaptation	The problem of responding appropriately to changes induced by the environment of the firm	Environment stable, simple and predictable; tasks routine. Adapting to change occurs in haphazard and adventitious ways. Unanticipated consequences abound	External environment of firm more 'turbulent', less predictable. Unprecedented rate of technological change
'Revitalization'	The problem of growth and decay	?	Rapid changes in technologies, tasks, manpower, norms and values of society, and goals of enterprise and society all make constant attention to the processes of the firm and revision imperative

collusions and coalitions. Particularly as organizations become more complex they fragment and divide, building tribal patterns and symbolic codes which often work to exclude others (secrets and noxious jargon, for example) and on occasion to exploit differences for inward (and always, fragile) harmony. Some large organizations, in fact, can be understood only through an analysis of their cabals, cliques, and satellites, their tactics resembling a sophisticated form of guerrilla warfare; and a venture into adjacent spheres of interest is taken under cover of darkness and fear of ambush.

(The university is a wondrous place for these highly advanced battle techniques, far overshadowing their business counterparts in subterfuge and sabotage. Quite often a university becomes a loose collection of competing departments, schools and institutes, largely noncommunicating because of the multiplicity of specialist jargons and interests and held together, as Robert Hutchins once said, chiefly by a central heating system, or as Clark Kerr amended, by questions of what to do about the parking problem.)[1]

4. The real *coup de grâce* to bureaucracy has come as much from our turbulent environment as from its incorrect assumptions about human behavior. The pyramidal structure of bureaucracy, where power was concentrated at the top – perhaps by one person or a group who had the knowledge and resources to control the entire enterprise – seemed perfect to 'run a railroad'. And undoubtedly, for tasks like building railroads, for the routinized tasks of the nineteenth and early twentieth centuries, bureaucracy was and is an eminently suitable social arrangement.

Nowadays, due primarily to the growth of science, technology, and research and development activities, the organizational environment of the firm is rapidly changing. Today it is a turbulent environment, not a placid and predictable one, and there is a deepening interdependence among the economic and other facets of society. This means that economic organizations are increasingly enmeshed in legislation and public policy. Put more simply, it means that the government will be in about everything, more of

1. For this quote, as well as for other major influences, I want to thank Professor Kenneth D. Benne.

the time. It may also mean, and this is radical, that maximizing cooperation, rather than competition between firms – particularly if their fates are correlated – may become a strong possibility.

5. Finally, there is the problem of revitalization. Alfred North Whitehead sets it neatly before us: 'The art of free society consists first in the maintenance of the symbolic code, and secondly, in the fearlessness of revision. . . . Those societies which cannot combine reverence to their symbols with freedom of revision must ultimately decay.' Organizations, as well as societies, must be concerned with those social conditions that engender buoyancy, resilience and fearlessness of revision. Growth and decay emerge as the penultimate problem where the environment of contemporary society is turbulent and uncertain.

Forecast of organizations of the future

A forecast falls somewhere between a prediction and a prophecy. It lacks the divine guidance of the latter and the empirical foundation of the former. On thin empirical ice, I want to set forth some of the conditions that will dictate organization life in the next twenty-five to fifty years.

The environment

Those factors already mentioned will continue in force and increase. Rapid technological change and diversification will lead to interpenetration of the government – its legal and economic policies – with business. Partnerships between business and government will be typical. And because of the immensity and expense of the projects, there will be fewer identical units competing for the same buyers and sellers. The three main features of the environment will be interdependence rather than competition, turbulence rather than steadiness, and large-scale rather than small-scale enterprises.

Population characteristics

The most distinctive characteristic of our society is, and will become even more so, its education. Peter Drucker calls us the 'educated society', and for good reason: within fifteen years, two-thirds of our population living in metropolitan areas will have attended college. Adult education is growing even faster. It is now almost routine for the experienced physician, engineer, and executive to go back to school for advanced training every two or three years. Some fifty universities, in addition to a dozen large corporations, offer advanced management courses to successful men in the middle and upper ranks of business. Before the Second World War, only two such programs existed, both new and struggling to get students.

All of this education is not just 'nice' but necessary. For as W. Willard Wirtz, the Secretary of Labor, recently pointed out, computers can do the work of most high school graduates – and they can do it cheaper and more effectively. Fifty years ago education used to be regarded as 'nonwork', and intellectuals on the payroll (and many staff workers) were considered 'overhead'. Today, the survival of the firm depends, more than ever before, on the proper exploitation of brain power.

One other characteristic of the population which will aid our understanding of organizations of the future is increasing job mobility. The lowered cost and growing ease of transportation, coupled with the real needs of a dynamic environment, will change drastically the idea of 'owning' a job – or 'having roots', for that matter. Participants will be shifted from job to job and even employer to employer with little concern for roots and homestead.

Work values

The increased leve l of education and mobility will change the values we hold about work. People will be more intellectually committed to their jobs and will probably require more involvement, participation and autonomy in their work.

Also, people will tend to be more 'other-directed', taking cues for their norms and values more from their immediate environment than from tradition. We will tend to rely more heavily on temporary social arrangements, on our immediate and constantly changing colleagues. We will tend to be more concerned and involved with relationships than with relatives.

Tasks and goals

The tasks of the firm will be more technical, complicated and unprogrammed. They will rely more on intellect than muscle. And they will be too complicated for one person to comprehend, to say nothing of control. Essentially, they will call for the collaboration of specialists in a project or team form of organization.

There will be a complication of goals. Business will increasingly concern itself with its adaptive or innovative–creative capacity. In addition, meta-goals – that is, supra-goals which shape and provide the foundation for the goal structure – will have to be articulated and developed. For example, one meta-goal might be a system for detecting new and changing goals; another could be a system for deciding priorities among goals.

Finally, there will be more conflict and contradiction among diverse standards of organizational effectiveness, just as in hospitals and universities today there is conflict between teaching and research. The reason for this is the increased number of professionals involved, who tend to identify more with the goals of their profession than with those of their immediate employer. University professors can be used as a case in point. More and more of their income comes from outside sources, such as foundations which grant them money and industries for whom they consult. They tend not to be good 'company men' because they divide their loyalty between their professional values and organizational goals.

Structure

The social structure of organizations of the future will have some unique characteristics. The key word will be 'temporary'; there will be adaptive, rapidly changing *temporary systems.* These will be problem-oriented 'task forces' composed of groups of relative strangers who represent a diverse set of professional skills. The groups will be arranged on an organic rather than a mechanical model; they will evolve in response to a problem rather than to programmed role expectations. The 'executive' thus will become a coordinator or 'linking pin' among various task forces. He must be a man who can speak the diverse languages of research, with skills to relay information and to mediate between groups. People will be differentiated not vertically according to rank and status but flexibly and functionally, according to skill and professional training.

Adaptive, problem-solving, temporary systems of diverse

specialists, linked together by coordinating and task-evaluating specialists in an organic flux – this is the organizational form that will gradually replace bureaucracy as we know it. As no catchy phrase comes to mind, I call this an organic-adaptive structure.

Motivation

The organic-adaptive structure should increase motivation, and thereby effectiveness, since it will enhance satisfactions intrinsic to the task. There is a harmony between the educated individual's need for meaningful, satisfactory, and creative tasks and a flexible organizational structure.

There will, however, also be reduced commitment to work groups, for these groups, as I have already mentioned, will be transient and changing. While skills in human interaction will become more important, due to the growing needs for collaboration in complex tasks, there will be a concomitant reduction in group cohesiveness. My prediction is that in the organic-adaptive system people will have to learn to develop quick and intense relationships on the job and learn to bear the loss of more enduring work relationships. Because of the added ambiguity of roles, more time will have to be spent on the continual search for the appropriate organizational mix.

In general, I do not agree with those who emphasize a new utopianism in which leisure, not work, will become the emotional–creative sphere of life. Jobs should become more rather than less involving; man is a problem-solving animal, and the tasks of the future guarantee a full agenda of problems. In addition, the adaptive process itself may become captivating to many.

At the same time, I think that the future I describe is not necessarily a 'happy' one. Coping with rapid change, living in temporary work systems, developing meaningful relations and then breaking them – all augur social strains and psychological tensions. Teaching how to live with ambiguity, to identify with the adaptive process, to make a virtue out of contingency, and to be self-directing will be the task of education, the goal of maturity, and the achievement of the successful manager. To be a wife in this era will be to undertake the profession of providing stability and continuity.

In these new organizations, participants will be called on to use their minds more than at any other time in history. Fantasy, imagination and creativity will be legitimate in ways that today seem strange. Social structures will no longer be instruments of psychic repression but will increasingly promote play and freedom on behalf of curiosity and thought.

Bureaucracy was a monumental discovery for harnessing the muscle power of the Industrial Revolution. In today's world, it is a lifeless crutch that is no longer useful. For we now require structures of freedom to permit the expression of play and imagination and to exploit the new pleasure of work.

One final word: while I forecast the structure and value co-ordinates for organizations of the future and contend that they are inevitable, this should not bar any of us from giving the inevitable a little push here and there. And while the French moralist may be right that there are no delightful marriages, just good ones, it is possible that if managers and scientists continue to get their heads together in organizational revitalization, they *might* develop delightful organizations – just possibly.

I started with a quote from de Tocqueville and I think it would be fitting to end with one: 'I am tempted to believe that what we call necessary institutions are often no more than institutions to which we have grown accustomed. In matters of social constitution, the field of possibilities is much more extensive than men living in their various societies are ready to imagine.'

8 W. F. Whyte

Models for Building and Changing Organizations

Excerpts from W. F. Whyte, 'Models for building and changing organizations', *Human Organization*, 1967, vol. 26, nos. 1 and 2, pp. 22–31.

When we set out to build an organization, we have in mind a theoretical model of that organization. When we set out to change an organization, we have in mind a theoretical model of what the reorganized structure should resemble. A man of action may deny that he is guided by any theoretical model. That is only to say that his assumptions about organizations remain implicit and are thus not available for conscious analysis and evaluation. This article is based on the assumption that man can act more effectively if he recognizes the organization models he carries around in his head and tests them against the realities of experience.

I believe that many organizational problems arise because the leaders of those organizations are attempting to apply to the human problems they face an inappropriate theoretical model of organization. I also believe that most men carry in their heads an extremely limited repertoire of models. They could act with more understanding and effectiveness if they made their own models explicit and if they could become more flexible and inventive in developing and applying models to the problems they face. The purpose of this article is, therefore, to make explicit some of the common models upon which people act, to examine some of the problems that arise when people use inappropriate models, and finally to suggest how model building may be more effectively applied to the problems of organization building and administration.

The community democracy model

The community democracy model is very popular in our culture. It assumes that every member of the organization should participate in the decision-making process. This means that people should be free to choose their own representatives, but it means much more than that. Participation itself on the part of all citizens is emphasized, and the exercise of authority is de-emphasized. In fact, it is thought that authority is anti-democratic and should be minimized if not done away with altogether.

This model is often applied to labor unions. People criticize the meeting of the local union for not conforming to the community democracy model. They point out that, in most local unions, only a small fraction of the total membership attends the regular meetings and, the larger the union, the smaller this fraction is likely to be. Curiously enough, local union leaders seem to have the same model in mind. Whenever I attend a meeting of a local union, I expect one of the officers to apologize to me for the small number of members in attendance. They feel ashamed that they are not living up to this model of pure democracy.

The model represents an ideal, which is, of course, never realized. We might think that the New England town, with its town meeting, approximates this model, but even there the resemblance is not close. As towns have grown, they have abandoned the town meeting. Even where it survives, it is generally held once a year and probably has more ceremonial than practical significance. The business of governing the town is carried on by the elected selectmen. In the course of a year, individuals and groups of citizens may discuss their problems and points of view with their elected representatives, but the citizens do not participate on a mass basis in discussing and voting upon the affairs of their town.

Most local unions hold monthly meetings and some even meet every two weeks. The leaders have a variety of ways in which they can assess the opinion of the membership, and the members have a number of ways in which they can make their views known to the leadership, outside the formal meeting. Nevertheless, many local union leaders seem to suffer from guilt feelings because they cannot get for their monthly meeting the same kind of turnout that a small New England village may get for its annual meeting.

In referring to the guilt feelings of union leaders, I am not concerned with their mental health. I am arguing that if they abandon the ideal and unrealistic model, they will become more skillful in handling the problems of union administration. They will then recognize that the union meeting is not, in fact, and never can be, primarily a decision-making body – though occasionally it may be called upon to ratify decisions made by its officers. Instead, they will see that its functions are primarily ceremonial, while it also provides for a certain amount of communication from members to leadership and from leadership to members.

As they abandon the inappropriate model, the leaders will also be freer to ask questions about other structures and procedures of the union. For example, particularly in a large local, they will not expect the union meeting to bring out a cross-section of membership opinion. They may then consider whether they should promote regular meetings of smaller segments of the union, such as departments of the plant. If each department has an elected steward representing it, then the top leaders will need to think whether the steward should conduct these meetings, with or without the presence of higher officers. They may have to explore further ways in which the steward can bring the problems of his constituents to the leadership and the leadership can use the steward to get its views across to the constituents. As long as union leaders continue to hope that some day they may stir the civic conscience of the members and have a great turnout so that union meetings can fulfill the purpose of the town meeting model, just so long are leaders inhibited from exploring practical measures to meet the real problems of the organization.

Such a democratic model was also at the base of some of the human problems that arose in the Japanese relocation camps during the Second World War. John Collier and others who were responsible for the policy in these camps recognized the ambiguous situation in which they and the Japanese-Americans found themselves. These were, in effect, concentration camps. People were sent there against their will and for many months were not allowed to leave. Nor were they taken into custody because of any crimes they had committed. In a burst of war hysteria, they were herded together to prevent them from engaging in acts disloyal to United States.

Recognizing that the very existence of the relocation camps was a violation of our democratic rights, the policy makers undertook to make the best out of a bad thing. They hoped that the camps could be administered as democratically as possible.

Therefore, the Japanese-Americans were given the opportunity to elect representatives to a local government of their own. It was thought that these elected representatives could handle some of the decision-making of the community and could present the views of the inmates to the administration. The whole effort was clothed in democratic ideology. In saying this, I am not accusing the policy makers of hypocrisy. They sincerely hoped to make an inherently undemocratic situation as democratic as possible.

The best account of the problems that arose in their effort to apply this democratic model is Alexander Leighton's book, *The Governing of Men* (1947),[1] which examines the situation in the Poston, Arizona relocation camp. There he describes how grievances built up among the inhabitants, how communication broke down between the elected representatives and the camp administration, and how a crisis arose when the elected leaders called a strike.

When this sort of crisis arose in some of the other camps, the administration had no way of meeting it except outright repression. Fortunately, in the Poston situation, the camp administrator was a flexible and imaginative person, and he had Leighton to advise him. In the crisis, he sat down with the community leaders and began to negotiate. This led to agreement that rapidly reduced tension. Periodic bargaining meetings continued for some time and resulted in a handling of problems that was reasonably satisfactory to all concerned – given the limits imposed by federal policy.

In effect, what the camp administrator did in the crisis was to abandon the community democracy model and substitute a labor relations model. I would argue that a labor relations model represents a much more realistic fit for the kind of situation faced by these participants. If a labor relations model had been in the minds of administrators of other camps, they would have had a better chance of meeting their crises effectively, and, if the Poston administrator had had this model in mind to begin with he too would have been better prepared for his crisis.

A labor relations model is superior to the community democracy model in this type of situation, for it allows one to deal

1. Leighton acknowledges particularly the contribution of Ned Spicer in developing this study.

realistically with authority as well as with participation. In a labor relations model, there is never any question as to who has the power to make administrative decisions. On the other hand, as in union–management relations, the people have a chance to protest and suggest changes to their elected representatives, and they also have the possibility of exercising pressures on the administration through withholding cooperation with administrative decisions, and ultimately, through the strike. When these facts are clearly recognized on both sides, the result is not an impasse but a bargaining situation in which the administration learns what it has to give in order to get the cooperation it requires.

The relocation camp example is a dramatic one, but the kinds of problems faced there are found every day in student government in educational systems. Educational administrators often propound the ideology of community democracy and talk as if they were really going to let the students govern themselves. The students find out soon enough that authority remains in the hands of the administrators. The result is either a demoralization of student government, with the elected representatives refusing to take any responsibility, or else the students band together to resist the administration collectively, perhaps even to the point of a strike. Here again it would be more realistic for educational administrators to think at the outset in terms of a labor relations model. Clearly a school or college is not a community governed by its students. The administration is in control, and nothing is gained by telling the students that they can really run their own affairs, when they know full well that this is not the case.

We see the same type of problem with an organizational model in the case of the 'therapeutic community' concept of mental hospitals. Reacting against the strictly authoritarian program of the traditional mental hospital, which emphasizes custodial care, Dr Maxwell Jones has converted his Belmont Hospital into a 'therapeutic community'. While the Belmont Hospital has not been taking in every patient referred to it, it has been accepting a number of patients who display psychopathic tendencies, which means in some cases that these are very unruly people who present severe problems of discipline to the ordinary mental hospital. According to the philosophy of the 'therapeutic community', the differences of status and authority among patients, doctors, nurses, attendants, occupational therapists, and so on, should be minimized. The problems that the patients have should be discussed freely among themselves and with the staff, and, as much as possible, decisions that are made should arise out of this group process and should not be simply the orders of some super-ordinate individual.

It may well be that this model is superior to the old-fashioned custodial model. Indeed it would be difficult to find an alternative to the custodial model that promised poorer results than that traditional institution. On the other hand, studies of anthropologists clearly reveal that 'the therapeutic community', at least as originally conceived and established, has not been fulfilling the expectations of its designers. On the basis of the evidence available, I would conclude that the reported difficulties arise out of the lack of fit between the organizational model and the conditions affecting the existence and functioning of the organization.

As anthropologists Robert Rappaport (1958) and Seymour Parker (1958) point out, there have been two typical problems in the therapeutic community. One problem involves the hospital's relation with the surrounding population. In the case of the Belmont Hospital, since patients were free to leave the hospital and spend some of their time in the community, there were inevitably occasions when a given patient would become drunk or otherwise unruly, cause some disturbance, or even damage someone's property. This naturally led to protests to the hospital from community authorities and recurring discussions in the administration as to how the patients might be controlled, within the limits of the democratic therapeutic community.

An internal problem, not entirely separate from the community relations problem, involved the decisions of the psychiatric staff regarding the disciplinary discharge of patients. Within the therapeutic community, the doctors retained the authority of determining who should be discharged, and when such a discharge should take place. According to the ideology of the therapeutic community, doctors were to discharge a patient only when they determined that he had recovered sufficiently to function reasonably normally in society or, on the other hand, when his behavior was such that, in their professional judgement, he could not benefit from further stay in the hospital. It was this latter type of discharge decision that led to bad feeling between patients and doctors, to a general breakdown of communications, and to disillusionment of the patients regarding the whole concept of the therapeutic community.

Patients argued that these decisions regarding disciplinary discharges were not being made strictly in terms of considerations of the welfare of the individual patients. Rather, they claimed, the doctors were using this weapon to get rid of patients they considered troublemakers. In fact, the patients claimed that the therapeutic community should be a particularly appropriate treatment setting for the aggressive, acting-out personalities that the doctors were inclined to discharge. This interpretation led many patients to conclude that the whole concept of the therapeutic community was hypocritical. The same old power structure was in effect, but the doctors and the administration were trying to dress it up with fancy, democratic-sounding language.

Whenever I have tried to propose a labor relations model for a mental hospital, I have found psychiatrists vigorously objecting on the grounds that the labor relations model is built upon the assumption of a conflict of interest between the workers and management, whereas in a mental hospital the psychiatrists and the patients have the same interest in getting the patients well.[2] I see no validity to this objection.

Actually, any large organization embodies a variety of interests among the participants, some of them shared, and some of them conflicting. Managers often argue that it is in the interests of the workers as well as of management to keep wages from rising too high and to introduce technological changes that displace workers, because only in this way can the economic health of the organization be maintained and the jobs of the workers protected. Furthermore, in trying to explain or control the behavior of people, we are not concerned with determining whether their interests are *really* in harmony or in conflict. What we need to know is how they perceive these interests. It is now a well-established uniformity of organizational behavior that wherever groups of people

2. There is, however, research literature that recognizes such structural and interest problems. See, e.g. Stanton and Schwartz (1954).

occupy widely differing positions in a hierarchy and carry out different activities, they are bound to see their interests as being different. This does not mean that doctors and patients will disagree on broad general values such as that of having the patients get well. It does mean that they are bound to differ from time to time on specific issues having to do with the control of the interactions and activities of patients.

I would suggest furthermore that harmony is an undesirable goal for the functioning of a complex organization. The objective should not be to build a harmonious organization, but rather to build an organization capable of recognizing the problems it faces and of developing ways of solving these problems. Since conflicts are an inevitable part of organizational life, it is important that conflict-resolution procedures be built into the design of the organization.

This does not mean that the conflicts must necessarily be bitter and contested in a destructive fashion. There are many well-documented cases in the union–management literature where the two parties have been able to work out a highly cooperative relationship. Such a relationship does not arise when underlying conflicts of interest are ignored, but rather when the two parties have worked out procedures whereby the problems each faces are argued vigorously with the other. In such cases, management gains the advantage of being faced with the direct expression of grievances that otherwise would fester at lower levels of the organization; also management has a better chance of implementing policies if they have been thrashed out in discussion with union leaders rather than simply imposed by management.

When ideology prevents the recognition of conflicts of interest in the complex organization, then we can expect that there will be no structures and procedures provided in the design of the organization for confronting and resolving such conflicts. Studies now coming to us from behind the Iron Curtain suggest that this is one of the human problems of the Communist world. In his study of *A Polish Factory*, Jiri Kolaja (1960) found both a labor union and a branch of the Communist Party functioning within the plant. However, according to Communist ideology, the factories are owned by the state and therefore by the people as a whole. In such a case, there can be no conflict between the managers and the workers, who share in the factory ownership. Against this ideological background, it is hardly surprising to find that conflicts of interest are not recognized, nor are there any stable procedures for resolving them. The labor union carries out certain social work functions but provides no channel for the airing of individual or group grievances or for the negotiation of issues with management. Instead we find leaders of the union, like leaders of the Communist Party and the factory management people themselves, exhorting workers to work harder and more efficiently.

The bureaucratic model [3]

While innovators have tried to apply the therapeutic community model to mental hospitals, the more common model for large hospitals and for large business and governmental organizations is what we might call the bureaucratic model. This is conceived in the form of a pyramid, with the policy makers on the top and those that carry out policies and do the work of the organization at successively lower levels. There is a chain of command in which the work of functionaries of each level is directed and supervised by an individual at the next higher level. Much has been written about the number of individuals that a given supervisor can adequately supervise.

There are, of course, variations in the model according to the type of organization that is designed. A hospital can be expected to have a different sort of structure from a factory. However, this may involve simply a different number of sub-hierarchies, without basically changing the hierarchical nature of the model.

The organizational model of a large institution tends to be reflected in a certain type of physical structure. In fact, some have called the building that houses such an organization 'a frozen organization' because the size, location and furnishings of the offices tend to fix the status structure in the minds of members and observers and to facilitate communication among certain individuals and inhibit it among others.

Those who think of innovation in organization models would do well to think of innovation also in physical structures. This is

3. Paul Van Riper calls this the 'production organization'. See his 'Toward a typology of organizations and related matters' (mimeo).

well illustrated in the case of the Aro Hospital for Nervous Diseases in Nigeria.[4] Fortunately, Dr T. Adeoye Lambo was appointed to the directorship of this particular hospital before the structure was actually built, and therefore he had a chance to plan both the organization and its physical setting. When Dr Lambo took office, he confronted an architect's drawing for a large mental hospital building meeting the highest standards of hospital construction in the advanced medical centers of industrialized countries. Dr Lambo felt that this type of structure not only would freeze the organization in an undesirable pattern but also would prevent the hospital from reaching its patients. The hospital was to be located in a rural area, whose inhabitants had had little, if any, previous contact with such large and imposing physical structures. Family ties were strong in that area, and Dr Lambo was concerned about the disruptive effects of taking the patient away from his family and about the difficulties of re-integrating the patient into family and community after the treatment had been completed.

With these considerations in mind, Dr Lambo worked out arrangements with the chiefs of neighboring villages to use the villages as wards for the mental health patients. This meant that each patient was placed in an existing household, accompanied by at least one member of his family to look after him. Doctors and nurses then circulated about these village wards, seeing their patients in an environment that was much closer to the one from which they came and to which they would return than would have been possible in the large modern mental hospital.

These innovations in physical and social structures can be described in a few words, but their simplicity conceals their extraordinary nature. Since the hospital and mental health program of Dr Lambo fit so well into the existing culture of the area, why should these innovations be considered extraordinary? I make that evaluation because the innovations seem to run counter to the well-established trends of culture diffusion.

In the relations between industrialized societies and the developing nations, we are inclined to think of the experts from the industrialized nations as selling their models of institutions, physical structures, procedures and practices to the developing

4. I am indebted to Alexander Leighton for this account.

nations. We fail to recognize an influence that may be equally strong: the tendency of the emerging specialists in the developing nations to imitate the organization models, physical structures, practices and procedures that are to be found in the advanced, industrialized nations. The doctor in Nigeria, Peru or Pakistan gains satisfaction from thinking that he is associated with a hospital that measures up to the best standards that are to be found in the metropolitan centers of the industrialized nations. He is likely to accept such a model for imitation and emulation, to urge it upon his government, regardless of the way it fits or fails to fit into the local situation. [. . .]

Summary and conclusion

The purpose of this paper has been to show that all organized activity is carried out in terms of organizational models that are at least implicit in the thoughts and actions of those making the key organizational decisions. If the designers of the organization are operating in terms of an inappropriate model, efficiency will be reduced and frustrations and frictions increased.

I have also sought to show that people tend to operate with an extremely limited number of organizational models. This suggests that if people are more flexible and imaginative in organizational model building, it will be possible to devise models that will operate more effectively.

How does one go about such model building? In the first place, it seems to me, we need to examine the activities that are to be carried out. Instead of designing the structure from the top down, we need to begin with relating people to activities where the basic work is to be carried out. Then we can consider how the people doing the work need to be related to each other, supported and guided. We need also to consider the way our organizational model will fit into the surrounding social and economic environment.

Finally, it seems to me that it is helpful in organizational model building to try to become more consciously aware of the types of models that are actually in operation in various fields of organized activity. If we do this, we may find that a model that is normally thought of in terms of one area of activity (for example, union–management relations) can be appropriately used to solve some of the ambiguities and frictions that arise in quite a different field of activity (let us say, a mental hospital whose director is trying to develop a new community-oriented program of therapy).

References

LEIGHTON, A. (1947), *The Governing of Men*, Princeton University Press.

PARKER, S. (1958), 'Changes in the administration of psychotherapy during a collective upset', *Human Organization*, vol. 16, no. 4, pp. 32–37.

RAPPAPORT, R. (1958), 'Community as the doctor', *Human Organization*, vol. 16, no. 4, pp. 28–31.

STANTON, H., and SCHWARTZ, M. S. (1954), *The Mental Hospital*, Basic Books.

9 J. Q. Wilson

Innovation in Organization: Notes Toward a Theory

J. Q. Wilson, 'Innovation in organization: notes toward a theory',
in J. D. Thompson (ed.), *Approaches to Organizational Design*,
University of Pittsburg Press, 1966, pp. 195–218.

The process of organizational change is perhaps the least developed aspect of organizational theory. Innovation (somehow defined) occurs, as we all know, but it has rarely been studied systematically except at the small group level (Blau and Scott, 1962, p. 223). It has always seemed easier, and even more interesting, to analyse organizational 'failures' to adapt, the displacement of goals, and the dysfunctional consequences of bureaucratization.

Although more has been written about innovation in the firm than in voluntary associations or government agencies, the state of the literature in economics is not much more satisfactory than in sociology or political science. For example, there appears to be little agreement as to whether monopolistic or competitive firms are more likely to innovate; for every case of a monopolistic firm that does innovate, e.g. du Pont introducing synthetic fibers, there is another monopoly that does not, e.g. General Electric failing to introduce the fluorescent lamp or Western Union failing to introduce the telephone. For every competitive industry with a high level of innovation, e.g. electronics firms, there seems to be another with a low propensity to innovate, e.g. textile firms (Nelson, 1959; Fellner, 1951; Phillips, 1956; Brown, 1957; Maclauren, 1950).

Not only can little be said about the effect of market structure on innovation, but little can be said about the correlation between firm characteristics and innovation. Mansfield has shown that for certain industries firm size and the expected profitability of an innovation are positively correlated with the rate of innovation, but for these same industries there seems to be no statistically significant relationship between innovation and a firm's rate of growth, profit level, liquidity, profit trend, or age of management. Further, there is only a slight tendency for the same firms to be consistent innovators; the leaders in one innovation are very, often the followers in another (Mansfield, 1961, 1963).

Although few comparably systematic studies have been made of organizations other than firms, historical and cast study evidence has been assembled to show that some voluntary associations (such as the National Foundation for Infantile Paralysis, the YMCA, and the Red Cross) have adapted 'successfully' to a changed environment, while others (such as the WCTU and the Townsend Movement) have not (Sills, 1957, pp. 253–70). Among government agencies, the New York City Fire Department rarely innovates, while the Port of New York Authority continually innovates (Sayre and Kaufman, 1961). Innovation in a federal enforcement agency has been extensively analysed (Blau, 1955).

It may be, of course, that what Wilbert Moore has said about theories of social change applies also to theories of organizational innovation: a 'pure' theory of change, independent of some specification of *what* is changing, would be either impossible to formulate or, if formulated, empirically uninteresting (Moore, 1960). Nonetheless, there is some point in trying to think in the broadest terms about innovation generally, if only to prove that not much can be learned that way.

Organizations

We begin with a conception of any formal organization, the central analytical attribute of which we assume to be its economy of incentives (Clark and Wilson, 1961). An incentive is any gratification, tangible or intangible, in exchange for which persons become members of the organization ('the decision to participate') and, once in the organization, contribute time, effort or other valued resources ('the decision to work') (March and Simon, 1958). Whatever the purpose, product or technology of the organization, this inducements–contributions balance must first be maintained.

The executive of the organization is that person who, whatever else he does, has particular responsibility for maintaining the inducements–contributions balance. The executive may be more than one person, of course, e.g. a committee or a partnership.

Each person in the organization is performing a task – a task is all those activities that add up to the full time in the organization of one member. It is assumed that all members of the organization endeavor to act rationally, i.e. to minimize the costs and maximize the benefits to themselves of performing an organizational task, but that no two members may have precisely the same preference orderings. What is a cost to one member, e.g. the need to spend much time in conferences, may be a benefit to another (Homans, 1961).

An innovation (or, more precisely, a major innovation, since we are not concerned with trivial changes) is a 'fundamental' change in a 'significant' number of tasks. What is 'fundamental' and 'significant' cannot be given a precise, *a priori* definition, for in our scheme the meaning of these terms can only be determined by the organizations themselves. Each organization, we assume, can rank proposed, or actual, changes in terms of how 'radical' they will be, or are. A change in tasks performed by ten typists may be less 'important', i.e. less radical, than the change in the task of one vice president. The executive measures proposed or actual changes in tasks in terms of the inducements–contributions balance. The greater the cost in scarce inducements, the more radical the innovation, regardless of the prospective benefits. Since these incentives include not only money payments but also prestige or status in the organization, the power of office, opportunities for rewarding social relationships, organizational purposes, and the like, the cost of an innovation is the extent to which any of these incentives must be redistributed or their supply increased. Loosely speaking, the executive of the organization assesses the cost of any innovation in terms of how much must be done to keep affected parties happy or (if the innovation calls for adding new members to the organization) what must be done, or 'spent', to induce new members to contribute. Money costs are often very important, of course, but other costs may be of equal or greater importance: soothing ruffled fur, reducing uncertainty-induced anxiety, bolstering members' self-conceptions, appealing to their sense of duty, eliminating interpersonal tensions and hostilities, changing the norms of informal work groups, familiarizing workers with new technologies, finding ways to compensate demoted members for their loss of prestige and power, reformulating statements of organizational purpose. The more of these expenditures of money and effort that are required by the innovation, the more radical it is.

The prospective benefits of an innovation are assessed in the same way. The expected utility of an organizational innovation is the product of the amount by which, if successful, it will enhance the supply of incentive resources and the probability that it will be successful. For some organizations wages and salaries may be the prime incentive to members, and thus net money income will be the prime incentive resource; for other organizations (including, perhaps, some business firms under certain circumstances), an intangible gratification such as organizational or personal prestige may be a crucial incentive for essential members, and thus opportunities for enhancing the organization's social standing, or the deference accorded members of it, will be the incentive resource in terms of which the benefits of a proposed innovation will be assessed.

The remainder of this paper will be an effort to indicate, in the perspective of the foregoing model of organizations, how proposals for innovations arise and how likely is their adoption. The 'theory' of innovation here presented will be, of necessity, an indeterminate one. Since the members, and especially the executives, of large organizations differ in both their personal preferences for incentives and their tastes for risk, it will be impossible to say that under a specified set of circumstances any single organization or any class of organizations will respond in a particular way. All that can be said is that various circumstances increase or decrease the probability of innovation. Furthermore, we make no assumption that innovation is always good for organizations, and we do not intend our description of why some organizations are more likely to innovate to be taken as a prescription for other organizations that in some sense 'ought' to innovate.

The unit of analysis is the organization, not the organization in its environment. For a variety of reasons we will not attempt to specify how environmental changes, for example, the action of a competitor or a change in the availability of resources, 'cause' or 'require' innovations in the organization. One reason is that we are not certain that they do in any obvious sense; the problem to be explained is why some organizations and not others respond adaptively to environmental changes. Further, we hope to show that for purposes of analysis it is useful to conceive of the organization as 'sensing' its environment by means of a certain mechanism – the incentive system and the task structure – and as assessing environmental changes not directly but indirectly as they are presented to it through the demands of organization members.

We make two assumptions about the environment: that it is organizationally complex and that it is rich in potential resources – capital, skills, consumers, attentive elites. What is said here about organizational innovation may thus be wholly inappropriate for other societies, or even parts of our own society, that have relatively few organizations and a scarcity of potential resources.

The central hypotheses

Innovation in an organization occurs in three stages: the conception of the change (strictly speaking, this is invention, not innovation), the proposing of the change, and the adoption and implementation of the change. We hypothesize that the probability of innovation activity at any of these three stages is principally a function of the diversity of the organization. Diversity in turn is a function of both the complexity of the *task structure* and the *incentive system*.

The *task structure*, i.e. the sum of all tasks, or one-man duties, in the organization, increases in complexity as the number of different tasks increases and as the proportion of nonroutine tasks increases. By nonroutine tasks we mean tasks that involve a minimum of prescribed, repetitive operations. If all operations in a given task are prescribed in advance and if those operations are essentially repeated from day to day, the task is entirely routine. In Herbert Simon's terminology, the task is highly 'programmed'. Routine or programmed tasks are more easily made subject to organizational control than are nonroutine tasks, either through supervision (checking on the performance of prescribed operations or on the attainment of certain rates of production, a certain quality of production, or both) or through mechanical and organizational 'linkages', e.g. linking a number of routine tasks by arranging them on an assembly line moving at a predetermined pace.

The *incentive system*, i.e. the sum of all rewards given to members, increases in complexity as the number of sources of incentives increases, and these in turn increase in number with an increase in the number of groups (both membership and reference groups, both inside and outside the formal organization) with which each member is affiliated. Affiliation with any group is based – in accordance with the general conceptual framework underlying this theory – on receiving gratifications from that group; the more different groups with which the member is affiliated, the more potentially varied the kinds of satisfactions the member receives. Naturally, not all affiliations are relevant to organizational innovation; only those affiliations that require the member to conform to some extent to expectations relevant to the innovating organization's activities in return for whatever gratifications he receives will constitute an affiliation that acts as a constraint on his behavior in that organization.

Obviously, one important source of an increase in the complexity of the incentive system is an increase in the complexity of the task structure, and thus the two aspects of organizational diversity are in part related. If the task structure becomes more complicated, it will in the typical case require the creation within the organization of sub-units, the adding of more supervisory positions or levels, and perhaps the decentralization of operations. The creation of such sub-units, particularly ones that are geographically dispersed or organizationally decentralized, normally results in the generation of sub-unit loyalties among members of the organization. If the sub-unit is sufficiently autonomous, more than simple loyalty may be at stake: the sub-unit may play as great or greater part than the organization as a whole in determining salary, promotions and assignments. Thus, the larger the number of organizationally defined sub-units, the greater the diversity of the organization – because both the task structure and the incentive system become more complex.

But the incentive system may be complex for reasons having nothing to do with the task structure. Organization members may be affiliated with, or identify with, informal work or social groups within the organization or with external associations and groups, such as trade unions, professional societies, colleague groups, political factions (Blau and Scott, 1962, pp. 60–74; Gouldner, 1958). The number and strength of such attachments complicate the incentive system by providing rewards that are not under direct organizational control. These extra-organizational, or non-organizational, incentives are important to the extent that the member values them and to the extent that the behavior they reward is clearly defined. Some such groups, e.g. an association of professional educators, may provide rather vague cues to action; others, e.g. an association of mathematicians, may provide very explicit ones. Further, some persons may value such rewards very highly, e.g. an economist who plans to return on the strength of his professional reputation to a university he left for service in a government agency, while others value them only slightly, e.g. an economist who has decided to forsake academia in favor of a position in private enterprise.

These two attributes of organizational diversity – task structure and incentive system – are, of course, related. The tasks of the member are the costs he must bear; in exchange for so doing he receives rewards. The task structure is the manner in which the organization (more precisely, its executives) has allocated effort; the incentive system is the manner in which the organization and other groups and associations over which the organization is likely to have little control have allocated rewards. Organizational maintenance requires the executive constantly to find and distribute incentives. The role would be a simple one if there were a perfect 'fit' between effort and reward such that a task once defined would be repeatedly performed by an individual once induced. This is rarely the case. The act of performing the task generates over time slightly different expectations, which are met with slightly altered incentives. The effort to find incentives for others, e.g. by making the organization increase in productivity, alters the existing distribution of effort and rewards, and further – indeed, endless – adjustments are necessary. Incremental changes are thus a constant feature of organizational life.

We argue here that the greater the diversity of the organization (in either its incentive system or its task structure or both), the *greater* the likelihood that some members will *conceive* major innovations, the *greater* the likelihood that some members will *propose* innovations, and the *less* likelihood that the organization will *adopt* the innovations. The reasoning behind these hypotheses follows.

Hypothesis 1. The greater the diversity of the organization, the greater the probability that members will conceive of major innovations.

A highly complex task structure inhibits close supervision, the precise specification of operations, and the linking of tasks in some mechanical fashion. Either ends or means will be only vaguely specified. (In the most complex task structure of all – organizationally uninhibited 'basic' research – neither the ends nor the means of the member's task can be specified at all.) In a complex task structure each member's task will to some extent be tailored by him to suit his own methods and style. There will be few standards the organization can use to maintain conformity among members. Each member can plausibly claim some justification for conceiving his job differently than others conceive their outwardly similar jobs. This complexity means that activity anywhere in the organization will probably affect its members differentially. In the absence of clear performance criteria and in the presence of a variety of conceptions of nominally identical tasks, each member will try to define his own job for himself.

A highly complex incentive system maximizes the probability that each member will be confronted with slightly – even considerably – different expectations governing his membership and performance. The greater the variety and complexity of rewards, the greater the incentive to conceive of ways in which one's task can be altered to maximize the attainment of some particular mix of rewards that the member values.

The most diverse organization, such as a collection of loosely organized scientists conducting basic research in a variety of fields, will produce the highest number of innovative conceptions.

Hypothesis 2. The greater the diversity of the organization, the greater the probability that major innovations will be proposed.

A task structure and incentive system that encourages new ideas will tend to encourage proposals embodying these new ideas. Behavior in a large formal organization is likely to be different from behavior in a small group – in part because in a small group tasks are, at any given moment, likely to be simple and the incentives almost entirely intra-organizational. But in addition, the suggestion of new ideas in the small group is likely to be low if any member feels threatened by the possibility that his idea will be rejected or even scorned. He has no support other than his own daring and the possible goodwill and approval of his associates. In a large, diverse organization with many sub-units there are likely to be many innovative proposals that are likely to find support in some face-to-face group even though they run the risk of organizational rejection. In short, the more diverse the organization, the greater the likelihood of finding allies. Further, in a highly diverse organization the social distance between members and executives is likely to be great; proposals can be made and rejected impersonally, thus minimizing the cost of both proposing and rejecting.

Proposals are made both to adapt tasks so that costs, i.e. effort, are reduced and to increase rewards. The greater the diversity of the organization, the greater the likelihood that costs and benefits are in an unstable equilibrium. Since diversity means that any activity, including an innovation, is likely to affect members differentially, new activity will require a widespread readjustment of efforts and rewards. This is the chain-reaction effect. The chain reaction does not continue indefinitely, of course, because (as explained below) there are limits to the tolerance organizations will extend to even those innovations that are adaptive responses to changes it has already approved.

If members make proposals only after balancing the expected utility of the change against the costs of proposing it, then it may not be self-evident that even a highly diverse organization encourages innovative proposals. If, as we shall argue below, organizational diversity *reduces* the probability that a proposal will be adopted, and if a rejection would be counted as a cost by the person making the proposal, then it could be argued that diversity, by minimizing the chances of getting a proposal adopted, also minimizes the likelihood that anyone will make it.

There are several answers to this. First, many proposals must be rejected not because their prospective benefits to the organization are negligible but because the cost of obtaining consent to them is too high. In short, many are rejected, not 'on their merits', but for essentially political reasons: it is too costly to concert the wills of organization members sufficiently to implement the proposal. Thus, the proposer may be rewarded (by being thought a 'bright fellow') even if his idea is turned down. Second, the greater the diversity of the organization, the greater the incentive members and sub-units have in acquiring bargaining power, one against another. Whatever value a member attaches to the probability of being made better off by an innovation, he will invariably have an interest in avoiding being made worse off. To protect the status quo, the member will make counter-proposals, offer suggestions to acquire bargaining power, or initiate limited changes in order to forestall greater, and less desirable, changes.

Hypothesis 3. The greater the diversity of the organization, the smaller the proportion of major innovative proposals that will be adopted.

To adopt a proposal the executive of a large organization must exercise influence over affected organization members. The more complex the task structure and incentive system, the greater the difficulty, i.e. the greater the cost, in wielding the influence. A complex task structure makes detailed control of the members' activities by the organization difficult: either means or ends or both will be difficult to specify. To the extent that such specification and supervision are not possible, it will be difficult to make the distribution of rewards dependent upon changing behavior. Further, the more complex the task structure, the less likely it is that the executive will be sufficiently knowledgeable about members' work to run the risk of instituting an innovation without obtaining their consent (Clark, 1961). Only to the degree that he understands the organization's technology can he innovate entirely on his own authority; lacking this understanding, he must rely to some significant extent on the opinions of subordinates as to the feasibility, costs and benefits of the proposed change. But a complex task structure also means that many members will be affected differentially by any major change; this in turn increases the probability that there will be disagreement among members about the merits of the change. Unless the executive has a high taste for risk, he must attempt to resolve this conflict, usually by redistributing incentives in such a way that aggrieved members are somehow compensated for the losses they will incur because of the innovation.

But if the organization also has a complex incentive system, such compensating moves by the executive will be difficult to carry out. The larger the number of incentives from extra-organizational sources (or other sources not directly subject to the executive's control), the greater the difficulty in using incentives to induce members to accept innovations (except, of course, in those cases where there happens to be a congruence between the activities required by the innovation and the activities rewarded by the extra-organizational incentives). The greater the value members attach to rewards they receive from informal work groups, professional societies, external colleague groups, trade unions, and the like, the less the relative value of those rewards the executive controls, e.g. pay, definition of purposes, prestige of office.

The process of adopting innovations can be looked upon as essentially a political one characterized by bargaining; the more diverse the organization, the more bargaining must occur before changes can be made. Inasmuch as incentives are by definition scarce, gratifying one member's demands for change, i.e. adopting his proposals, can usually be done only at a cost to other members – and the cost rises with increases in task complexity. Such proposals therefore elicit counter-claims (resistance, alternative proposals, threats). The executive seeks to reconcile the competing claims by mediation, by slowing the pace of events to insure that all affected parties are heard from, by finding new or alternative incentives to compensate members for losses (in game-theory language, by distributing side payments to convert zero-sum games into non-zero-sum games), and by searching for information that will indicate the limits of 'tolerable' innovation.

The winning of consent for proposed innovations is costly to the executive *at the level at which the innovation is to take effect*. A highly diversified organization may also be a decentralized organization, that is, one in which authority over a predetermined range of choices is delegated to particular sub-units. A certain proposal may more easily be adopted if it is dealt with by a sub-unit rather than by the organization as a whole because in the sub-unit there are fewer wills to concert. This fact might lead one to suppose that decentralization (and thus diversity) increases rather than decreases, the probability of adoption of innovations. This supposition, however, is unwarranted, for it is based on a confusion of levels of analysis. The diversity of the organization must be determined for the unit or level to be affected by the innovation; the problem of adoption is a problem for the executive(s) of the unit affected. That a sub-unit of a decentralized organization can adopt a proposal does not mean that diversity has facilitated adoption, for the diversity of the whole organization is irrelevant to the politics of the sub-unit so long as the adoption of the proposal is irrelevant to the whole organization. In short, the application of all three central hypotheses requires first a careful specification of the organizational level to which they are to refer.

Finally, the limited resources available to the executive prevent the chain-reaction effect discussed earlier from continuing without end. In the short run, however, there will be a chain reaction; viewed retrospectively, innovations will seem to have occurred in clusters (Sofer, 1961). This is in part because the price of obtaining the consent of members to one innovation is often to adopt other innovations that will benefit them (or at least reduce the cost to them of the original change). A 'package deal' will be negotiated. The chain-reaction effect may also be in part the result of a temporary lowering of the resistance to change: the organization is seized with an enthusiasm for change, perhaps because the successful adoption of one change encourages others to think that further changes are not so costly as they had believed. As with human passions, however, the enthusiasms of organizations are typically short-lived.

Some related hypotheses

This general orientation (it is too much to call it a theory, since its main elements have not been stated in 'operational' form) to the study of innovation suggests certain more specific hypotheses:

1. If organizational diversity is directly proportional to the rate of proposals and inversely proportional to the rate of adoptions, little

can be said about the total number (or the frequency) of adopted innovations in organizations. The net effect of these contrary tendencies would depend entirely on the steepness of the two curves; all that can be suggested from a theoretical point of view is their direction. This in itself may explain why the evidence on whether large or small organizations are more innovative is inconclusive. Nor can practitioners of organizational design find much use in the theory presented here; unless (as seems unlikely) numerical values could be attached to the rates of proposal and adoption for whole classes of organizations, there will be no way to determine an optimum point where, in effect, a marginal increase in the probability of additional proposals will just equal the marginal decline in the probability of their adoption.[1]

Such considerations as these may shed light on a problem familiar to the author: how can one compare the innovative capacities of two city governments, one of which is characterized by a high degree of centralization, the other by a low degree? Chicago's government is informally centralized by a political boss whose machine has almost complete control of the incentive system of key members of the administration and of almost all members of the city council (Banfield, 1961). New York has a city government that is decentralized; the formal, legal dispersion of power is not overcome by informal centralization under party auspices. Key administration members are attracted by a wide variety of rewards over which the nominal head of the administration, the mayor, has little or no control, e.g. the possibility of an independent political career, of advancement to higher posts within semi-autonomous boards and commissions, of conforming to internally valued or externally rewarded professional expectations and standards, of entering into alliances with civic associations and newspapers for whatever benefits they can bestow, and so forth. In New York, new proposals are constantly being generated by many persons within the administration; each pro-

1. This is not merely a difficulty, but an impossibility. Material incentives are the cornerstone of economics precisely because they may have money prices – and hence numerical values – assigned to them. Once nonmaterial incentives are introduced (as they almost inevitably must be in a discussion of organizational innovation), such values cannot be calculated and determinate solutions cannot be obtained.

posal, however, 'must run a gauntlet that is often fatal' (Sayre and Kaufman, 1961, p. 716). There are literally scores of opportunities for others to intervene and register a decisive veto. In Chicago there is no such gauntlet; only the mayor's, i.e. the boss's, views count, and what he decides becomes policy. At the same time, relatively few proposals are generated within the administration; the real sources of innovations are private associations and groups that compete for the mayor's attention. (Such outside groups are also active in New York, of course, but there they can usually count on having a governmental agency or bureaucrat as their overt ally.) Whether Chicago or New York is more innovative depends on the result of the operation of these contrary tendencies (Banfield and Wilson, 1963, ch. 23).

Although the inverse relationship between the rate of proposals and the probability of their adoption makes it difficult to predict in the ordinary case which of two organizations is more likely to be innovative, *extreme* differences in organizational diversity seem to be clearly related to differences in the level of innovation. A university research team is probably more innovative than a stenographic pool; apparently there is some (unknown) point beyond which further increases in diversity cause the rate of proposals to increase faster than the difficulty of securing their adoption – at least for some kinds of tasks. (The researchers' innovations may not be more significant, however, if the cost in inducements of their adoption is lower than is the cost of the adoption of the stenographers' innovations. The significance or radicality of the innovation from the organization's point of view should not be confused with its significance from society's point of view.) The pessimistic conclusion that organizational designers cannot use this theory of innovation to make any given organization 'more innovative' must be modified to allow for the gross differences in levels of innovation between two quite dissimilar organizations. (In practice, of course, this concession probably will not offer much real solace, for the task of organizational designers is typically to introduce marginal changes in a single organization, not to convert it into a wholly different kind of organization. The theory does not permit one to predict whether diversifying a stenographic pool will make it more innovative;

reality does not permit one to convert stenographers into physicists.)

There is considerable evidence that organizations with large proportions of 'professional' personnel are more innovative than those with small proportions of professionals.

Stinchcombe (1960) has shown that 'progressive' firms (impressionistically determined) have a higher proportion of professionals among their top workers than 'stagnant' firms. Hill and Harbison (1959) have shown that industrial firms that innovated extensively between 1947 and 1955 also increased their employment of professionals during that period. Stinchcombe (1960) has re-analysed their data to show that the innovating firms not only hire more professionals but also entered the period of innovation with more professionals.

Browning (1963) has compared two departments in a state government, one of which was, by a variety of measures, more innovative than the other. The innovative agency was far more 'professionalized' than the other and had, in my terms, a much more complex incentive system (for example, the innovative department subscribed to 105 professional journals and sent its personnel on 281 trips to ninety-one out-of-state professional meetings; the other departments subscribed to only eleven journals and sent its personnel on only nine trips to five different meetings). Browning concludes that neither political nor technological changes accounted for the innovative department's behavior, but rather its own incentive system: 'The main sources of new policies for the innovative, rapidly growing Welfare Department are neither local clientele demands nor shifting technology. They are the members of several professions, usually working in . . . universities, in private nonprofit welfare institutions, and in [other government agencies]' (p. 14).

That persons who are 'cosmopolitans' are more likely to adopt innovations than 'locals' has been well established for individuals outside the context of large formal organizations (Rogers, 1962, pp. 42, 44, 51, 228, 310). Carlson (1961) has shown that school superintendents recruited from outside the system are more likely to propose innovations than those recruited from inside. Few studies exist, however, relating the implementation of innovations within organizations to the professional or cosmopolitan character of the personnel. And as Benson (1961) has suggested, the great complexity of the instructional task and difficulty of supervising its execution have been two important reasons for the slowness of schools to innovate despite the professional orientation of the staffs.

2. It is easier (less costly) to increase an organization's capacity to generate new proposals than it is to increase its capacity to ratify any given proposal. The former requires adding new and somewhat differently motivated personnel, increasing the autonomy of sub-units, or increasing the number of different tasks being performed, but the latter requires assembling power (enhancing the supply of valued incentives at the executive's disposal). Furthermore, increasing the proposal-generating capacity of the organization may not only make adoption more difficult by increasing the number of wills to be concerted but may also make it harder by increasing all member's valuation of the status quo. For example, in an effort to get new ideas introduced into the organization, 'idea men', e.g. a Vice President for Innovation, might be hired. The cost of such a move may well be an increased resistance to change by other members, who feel threatened by this move; it seems to increase the probability of unpredictable changes, so members respond by taking whatever steps they can to reduce that probability, e.g. by bestirring themselves to point out to others the risks of change.

This hypothesis may help account for the finding by Mansfield (1961) that the productivity of expenditures on research and development is lower in the largest firms than in the medium-sized ones (holding the absolute amount of such expenditures constant). While it is true that for any given firm size bigger R & D expenditures lead to more significant inventions for the firm, firms whose R & D expenditures are a larger proportion of the firm's total budget are more inventive than firms in which the proportion is smaller. Mansfield suggests that may be due to 'looser controls and greater problems of supervision and co-ordination in a very large organization' (p. 15). In terms of the present theory, this apparent anomaly would be explained by the fact that the political influence within the firm of the R & D unit, and thus the ability of the unit to win acceptance for its proposed innovations (and for its research plans), increases the larger the share of the firm's resources it commands. Sheer size may produce more ideas, but insofar as innovation requires getting persons to accept the ideas, influence is necessary; the greater the *share* of the firm's resources spent by R & D, the less the diversity of the firm *as a whole*, and thus the less the influence required.

3. *Proponents of a particular innovation are not likely to perceive fully the difficulties that stand in the way of successful innovation* (Levitt, 1963). The proponent of a change is likely to see the benefits of the proposal in personal terms and the costs in organizational terms; everyone else is likely to see the benefits in organizational terms and the costs in personal terms. To the proponent the prospective benefits are (in most, though not all, cases) direct and easily conceived; the costs are remote, something 'the organization' will deal with. To organization members who will be affected by the change the costs to them are likely to be directly and immediately felt; the benefits are something that will accrue remotely to 'the organization'. The executive is the person who must discover whether there are any terms on which objections can be overcome; he is likely to be the only person (or persons, if it is a collective executive) to whom *both* costs *and* benefits are directly perceived in personal terms – success or failure of the innovation is ultimately his responsibility, and the effort to adopt it is inevitably his task.

4. *Many organizations will adopt no major innovation unless there is a 'crisis'* – an extreme change in conditions for which there is no adequate, programmed response. A crisis increases the probability that innovations will be ratified by increasing the cost to any member of opposing the ratification. If all members are persuaded that a crisis exists (if, for example, the firm cannot meet its payroll, or if the voluntary association is in danger of losing most if its members), then those who resist adopting the most favored innovation place themselves in the position of, in effect, favoring the death of the organization and therefore favoring the imposition of heavy costs on all other members. Further, a crisis leads members to devote themselves to *organizational* interests rather than to task interests; the diversifying influence of the task

structure is thereby temporarily set aside. Similarly, the crisis tends to eliminate the normal discrepancy between individual and organizational objectives, which it is the function of the incentive system to reconcile. The short-term value of organizationally controlled incentives increases because they are being threatened by the crisis; other incentives are presumably not in jeopardy, and, although their long-term value may remain unchanged, they are in effect discounted in the short term.

Empirical studies of the relationship between crisis and innovation have shown that an economic crisis led to faster rate of adoption of local industrial-development commissions in Iowa towns and that labor shortages led to a faster rate of adoption of a cotton-spinning innovation in English firms and to increased farm mechanization in Louisiana (studies summarized in Rogers, 1962, p. 125).

5. Organizations that rely primarily on intangible incentives (as do voluntary associations) will display in exaggerated form the contrary tendencies that determine the innovative capacity of all organizations. They will have a higher level of diversity and, as a consequence, the number of innovative proposals will be higher than in organizations that rely primarily on material inducements (such as business firms or government agencies). In the typical voluntary association, for example, the organization occupies a position of relatively low salience in the lives of most members; within the association, roles and tasks are less specialized, less clearly defined, and less demanding of a member's time than is typically the case in an organization that offers gainful employment to the member. As a result, demographic and personality variables, e.g. class, education, political affiliation, religion, marital status, become highly important as sources of diversity. The less structured the role, the less likely that individual behavior can be predicted on the basis of role occupancy; the personal characteristics of the member control behavior to a much greater extent, producing thereby a highly diverse organization. Furthermore, the organization has less opportunity to control behavior because it can only utilize incentives that are more general or indivisible than specific, money incentives (if a general incentive is given to one person, it must be given to all) and because such incentives are often not so highly valued as money incentives. Finally, the organization convenes *in meetings* rather than *around tasks*; in the nature of the case, the organization's business is everybody's business, and members are typically expected to make proposals.

All of these factors might be summarized by saying that a nonpecuniary organization must tolerate a great deal of foolishness if it is to survive. Whether it will adopt a greater or lesser proportion of these innovative proposals than will a pecuniary organization depends on the case. If the organization has a high salience for members (as, for example, the Socialist Party had for its members in the 1920s), a high value will be attached to the costs and benefits of new proposals and – lacking control over comparably highly-valued incentives with which to obtain compliance – the executive will find it exceptionally difficult to ratify any new proposal that is not widely supported (and few proposals *will* be widely supported). If, on the other hand, the association has a low salience for its members, few may care enough what the organization does to block any plausible proposal, although they may well care how they are regarded personally by other members, and thus actively make proposals.

Looked at in organizational rather than in individual terms, a voluntary association with broad, diffuse goals (typically associated with relatively low salience) will adapt more readily to environmental changes than will organizations with narrow, precisely stated goals (typically associated with high salience). Zald and Denton (1963) found that broad, diffuse goals contributed to the adaptability of the YMCA; Messinger (1955) suggested that the precise goals of the Townsend Movement inhibited its adaptability. In the former case the organization was able to offer a wide range of membership inducements without alienating any significant group of members; in the latter case, a change in inducements could only be accomplished at the cost of driving out one set of members in favor of another.

6. *Environmental changes that to the outside observer 'objectively' seem to 'require' innovation by the organization are likely to lead to such innovation only insofar as these changes alter the preferences of members for incentives (by changing present or prospective costs*

or benefits of participation in the organization). The many organizations that observers describe as having 'failed' to 'adapt' are often organizations that are being judged exclusively in terms of their goals (and then only in terms of their public, stated goals) and what is 'objectively' necessary to attain those goals. Whether a failure to attain a goal will lead to innovation depends on whether members regard attainment of (or work toward) that goal as a reward of participation. Many organizations, of course, do have such goals – we call them 'purposive' or 'ideological' organizations; many more do not.

The distinction between goal and incentive may help account for the oft-noted tendency of many business firms to sacrifice short-run profit maximization for other objectives. As William Baumol suggests, many – perhaps most – oligopolistic firms act as if they were trying to maximize sales revenue (or, perhaps more correctly, growth of sales revenue) subject to a minimum profit constraint (Baumol, 1959, 1962). Among the reasons for this is that the interests of management are often better served by a sales, rather than by a profit, objective; a favorable sales position produces more rewards for management than a favorable profit position, particularly if management has only a minor equity stake in the firm. Declining sales, whatever the profit level, may create a state of affairs in which certain members, such as distributors and salesmen working on commission, threaten to withdraw, in which firing rather than hiring becomes the order of the day, thus making personnel relations in the firm unpleasant, and in which management salaries may suffer, since salaries are empirically more closely correlated with the scale rather than with the profitability of operations (Roberts, 1959).

The goal–incentive distinction also suggests some crucial differences in the behavior of voluntary associations that help explain why some associations 'adapt' while others do not. Some associations are 'enrollment' organizations, while others are 'membership' organizations. The YMCA (Zald and Denton, 1963) and many adult education programs (Clark, 1956) are examples of the former; reform political clubs (Wilson, 1962) are examples of the latter. Organizations that sustain themselves by enrolling 'users' are sensitive to user tastes for programs. They view the organization as a source of divisible benefits; they use services rather than attend meetings, they feel free to select their satisfactions from among those offered, and they withdraw if nothing suits them. Membership organizations, on the other hand, offer largely indivisible benefits; members benefit from, and identify with, the whole organization rather than consume its services. It is the total character of the organization – particularly its goals and general associational attractiveness – that constitute its inducements. Under such circumstances the organization's executive finds it harder both to know the tastes of the members (they can vote, but only in elections, not in a service 'market') and to change goals and associational attributes to meet altered tastes. Thus, although the nominal goal of two organizations might be the same, e.g. serve the neighborhood, failure to attain the goal – or environmental changes that require new strategies to attain it – is more likely to lead to organizational innovation in the enrollment organization, in which the value of incentives are precisely measured against users' tastes, than in the membership organization, in which the value of incentives depends on members' *commitments* rather than tastes.

7. Decentralization can be regarded as a method for increasing the probability of ratification of new proposals by confining (in advance) their effect to certain sub-units. It is often regarded as a means of increasing efficiency (i.e. the ratio of valued output to valued input), and, of course, that is frequently the case; but it can just as easily be viewed as a way of reducing the obstacles to ratification without seriously increasing the risk. By decentralizing an organization, that is, by giving to sub-units a high degree of autonomy in the control of their own incentive and task structures, the organization as a whole reduces the number of wills that must be concerted before a proposal generated within the sub-unit can be adopted. A sub-unit can ratify a proposal that would be smothered if it had to compete with all proposals from all sub-units. There is a cost to such decentralization of course: the parent organization, by increasing the autonomy of sub-units, may make it more difficult for it to manage these sub-units with respect to those matters over which the parent organization retains control. In addition, only certain kinds of organizations – generally those that have tasks and objectives that can be unambiguously specified and measured – can risk extensive decentralization. If sub-unit performance cannot be precisely assessed, its behavior cannot be controlled and thus kept consistent with overall objectives.

The decentralization of the YMCA, according to Zald and Denton (1963), facilitated the adoption of innovations by various local units before other, apparently similar, units were even aware of the need for such changes. The National Foundation, on the other hand, was sufficiently centralized so that, according to Sills (1957), the *entire* organization was able to innovate quickly in response to a threat to its very existence even though no sub-unit had previously experimented with such changes.

8. *The extent to which 'participative management' will stimulate the production of proposals or facilitate the adoption and implementation of innovations will depend upon, among other things, the extent to which the decision-making group itself becomes a highly valued source of incentives and the extent to which these group-based incentives are congruent with those offered by the larger organization.* The great theoretical importance attached by certain students of organization to group decision-making, participative management, and power equalization in organizations (especially business firms) stands in rather sharp contrast to the meager empirically verified results of the application of such theories. Strauss (1963) and Bennis (1963), summarizing the literature on this approach, conclude that it is by no means clear how likely or under what circumstances participation will improve worker satisfaction, increase productivity, or stimulate organizational innovation.

Substituting collegial for hierarchical methods of making decisions is widely advocated, yet there has been little effort to specify the organizational conditions under which collegiality will facilitate innovation; furthermore, few clear data have been produced to establish a relationship between the method by which a change is developed and improvement in the performance of the individual or the organization (Bennis, 1963, p. 159). Such devices as 'T-group' training conducted under laboratory conditions often change the behavior of the subjects of the experiment, but we cannot be certain that this altered behavior persists after the subjects return to the organization or, if it persists, that it facilitates organizational change. Shepard's evaluation of his work with the Esso Company suggests that the laboratory experience was 'slightly more helpful than useless' in changing the organization (Bennis, 1963). The experiment of Morse and Reimer (1956) was one of the few done in an organization rather than in the laboratory. While the group of clerical employees subjected to participatory supervision seemed to manifest more worker satisfaction, the group exposed to hierarchical supervision was the more productive. Likert (1961), on the other hand, indicates some evidence favoring the belief that organizational as well as personal benefits flow from participation.

On the basis of the theory of innovation presented here, one would expect a well-established participative management group would propose a larger number of innovations than isolated individuals working in a hierarchy in which innovative suggestions are rewarded by the group. In short, the organization has been made more complex by increasing the diversity of sources of incentives. One would also expect, however, that the probability of the adoption (including implementation) of any given proposal would depend on (a) whether the incentives offered by the decision-making group were valued sufficiently to induce members to alter customary behavior in order to obtain them and (b) whether the behavior induced by group incentives was compatible with that required by organizational incentives. As critics of the participative management movement point out, not everyone has the same taste for collegial decision-making and the opportunity it supposedly affords for cooperation, problem-solving, and 'self-actualization'. Some persons have a taste for routine, deference, power, and certainty or a desire to reserve for non-organizational settings their self-expression.

That the effect of participative management on organizational change depends on member preferences for certain incentives is suggested by Strauss's explanation (1963, p. 67) of the difference between the results of the Harwood and Norway experiments. In the Harwood case (Coch and French, 1948) participation led to higher productivity because the opportunity to participate was highly valued by low-status rural female employees; participation did not lead to productivity increases in Norway (French, Israel and Dagfinn, 1960) because such inducements had a much lower value for the more sophisticated urbanized male workers.

Participation in the simplest case may reduce resistance to planned change insofar as it provides an opportunity whereby certain *dis*-incentives can be eliminated or reduced (by giving members a chance to talk out their grievances, discharge generalized resentment, and partially overcome feelings of inferior status). Whether participation can go much further cannot be predicted in advance for all cases, because too much depends on preferences for incentives. The fact that the theory of participative management, seen from the present theoretical viewpoint, cannot lead to unique predictions about outcomes might be grounds for qualifying some of the claims made on its behalf. It is worth remembering that informal work groups that *restrict* production and enforce quotas are also examples of a kind of participative management.

9. *Innovative proposals will be more frequent in organizations in which a high degree of uncertainty governs the members' expectation of rewards.* If incentives are not routinely received for the performance of specified acts, there will be a tendency for members either to quit the organization (having a low taste for risk and uncertainty) or to bid competitively with one another for a share of available incentives by advancing proposals. This pattern of management has been institutionalized, as Burns and Stalker (1961) point out, in certain British electronics firms. Committee management and group decision-making were instituted in the first place to deal with a special organizational environment – one characterized by a high rate of technological invention, a high level of competition, and the domination of a single, unpredictable buyer (the government). These electronics firms attempted to deal with their highly uncertain environment by organizing themselves in such a way as to maximize the flow of information, extend the search for alternatives, and develop a generalized commitment on the part of all members to the survival of the firm. The cost of this management system is a high degree of personal insecurity, because members have no clear conception of their duties, status, authority or prospects. These costs must be met by the incentive system in some way. In this case one would

expect the firm to stress that the unstructured situation eliminates seniority barriers to advancement, to distribute widely such intangible gratifications as titles and opportunities for access to the president, and to emphasize the importance of the work to the scientific community and to the nation as a whole. Once instituted, these arrangements (a highly complex task structure and incentive system) could be expected to increase markedly the number of innovative proposals but reduce (whether by a corresponding amount is not clear) the ability of the organization to win consent for any single proposal.

Burns and Stalker draw the contrast of certain rayon textile firms (also in Great Britain) whose environment was much more stable (they dealt with a large number of small buyers with predictable tastes) and who could consequently organize themselves along more traditional, hierarchical lines with little reliance on non-monetary incentives and a heavy emphasis on highly specific tasks.

10. *To the extent that members of a society attach a high value to extra-organizational, particularly non-material, incentives, there will be an increased number of inventions, i.e. proposals, but a decreased probability of organizational innovation.* This may be an important policy implication of the foregoing analysis. In an affluent society in which a high standard of living is coupled with government measures that tend to equalize income (a steeply progressive income tax) and to prevent citizens from receiving private gain for performing public tasks (the elimination of political patronage, for example), organizations – especially those that act in the public sphere – may find themselves relying on incentives that stimulate invention but hamper the adoption of innovations. As money payments diminish in value (at the margin) and non-money payments increase in value, the organization will rely more and more on the latter. This will not only make life more difficult for the social scientist (behavior is harder to predict unambiguously when unmeasurable objectives such as prestige, power and ideology are being sought), but it will also weaken the influence of organization executives, partly because non-material rewards are less specific in their effect and partly because they are harder to bring under the control of the organization.

This may account for the apparently paradoxical fact that communities with high proportions of persons who individually favor such innovations as fluoridation and urban renewal are also communities with the lowest rates of adoption of such proposals (Hawley, 1963; Pinard, 1963). Banfield and Wilson (1963) have suggested that since the preference for such controversial innovations is higher among middle-class than among lower-class individuals and that since communities with a high proportion of middle-class citizens are more likely to be governed in accordance with the 'good government' ideal, the inability to translate personal preferences into public policy may be the result of the weakness of the political structure. The political and governmental arrangements characteristic of middle-class communities tend to emphasize honesty, efficiency and impartiality but are often incapable of assembling the amounts of influence necessary to adopt a controversial innovation. Perhaps this is because a preoccupation with procedural proprieties makes it impossible for the government to offer specific, material incentives to politicians and voters in order to permit the centralization of influence sufficient to ratify any but generally accepted proposals.

To the extent that innovation involves inter-organizational relations (such as relations between political parties and interest groups), the changes described in the preceding paragraph may make such relations less stable as executives find it increasingly difficult to control the behavior of members and thus to deliver on commitments made to other organizations. Such considerations may in turn have the profoundest implications for social change generally, and not simply for innovation within organizations.

References

BANFIELD, E. C. (1961), *Political Influence*, Free Press.
BANFIELD, E. C., and WILSON, J. Q. (1963), *City Politics*, Harvard University Press.
BAUMOL, W. J. (1959), *Business Behavior, Value and Growth*, Macmillan.
BAUMOL, W. J. (1962), 'On the theory of expansion of the firm', *American Economic Review*, vol. 52, pp. 1078–87.
BENNIS, W. G. (1963), 'A new role for the behavioral sciences: effecting organizational change', *Administrative Science Quarterly*, September, vol. 8, pp. 125–65.

BENSON, C. S. (1961), *The Economics of Public Education*, Houghton Mifflin.

BLAU, P. M. (1955), *The Dynamics of Bureaucracy*, University of Chicago Press.

BLAU, P. M., and SCOTT, R. M. (1962), *Formal Organizations*, Chandler.

BROWN, W. H. (1957), 'Innovation in the machine tool industry', *Quarterly Journal of Economics*, vol. 71, pp. 406–25.

BROWNING, R. P. (1963), 'Innovative and non-innovative decision processes in government budgeting', paper read before the annual meeting of the *American Political Science Association*, September.

BURNS, T. and STALKER, G. M. (1961), *The Management of Innovation*, Tavistock.

CARLSON, R. O. (1961), 'Succession and performance among school superintendents', *Administrative Science Quarterly*, vol. 6, pp. 210–27.

CLARK, B. R. (1956), *Adult Education in Transition*, University of California Press.

CLARK, P. B. (1961), 'The business corporation as a political order', paper read before the annual meeting of the *American Political Science Association*, September.

CLARK, P. B., and WILSON, J. Q. (1961), 'Incentive systems: a theory of organization', *Administrative Science Quarterly*, vol. 6, pp. 129–66.

COCH, L., and FRENCH, J. R. P. (1948), 'Overcoming resistance to change', *Human Relations*, vol. 1, pp. 512–32.

FELLNER, W. (1951), 'The influence of market structure on technological progress', *Quarterly Journal of Economics*, vol. 65, pp. 556–77.

FRENCH, J. R. P., ISRAEL, J., and DAGFINN, A. (1960), 'An experiment in participation in a Swedish factory', *Human Relations*, vol. 13, pp. 3–19.

GOULDNER, A. W. (1958), 'Cosmopolitans and locals: toward an analysis of latent social roles', *Administrative Science Quarterly*, vol. 2, pp. 281–306 and 444–80.

HAWLEY, A. H. (1963), 'Community power and urban renewal success', *American Journal of Sociology*, vol. 68, pp. 422–531.

HILL, S. E., and HARBISON, F. (1959), *Manpower and Innovation in American Industry*, Princeton University Press.

HOMANS, G. C. (1961), *Social Behavior: Its Elementary Forms*, Harcourt, Brace & World.

LEVITT, T. (1963), 'Creativity is not enough', *Harvard Business Review*, May–June, pp. 72–3.

LIKERT, R. (1961), *New Patterns of Management*, McGraw-Hill.

MACLAUREN, W. R. (1950), 'The process of technological innovation' *American Economic Review*, no. 40, pp. 90–112.

MANSFIELD, E. (1961), 'Technical change and the rate of imitation', *Econometrica*, no. 29, pp. 741–66.

MANSFIELD, E. (1963), 'The speed of response of firms to new techniques', *Quarterly Journal of Economics*, no. 77, pp. 290–311.

MANSFIELD, E. (n.d.), 'The expenditures of the firm on research and development', working paper prepared at the Graduate School of Industrial Administration, *Carnegie Institute of Technology*.

MARCH, J. G., and SIMON, H. A. (1958), *Organizations*, Wiley.

MESSINGER, S. L. (1955), 'Organizational transformation: a case study of a declining social movement', *Administrative Science Quarterly*, no. 20, pp. 3–10.

MOORE, W. E. (1960), 'A reconsideration of theories of social change' *Administrative Science Quarterly*, no. 25, pp. 810–18.

MORSE, N. C., and REIMER, E. (1956), 'The experimental change of a major organizational variable', *Journal of Abnormal and Social Psychology*, no. 52, pp. 120–29.

PHILLIPS, A. (1956), 'Concentration, scale and technological change in selected manufacturing industries, 1899–1936', *Journal of Industrial Economics*, no. 4, pp. 179–93.

PINARD, M. (1963), 'Structural attachments and political support in urban politics: the case of the fluoridation referendums', *American Journal of Sociology*, no. 68, pp. 513–26.

ROBERTS, D. R. (1959), *Executive Compensation*, Free Press.

ROGERS, E. M. (1962), *Diffusion of Innovations*, Free Press.

SAYRE, W. S., and KAUFMAN, H. (1961), *Governing New York City*, Russell Sage Foundation.

SILLS, D. L. (1957), *The Volunteers*, Free Press.

SOFER, C. (1961), *Organizations From Within*, Tavistock.

STINCHCOMBE, A. L. (1960), 'The sociology of organization and the theory of the firm', *Pacific Sociological Review*, vol. 3, no. 2, pp. 75–82.

STRAUSS, G. (1963), 'Some notes on power equalization', in H. J. Leavitt (ed.), *The Social Science of Organizations*, Prentice-Hall.

WILSON, J. Q. (1962), *The Amateur Democrat*, University of Chicago Press.

ZALD, M. N., and DENTON, P. (1963), 'The YMCA: from evangelism to general service', *Administrative Science Quarterly*, no. 8, pp. 214–34.

Part Four
The Practice of Planned Organizational Change

We need greater awareness of the diagnostic 'maps' which we
characteristically use in developing strategies for change and
these should be continually informed by theories and concepts
which draw attention to the important, new problems. Reading
10 by Lorsch and Lawrence presents such a theory – the
differentiation–integration model – which focuses on the
problem of the interaction between the organization and its
environment.

For our purposes, a significant aspect of the 'differentiation–
integration model' is its capacity for linking the problem of
planned organizational change with the management of conflict.
Elsewhere, for example, the authors have stated:

This model also points to another set of variables which are
important – the behavior patterns used to manage intergroup
conflict. . . . Our work indicates that the pattern of behavior which
leads to effective conflict resolution varies in certain respects
depending upon environmental demands, and in other respects is
the same regardless of variations in environmental demands. . . . If
conflict is to be managed effectively, this influence must be
concentrated at the point in the various group hierarchies where the
knowledge to reach such decisions exists. Obviously, this will vary
depending upon the certainty of information in various parts of a
particular environment (Lawrence and Lorsch, pp. 13–14).

Similarly, we need to be more explicit about our 'theories of
changing'. Such 'theories' involve the assumptions made about
key leverage points for change in the organization. Leavitt
(1964), for example, has developed a typology of three such
leverages: structure, technology and people; he has been

particularly critical of the limiting assumptions of the latter, which has become known as the power-equalization strategy. Moreover, recent empirical work has demonstrated the interdependence of the three leverage points. Joan Woodward's studies, which have been mentioned at several points, have shown the dependence of structure on technology. And Fiedler's exhaustive studies of work teams have shown the consistent dependence of supervisory style (a 'people' leverage) on the nature of the task, leading him to advocate the change aphorism: 'Engineer the job to fit the manager' (see Fiedler, 1965, 1967). Prescriptively, this means that it is incumbent on the manager to be as aware as possible of the causal linkages he implicitly makes among these kinds of leverages. Whyte's readings in Part Three discussed the significance of what might be termed our implicit theories of organization; similarly, we have and use implicit theories of changing organizations.

Both the Terreberry (in Part Two) and Lawrence and Lorsch papers describe the emerging importance of an organization–environment perspective on the management of change. Reading 11 by Clark and Krone develops a model for relating this to (a) Vickers's concept of 'the appreciative system' of the manager – the image of the organization and environment available to him; and (b) those approaches to organization development aimed at enhancing communication processes and the utilization of task groups for promoting individual growth. The goals of the 'theory of practice' described in this article include expansion of the manager's 'environmental realities' and the way he values them, and the redesign of organization structure so that it can effectively influence these environmental realities in valued directions.

Clark and Krone are refreshing in their explicitness about the values which have guided the development of what they term 'open-systems consultation'. This strategy involves an effort to integrate humanistic assumptions about man-in-organization[1] with the belief that a healthy organization is one able to proactively engage all facets of its environment – physical, technological, social and biological.

1. For further discussion of this concept, see Tannenbaum and Davis (1969) and Harman (1969).

To conclude this section, Katz and Kahn (Reading 12) elaborate the criticism that individual, people oriented approaches to organizational change often fail to account for the systemic properties of organization and confuse changing individuals with changing organizations. In contrast, they comment positively on several studies, which have become known as *socio-technical* strategies, where the systemic linkages between tasks, roles and interpersonal relationships provide the basis for a 'theory of changing'.

One of the guiding assumptions in the design of this collection of readings has been that the effective management of change requires an understanding of the major forces of change shaping the environment of the organization. The open systems concept developed by Katz and Kahn underscores the importance of cultivating this awareness. In concluding their essay, they state: 'We would predict . . . that in the absence of external changes, organizations are likely to be reformed from within in limited ways. More drastic or revolutionary changes are initiated or made possible by external forces.'

References

FIEDLER, F. (1965), 'Engineer the job to fit the manager', *Harvard Business Review*, Sept./Oct.

FIEDLER, F. (1967), *A Contingency Theory of Leadership*, McGraw-Hill.

HARMAN, W. W. (1969), 'The new Copernican revolution', *Stanford Today*, Winter, series 2, no. 1.

LAWRENCE, P., and LORSCH, J. W. (1969), *Developing Organizations*, Addison-Wesley.

LEAVITT H. (1964), 'Individual, structural and technical approaches to organizational change', in W. Cooper *et. al* (ed.), *New Perspectives in Organization Theory*, Wiley, pp. 55–70; this paper is available in Vroom (ed.), (1970), *Management and Motivation*, Penguin Books.

TANNENBAUM, R., and DAVIS, S. (1969), 'Values, man and organizations', *Industrial Management Review*, vol. 10, no. 2.

10 J. W. Lorsch and P. Lawrence

The Diagnosis of Organizational Problems

J. W. Lorsch and P. Lawrence, 'The diagnosis of organizational
problems', in W. G. Bennis, K. Benne and R. Chin, *Dynamics of Planned
Change*, Holt, Rinehart & Winston, 1968, pp. 468–78.

The need for diagnostic models

In this paper we would like to discuss an approach to organizational change which puts considerable weight on the diagnosis of organizational problems prior to the change effort. As a first step in this discussion, it is necessary to examine the need for diagnosis of organizational problems and some of the current thinking about diagnosis.

There is no doubt that change agents have various analytic models of organizations and of how to alter behavior in them. Their analytic schemes are both implicit and explicit, but it seems that there has been an increasing attempt to make them more explicit and particularly to gain an increased understanding of the change process. An interesting example of this trend is the recent *Harvard Business Review* article by Blake and Mouton, Barnes and Greiner (1964). The authors describe an attempt to systematically investigate and evaluate one of the 'Managerial Grid' organizational development programs. While it is possible to be critical or skeptical on specific grounds about this and other attempts to describe and understand organizational change, the fact remains that these attempts are being made with the best methods currently available and the eventual payout should be improved understanding of the dynamics of the change process.[1] These studies are mentioned, not as a prelude to discussing their particular strengths and weaknesses, but rather to indicate that the focus of much of the current work in the area of organizational change is toward an understanding of the change process itself. Much less attention is being devoted to the development of

1. For example, Seashore and Bowers (1963).

analytic models which could be useful in diagnosing organizational problems prior to the change effort.

This is not to suggest that change agents do not have some implicit analytic model in mind. Nor are we suggesting that they do not undertake a diagnosis before beginning a development or a change program. In fact, as Greiner has pointed out, one characteristic of effective change efforts is the fact that some attempt, even though limited, had been made to gather data about organizational problems before the change effort was attempted (Greiner, 1965). Apparently, this helps to create an awareness of the need for change and often provides the motivation to begin the effort. It therefore seems to us that there is a need for some diagnosis and we now want to examine in more detail what these diagnostic steps usually entail and how the approach we have been using may differ from other attempts at diagnosis.

There are two aspects to the diagnosis of organizational problems: first the question of what data is gathered, and second the manner in which the data is interpreted and presented to members of the organization. The diagnostic data-gathering preceding change efforts seems to be typically carried out through interviews with a few significant managers at various levels of the organization. Less frequently, more systematic and thorough attempts have been made to gather data through the use of surveys (Seashore and Bowers, 1963). One limitation of these diagnostic attempts as usually practiced is that they tend to be somewhat cursory and often tend to be conducted in spite of the fact that the action program has already been well planned in advance by the change agent. A second problem is that the change agent during the diagnostic phase is often more concerned with understanding and improving his relationship to the client organization than he is with understanding specific organizational problems. For example Seashore and Bowers indicate that the reason they decided to conduct their diagnostic survey was 'to introduce a note of calmness and realism, while still advancing the intended work'. They decided on this diagnostic step to signal to the organization's membership what the project was all about and thus to strengthen their relationship with the client. While this is important, it tends to support the view that insufficient attention is given to gathering data about organizational problems, prior to planning the change program.

Turning to the second aspect of diagnosis – the manner in which the data are presented and interpreted to members of the organization – this is generally accomplished in one of two ways. First, the raw data are discussed with top management, who are asked to make the diagnosis within their own framework; or second, the change agent may present his own diagnosis without making his model for analysing organizational behavior explicit. The problem with the first approach is that management is limited by its own framework and it tends to see each problem separately, failing at times to recognize the interrelationship between problems and what may lie behind them. The second approach has inherent in it the problems of communication in getting management to see why the change agent sees the problems the way he does. One example of this problem is cited by Rice (1958) when he describes the difficulties in getting management to understand his diagnosis and the necessity for making his conceptual scheme more explicit.

A more general difficulty with either of these approaches derives from the close relationship between diagnosis and action. The action which is taken cannot be separated from the diagnosis made. Yet in many of the current change efforts, the emphasis seems to be on action and there tends to be a general action program which the change agent will apply to any organization regardless of its specific problems. For example, Blake has his well conceived action program based on the management grid which he is applying to many organizations, and Seashore and Bowers and their associates at Michigan had designed an action program for the Banner organization based on participative management prior to the diagnosis of any specific problems. In thinking about these matters, we have concluded that if more weight were given to prior diagnosis before planning a change program, the action program could be better designed for the specific needs of the particular situation.

It is sometimes argued that diagnostic analysis is overdone. It is undoubtedly true that the request for 'further study' can be a dodge to delay needed action in organizational problems. This is most apt to happen, however, when the diagnostic effort is, in effect, a general fishing expedition guided neither by a well developed conceptual framework or by a clear problem focus. The fact that diagnostic work is sometimes done in a weak and ineffective manner should not lead to a general short-circuiting of this step. Quality diagnostic work leads toward action and not away from it.

Recognizing the limitations of current diagnostic efforts and the relative absence of change attempts made on the basis of analytic models which were outlined to members of the organization, we have in a recent change effort placed much more weight on a careful diagnostic study and then have discussed in considerable detail both our analytic framework and the data collected.

Our general approach, then, has been to spend considerable time and effort through the use of questionnaires and a systematic interviewing program in gathering data to be analysed in terms of a conceptual framework developed in our research efforts.[2] Having collected and analysed this data we have then educated management to our conceptual scheme and have fed the data back to them, working through with them the meanings and the limitations of the data. The managers themselves have worked out whatever structural changes seemed required and have collaborated with us in the formulation of specific development programs to alleviate specific reorganizational problems. In the balance of this paper we will describe briefly the analytic framework we have used, some of the problems identified in this particular organization and some of the resulting change steps.

The differentiation and integration model

At the outset of describing this analytic scheme, it is important to stress that it has been developed primarily for the study and understanding of intergroup or interdepartmental issues in organizations, and it is in designing change programs aimed at this general class of problem that it has been useful. It is based on a set of ideas in the social sciences which go back to Herbert Spencer (1904, p. 56) and probably beyond, differentiation and integration. It is not either of these concepts, by themselves, but the

2. For a detailed explanation of this conceptual scheme, see Lawrence and Lorsch (1967).

intriguing interrelationship between them that is important. Any complex social system, which is the basic way we conceive of an organization, is made up of differentiated parts, the activities of which must be integrated into a unified effort if the organization is to cope effectively with its environment. In the case of business firms, the differentiated parts are the major departments. In the specific case of the organizations in this change effort, they consisted of the sales, production, research and development units involved in the innovation of products, which was the major external issue confronting these particular organizations. (The change program we shall describe here actually involved two unrelated product organizations and we shall treat each of these as a separate entity.)

The functional units in these organizations were each required to cope with quite distinct segments of the organization's environment – sales with the market, research with the scientific environment, etc. They each performed different tasks and in relation to these tasks the units developed distinct attributes. The conceptual scheme which we have been developing identifies four of these characteristics, the time orientation of members, the interpersonal orientation of members, and the unit's internal formal structure. As the organizational units engage in their separate tasks they become differentiated along these four dimensions. For example, our scheme hypothesizes and our findings confirm that a research laboratory has a low degree of structure (few rules, broad spans of control, few levels in the hierarchy, long time spans of reviews, and very general reviews). It has members whose primary goal orientation is toward science, whose primary time orientation is toward longer term matters and who mildly prefer a task oriented interpersonal style over a relationship oriented style. On the other hand a production unit has high structure, and personnel whose goal orientation is toward production costs and processing problems; whose time orientation is toward immediate problems; and whose interpersonal orientation is more strongly task oriented.

Basically what this way of looking at organizations suggests is that each of these units is different along these (and perhaps other) dimensions, but they are differentiated from each other for good and proper reasons – because they are working on quite different tasks. For them to perform their individual tasks, they must be differentiated. The fly in the ointment, however, is the fact that these differences between units tend to be related to the problems of achieving effective integration. Our data indicate that the more different any pair of units in an organization are along these dimensions, the more problems are experienced in achieving collaboration between them. Thus two units which are quite similar in these organizations and in structure will achieve effective integration with each other while units which have quite different orientations and structures will have difficulty in achieving collaboration with each other. Differentiation is thus a two-edged sword – it is important for individual unit performance, but can be costly in achieving coordinated total performance.

While the processes of differentiation and integration seem to be basically antagonistic between pairs of units within one organization, we have found in comparing several organizations that an organization can achieve both the high differentiation required for individual unit performance and the effective integration required for effective total organizational performance. The key to the achievement of both high differentiation and integration seems to reside in the development of what we have conceptually identified as integrative devices, which function effectively. These integrative devices can be managers in linking roles, a separate departmental entity which has a coordinating function, or cross functional committees which are intended to facilitate the resolution of conflict and decision making between functional units.

In studying the processes of differentiation and integration in organizations we have identified some variables which seem to be related to the effectiveness of these integrative devices. For example integrating departments, whether they be called new products, development, marketing, etc., seem to be effective when their members have task, time and interpersonal orientations as well as structures which are at some intermediate point between the units they are linking. If an integrative department is linking a sales and a research unit we have found that it will be most effective if its members do not have either a long-term orientation, as in research, or a short-term orientation, as in sales, but instead have a balanced time orientation. The same factor seems to hold for goals and interpersonal orientations and for structure. Similarly, we have identified some factors which seem to be related to the effectiveness of integrating committees. The most important of these seems to be the presence of norms for resolving conflict which sanction what Blake would call a 9.9 approach, that is, a problem-solving confrontation of conflict rather than a win–lose or avoidance mode (Blake and Mouton, 1964).

This brief description of some of the factors influencing the performance of integrative devices and of the complex inter-relationship between the processes of differentiation and integration should give some understanding of the conceptual framework we are using and perhaps a crude idea of the type of data we attempt to collect. It can be concluded by pointing out that our work suggests that effective organizational performance is related to the presence of both the differentiation and integration that are required by the characteristics of their immediate environment. In the particular industry in which we have been conducting our activities, the nature of the external environment dictates that high differentiation and high integration are required for effective performance. What this pattern will look like in other industries is something we have also investigated and on which we will subsequently report.

Some problems identified and action steps taken

Having quickly laid out the concepts we have utilized in our diagnostic work, it may now be useful to add some life to them by demonstrating briefly how we have identified some specific problems in the organizations with which we have been consulting, and what action steps have been taken. The problems upon which we will focus are representative of an interrelated set of differentiation and integration issues identified in each of the two organizations, and were presented to the managers involved by comparing these two organizations with each other and with a third more effective organization in the same corporate structure which we had studied earlier.

In one of the organizations there were two research sub-units, one of which theoretically was supposed to be engaged in fundamental long-range research and the other of which was supposed to be an applied shorter range operation. The data which we collected indicated two things. First, that the research units were achieving extremely poor integration as compared to the effective organization. There were frequent conflicts between them and according to members of the organization their ability to achieve unity of effort with each other was limited. Second, we found that while these laboratories were highly differentiated in their structural and interpersonal attributes, they were quite similar in time and task orientations. In effect both laboratories seemed to be trying to perform essentially the same tasks with quite different structures and interpersonal orientations. Our interviewing also indicated to us that members of these laboratories often saw each other as competitors, rather than potential collaborators who were performing a different phase of the organization's total task.

Armed with this and similar data about other problems from questionnaires and interviews, we sat down with the teams of top managers responsible for all the functional activities related to this group of products. We first spent some time discussing our conceptual scheme and then relating these data to it. We explained that the high differentiation in interpersonal and structural attributes was related to the problems of achieving integration, but that the fact the units were occupying the same task and time space seemed to be intensifying the difficulties in achieving collaboration. In this discussion the managers recognized that two things were needed: first, a clearer differentiation of the role of the laboratories, and second, the development of improved integrative devices.

Management's reaction to this presentation and discussion was fairly typical of what we found in both organizations. The data supported their intuitive hunches but also clarified the factors underlying the problem. After considerable discussion about potential action steps, in which we took a minor role, the managers decided as a first step to begin a series of discussions with laboratory personnel and among themselves to clarify the tasks they wanted each unit to perform. Once these discussions have been concluded we will work with them in developing a tailored training program to sharpen the integrative process.

A problem which appeared similar on the surface can be used as an example from the second organization with which we were working. Here the two laboratory units were finding great difficulty in working with the coordinating unit. They complained that the coordinating unit was a 'filter' which closed up and inhibited the flow of ideas. The data collected indicated that the coordinating unit was overly concerned with immediate customer problems rather than having the balanced outlook that effective coordinating units developed. In discussing this with the team of managers responsible for this product group, it became apparent that the short-term customer orientation of the coordinating unit was the result of environmental pressure it felt to provide frequent and detailed service to customers. The managers in this instance also saw the data as supporting their hunches about their problems, but also saw that there was no way, given the competitive situation, to redesign the task of the coordinating unit. After considerable discussion of this issue both the managers and we saw the need for a training program which would have as its objective a greater awareness on the part of researchers and coordinators of the differences in their ways of thinking, so they would appreciate these differences and develop a greater tolerance for them and greater skill at resolving conflict caused by their different ways of thinking. On the basis of this plans were made for a training program.

As a first step in this brief training effort we fed back the same data to the participants as we had to the managers. Again, as with the managers, the data were received as being congruent with the experience of the scientists and coordinators in the session. But we had designed the training to move beyond this and to give the participants some appreciation of the way their concrete actions and behavior patterns affected persons in other departments and also to provide each group with some understanding of the task realities which were influencing the other group to have a differentiated behavior pattern. To accomplish this we divided the participants into three-way teams with representatives from each of the laboratories and the coordinating department. Each of these groups then met for four sessions. The first session was devoted to each man describing his own work activities and the factors that gave him the most satisfaction and the most dissatisfaction with his job. The second and third sessions were used for the participants to discuss the activities and behavior of other units which most facilitated and most blocked performance in their own groups. Out of these discussions the long-range researchers began to see what pressures the coordinators were operating under as they fought customer fires, and the co-ordinators literally blinked in disbelief as they realized that the scientists actually worked for months or years on a single project without any concrete feedback. Thus researchers became aware of why the coordinators were not able to drop everything and discuss their problems and the coordinators recognized that some of the decisions which they made in a very few minutes with little fore-thought could influence the work of an individual researcher for several months or years.

At this stage of the program an awareness of the differences between these groups had been created and hopefully some appreciation of the importance of these differences had developed. The fourth, and final, session was devoted to a discussion of how these differences were characteristically resolved and some of the factors underlying these modes of resolving conflicts. The funda-mental researchers, for example, began to recognize that they had characteristically resolved conflict by smoothing it over. When they saw a problem they retired to their laboratories and waited. The coordinators, on the other hand, tended to be more aggres-sive, often forcing the more compliant researchers to alter courses.

The immediate response to this session was gratifying, since the participants recognized its relevance to their jobs and felt it had altered their perception of members of other units. While it is much too soon to make any final claims of success, a preliminary survey taken six months after the training indicates that in general the training and feedback sessions had many of the intended consequences. Members reported to an in-house behavioral scientist, who was not involved in the change program, that they were able to work more effectively together on inter-departmental teams.

One interesting exception to these generally positive results is the case of the fundamental research scientists. They reported a general worsening of relations with other units, particularly with the coordinators. The reason for this, which was developed in interviews, was that as a result of these training sessions these scientists felt that the coordinating personnel were going to take some concrete steps to improve collaboration with them. When this did not happen, apparently because of continuing time pressures with the coordinators, the researchers became further antagonized. This suggests that one danger of any such change effort is the raising of expectations which cannot be satisfied. In any case, these additional data have been fed back to the co-ordinating group and further efforts are being made to work through this problem.

This brief report of progress is not presented as a final evaluation of this change effort, but rather to indicate our continuing concern throughout the change effort of gathering data about the state of the organization as a guide to future change steps. It is consistent with our thesis that a change effort will be most successful if it is based on a careful diagnosis of the organization's problem.

Conclusions

We would now like to step back to look at what we have been trying to accomplish – first by using this particular conceptual scheme, and second by generally placing more emphasis on diagnosis. In doing this, it is most important to recognize that our evidence about whether we have succeeded, while encouraging, is still tentative and only suggestive.

First, looking at the value of this particular scheme, it enables us to focus not on just the problems of developing more effective integration, but also on the relationship between integration and differentiation, and the necessity for differentiation in achieving effective task performance. The change attempts described by Blake, Argyris and others place emphasis on the development of mutual trust, openness, and problem solving, all of which are important to facilitate organizational integration, but these change efforts may not be directed at the important problems of achieving clear differentiation so that units can work at their separate primary tasks (Blake, Mouton, Barnes and Greiner, 1964, and Argyris, 1964). The use of this conceptual scheme has enabled us to focus on both of these problems and to help in the development of an action program aimed at both issues.

Turning to the more general value of placing greater emphasis on diagnosis, it has permitted us to develop a more 'tailored' approach to organizational change and development. As the examples cited demonstrated, we have attempted to design interventions which fit the particular problems of the organization, rather than relying on a general program aimed at influencing behavior throughout the organization. Obviously this has cost less in time and money for the organization, but more important, it provides strong guidance as to whether an educational or a structural intervention is more appropriate as a first step in the change process. Regardless of which of these intervention steps is taken first, it can, and in most instances probably should, be followed up with the other. If the first step is to be an educational one, the data can guide the design of a program that can present the participants with an educational experience which hopefully has some immediate relevance to problems they are encountering in their daily experience, and this provides them with more rewards for altering their existing behavior patterns. This is especially likely if the development program is followed or preceded by appropriate attention to task and structural redesign that grows out of the same diagnosis.

The emphasis on prior diagnosis also presents managers with some hard data which confirm or challenge their hunches. Based on these interpreted data, they can take charge of their own programs of actions. We have so far avoided making detailed recommendations to the management about either structural changes or educational change programs. Instead we have made ourselves available as resource people as the management group discussed the problem. Our limited experience seems to suggest that this enabled managers to engage these problems, become involved with them and to attempt to solve them. This experience is supported by Floyd Mann's view that, 'Change processes organized around objective new social facts about one's own organizational situation have more force for change than those organized around general principles about human behavior' (Mann, 1962).

In this particular case we have been fortunate that we had made a comparative diagnosis of three separate organizational elements, one of which was outstanding in performance. The presence of this example provided the managers with a concrete comparison, which they could examine in relation to our conceptual scheme and our data. It presented a model of the desirable which was not an abstraction, but a real going concern. Our experience coupled with Dunnington's report of a similar experience in changing behavior in several IBM plants suggests that this is an important leverage point to be utilized whenever possible.[4] But the use of these real organizational models is not possible unless a thorough diagnostic study has been conducted.

By emphasizing diagnosis and data feedback, we have also left the management group with a new kit of tools which they can continue to apply to similar problems in the future. Too often, the change agent takes his conceptual scheme with him when he leaves and the organization must seek help for each new set of problems. It is our hope that by making our conceptual scheme explicit and by helping the managers to work with it, we have given them a new cognitive map to think about future organizational issues.

4. R. Dunnington in a talk before the MBA students at the Harvard Business School.

References

ARGYRIS, C. (1964), *Integrating the Individual and the Organization*, Wiley.

BLAKE, R., and MOUTON, J. (1964), *The Managerial Grid*, Gulf Publishing Co.

BLAKE, R., MOUTON, J., BARNES, L., and GREINER, L. (1964), 'Breakthrough in organization development', *Harvard Business Review*, November/December.

GREINER, L. (1965), Organization Change and Development, *Harvard Business School*, unpublished doctoral thesis.

LAWRENCE, P., and LORSCH, J. (1967), 'Differentiation and integration in complex organizations', *Administrative Science Quarterly*, vol. 12, no. 1, pp. 1–47.

MANN, F. (1962), 'Studying and creating change', in W. G. Bennis, K. Benne and R. Chin (eds.), *The Planning of Change*, Holt, Rinehart & Winston.

RICE, A. (1958), *Productivity and Social Organization*, Tavistock.

SEASHORE, S., and BOWERS, D. (1963), *Changing the Structure and Functioning of an Organization: Report of a Field Experiment*, Survey Research Center, Institute for Social Research, Monograph #33.

SPENCER, H. (1904), *Autobiography*, New York, vol. 2.

11 J. V. Clark and C. G. Krone

Towards an Overall View of Organizational Development
in the Early Seventies

J. V. Clark and C. G. Krone, 'Towards an overall view of
organizational development in the early seventies', UCLA, 1971,
unpublished manuscript.

Our goal in this paper is to provide an integrated overview of
the changing field of organizational development, into which new
concepts and new intervention processes can be placed. We
start from two premises:

1. A healthy organization is one capable of integrating proactively with its physical, social and biological environment
(Clark, 1963).

2. An effective organizational development practitioner is someone who enables an organization to develop the attitudes and
processes which will allow it to integrate proactively with its
environment.

The individual and his small group – communication

Starting from these two premises, one can think about the interpersonal communications type of interventions (task-group team
meetings, management development laboratories, Blake grids,
etc.) in the following way. At the outset of such small group
meetings, one is aware that very little information about the
present situation in which the members find themselves is being
exchanged. They suppress thoughts and feelings they have about
themselves and others and they are insensitive to thoughts and
feelings others have about the same subject.

From the standpoint of an individual member, his 'life-space'
looks something like the diagram on page 285.

As the diagram suggests, Member 1 is insensitive to many of
his own feelings, nearly all the feelings and most of the thoughts
of others. He sends a few thought messages to a few members
and has, but doesn't send, considerably more.

This situation exists from the very outset of a group because all the members have brought to it a set of socially acceptable rules about appropriate things to see and say. So there is a structure operating which, for good or bad, consistently separates

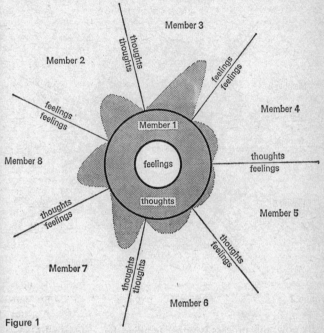

Figure 1

individuals one from another, since without information there can be no relation. As the group develops, a great deal more information gets exchanged, usually preceded by heated debates on whether or not it is appropriate to change the social rules which govern information exchange between people. As more information gets exchanged, an individual wants to connect with more members and with more aspects of any one member and so frequently chooses to communicate more aspects of *himself* to more people. It is this process which is so exciting to people in such groups. They are often delighted with these new choices and capacities. They speak of new-found potentialities in themselves and others and remark often of getting out of 'boxes', 'ruts' and 'grooves'. At this stage, a member's life-space looks like this:

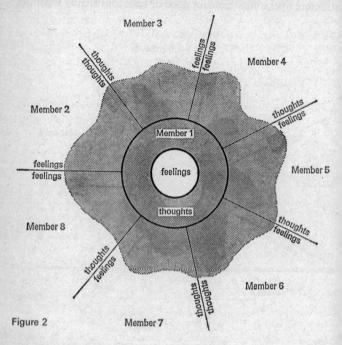

Figure 2

By now, this process is rather familiar, but readers wishing to delve into it further, as well as the process of enabling it to occur in task groups, can consult Clark (1963, 1970a, 1970b).

The individual and his world – appreciation

Another typical result of attending small group communication programs has been that, outside the group, an individual begins to feel that he understands and perhaps is even somewhat similar to many different kinds of people. If, in his group, he has gotten to know persons of different ages, colors, hierarchical positions, religions, political persuasions, etc., he has come to feel the excitement of relating more openly with them. Consequently he may feel he perceives all 'young people', 'blacks', 'women', etc., more accurately and can therefore relate more adaptively with them. One of the most common results of organizational development programs in industry, by way of illustration, is that people feel they get along better with their wives and children. Again, to illustrate graphically, a member's life-space in regard to social groups may look something like this before entering into the training experience:

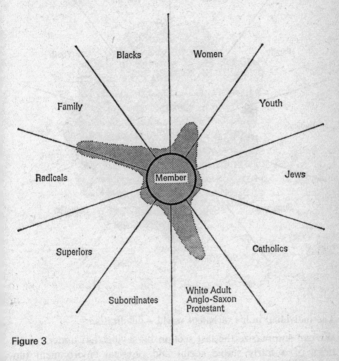

Figure 3

And, after, if he has been in a fairly heterogeneous group, perhaps something like Figure 4.

In moving from Figure 3 to Figure 4, several things have happened. First, new judgements about reality were made and, second, these new realities came to be *valued* in a different sort of way – new aspects of new people were, so to speak, 'appreciated'. Thus, for example, not only were another member's feelings perceived, but it became *important* to understand them. Thus what Geoffrey Vickers calls the 'appreciative system' of the individual has changed (Vickers, 1968); he sees more of his environmental realities and he values them differently.

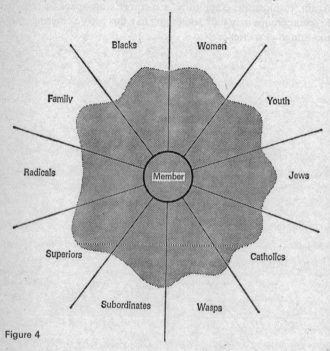

Figure 4

The individual in his turbulent world – debilitation

We can summarize the last section by saying that under conditions of a fairly stable social and physical environment (an individual's 'world'), he feels excited and growthful when his appreciative system changes. In a sense, this was the situation during the middle 1960s when our organizational development programs were focusing on interpersonal communication processes. However, in the late 1960s, people's worlds started changing much more rapidly than their appreciative systems.

The external part of this problem, the changing world itself, has been discussed by Emery and Trist (1965) in their paper on 'The causal texture of organizational environments', where they point out that environments become unpredictable and increasingly unmanageable for people when aspects within those environments interact upon one another regardless of the behavior of any single person or organization within it.

Clearly, such social-physical-biological environments are becoming typical today. And the consequences of living in that kind of world have been well described by Alvin Toffler (1970) in his book on *Future Shock*. He took the description and the label 'future shock' from the rather well documented experience of culture shock, which is a state of extreme anxiety, disorientation and debilitation suffered when one is unable to predict the meaning of his own or others' social actions. Toffler cites the Peace Corp's experience in this regard, which is that its members require six months or more to recover. Future shock is the same thing, only worse, because in culture shock the culture more or less stays put while the individual figures out its structure and meaning. But hardly anyone's world stays put, nowadays. And so what people in the early throes of future shock try to do is to reintroduce a sense of structure and predictability by reiterating and reinforcing the values of the sector of the world they are most familiar with. They are much like the frustrated tourist who speaks his own language slowly and loudly upon encountering someone who speaks a different one.

Toffler describes many ways of alleviating the symptoms of future shock, but the most penetrating analysis of the process of adaptation in turbulent environments has been made by Vickers (1968) in his paper on 'The limits of government'. He maintains bluntly that either mankind learns to develop new appreciative systems rapidly and constantly or it is caught in the 'ecological trap' of being unable to adapt to a changing environment, as was the dinosaur. In discussing this trap, Vickers observes that the conditions necessary to regulate large-scale social and political systems become increasingly difficult to obtain as the lead time needed to mount any regulative action becomes ever longer (due to the increasing complexity of most social and technical problems), while the future span over which any reliable prediction can be made grows ever shorter. He sums it up, quite pessimistically, when he says, 'It is quite possible for the world as we know it to become unregulable in important fields, in that it might pass the point beyond which *any* considered action might have a statistical probability of becoming worse than random.'

But, he continues, 'the condition which produces this unhappy result is not primarily due to exploding technology, but to the limitation of human communication (to generate) a sufficiently agreed view of the situation, a sufficient consensus on the course to pursue and sufficient common action to achieve it.' By communication, he means the failure to maintain 'appropriate shared ways of distinguishing the situation in which we act, the relations we want to regulate, the standards we need to apply and the repertory of actions available to us.'

Graphically, the connection between Vickers's point and our discussion here can be illustrated by our Figures 3 and 4. If someone is in a real-life situation with the Figure 3 groups as its main actors (a university president comes to mind, for example), then the appreciation of that situation represented by the shaded area in Figure 3 is clearly maladaptive. His appreciation must shift toward Figure 4, as must the appreciation of *all* involved.

The organization and its future in a turbulent environment – open-systems planning

As a result of this contemporary necessity to develop appreciative skills in order to mediate between an organization's turbulent environment and the future shock of its members, Charles G. Krone, in collaboration with James V. Clark and G. K. Jayaram, has been developing a technology of so-called 'open-systems planning' based on Miller's general systems behavior theory (Miller, 1965). While it will be described in detail in a subsequent paper, open-systems planning is, briefly, a set of procedures whereby groups can:

1. Rapidly identify and map out the dynamic realities which are in their environment.

2. Map out how the organization represented by the members of the group presently acts toward and hence values those realities.

3. Map out how the organization wants to engage with those realities in the future (that is, to set value-goals).

4. Make plans to restructure the 'architecture' of the organization in order to influence the environmental realities in the valued directions.

We have developed this method with the help of nearly a hundred client systems of many types and levels, working with industrial, religious, community, educational and governmental groups. Our experience to date has been that, while considerable discouragement and even depression are encountered along the way, such systems can, as a result of seeing more of and valuing differently the complicated texture of their environments, generate a considerably more varied range of action possibilities from which to choose directions and strategies. Moreover, they are able to visualize *alternative* futures and to take action against *them* instead of an assumed 'it'.

Before we proceed, we would like to draw attention to the temptation we and some of our clients have experienced to see open-systems planning as an organizational development intervention which ought to supercede team meetings which 'only' change norms and styles of communication. But notice that communication is the skill necessary in order to develop common appreciative systems between individuals or groups. And it is surely large groups of people who must, *together*, develop new appreciations before organizations can survive in turbulent environments. We have learned and relearned what we should already have known, that open-systems planning is likely to be unsuccessful as an organizational intervention unless it is introduced into groups with well developed communication skills – groups, that is, whose members have learned to perceive and value one another's thoughts and feelings. It will *surely* be unsuccessful unless such groups come to value, early in the process, the necessity of special work on communication improvement. We will return to this point in a more general sense at the conclusion of this paper.

By way of illustration, we can look at the familiar situation of an organization investing huge amounts of capital to build a product which it believes to be technically superior, only to discover almost overnight that it had failed to consider the effects on the product of the rapidly changing value shifts in the society in which it is being made and sold. Had certain social and political realities been better perceived, corporations might have wished not to invest so heavily in certain market capacities.

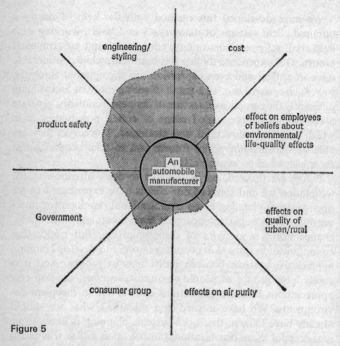

engineering/
styling

cost

product safety

effect on employees
of beliefs about
environmental/
life-quality effects

An
automobile
manufacturer

Government

effects on
quality of
urban/rural

consumer group

effects on air purity

Figure 5

On the other hand, appreciative systems include both reality judgements and value judgements. Situation, if perceived more accurately at the outset, can be valued differently and, as a consequence, acted upon differently.

Continuing in the vein of the above example, one can appreciate what is happening in the automotive industry in different sorts of ways, depending on the scope with which they are dealt. If one is valuing only the narrow sphere of what might be called the 'primary effects' of automobiles – transportation – one can say, eyeing some of the criticism one sees today, 'the public does not appropriately value the transportation and beauty of my products'. The appreciative map of such an hypothetical observer is seen in Figure 5. Doubtless he would consider the domains he pays attention to as primary and all the others as secondary. Moreover, he would have created organizational forms that reflect that division, placing immense resources against the primary domains and scant ones against the others.

On the other hand, if an appreciative system allowed one to deal with and positively value not only knowledge about primary but also about secondary effects, one would look at the problem of studying the effects of automotive transportation as follows:

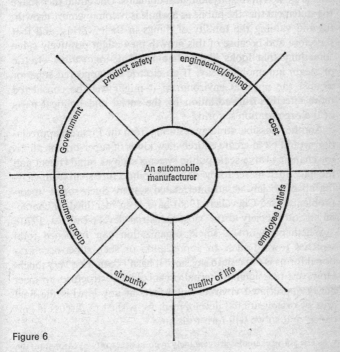

Figure 6

Moreover, one might put considerable organizational resources against monitoring and otherwise engaging with those parts of the organization's world from which it hears about secondary effects, be they technical, social, political, physiological or whatever.

Thus, if one were convinced of the truth of negative second level social and physiological effects, a more growthful response might be 'The second level effects of my products are so great that I need to create a new form (perhaps even an earlier form) which is more effective when I take into consideration the *whole* of both the first and second level effects'.

On the other hand, one can appreciate these other second-level domains of the organization's world – the social and political, for example – whether or not one were convinced that negative effects existed in the physiological domains. One could then make the statement that the public as a whole is becoming more growthful and valuing the totality of things in their worlds, and that therefore and because of this growth they might positively value something that looks like technological de-innovation, electric or steam automobiles, say. If an electric car appeared superior against the physical environment it might well be considered more effective transportation by the social and political parts of the organization's world.[1]

Another possible strategy resulting from the Figure 6 appreciation would be to create entirely new kinds of super-organizations for changing large-scale public systems such as rapid transit and the like. Such newer forms of social architecture stem from viewing all of society as an interrelated system. Such social 'meta-problems' (see Chevalier, 1966) have been identified as characteristic of a society at the 'post-industrial' level (see Trist, 1970).

Whether or not a single organization can influence total societies toward such an appreciation or such super-organizational forms is difficult to say since it hasn't been tried very much. However, redesigning internal organizational structures to meet newly appreciated environmental facts at any level is the final area of organizational development we wished to discuss in this paper, and so we will turn to it now.

1. The above examples are genuinely hypothetical for two reasons: (a) the authors have considerable hindsight about the physical and political domains of the automotive industry and, (b) very little technical knowledge of the secondary effects on social and physiological environments. We don't feel particularly lonely along either dimension.

The organization and its presence in a turbulent environment – open-system designing

Briefly stated, open-system organizational redesigning is the practice of creating organizational processes such that members are allowed to make dynamic responses to the dynamic environments of the technologies that form the core of their work. While no one has exactly elaborated this concept in the literature, a good basic first approximation is contained in *A System Approach to the Design of a Descriptive Model of Organizational Structure* by Driggers (1966).

We will try to illustrate, however, by taking some examples from some open-systems design projects on which we are working (see Krone, 1970, for a discussion of one of these projects). Consider, first off, the usual manufacturing organization in which everyone is given instructions to play roles which focus their attention on some aspect of their technology. Jobs are prescribed such that nearly everyone is assigned a particular part of the internal operation to 'run' (line) or 'audit' (staff) or 'improve' (often uncertain). A typical linear technology (assembly line, packing line, etc.) then, would look like Figure 7.

In the center can be seen five 'operators' who have been planned for by the five management personnel seen in the outside circle and maintained by the four maintenance personnel seen in the middle circle. The arrows going out from each person indicate the areas he is to appreciate and attend to, according to his job description and the other prescribed behaviors coming in from the different environmental domains attended to by the managers (illustrated in Figure 7 by the outward arrows).

Such a system is familiar to all of us and requires no elaboration here, although Drigger's discussion of the assumptions underlying it is interesting. Before passing on to an open-system design, however, we would like to call attention to the fact that the organizational structure depicted in Figure 7 is designed to produce the constricted appreciation patterns we have seen throughout our discussion in Figures 1, 3 and 5. In fact, members attempting wider appreciation patterns such as those seen in Figures 2, 4 and 6 above and 8 below are typically punished for such offenses as 'rate-busting', 'crossing craft-lines', 'usurping management prerogatives', or just plain 'sticking your nose in where it doesn't belong'.

In some of the open-systems redesign projects in which the authors are involved, this form of organization is abandoned in

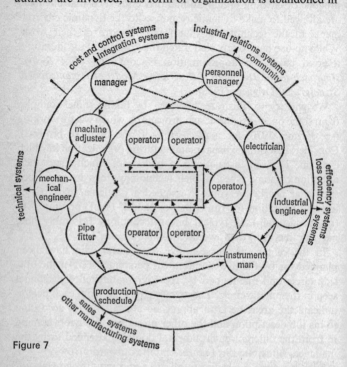

Figure 7

favor of a system in which the people who have direct responsibility for maintaining the flow of product of one form or another (a product concept can be the product of an information processing system, for example) also have direct responsibility for identifying and proactively engaging with the environments of that production flow. For example, in the project described in Krone's paper, packing line workers identify, ahead of time, changes in sales volume, product formulation, social processes in the community, and so forth, and restructure their system so as to appropriately engage it with those forthcoming environmental changes.

In graphic form, such an organization might appear as in Figure 8.

One aspect of this organizational form is difficult to depict graphically, and that is the portion of the world around the core technology to which particular operators often attend shifts, by

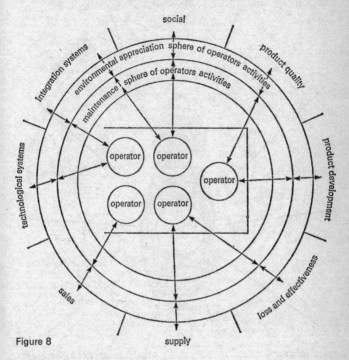

Figure 8

common consent. It may shift during a day, or over a period of weeks or months.

In any case, as we mentioned earlier, an operator moves from an appreciative map such as seen in Figure 9 towards one similar to Figure 10.

As mentioned earlier, a particular operator may have a somewhat differently shaped appreciative 'profile', but he surely will have a considerably larger life-space within which to operate than he did when his appreciative map was similar to Figure 9.

Under such an organizational design, the role of management moves away from identifying environmental changes and directing the system's responses to them, toward identifying changes in the capacity of the work force itself to engage in that process.

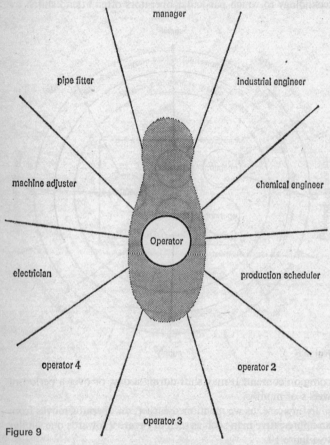

Figure 9

Management, then, in fulfilling its functions asks questions such as, 'Does the system have enough information about the environment?', 'Does it have enough information about its responses to the environment?', 'Are its members helping one another to more effectively engage in appreciative acts?', etc. It monitors, that is, whether or not people who directly engage with the technology have the appropriate capacities, information and organizational forms to engage directly with the environment of that technology.

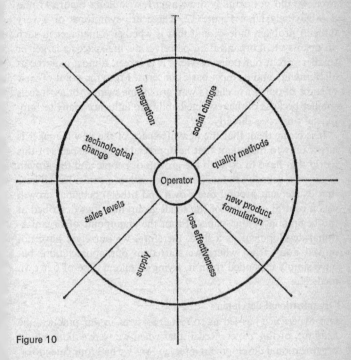

Figure 10

When the manager shifts to these kinds of concerns, his map, from our point of view, shifts from a narrow one where he is directly concerned with cost and control of the technological processes towards a broader one where he is concerned directly with the processes that result in effective costs and control of the technology. These new concerns are with the growth of people, with his own ability to create systems which allow for the identification and linkage between appropriate people and appropriate environmental domains, his own ability to create systems which allow for appropriate 'links' with the future, his own ability to create systems that can generate values, and even valued values (although that gets a little tricky), and the like.

The attentive reader may have noticed that, at the beginning of the last paragraph, we said 'from our point of view'. Moreover, we did not actually draw a narrow looking Figure 11 and a satisfyingly large Figure 12. These are symptoms of a very difficult problem indeed, and that is whether a manager in such an open-system organization perceives his life-space as larger or smaller. From our point of view, it is larger, almost as large as all humanity and its most basic concerns. From the point of view of some of our brave clients who are in this swim with us, it feels smaller because of the restricted ability to influence many technological processes directly.

It is clear, then, that the new life-space of the new manager is larger only to the extent that he appreciates those aspects of this world that have to do with the growth of people and the growth of his own capacity to facilitate the growth of people. Recall here that excitement around one's own and others' personal growth was a central outcome of the small group meetings described at the beginning of this paper. From the standpoint of organizational development as a field, therefore, we ourselves have not moved away from where we started in our appreciation, but have simply expanded from it, trying to take a dose of our own medicine.

Organizational developing

Our experience has led us to value, as steps in our practice, the headings of this paper. Recall that when we were talking about organizational development interventions we had four categories: (a) the individual and his small group – communication, (b) the individual and his world – appreciation, (c) the organization and its future in a turbulent environment – open-systems planning, and (d) the organization and its present in a turbulent environment – open-systems designing.

It was only when we introduced a symptom we hadn't anticipated along the way that we inserted another category between (b) and (c); the individual in his turbulent world – debilitation.

Our categories form a map which looks like this:

Aspects of organizational developing

	Intervention structures	Intervention processes
Internal to a system	open-systems designing	communication
	4	1
External to a system	open-systems planning	appreciation
	3	2

Our own view is that an organizational development program is not complete until activities occur spontaneously and continuously in all boxes, without professional outside intervention.

Our experience with several such programs has been that, while they are developing, they need to proceed clockwise and also that they tend to fade out if they fail to proceed onward until all four steps have been covered. Neither proposition has been tested in the experimental sense, of course, but our best clinical judgement supports them both at the present time, and so we pass them on to our clients and colleagues. Where you start on the circle, by the way, seems to depend on a number of situational factors, including the culture in which the organization is embedded. In most American projects with which we are acquainted, projects start with communication (1), but we have been involved in varying degrees with a large-scale project in England which started with a version of open-system planning (3).

However, as implied earlier, our experience is also indicating that, regardless of where you start, the Figure 11 process is iterative, primarily because of the difficulties encountered by the manager who is fostering open-systems redesign activities. If he has started with (1) and proceeded on through (2) and (3) he has experienced, so far, largely the delight of enlarged appreciations of and within his own personal world. But, in open-systems redesign, it is the system as a whole which enlarges its potentialities,[2] and, as we stated before, it is often difficult for managers to conceive of their own individual worlds as expanding under those conditions. We repeat this point because it is troublesome to us, troublesome both as consultants to, and as friends of, our clients. At the present time it is difficult to know ahead of time which managers will, and which will not, enlarge their appreciative systems to include the growth-monitoring and growth-inducing aspects central to the open-systems manager's 'core technology'. In our framework, of course, which might at this point be called 'open-systems consultation', this problem must be identified and shared with managers as soon as it is perceived. We hope very much to participate in its resolution whenever we can, but it would be presumptuous and inaccurate to imply, in a closed-system sense, that we can 'solve' it. This paper was generated, in large part, by the desire to enlist the help of our clients with this extraordinarily difficult problem.

References

CHEVALIER, M. (1966), 'Towards an action framework for the control of pollution', *Canadian Council of Resource Ministers' Conference on Pollution*, Montreal.

CLARK, J. V. (1962), 'A healthy organization', *California Management Review*, vol. 4, no. 4, Summer, pp. 16–30.

CLARK, J. V. (1963), 'Authentic interaction and personal growth in sensitivity training groups', *Journal of Humanistic Psychology*, Spring, pp. 1–13.

CLARK, J. V. (1970a), 'Task group therapy 1: goals and the client system', *Human Relations*, vol. 23, no. 4, pp. 263–77.

CLARK, J. V. (1970b), 'Task group therapy 2: intervention and problems of practice', *Human Relations*, vol. 23, no. 5, pp. 383–403.

DRIGGERS, P. F. (1966), *A System Approach to the Design of a Descriptive Model of Organizational Structure*, unpublished Ph.D. dissertation, University of Illinois.

EMERY, F. E., and TRIST, E. (1965), 'The causal texture of organizational environments', *Human Relations*, vol. 18, February, pp. 21–32.

KRONE, C. G. (1970), 'Organizational response to technological change', the Procter and Gamble Company, unpublished mimeo; paper presented to the 1970 meetings of the Institute for Management Sciences, U.C.L.A.

2. A point clarified for us during a conversation with our colleague, W. H. McWhinney of U.C.L.A.

MILLER, J. G. (1965), 'Living systems: basic concepts', *Behavioral Science*, vol. 10, nos. 3, 4, July and October, pp. 337 *et seq.*

TOFFLER, A. (1970), *Future Shock*, Random House.

TRIST, E. (1970), 'Urban North America in the next 30 years', in W. Schmidt (ed.), *Organizational Frontiers*, Wadsworth.

VICKERS, G. (1968), 'The limits of government', ch. 4, pp. 73–95, in *Value Systems and Social Process*, Basic Books.

12 D. Katz and R. L. Kahn

Organizational Change

Excerpts from D. Katz and R. L. Kahn, 'Organizational change', in *The Social Psychology of Organizations*, Wiley, 1964, chapter 13, pp. 390-451.

The major error in dealing with problems of organizational change, both at the practical and theoretical level, is to disregard the systemic properties of the organization and to confuse individual change with modifications in organizational variables. It is common practice to pull foremen or officials out of their organizational roles and give them training in human relations. Then they return to their customary positions with the same role expectations from their subordinates, the same pressures from their superiors, and the same functions to perform as before their special training. Even if the training program has begun to produce a different orientation toward other people on the part of the trainees, they are likely to find little opportunity to express their new orientation in the ongoing structured situation to which they return.

Almost all psychotherapy, including group therapy, suffers from this same weakness. Its immediate target is improved insight by the individual into his motivations. Even if individuals and small groups emerge from the therapeutic sessions with improved understanding of themselves and others, the effects of such individual change on social structures tend to be minimal. With respect to the supersystem of the nation-state the same confusion of individual and system functioning is often apparent. It was conspicuous, for example, in the objections to changing Negro–white relations by law. A common point of view was that individuals would have to change their attitudes and habits first. The fallacy in this position has been demonstrated by the revolution created by changes at the top of the legal structure, specifically the Supreme Court decision of 1954.

The confusion between individual and organizational change is due in part to the lack of precise terminology for distinguishing between behavior determined largely by structured roles within a system and behavior determined more directly by personality needs and values. The behavior of people in organizations is still the behavior of individuals, but it has a different set of determinants than behavior outside organizational roles. Modifications in organizational behavior must be brought about in a different manner.

Let us examine the individual approach in more detail. Its essential weakness is the psychological fallacy of concentrating upon individuals without regard to the role relationships that constitute the social system of which they are a part. The assumption has been that, since the organization is made up of individuals, we can change the organization by changing its members. This is not so much an illogical proposition as it is an oversimplification which neglects the interrelationships of people in an organizational structure and *fails to point to the aspects of individual behavior which need to be changed*.

Some psychoanalysts, for example, assume that wars are caused by the aggressive impulses of man and that if we can lessen frustrations and redirect aggressive impulses, we can change the belligerent character of the state and eliminate war. Reasonable as this sounds, it has very little to do with the case. The finger that presses the button unleashing a nuclear warhead may be that of a person with very little repressed hostility, and the cabinet or state directorate behind the action may be made up of people who are kind to their families, considerate of their friends, and completely lacking in the psychopathology of aggression. They are merely carrying out their roles in a social system, and unless these roles and the social structure which gives them definition are changed, we will still have wars. Yet we persist in attempting to change organizations by working on individuals without redefining their roles in the system, without changing the sanctions of the system, and without changing the expectations of other role incumbents in the organization about appropriate role behavior.

In short, to approach institutional change solely in individual terms involves an impressive and discouraging series of assumptions – assumptions which are too often left implicit. They include, at the very least: the assumption that the individual can be provided with new insight and knowledge; that these will produce some significant alteration in his motivational pattern; that these insights and motivations will be retained even when the individual leaves the protected situation in which they were learned and returns to his accustomed role in the organization; that he will be able to adapt his new knowledge to that real-life situation; that he will be able to persuade his co-workers to accept the changes in his behavior which he now desires; and that he will also be able to persuade them to make complementary changes in their own expectations and behavior.

The weaknesses in this chain become apparent as soon as its many links are enumerated. The initial diagnosis may be wrong; that is, the inappropriate behavior may not result from lack of individual insight or any other psychological shortcoming. Even if the initial diagnosis is correct, however, the individual approach to organizational change characteristically disregards the long and difficult linkage just described. This disregard we have called the psychological fallacy. In warning against it, however, we do not propose to commit a complementary sociological fallacy. We do not assert, in other words, that *any* alteration in human behavior can be brought about in organizations provided the process of change is initiated with due attention to organizational structure. The problems of change are too complex for such simplistic generalizations and require further specification.

Perhaps the best way of introducing such specification into problems of social change is to examine two separate aspects of the matter: the methods employed to bring about change, and the targets at which such methods are directed. Although a single method may be directed at different targets or at a sequence of targets, it can be argued that there is inherent in each method a primary or preferred target and a hypothesized linkage by which other targets may be reached. We shall discuss a primary target in relation to our presentation of each method of change.

These methods for bringing about organizational change include the direct use of information, skills training, individual counseling and therapy, the influence of the peer group, sensitivity training, group therapy, feedback on organizational functioning, and direct structural or systemic alteration. The primary target of change may be the individual as an individual personality, the interpersonal relationships between members of peer groups, the norms of peer groups, the interpersonal relationships between members of an organizational family, the structure of a role, the role relationships of some segment of organizational space, or the structure of the organization as a whole. The difficulty with many attempts at organizational change is that the changers have not clearly distinguished their targets and have assumed that the individual or group-level target was the same as the social-structure target. [. . .]

Group therapy within organizations

An interesting attempt to produce organizational change through group therapy introduced into the organization itself has been utilized by the Tavistock Institute in England and is reported by Elliot Jaques (1951). The factory in question is an engineering and metals concern, the Glacier Company. The essence of the procedure is to have the organization change itself by means of group processes occurring at every level in the organization. The immediate target in this approach is the improvement of people's understanding of their organizational interrelationships and their own personal motives. The remote target is organizational restructuring by responsible organizational members themselves. The basic philosophy flows from individual therapy. The research team of outsiders is only one change agent; the major agents of change are the organizational members themselves. To quote Jaques, the research team is 'to act only in advisory or interpretive capacity. The team is not here to solve problems for Glacier. They may, however, be able to help with the continuing development of methods of getting a smoother organization.'

In accordance with this philosophy the research team began its program only after gaining acceptance from the Director, the Works Council (a body composed of management and elected union representatives), and the factorywide committee of shop stewards. Instead of applying the therapeutic approach in literal fashion, the Tavistock researchers focused upon organizational problems. Their preliminary move was a historical investigation of the plant, followed by an organizational study to establish the role structure of the system. This latter study included 'an examination ... of how far the social structure of the factory had proved effective in coping with the forces which affected production and group relations.'

After the presentation of these background reports to the Works Council, various sections of the organization began to ask the research team for cooperation on specific problems. The procedure of the research team was to direct the groups with which they worked toward the discovery of underlying causes and the expression of partly unconscious motives. Resistances emerging in group sessions were sometimes interpreted by the research teams; in other instances the group was left to make its own discoveries. To use Jaques' words:

The method used was to draw attention to the nature of the resistance on the basis of the facts known to those concerned. Opportunities were taken to illuminate in the specific situation the meaning of the feelings (whether of fear, guilt, or suspicion) that constituted the unpalatable background to anxieties that were present about undergoing changes that were necessary. When successful, interpretations of this kind allowed group members to express feelings which they had been suppressing, sometimes for years, and then to develop an altered attitude to the problem under consideration. Even awkward or over-blunt comments often came as a relief (p. 306).

And in the same context Jaques observes:

The process of helping a group to unearth and identify some of the less obvious influences affecting its behavior is one borrowed from medical psychotherapy, from which is borrowed also the technical term *working-through*. It presupposes access by a consultant trained in group methods to a group accepting the task of examining its own behavior as and while it occurs, and a group able to learn, with the aid of interpretive comment, to recognize an increasing number of forces, both internal and external, that are influencing its behavior. The expectation, then, is that the group will acquire a better capacity to tolerate initially independent insights into phenomena such as scapegoating, rivalry, dependency, jealousy, futility and despair and thence a greater ability to deal effectively with difficult reality problems. When we speak of a group working through a problem we mean considerably more than is ordinarily meant by saying that a full discussion of a problem has taken place. We mean that a serious attempt has been made to voice the unrecognized difficulties, often socially taboo, which have been preventing it from going ahead with whatever task it may have had (p. 307).

The Tavistock researchers regard two factors as necessary for successful working-through, and a third is desirable though not always essential. The first factor is similar to Dewey's old initial condition for problem-solving, the existence of a felt difficulty. The group must be hurting; its members must recognize a severe and painful problem. The second factor is group solidarity or cohesiveness. Members must have commitment to the group and its objectives. Otherwise they will not have the motivation to overcome the additional anxieties involved in problem solution. The third condition is a state of frustration created by the failure of denial and other mechanisms of defense to function in their accustomed manner. Groups tend to avoid facing up to the basic causes of their problems through various devices of avoidance and denial. When group members, through the help of a consultant or by other means, find that running away from the problem gives them no relief, they are ready for more realistic exploration.

The group-therapy procedure had an interesting outcome in the Glacier Company, an outcome illustrative of the strengths and weaknesses of the approach. No fundamental restructuring of the organization took place, but inconsistencies and ambiguities were resolved and the pseudo-democratic stance of management was replaced by a clearer authority structure. The Works Council was reorganized to include representatives of various levels of management in addition to top management and union stewards, and its function as an advisory rather than a decision-making body was explicitly formulated. The executive system was clearly separated from the functions of the Works Council so that the line of authority was not interfered with in everyday operations.

The target of change and the nature of the changes attempted and achieved in the Glacier project deserve careful consideration. The group therapy was nondirective in the sense that the research team did not propose specific answers to problems in organizational functioning. Instead, they emphasized a method by which organizational members could discover their own solutions. The focus was upon procedures for enabling groups to gain better understanding of themselves and others. Essentially the approach was aimed at the removal of unrecognized and unconscious forces which impede the rational functioning of people in group relationships.

To the extent that there is a commonality of interests and goals among all subsystems and groupings within an organization, much can be accomplished by aiding people to make full use of their rational faculties in problem solution. The result should be more efficient organizational functioning and improved morale and interpersonal relations. Many of the anxieties of people, whether about their personal lives or about their roles in a social system, are crippling in their effects and often groundless in relation to objective facts. These irrational worries and emotional difficulties can gain group reinforcement and so be more potent in their undesirable consequences. The insecurities of one group can lead to scapegoating and uncooperative behavior toward another group in the same organization and so make the task of the second group unusually difficult.

The great limitation in the use of group therapy is that all conflicts and problems in organizational functioning are not irrational in nature. Many difficulties are based upon genuine conflicts of interest, and the more the irrational anxieties are stripped away, the more clearly these interest conflicts come into focus. In the early history of American industrialism some employers exploited the antagonism of one nationality group against another. To have the Irish at odds with the Poles obscured their common interest and made unionization more difficult. Group therapy in this situation could have reduced the tensions between the different nationality groups, but it would not have solved the basic conflicts between workers and management.

In the Glacier Company, then, the organizational changes should not be construed as a basic restructuring of the organization and a democratic resolution of competing interests within the organization. It is true that the Works Council was to some extent revitalized as a policy-making body, but the broadening of its representative character revitalized the management representatives on the Council more than the workers. Previously, management had appointed all its representatives to the Council; now the various echelons of supervisory and management personnel elected their own representatives. In his own account of the later functioning of the company, the Director, Brown (1960), is honest and straightforward in describing the changes which took place. The changes essentially clarified and made consistent the basic philosophy of management and its operational procedures. Some degree of employee representation does not mean that the organization is a democratic political system. In such a system the constituent members elect their officers and legislators, who in turn appoint executive officers; policy on all matters is determined by the constituents or their duly chosen representatives.

The Glacier Company, according to its stated policy as an industrial enterprise concerned with profits, is not governed basically by its Works Council. The Company recognizes three other influential systems: the executive system, the shareholders and their board of directors, and the customers. The representative system comprising both managerial and nonsupervisory employees is only one system, and very limited in the decisions it can make. Neither the written policies of the Company nor its philosophy as described by its Director define an area of discretionary judgement for the Works Council, except to assert that its decisions should not interfere with what the stockholders think desirable in terms of costs and profits, what the customers want in terms of services and products, or what the executive system should handle as the implementation of policy. Moreover, the Director, who is chairman of the Works Council, speaks with several voices in the deliberations of that body. He is the chief representative of the executive system, he speaks for the stockholders and their interests, and he also is the self-admitted spokesman for the customers or clientele of the organization. If the discussion should enter an area which he regards as belonging within the province of the stockholders, or of executive management, or of the customers, he can merely say, 'Gentlemen, that is not the legitimate concern of this group' or 'Gentlemen, the *given* in this situation by which we must abide is the following wish of our stockholders.' Small wonder that few crucial decisions are made by the Works Council.

The Company formula frankly states that the area of discretion or contribution to policy by the employees is defined by their willingness to mobilize whatever power they possess to oppose or support a proposal. If management proposes changes which are likely to lead to rebellion among the employees, this can be tested out in the Works Council. If the representatives of the employees rise up in their wrath and predict that a given change will lead to a strike, management may then back down. The wise use of Council meetings by management can avoid widespread discontent in the company, since management will be guided by what they gauge the opposition forces to be. On the more positive side, management has an opportunity to gain the assent and sanctioning power of the Works Council for those proposals accepted by the Council after discussion.

Fundamentally, the representation of employees on one of the policy-making boards of the Company gives the workers a feeling that they will not be pushed too far or too fast by management. Precedents will be followed, people will be heard if drastic changes are contemplated, and management probably will accept a veto which the employees are ready to implement by a strike or a slowdown. Employees are confident that they will have some voice in any change that would fundamentally alter their way of life in the organization, and they have a means of getting a hearing for proposals of their own.

Though the representative system must rely on the power it can mobilize to affect decisions, the full power of the employees is not lodged in it. The trade union and the shop stewards constitute the organized power with which management negotiates, and the union is outside the representative system, though there are relations between the two. In fact, the Works Council includes union men, though they are not elected as such, who can informally represent the point of view of the union and in turn carry back to the union the views of the management. This division keeps clear the struggle between management and union over contracts and does not involve the employees in negotiations with the company as representatives in the Works Council. By the same token, it reduces the power of the representative system in the overall legislative process.

The group therapy process at Glacier thus helped management clarify its policies and procedures with respect to management responsibility, make unambiguous the character of the executive structure as an order-giving system, and stipulate the part to be played by the representative system and by the union. In the past management had suffered from confusion about the use of consultative democratic procedures, the pretense of democratic participation, and the abdication of management from some of its responsibilities. The Director was reluctant to assert his authority among the divisional managers. At times he refused to take the chair and lead the group, and wanted to appear merely as one of the group members. The role of middle management was weakened because it saw itself as being bypassed. The workers' representatives sat in council with top management and were in fact closer to top management than managers down the line. The very concept of role with its clear demarcation of duties was avoided. The assumption was made that if management and workers could get along amiably, all problems would be solved. The group processes instituted by the Tavistock research team enabled members of management to see clearly what they had been doing and what was necessary for effective operation as the sort of organization they wanted to be.

As leaders of a marginal operation in a competitive industry, top management probably made a correct assessment of the situation with respect to survival. It was not, however, the only possible course of action. They could have attempted to clear up the contradictions of democratic and authoritarian philosophy and practice by moving toward a cooperative enterprise, with employees sharing in the profits and policy decisions and electing the company officials. One difficulty with this solution is that the workers themselves may not have wanted it. To have become true partners in production with management would have meant breaking with the trade union structure and losing the security of long-standing membership in the union, for the sake of becoming members of an unusual partnership which the next turn of the market might wipe out. Moreover, the investment of the stockholders and their legal control of the company also represented a limiting factor in organizational change. Finally, top management was not willing to turn over the direction of the company to employees and perhaps to throw away its years of experience and its special competence in running the company. Management saw itself as dependent upon stockholders and the consuming public, no less than upon employees. As a marginal enterprise the company was very much an open system, and management had been trying to reconcile the demands from outside the organization with the internal needs of the employees.

For all these reasons, the Glacier management rejected a democratic political model as inappropriate for the organization. They did not, however, want to move toward the other logical extreme of machine theory, in which the organization is seen solely as a mechanism for task accomplishment and the people in it as objects to be molded to their job assignments. Management, though giving priority to the nature of the task as determined by the customer system and the stockholder system, also recognized the needs of employees. They hit upon the Glacier formula as an excellent means of preserving the best in machine theory with a clear enough concession to the democratic trend of the times to avoid serious discontent in the plant. This formula swept democratic consultative practices in everyday task decisions out of the door. The executive system was given full and complete authority for getting the job done within the scope of policy decisions made by the Board of Directors and the Works Council. The employees could be heard in the Works Council and when they felt very strongly about a given policy, could get it modified. Moreover, they had their own union to fall back upon for the protection of their interests. Management's recognition of the veto power of employees and its willingness to listen in advance to their wishes helped to sanction the workings of the executive system and to give psychological security to the members of the organization. Clarity of responsibility and authority in the executive system enabled the organization to get the most out of hierarchical authority.

The solution achieved in the Glacier Company is thus a viable compromise, probably well suited both to its immediate situation and to the larger context of British industrial society, with its well established trade union movement and its value emphasis upon gradualism and precedent. The compromise arrangement, however, does not permit the full use of the democratic process with all its potentialities for problem solution, for the development of people, and for motivating them to use their full abilities. Two of the traditional difficulties of machine theory remain unsolved at Glacier: (a) The conflicts of group interest still persist. The deep-seated problems of restriction of production, of worker reliance upon the seniority principle, and of resistance to mechanization and automation have not been touched by the Glacier formula. Such problems do not yield to the use of group therapy. They can be solved only through the internalization of organizational goals by employees, which in turn requires accepting them as real partners in production. (b) The clear change of authority and responsibility in the executive system makes for precise allocation of duties but in so doing loses the advantages of group responsibility and of innovative and cooperative behavior beyond the line of duty.

The use of group therapy in the Glacier Company was, however, a landmark in the theory and practice of organizational change. The Mayo tradition with its emphasis upon informal groups, the Lewinian approach with its use of group process for organizational reform, and the extension of that approach to the sensitivity training of individuals apart from the organizational context had neglected the facts of organizational structure and the properties of organizations as social systems. Individual change was equated with organizational change and small groups were equated with large organizations. It was the genius of the Tavistock workers to combine a knowledge of therapy with a knowledge of the social psychology and sociology of organizations. Their theoretical approach took account of the systemic character of the situation with which they were dealing, even though the method for modifying social structure was that of group therapy. Their first step to gain access to the company was to gain acceptance from the component subsystems of the organization. Their next step was a background study of the system as a whole and its functioning. In working through problems for various sections of the enterprise they were guided by their awareness of the relations of one subsystem to the other subsystems of the organization. Finally, they were perceptive of the high degree of the openness of the company to related systems in the environment which helped to determine its input and the market for its output.

Recently there have been promising attempts to adapt small-group approaches, especially sensitivity training and its variants, to an account of the organizational context. The work of Schein and Bennis (1965), Argyris (1964), and Blake and Mouton (1964) are outstanding examples. The final pages of the work by Bradford, Gibb and Benne (1964) speak of the 'extended use of T-groups and laboratory methods in nonlaboratory (i.e. organizational) settings.' The Tavistock work deserves to be recognized, however, as the first purposeful and successful fusion of the therapeutic and organizational approaches.

The systematic use of feedback and group discussion: the approach of Floyd Mann

Most organizations have at least one kind of feedback from the environment to guide their operations and indicate the need for organizational change. This feedback is from the reception of their product accorded by the clientele or market. When an automobile company cannot sell its cars it must make changes in the nature of its product. But there is another kind of feedback to the organization which derives from its own internal functioning. Two types of such internally generated information are frequently used by organizations. One concerns the technical side of internal functioning and implies an accounting for each production job in the organization. Some factories still follow the Taylor system in this respect, and at the close of everyday report forms are passed up the line from each level of the organization describing the number of pieces produced, the utilization of materials, the amount of scrap and waste material, and the number of hours each employee spent on the various aspects of his job.

The second type of internal information concerns the human side of the productive and production-supportive processes of the organization. Typically, such feedback reaches the upper echelons only when some problem has become acute. Top management learns that there has been a disastrous slowdown in the foundry and that castings are not reaching the assembly line on schedule, or that some key engineers and research people have resigned to take jobs with competing companies.

Suggestion systems are sometimes employed both to get ideas about technical improvement and to get feedback on the human problems of organization. Surveys of morale and of employee feelings, attitudes and beliefs are also conducted by companies to give the latter type of feedback. If there were full and accurate communication up the line such surveys would not be needed, but the barriers to such upward communication are too numerous and too strong to ignore. Nor are these barriers only to peripheral data about employee attitudes. A sharp distinction between information about technical and human processes is false. The concept of the socio-technical system of Emery and Trist (1960) rightly gives emphasis to the complex interrelationships of social and technical processes. An adequate morale survey will furnish information both about the feelings of people and the actual operations of the technical or work system.

The great weakness in the use of surveys of employees' ideas and feelings is the inability of management to utilize this type of feedback about the internal functioning of the organization. Sometimes top management feels that it has done the proper thing just by conducting a survey, and proceeds to file the reports in the personnel office; at other times it will pass the findings along to lower echelons with no specific directives about their use. If the results of the survey are read by these subordinates, the natural tendency is to select the items that reinforce their present biases and to discount findings that run contrary to their own ideas.

Employees have two reactions to such unutilized surveys. The first and perhaps the dominant one is satisfaction in having been asked to express their views and in actually ventilating their feelings. The other reaction, which arises particularly when they have been led to expect positive action, is one of frustration in that nothing happens after all their efforts to tell the company what was wrong and what should be done.

To make the survey an effective form of feedback for organizational change, Floyd Mann and his colleagues at the Survey Research Center developed a plan for group discussion of survey results by appropriate 'organizational families'. Mann's approach was first used in a fairly large company in which there had been a thorough survey by questionnaire and interview of all officers and workers. The concept of the organizational family refers to a supervisor at any hierarchical level and the employees reporting directly to him. Any supervisor thus would have membership in two organizational families. He would be involved in the group he supervises and he would also be a member with his coordinate supervisors of the family reporting to the officer above him. Thus the concept of organizational family takes account of the linking of subgroups in an organizational structure through the dual membership of their top men.

Mann's use of group discussion by such organizational families is like the Tavistock approach in taking into account the realities of organizational structure. Moreover, the hierarchical character of an enterprise is recognized by starting the feedback process with the top organizational family, for example the president and the vice-presidents reporting to him. The next series of feedback discussions might include each vice-president and the department heads who report to him. Starting at the top of the structure means that the serious examination of survey results is sanctioned or legitimized by the executive system. Every supervisory officer who calls a meeting of his subordinates has already been through a comparable discussion session with his coordinate officers and their chief.

The feedback material prepared for each session by the research team is, moreover, of special relevance for the particular organizational family into which it is introduced. The branch chief meeting with his department heads will be given companywide totals of employee ideas and feelings about all issues as well as branch totals, but, in addition, the branch totals will be broken down for the departments represented at the meeting. Thus, at the meeting the participants can see how their branch compares with the company as a whole as well as the strong and weak points of the departments within the branch. In turn, when the department head meets with his supervisors, they will have before them data to show how their department compares with the branch of which it is a part and how the sections within the department, manned by the supervisors present, compare with one another. In general, then, each organizational family is presented feedback about its own problems in detail and comparative information about the company as a whole or the larger part of the company to which it belongs.

For example, in one company studied by Mann, the top echelons of one department could immediately see that they compared very unfavorably with the company as a whole on certain aspects of employee morale. A much higher percentage of workers in that department than in the rest of the company had thought about quitting their jobs during the past year and were apparently waiting for the first good opportunity to leave; identification with the company was much lower in that department and dissatisfaction with supervision was higher. These findings brought home forcibly to the departmental officers and to their superiors what they had long been aware of to some degree, namely that top management had at times considered the department as expendable, its services always replaceable by contractual arrangements with outside firms. That company policy had affected rank-and-file employees so deeply was, however, something of a surprise.

The presentation of survey findings to the various organizational families sometimes brought new problems to light. More often it gave an objective and factual basis to problems that had either been brushed aside or dealt with by some opinionated gesture. Not only had vague reports about the perceptions and feelings of employees been reduced to facts and figures, but comparisons could be made among similar groups and the findings could be related to possible causal factors. In this objective atmosphere questions could be raised about the data, many of which could be answered by further analysis of the same data. And this was the emphasis of the Mann feedback procedure – group discussion of facts and figures in a task-oriented atmosphere where people were seeking to analyse the problem, identify possible causes as objectively as possible, and agree upon possible solutions. The reason for utilizing organizational families and presenting to them the relevant data about their operation, thus becomes clear. The members of a specific organizational family have been involved in these very problems, already know a good deal about them, and know what questions should be asked to dig deeper into the available data for answers. Moreover, the group members are the immediate agents for implementing any policy changes with respect to problems at their own level. If they understand the causes, have been involved in a discussion of solutions, and perhaps have proposed the new policy, they will be more effective agents for achieving change.

The feedback technique, utilizing group discussion and group involvement, must be used under certain conditions if it is to realize its potential strength. Mention has already been made of the need for a factual, task-oriented atmosphere. A second necessity is the discretion of each organizational family to consider the implications of findings at its own level. Again, an area of freedom is required to utilize group process. General problem areas may be designated at higher echelons, but the detailed answers must be worked out by people closer to the problem.

For example, when the top management family looks at departmental comparisons they may become immediately aware of the low morale in a given branch. They may also note that there is more dissatisfaction with supervision in this branch and may want to attribute its morale problems to the practices of its first-line supervisors. This, however, is something the branch head can look into more definitively when he meets with his own department chiefs. At this meeting they will have a more complete breakdown of survey findings by sections and type of work, and it may become apparent that discontent with supervision is concentrated among the unskilled laborers.

Suppose problems of supervision are revealed to be specific to certain sections and independent of the general disaffection in the department. It becomes apparent that supervisors of unskilled laborers were not helped by the supervisory training program as much as other supervisors. The men under them are more accustomed to authoritarian methods than were other workers. Supervisory training in human relations had confused rather than helped these foremen, in that they were not really enabled to use more consultative methods and yet were made insecure in their use of older authoritarian approaches. They are also of lesser education and ability than the other groups of foremen, and feel the double insecurity of being men in the middle in a marginal department. It is difficult to imagine the revelation and discussion of such material except in the organizational family of its greatest relevance, acting according to its own discretion.

A third requirement for the effective use of the feedback procedure is a reporting back up the line of the outcome of meetings at the lower organizational level. When a department was satisfied that it had some answers to its problems and some recommendations about them, its head could present these findings at a subsequent branch meeting. He could report to the branch meeting to what extent various difficulties could be met at the departmental level and to what extent they seemed to arise from branch and company policies which would have to be changed at higher levels in the organization. The branch then could discuss all departmental reports and could attempt a summary report to go to the sessions of top management. At any point in the procedure the research team might be asked to bring back further breakdowns of relevant data.

One great advantage in this type of feedback with group discussion is its utilization of existing organizational structure. The executive line is not bypassed in securing information and implementing policy. Effective working relationships between supervisory levels are improved and two-way communication facilitated. Management policy is better understood and more fully put into practice, and the special knowledge and competence of all levels is more fully utilized. Mann (1957) recognizes that improving organizational functioning means dealing with the systemic properties of organizational structure:

Organizations, as systems of hierarchically ordered, interlocking roles with rights and privileges, reciprocal expectations, and shared frames of reference, contain tremendous forces for stability or change in the behavior of individuals or subgroups. Change processes need to be designed to harness these forces for creating and supporting change (p. 162).

Mann also points out five other related sets of facts which make for the efficacy of systematic feedback of survey data through organizational families.

Participation in the interpretation and analysis of research findings leads to the internalization of information and beliefs. When ideas are a person's own, they are much more likely to be translated into meaningful practices than when they are the suggestions of an outside expert.

The feedback of information and its discussion by the appropriate organizational family makes it highly relevant to the functioning of the subgroup and its members. Principles taught at a general level of abstraction are more difficult to apply than the discovery of principles from a person's own immediate experience.

Knowledge of results can in itself motivate people toward improving their performance. Level-of-aspiration studies indicate that individuals tend to raise their sights when they see the outcome of their efforts. If there is continuous feedback on the basis of some objective criterion of behavior, people will be motivated to attain better scores.

Group support is especially effective where there is continuing membership in a particular group. The members of an industrial organization during most of their waking hours are part of one or two organizational families. If the other members of these permanent groupings also change, there is a continuing reinforcement for individual change. More remote and fleeting group memberships are occasionally significant but one cannot escape the constant pressures of the here and now.

Finally a hierarchical ordering of roles with respect to authority is characteristic of most organizations, or at least of their executive systems. Hence the introduction of feedback starting at the top of the structure not only gives organizational legitimacy to the process but ensures that for every individual in the organization there will be expectations from his immediate superior about his behavior. The changes will have been worked out in part by lower levels in the organization, but in their final implementation will have the authority of the organizational line of command.

The effectiveness of this type of feedback program was demonstrated in the accounting branch of an industrial enterprise. All employees of the company had been included in a companywide study in 1948, and the results had been fed back to all branches of the organization. In 1950 a similar questionnaire was filled out by all employees of the accounting branch and these returns furnished the basis for the feedback experiment. Four accounting departments participated in the feedback process, which was initiated with a meeting of the accounting executive and his eight department heads. Two of the eight departments were eliminated from the research design because of changes in their key personnel since the 1948 survey was conducted. Two other departments were held out of the feedback process to serve as controls. In the four experimental departments the feedback activities varied somewhat, especially in the extent to which the nonsupervisory employees were involved. The basic pattern was essentially as described above, however, with meetings of organizational families down the line at which were also present a member of the research team and a member of the personnel department of the company. These latter two individuals were not active participants in the discussions except when called upon as resource people for certain types of information.

After an eighteen-month period in which the natural variations of the feedback programs in the four departments had run their course, a new survey was conducted in the accounting branch. The before and after measures indicated that more significant changes had occurred in the four experimental than in the two control departments. As Mann (1957) states:

Two measures of change were employed: a comparison of answers to sixty-one identical questions which had been asked in the previous surveys and a comparison of answers to seventeen questions dealing with changes perceived by the workers since the 1950 survey. In the experimental group (comprising four departments), a fourth of the sixty-one items showed relative mean positive changes, significant at the 0.05 level or better; the change for another 57 per cent of the items was also positive in direction, but not statistically significant. Major positive changes occurred in the experimental groups in how employees felt about (1) the kind of work they do (job interest, importance and level of responsibility); (2) their supervisor (his ability to handle people, give recognition, direct their work, and represent them in handling complaints); (3) their progress in the company; and (4) their group's ability to get the job done. The seventeen perceived-change items were designed specifically to measure changes in the areas where we expect the greatest shift in perceptions. Fifteen of these showed that a significantly higher proportion of employees in the experimental than in the control departments felt that change had occurred. More employees in the experimental departments saw changes in: (1) how well the supervisors in their department got along together; (2) how often supervisors held meetings; (3) how effective these meetings were; (4) how much their supervisor understood the way employees looked at and felt about things, etc. These findings indicate the extent to which the feedback's effectiveness lay in increasing understanding and communication as well as changing supervisory behavior.

Comparisons of the changes among the four experimental departments showed that the three departments which had two feedback sessions with their employees all showed positive change relative to the control departments. The change which occurred in the fourth was directionally positive, but it was not significantly different from the control departments. In general, the greatest change occurred where the survey results were discussed in both the departmental units and the first-line organizational units. The greater the involvement of all members of the organization through their organizational families – the department heads, the first-line supervisors, and the employees – the greater the change (pp. 161–2).

The procedure of feedback to organizational families as developed by Floyd Mann is similar in many ways to the group therapy approach of the Tavistock Institute. It has the same objective of clarification and improvement of organizational functioning through an objective assessment of problems by the organizational members themselves. It differs in four respects:

Mann had the considerable advantage of providing objective feedback on organizational functioning through detailed data furnished by his comprehensive survey. This made possible a task-oriented atmosphere where facts and figures were the guiding criteria. It also made possible the setting of performance norms, and ensured a representation of the views of all employees in the consideration of problems by the various levels of management.

Mann's technique covered the entire organizational structure in systematic fashion. The Tavistock research team entered only those sections and groups of the organization to which they were specifically invited, and tended to spend more time with top management than with the lower echelons.

The Tavistock investigators were more active participants in the change process than were Mann and his colleagues. Though the Glacier people were not presented with solutions, they were led persistently to re-examine their thinking and to become aware of unrecognized and unconscious forces in the situation.

This meant that the focus in the Glacier study was more upon irrational sources of difficulty and in the Detroit Edison Company more upon reducing areas of ignorance through the acquisition of facts and modifying vague opinions with documented beliefs. It would be interesting to have a research comparison of the amount of personal and organizational change produced by the two methods and of the mediating processes responsible for whatever changes did occur.

Both methods by choice avoid identifying in advance desired changes in organizational structure and functioning. The objective is to induce the organization to change itself. This has a tremendous advantage in removing from the researcher the onus of deciding what needs to be changed. It has the possible disadvantage of making an organization more vigorous in its present mode of operation even when there may be basic defects in its operating philosophy. For example, a non-union factory, if subjected to the Tavistock group therapy, might emerge with a management clearer in its conception and more ingenious in its pursuit of ways to prevent union organization. In general, the organizational change attained by either the therapy or the feedback technique is likely to be in the direction of more efficient functioning but not in the direction of basic structural change. The oligarchy will still remain an oligarchy, the autocracy still an autocracy. These methods represent the philosophy of mild and bland reform, not radical change.

To state it more precisely, the primary target of the feedback technique employed by Mann is improvement of both personal and role relationships within the organizational family. The objective is not to introduce a systemic change but to improve the relationships among the members of each organizational family and between organizational families, through their discussion of their common problems. The specific changes which occur may vary from one sector of organizational space to another and they may all add up to better understanding and clearer communication in the organization as a whole. But the target has not been to change the system as a system.

This approach thus raises the question of the effective limits of change which is not systemwide in its character. Lippitt, Watson and Westley (1958), in their incisive analysis of planned change, point out the problems raised by interdependence among the subparts of a system with respect to change processes. Change in one subpart can generate forces in other parts to produce related modifications, but interdependence can also mean that more sources of resistance are mobilized against any alteration of established procedures. Hence these authors emphasize the need for defining the unit in the organization appropriate to the change attempted. They write:

If the subpart is too small to cope with a given problem, it will be unable to change because of resistance originating outside the subpart, coming either from the larger systems in which it is embedded or from parallel systems to which it is related. If the unit is too large and includes semi-autonomous sub-systems which are not directly involved in the change process, it may be unable to change because of resistance originating within the system. On the other hand, if the size of the unit selected as a client system is appropriate for a particular change objective and if several subparts of this system all become committed to achieving the same objective, the motivation and energy available to the system for working on change will be intensified by the interdependence and interaction among the subparts (p. 77).

Systemic change: changing organizational variables (the Morse–Reimer experiment)

Most of the experimental attempts to produce change in organizations have been directed at individuals and not at the organization itself. This is true of the typical psychological approach with its emphasis upon individual training programs and of the group dynamics movement with its concentration on the small group irrespective of its organizational dependence. The group therapy approach of the Tavistock team recognized the organizational structure but made no direct attempt to change it. Similarly the feedback procedure of Mann recognized the interlocking organizational families but left all change to these families themselves. In everyday life, however, attempts are made to change an organization as a social system, i.e. to deal directly with organizational characteristics as properties of the organization rather than as the outcome of group and individual properties. Such an attempt involves the legitimation of changes in the role relationships making up the system. It is sometimes done by executive order, as when two companies merge and large sectors are reorganized or even eliminated. It can come about from revolution from within, as when young reformers capture a state or local political organization, oust the old guard from control, and reorganize the functioning of the political party. Systemic change can come about from pressures from without, as when the government orders the reorganization of an industrial empire which has achieved something of a monopolistic position in a given field of enterprise. Or the outside pressure can be the power of a labor union, which moves in on some of the old management functions of employee discipline, lay-off, and dismissal.

There have been very few attempts at the experimental manipulation of organizational variables by social scientists, partly because of the practical difficulties of attaining sufficient power to introduce organizational changes or of persuading organizational leaders already planning a change program to carry it out with experimental controls and measurements. To these difficulties must be added one which is self-imposed: research workers in this field have taken organizational variables as given, as the walls of the learning maze in which experiments on learning are to be run. Moreover, the individualistic bias of psychologists has prevented them from recognizing organizational variables as basic determinants of the social process.

One major experiment in which there was a direct and deliberate attempt to change an organizational variable was conducted by Morse and Reimer (1956) in one department of a large business enterprise. The organizational variable selected for modification involved the authority structure of the system, or more specifically the degree of organizational decision-making at various levels in the company. The experimenters, following the theorizing of Allport, conceptualized this variable as the degree of *axiality*, since organizations can be described as having an *axis* of control and regulation of their processes extending from the person or persons in the highest authority position down to the rank-and-file members of the organization. In the words of Morse and Reimer (1955):

The hierarchical location of the regulation and control processes on this axis is the degree of *axiality* of the organization. A description of the degree of axiality of an organization as a whole can be obtained by examining, for each hierarchical level in turn, the degree to which the organization is controlled and regulated by people at higher levels in the organization compared to the degree to which it is controlled and regulated by individuals at a given level or lower in the hierarchy (p. 1).

In this experiment the objective was to change the role structure with respect to decision-making and its accompanying activities so that the lower hierarchical levels in the structure would have more power and responsibility for carrying on the work of the organization. The essential idea was that all the advantages of small group democracy are lost in an organization in which the group has virtually no power to make decisions of any importance. Unless a given person or group in the legitimized authority structure is assigned responsibility for decision-making, all the training of individuals or of small groups to utilize group process and group decision are likely to be transitory or even abortive in their outcome.

We do not change organizations by occasional demonstrations of the value of the democratic process. The ongoing forces are structurally fixed in the system and the legitimate authority will not be affected to any appreciable degree without a direct attack upon its permanent structure. Hence the experimenters worked with the top echelons in the company to attain a legitimized change in organizational structure, so that the rank-and-file employees would be given the authority and responsibility for carrying out not only their own previous assignment but also the previous functions of the first-line supervisors. The first-line supervisors were to give up their previous decision-making for the people under them and were to take over the running of the division. In turn, the division managers gave up their former divisional responsibilities and were made responsible for the department. This left the department head without a major function and so he was asked to assume some of the executive vice-president's duties of coordination between the production department in question and the methods and personnel departments.

In other words, axiality, or the degree of control and regulation of the activities of the organization, cannot be changed at one level without affecting the whole organization. In fact, this is characteristic of any systemic property. If we are really dealing with an organizational or system variable, its manipulation will involve the entire organization. To achieve organizational change we have to deal with these systemic variables. Individual or group change applies only to specific points in organizational space and is more likely to be vitiated by the enduring systemic properties than to change them.

Change of organizational characteristics is regarded as inherently difficult to bring off because it means changing so much, and, of course, this is correct. What is overlooked, however, is that modification of major organizational processes by working with less relevant variables is infinitely more difficult to attain, even though working with such variables may entail less effort on the part of the change agent. For example, it is relatively easy to persuade many individuals to sign petitions renouncing war as a way of settling disputes between nations. Pacifist pledges of individuals have always been meaningless, however, when the latent war-making structure of the nation becomes its manifest structure in times of crisis. Unless national structures become modified to accept the jurisdiction of a larger international structure like the United Nations, war is inevitable.

The target of experimental change in the Morse and Reimer experiment was the variable of control and regulation of organizational processes. The proposed change was to shift the locus of control downward in the structure. To accomplish this purpose a variety of procedures was employed.

First in sequence was the persuasion of the executive vice-president and his assistants of the desirability of the change. Part of the persuasion was accomplished through group sessions of his own staff and the research team, part through the presentation of findings from a previous survey in his own company, the implications of which supported downward delegation. The results of the survey showed that the higher producing sections in the organization were less closely supervised and had more group involvement of their members than the lower producing sections. In the higher producing sections, for example, the clerks did not confine themselves to their own narrow job assignments but would help one another out. Supervisors in these sections gave the clerks more freedom in their tasks and gave extra time to training any clerk interested in moving up to a better job in the company.

A second procedure was the use of group discussion at various levels in the organization to prepare the employees for the anticipated change. This method of preparation also included the training of supervisors for their new roles.

The third procedure was the official introduction of the change as the new policy of the company, in a presentation by the executive vice-president himself to the employees. In other words, the change was legitimized as new role requirements by the proper authority structure. Finally, group discussion and decision-making was the mode of operation by which the rank-and-file employees and first-line supervisors implemented the new program.

Some nine months were spent in preparation for the experimental changes, including the early meetings for securing the approval of top management. The experiment itself ran for a year, with before and after measurements of productivity and morale. In all, four parallel divisions of one department were involved. Two of the divisions were assigned to the experimental treatment described above. The other two were placed in a change program which also involved manipulation of the axiality variable, but in the direction of tighter control and increased regulation from the upper echelons. In a field experiment the classical notion of a control group which operates as usual is not appropriate, since the experimental group has the advantage of special treatment no matter what the treatment. Accordingly, the design in this experiment called for the two opposed experimental treatments, to control for the effects of special attention. The divisions in the two programs were matched in productivity on the basis of their performance during the previous year. The program of downward delegation was called the *Autonomy Program*; the program of tighter control from above the *Hierarchically Controlled Program*. In the latter program of hierarchical control, decisions formerly made by first-line supervisors and by division heads were now made at the departmental level.

Some thirty-three supervisors and 204 non-supervisory employees constituted the four divisions in the two programs. Each division processed contractual forms and had separate sections dealing with lapses, cash surrenders, new business, and the like. Each was identical or similar to the other three in every respect which the company could control. Productivity was measured by the number of employees required to complete a given volume of work. The volume of work accomplished by a given section was not under its control, but what did vary was whether the section needed more or fewer clerks to get the job done. Increased productivity thus could be achieved only by out-placing some of the clerks, or not replacing those who left of their own accord. Decreased productivity would result from calling in extra workers (or floaters, in the company's terminology).

The experimental manipulations were successful in creating two different social subsystems for the two sets of divisions. In the Autonomy Program the clerical work groups did in fact make a variety of group decisions on matters of importance to them, such as recess periods, the handling of tardiness, work methods, and work processes. Some work groups were more active than others in getting together to discuss and decide on how their section should operate, but all groups in this program assumed group responsibility for the operations of the section. In the Hierarchically Controlled Program, on the other hand, the employees were less involved than before in the regulation and control of their own activities. Previously they had little direct influence on decisions, but they did have some degree of influence on their supervisors and division managers with whom they had direct contact. Now decisions were made at the departmental level, and employees were completely removed from affecting the control process. The measurement of the changes perceived by the employees in the two programs corroborates the effectiveness of the experimental manipulations. In the Autonomy Program the clerks saw decision-making activities as less a function of higher organizational levels than before the experiment, whereas in the Hierarchical Program the clerks now perceived all policies and procedures as determined to a very high degree at levels above their own.

It was hypothesized that the Autonomy Program would improve the morale of the employees in the following attitudinal areas: (a) self-actualization, (b) satisfaction with supervision, (c) liking for working for the company, (d) job satisfaction and (e) liking for the program. Correspondingly it was predicted that there would be a decrease in favorable attitudes in these areas in the Hierarchically Controlled program. It was also hypothesized that over time there would be an increase in productivity in the Autonomy Program and a decrease in productivity in the Hierarchically Controlled Program.

Self-actualization was measured by combining answers to the

following five questions into an index score. (a) Is your job a real challenge to what you think you can do? (b) How much chance does your job give you to learn things you are interested in? (c) Are the things you are learning in your job helping to train you for a better job in the company? (d) How much chance do you have to try out your ideas on the job? (e) How much does your job give you a chance to do the things you are best at? Significant differences were found in the predicted direction, with an increase in self-actualization in the Autonomy Program and a decrease in the Hierarchically Controlled Program.

The programs also had differential effects on attitudes toward supervision. Relations with the assistant manager and the division manager improved significantly in the Autonomy Program and deteriorated in the Hierarchically Controlled Program. Similarly, attraction to the company increased in the former program and decreased in the latter program. The results on intrinsic job satisfaction were less clear cut. As predicted, there was a significant decrease in the Hierarchically Controlled Program, but contrary to prediction there was no significant change in the Autonomy Program, though there was some slight improvement. Morse and Reimer speculated about this one failure of their predictions on attitudinal change as follows. 'The lack of change in the Autonomy Program may be due to the fact that the job content remained about the same. It is also possible that the increases in complexity and variety of their total work were offset by a rise in their level of aspiration, so that they expected more interesting and varied work' (p. 126).

There were marked differences between the two experimental groups in their liking for the programs to which they had been assigned.

The clerks in the Autonomy Program typically: wanted their program to last indefinitely, did not like the other program, felt that the clerks were one of the groups gaining the most from the program and described both positive and negative changes in interpersonal relations among the girls. The clerks in the Hierarchically Controlled Program, on the other hand, most frequently wanted their program to end immediately, liked the other program and felt that the company (rather than the employees) gained the most from their program. Not one single person in the Hierarchically Controlled Program mentioned an improvement in interpersonal relations as a result of the program. All of the noted changes were for the worse, with increases in friction and tension being most frequently mentioned (p. 126).

For example, whereas 24 per cent of the Autonomy group reported more cooperation and 18 per cent more friendliness among the girls than had existed prior to the program, not a single employee in the Hierarchically Controlled Program gave such a positive response.

Unfortunately there were no good overall measures of productivity, or total costs to the company in relation to amount produced by the two programs. Both experimental groups showed significant increases in productivity on the basis of company figures for the costs of clerk time to get the job done, whereas the original predictions called for an increase in the Autonomy Program and a decrease in the Hierarchically Controlled Program. As a matter of fact, the increase in the Hierarchically Controlled Program was greater than that in the Autonomy Program on the clerk-time measure of productivity.

On the other hand, the costs in terms of clerk time do not cover the costs of turnover. Of the fifty-four girls who left the company from the four divisions during the course of the experiment, twenty-three made unfavorable comments in their exit interviews with members of the personnel department about pressure and too rigorous work standards. Of these twenty-three, nineteen were from the Hierarchically Controlled Program. There is no doubt, however, that the productivity of the employees was increased by the direct expedient of assigning fewer girls to handle the same amount of work in the Hierarchically Controlled Program. This was achieved, however, at the cost of employee morale and may have been a short-run solution. What would have happened had the experiment run for a longer period can only be conjectured. A major reorganization, which had nothing to do with the experimental programs, but which called for decentralization of the whole clerical operation to divisional geographical offices, meant the end of the experimental groups.

Two other factors in extrapolating the results of this experiment to other situations should be kept in mind.

The first of these is the character of the employees. The overwhelming majority of clerks were girls recently graduated from high school who intended to stay only a few years with the company before getting married. They had little commitment to their jobs as a permanent occupation. Hence they were probably less responsive to either experimental treatment than men with more involvement in their occupation. Though they disliked the Hierarchically Controlled Program, these young, unorganized girls were not as likely to quit, go on strike, or rebel in an overt manner as more involved people might do. Management in the Hierarchical Program was able to increase productivity by tightening the screws. In other situations, management may not be able to overpower its workers in this fashion because of the presence of unions, or the presence of outside job opportunities for skilled workers, or the active resentment of a more occupation-conscious worker.

The second limiting factor in this experiment was the constant rate of work flow to all sections. This meant that the cooperative group spirit engendered in the Autonomy Program could not be fully expressed in increased productivity without disrupting the group. In effect, the girls would have had to tell their superiors that they were asking for the transfer of a group member because she was not vitally necessary for handling the volume of work. Increased productivity actually came about in the Autonomy Program when the girls decided not to replace a member who was leaving to get married or to have a baby. But they could hardly be expected to dismember their group if no one was willing to leave, and they showed no inclination to do so. If the girls themselves could have determined their quotas of work, there would have been more opportunity for increases in productivity, as in the Bavelas experiment, in which workers raised their sights about what was an acceptable, fair day's work. Under these circumstances, the Autonomy Program might well have showed larger gains in productivity. Alternatively, as Likert (1956) suggests, the continuation of the experiment might have produced continued gains in the productivity of the Autonomy Program and reversal of gains in the Hierarchical Program. However plausible these possibilities, they are only that, and await confirmation or rejection in future research. Meanwhile, the increases in productivity in the Hierarchical Program constitute a clear disconfirmation of the original prediction, and a reminder of the effective power of hierarchy under conditions favorable to it.

Field experiments of the Morse–Reimer pattern, which attempt to change an organizational variable and measure the outcome upon the functioning of the organization, are desperately needed to advance our knowledge of organizational dynamics and effectiveness. The great difficulty with the therapy and feedback approach is that, in the first place, we do not know if any significant organizational change will occur, and in the second place, if change does take place, what precisely has occurred. What is necessary in studies of this sort is a wide net of measures continued over time to discover the central change and its impact. Any organizational change which experimenters want to bring about to increase knowledge in this field must, of course, gain acceptance from the authority structure of the organization, and this itself imposes great limitations on scientific manipulations. Nonetheless, on many occasions organizations are open to modification and organizational leaders contemplate change programs themselves. Within this framework researchers can introduce the controls and measurements, and sometimes stipulate the means or sequence of change to yield more documented knowledge about social systems than we now possess.

The target of change as the fit between the technical and social subsystems

Organizational structure as the direct target for change includes all types of patterned relationships which comprise a system or subsystem. It is useful, however, to consider two dimensions of any production system, the technical system and the accompanying social-psychological system, and the fit between these two interlocking arrangements. Trist (1963) and his Tavistock colleagues have developed the concept of the socio-technical system to take account of these two related dimensions of the organization of work:

The concept of a socio-technical system arose from the consideration that any production system requires both a technological organization – equipment and process layout – and a work organization relating to each other those who carry out the necessary tasks. The technological demands place limits on the type of work organization possible, but a work organization has social and psychological properties of its own that are independent of technology. . . . (Rice, 1958, p. 4).

Some technical systems may make imperative a particular type of social arrangement; for others there may be alternative social-psychological systems possible within the technical requirements of the machines and tools for getting the task done. And yet one social-psychological system may be far superior to another, both with respect to member satisfaction and organizational productivity. The target for Trist and his research group has been to find the best fit between the technical and social systems, and to introduce into a given industry the reforms needed to attain that fit. Priority is accorded the technical requirements of task accomplishment, but this does not mean that any so-called technical improvement imported from another industry is accepted uncritically as an appropriate modification of an existing work structure.

The assumptions of this approach as presented by Rice (1958) start with the following proposition: 'The performance of the primary task is supported by powerful social and psychological forces which ensure that a considerable capacity for cooperation is evoked among the members of the organization created to perform it' (p. 33).

The sources of gratification in getting the job done are: (a) closure or a sense of completion in finishing a meaningful unit of work, (b) some control over their own activities by those engaged in a task, and (c) satisfactory relationships with those performing related tasks.

1. The completion of a whole task by an individual is of course difficult to achieve in many types of industry, but this feeling of completing a meaningful cycle of activities can be provided by the group assignment rather than the individual job. This necessitates, however, a group organization in which individuals share in some perceptible fashion a meaningful task. It has been shown in the experimental laboratory that there is a group Zeigarnik (1927) effect. Zeigarnik originally demonstrated that an interrupted task results in frustration and leads to perseveration of the interrupted

activity. People seek closure or completion of a process once begun. Moreover, if two or more people are given a common task, the logic of the Zeigarnik effect carries over to their joint activities. One member may achieve closure through the activities of his fellow member or may be stimulated to complete a task begun by his comrade. This is not conjecture. The experimental findings of Lewis and Franklin (1944) demonstrated that partners on a group task would remember the task if not allowed to complete it. If, however, one partner was allowed to finish the task, the other partner would also experience a sense of closure. And Horwitz (1954) found that groups of five college women experienced less tension for the tasks their groups had decided not to finish than for unfinished tasks which the group was committed to complete. The usual application of machine theory to the development of a technical work system overlooks the possibilities of worker motivation to perform a meaningful part of a cycle of activities which is completed by a group.

2. The need for autonomy in the control of one's own activities has already been discussed in relation to the need for self-determination and self-expression (Chapter 12). The autonomy need can find genuine expression at the group as well as the individual level. Not every person has to make all the decisions about his work in order to experience a feeling of autonomy or self-determination. If his own immediate group has some degree of decision-making, this can satisfy his needs very adequately. Moreover, it has the advantage of not] overwhelming him with responsibility for which he is not prepared.

3. The need for satisfactory work relationships with others has been discussed (Chapter 12). All that need be added here is the negative side of the coin. If the socio-technical system is not properly organized, workers may blame others indiscriminately, form cliques, and engage in reciprocal scapegoating activities.

To achieve better work organization, Rice makes the following additional assumptions:

Group stability is more easily maintained when the range of skills required of group members is such that all members of the group can comprehend all the skills and, without having, or wanting to have them, could aspire to their acquisition (pp. 37–8).

In other words the greater the differences in skill, the more difficult it is for members to communicate and the harder it is to develop group cohesiveness. Similarly,

The fewer the differences there are in prestige and status within a group, the more likely is the internal structure of a group to be stable and the more likely are its members to accept internal leadership (p. 38).

And finally,

When members of small work groups become disaffected to the extent that they can no longer fit into their own work group, those disaffected should be able to move to other small work groups engaged in similar tasks (p. 39).

These assumptions describe the conditions under which a social-psychological system can operate to further organizational goals and to increase member satisfaction. An ideal arrangement for a socio-technical system would be one in which the technical aspects of the work could be organized in such a manner that the immediate work group would have a meaningful unit of activity, some degree of responsibility for its task, and a satisfactory set of interpersonal relationships. And the greater the differences in skills, prestige and status among members of the work group, the more difficult it will be to establish and maintain satisfactory interpersonal relationships.

The Trist studies of British coal mines

The relationship between the technical and the social systems in British coal mines has been studied by Trist and Bamforth (1951) and other Tavistock researchers, with respect to problems of technological change in the industry. The production side of coal mining includes three different types of operations: (a) the winning of the coal by hand or machine from the coal face, (b) the loading and transportation of the coal from the face, and (c) the supportive and preparatory activities of advancing the roof supports and of bringing up the conveyor system as the mining cuts deeper into the coal face. The early organization of these technical operations in many British mines was a simple system of small, self-contained units working independently. For example, in some pits the primary work group would consist of six men, two to a shift. Each man would be a complete miner, i.e. would have all the skills for carrying out the three types of operations described above. The two men working during the day would go through that part of the cycle of activities which the work demanded. The two men who succeeded them on the next shift would take up the task at whatever stage in the cycle their predecessors had left it, and so on through the three shifts. All six men would be on the same paynote, i.e. they would be paid the same wages, the amount being based upon the productivity of the six-man group. The composition of the group was based on self-selection, with men selecting their own mates. Any primary work group tended, therefore, to have six men fairly equal in overall performance. The earnings and performance of different mate or marrow groups, however, varied greatly, with differences of 200 and 300 per cent between the most productive and least productive of them. Each work group enforced its own standards of production and had considerable autonomy in its task. This simple system of working had advantages in mines in which irregularities of coal seams put a premium upon the adaptability of work groups. Each team could set its own work pace as the conditions required, and each worker as a complete miner could adapt to the changing situation. Moreover, there were many psychological advantages in the system. Workers gained satisfaction from being engaged in meaningful cycles of activity, in having considerable autonomy and variety of work, and in being part of a group of their own choosing.

This traditional system of single place working was replaced in Britain by the longwall method of mining, partly because of the introduction of the face conveyor. As reported in the Trist studies:

The longwall system made possible by the face conveyor has a compelling economic advantage in that the proportion of stonework necessary for roadways in relation to extraction area is considerably reduced compared with what is necessary in single place layouts. ... There is also the question of extraction at greater depth where the lateral effects of pressure often crush short pillars and longwall faces are preferred even under high seam conditions (p. 41).

These technical changes in the coal mining process were accompanied by a reorganization of jobs and of work relationships.

The model was the machine theory of the mass production industries. Division of labor in which each worker was limited to a single task replaced the integrated task and complete miner of single place working. The three basic types of operations were separated, so that the first shift had the task of cutting into the coal face, the second shift the task of shoveling the coal into the conveyor, and the third shift the task of advancing the face and enlarging the gateways. Moreover, within each of these phases there was further job specialization. When mechanical cutters were used in the first phase, five different work roles were specified. In place of the single work group of the older system six or more task groups were established. Though the longwall technology clearly required some modification of the older social system of single place working, the kind of job fractionation introduced and the neglect of the motivational forces of the primary work group were mistakes of the first order.

The justification for job fractionation is the economy in training a worker to exercise only a single skill, and the greater efficiency of the person performing a single operation over the person performing a number of functions. But the skills which were separated out for specialization in the longwall system were not of such complexity or variety that their performance by a single worker prevented the attainment of a high level of efficiency. Moreover, the artificial distinctions between jobs failed to recognize a common underlying ability required of all miners. In addition to their direct role in the production process, miners must have the ability to contend with the dangers, threats and interferences which are part of the business of working underground. This is in fact a more basic skill than the separate acts of cutting, drilling, hewing or shoveling coal; it is, moreover, an ability which miners have in common. It is buttressed by involvement in a cohesive group, and it develops from the actual experience of working underground. It is essential for maintaining a high level of performance when difficulties arise. The conventional longwall system, because it failed to develop a work system appropriate to the utilization of this common experience and ability, depressed the productive performance of the miners.

A further difficulty with the conventional longwall system was its failure to maintain the natural or spontaneous coordination of the work cycle which had existed prior to its introduction. The longwall system organized work groups around task specialities, and each specialty had its own pay rate. Formerly each work group of six men had carried through all three phases of the mining operation, had taken joint responsibility for the amount of coal turned out, and had been paid accordingly. Now the fillers, the men who shovel the coal onto the conveyor, were given responsibility for this function alone, although they were dependent upon the previous shift for an adequate amount of work and in turn could hold up the succeeding shift if they did not make the expected progress. Each group was made pseudo-independent in its function, and was separated psychologically and socially from the other groups. The performance of the three phases of the cycle, which comprise an interdependent whole, is no longer a worker responsibility. To management fell the burden of coordination, and the longwall supervisor added for this purpose had a continual struggle meeting the crises which threatened the smooth flow of the continuing work process.

The institutionalization of the work system around specialized tasks carried over into the method of payment and produced further problems for management. Since miners were no longer paid according to the amount of coal turned out by their own group, each main task and its related sub-tasks became subject to negotiation. The result was a long list of itemized prices to cover all sub-tasks and related activities. Since objective measures were difficult to apply to many of these items, there was haggling on every payday and a constant flow of grievances from the miners. Moreover, the different specialized work groups were now in competition to increase their earnings, and anxious to put the blame for slowdowns on the other groups. Such competition does not mean greater production, because energy is channeled into making one's own task easier or better rewarded, at the expense of other jobs.

The psychological separation between work groups under the longwall system was increased by distinctions of status. The men who shoveled coal were doing a less skilled job and a less desirable job than the cutters or the hewers. New men were assigned to handling shovels in the filler group, and many of the older men in the group were resentful at not having moved to a more desirable status. They were not strongly motivated to cooperate with more privileged miners in ensuring a coordinated work cycle. An indication of the low morale of the fillers was the high rate of absenteeism found among this group.

Finally, the miners found the fractionation of their jobs distasteful. Under the old system there was variety and challenge in their work. They much preferred being multi-skilled complete miners to being hewers or cutters or fillers. In some mines where short conveyor faces made conversion to the conventional longwall system less urgent for technological reasons, the men exerted pressure to maintain the older form of group organization with the variety of tasks it entailed. There was no question that one of the most disliked features of the conventional longwall system was its tying the worker to a single, narrowly defined task.

A comparison of two different social systems for dealing with the same technical problems of production: the conventional longwall versus the composite longwall systems

The Tavistock researchers found that not all pits had moved to the conventional longwall method with its job specialization and machine theory applications. Especially in pits in which coal was found in short faces, the traditions of the single place system had sometimes been carried over into the new technological system, with its new face conveyors and its new cutters. A systematic comparison was therefore possible between two pits, one of which had taken over the conventional longwall method and the other of which had adapted the composite method of the older system to the new technology.

The composite longwall system. The composite method of the single working place originally had involved groups of six men, two on each of three shifts, with each group of six carrying major responsibility for completing the three basic phases of the production cycle. The adaptation of this system to longwall operation in the pit under observation involved forty-one men, divided among three shifts. The requirement of additional skills for handling the new machines was met, not by tying each worker to a specific job, but by the movement of the team from one task to another as the work demanded. The group would bring one phase of the operation to completion, then reassign its members for the next phase. It was not necessary for every member of the team to be completely multi-skilled; it was necessary for each team to contain enough skill in its total man power to handle any tasks that might arise. The major difference between the composite system in the single working place and in longwall mining was that in the former system there was complete rotation of tasks, while in the latter not all men were necessarily rotated through all the specialized tasks required by the new machines. There was still, however, variety in the work in that all men were rotated through a number of different jobs.

The composite work method applied to longwall mining thus restored the continuity of task effort so lacking in the conventional system. In the composite system little external coordination of activity is required because the men move naturally from one task to the next as part of the requirements of their overall role. There is no lag between phases and no group conflict over the difficulties created by one group for the succeeding group.

The cohesiveness of the composite group stems from several sources. The group selects its own members and so the marrow, or mate, relationships traditional in British coal mining are preserved. This is an especially important factor for difficult and hazardous occupations. Moreover, the group assumes responsibility both for the overall task and for the allocation of members to the various jobs. It provides not only for ready job rotation but for shift rotation as well.

Finally, the method of payment recognizes and increases the interdependence of the group members. Their monetary rewards are tied directly to their performance. To the base rate of payment is added incentive pay based upon the productivity of the group. This pooling of earnings does not require that each member draw exactly the same pay. The basic assumption, however, is that every miner in the group is a multi-skilled worker, interchangeable with his mates according to the requirements of the unfolding task, and hence entitled to the same reward. In short, the composite longwall system mobilizes the social-psychological forces of the immediate work group for maintaining a high level of production. Moreover, it saves management the cost of an external system of coordination and of the bickering each payday over payments for the itemized list of sub-tasks.

The observations of the Tavistock researchers on the functioning of the two longwall systems and their theoretical analysis of the superiority of the composite system were put to test by a factual comparison of the two systems in operation. Two panels of forty-one workers each were studied, one panel organized on the conventional longwall pattern, the other according to the composite method. Though the panels were in different pits, the conditions of work were basically the same – both coal faces were in the same seam; the geological conditions were very much alike; similar haulage systems were employed; and the same cutting technology was used.

One measure of the effectiveness of group functioning is the rate of absenteeism, both voluntary and involuntary. Absence rates usually are not sensitive measures, because the total rate of absenteeism under normal industrial conditions tends to be very low. Yet the differences between the conventional and the composite systems are striking; total absence rates in the conventional panel are two and a half times as great as in composite panels, and voluntary absence is ten times as great. A plausible explanation for these differences would emphasize two points: (a) the competitive, distrustful relations between workers on different tasks in the conventional system make the work situation less attractive psychologically than the composite system, with its supportive relationships among all workers on the panel; (b) the stresses produced by the work are greater in the conventional than in the composite method of operation. If some workers encounter heavy and difficult tasks in the conventional system there is no relief, whereas in the composite mode of operation the load can be spread among other members of the panel.

The productivity measures also implied clearly the superiority of the composite to the conventional method. Production was much more regular in the composite system. As Trist says,

... the conventional longwall with conditions quite normal ran for only twelve weeks before it lost a cut, and during these twelve weeks it needed reinforcement to enable it to complete its cycles. The composite longwall, on the other hand, ran for sixty-five weeks before it lost a cut, and never needed any reinforcement (p. 125).

Productivity as measured by output per man-shift was 3·5 tons for the conventional longwall, which was very close to the national norm; for the composite system it was 5·3 tons. When allowances were made for possible differences in seam sections and other factors, the composite system was found to be operating at 95 per cent of its potential and the conventional system to

Table 1 **Productivity as per cent of estimated face potential***

	Conventional longwall	Composite longwall
Without allowance for haulage system efficiency	67	95
With allowance	78	95

* Trist *et al.* (1963, p. 125).

be operating at 78 per cent of its potential (Table 1). Finally, a measure of organizational effectiveness must go beyond output per worker and include other costs such as supervision. It should be noted, therefore, that the greater need for external coordination in the conventional longwall method necessitated the assignment of a supervisor not required by the composite system. Not only were the forty-one men in the composite panel turning out more work than the conventional panel, but they were doing it without costing management the salary of a supervisor.

One reason offered for the greater productivity of the composite group corresponds closely to one of the types of behavior required, according to our analysis, for a high level of organizational functioning. That is the behavior which goes beyond specified role requirements and yet advances the organization toward its goals. In the conventional system men did their work without regard to the effects which their way of operating might have upon other groups.

Fillers, concentrating on tons of coal filled, were not greatly worried by the consequences for the pullers of how they put in their supports. Pullers, in their turn, were not very concerned to stack withdrawn supports behind the belt, and tended to leave them in the cutting track. For men in all groups, their view of the work of the face is limited to their own task. There is, therefore, a good deal of *unnecessary work* created by one group for another. On the composite longwall, on the other hand, where there is only one team all of whom share a single primary task and a single paynote, the effect of the work done by any shift group on their mates who will follow them on later shifts, was anticipated, and anything likely to cause extra work later was avoided. The standard of workmanship, therefore, tended to be better. The effect of these differences was very striking to the observer. On the composite face the coal was completely cleared off the face, with no band of coal left lying; the timber was always in a straight line; and the face gates and equipment were kept in very tidy order. On the conventional face, timber was badly set and out-of-line; the face always had a good deal of spillage left on it; and the gates and equipment were in noticeably less well-kept condition (p. 120).

The Tavistock research team extended its investigation to the socio-technical system emerging in other British coal fields with the introduction of new technology. For example, they compared two composite longwalls which varied in the degree to which the ideal of the composite system was approximated. One embodied all the features of the composite system, the other only some of them. This latter longwall system was organized as two face teams. Each worker was assigned one main task, supplemented by occasional involvement in other work roles. There was little movement of workers from one task group to another, and responsibility for each given task was on an individual rather a group basis. The other longwall group resembled much more closely the composite system described earlier, with multi-task jobs, rotation of work, and free movement of workers within the panel. Both the modified and the composite systems operated in the same seam, under similar technical conditions, and with workers very much alike in qualifications and experience. Again the 'pure' composite panel was definitely superior to the modified composite panel; it had a lower absence rate, a lower accident rate, higher productivity, and a more successful regulation of cycle progress.

The research team was not able to work directly with top management, government, and union officials to introduce a change program in the industry as a whole. They worked at the local level in those mines where local officials were willing to have research conducted and were interested in research outcomes. In some cases the research findings and the concepts of the researchers had an effect upon the ongoing change process. The availability of new machines had plunged the coal fields into a process of technological change, and the way was partly open to seek the most appropriate change in the accompanying social-psychological system. Nevertheless, the thrust of the Tavistock group toward developing the best fit between the technological system and the social system met with only partial success. Its efforts were limited by its inability to gain entry to the top-power circles in the industry, the difficulty of communicating the research results to groups who had not themselves been involved in the experimental comparisons, and the threat to the larger social system of the implications of a thorough rational reform. [. . .]

Change and stability

Though organizations are always in some degree of flux and rarely, if ever, attain a perfect state of equilibrium, major changes are the exception rather than the rule. They can be attributed to two sources: (a) changed inputs from the environment including the organizational supersystem, and (b) internal system strain or imbalance.

Changed inputs

Changes in information or energic input into the organization are of two types. The first – new or modified production inputs – has to do with modifications of quantity or quality in the inflow of materials and messages. These changes may be due directly to environmental changes, such as the discovery of new resources and the depletion of old ones, or to changes in the transactional process through which the organizational output provides energic return and reinforcement. The saturation of a market with a given type of product is a case in point; it demands a search for new markets, a change in product, or a revival of demand. Changes in input may also come from the supersystem which legitimizes various aspects of organizational functioning, as when new laws are enacted affecting taxes, labor relations or restrictive trade agreements.

A second type of change has to do with maintenance inputs, which represent the values and motivations of the organizational members. In general, this type of change is evolutionary. For example, in the United States the growth in intensity and extensity of the democratic ethic has slowly affected the character and expectations of the American people. When they assume their organizational roles today in industry, in government or in school, they expect, and if necessary demand, more democratic rights and privileges than most people asked or aspired to a hundred years ago. Such changes in maintenance inputs can be facilitated by outside systems, as labor unions have facilitated democratic developments within industry. Slower, more evolutionary changes in norms and values may go unnoticed until they accumulate at some critical point or threshold area and are consolidated around some precipitating event.

Internal strain and imbalance

Organizations function by means of adjustments and compromises among competitive and even conflicting elements in their structure and membership. These diverse elements produce system strain of two kinds: (a) the competition between different functional subsystems, or horizontal strain, and (b) vertical strain, the conflict between various levels in the hierarchy of power, privilege and reward.

We have already described horizontal strain in Chapter 4, in pointing out the different dynamics of the various subsystems, each with its own essential functions. Thus the research and development people, with the task of innovation and adaptation, may want to move the entire organization in a different direction than seems reasonable to people in the production subsystems. Or two divisions of a single subsystem – two departments in a university, for example – may be in competition for the same resources. Each represents to the dean the greater importance of its particular program.

In addition to conflicts engendered by differences in function, subsystems may be in conflict because of their differential rates of growth. One subsystem may for a variety of reasons show a very rapid rate of growth. It becomes a leading subsystem and other subsystems move to adjust to it, either by following its pattern or attempting to check its development. The interdependence of all units in producing a stable overall system means that no one subsystem can move very far out of line without evoking strain. Other subsystems catch up by acquiring more momentum, or the leading subsystem is checked in its expansion, or the entire organization undergoes some degree of restructuring to find a new equilibrium.

For example, suppose that the professional and technical schools of a university accept large increases in enrollment while the liberal arts college attempts to hold constant the number of new students accepted. The liberal arts college now finds its stable position threatened by the demands of the other schools of the university for more space and more resources. Moreover, service teaching of the college for other schools increases relative to its use of resources for its own students, since it must admit to its classes all qualified students in the larger university of which it is a part.

Hierarchical or vertical conflict. Every organization requires some commonality of goals which transcends the differential loyalties of sub-units and binds the organization together. Such commonality is difficult to achieve, particularly when there are large differentials in rewards and power between hierarchical ranks. The conflict evoked by such distinctions is made sharper if the different levels in the organization are defined more in terms of ascribed than achieved status. If the worker on the floor of the factory can never move up the rungs of the hierarchical ladder because of his limited education, he and his fellow workers have a common set of interests not identical with those occupying the officer positions or those eligible for them. This source of strain takes on greater significance in a democracy than a tradition-oriented society, since the values of the democratic society emphasize equality of opportunity.

It is our thesis, however, that these sources of internal strain are not the most potent causes of organizational change. The set of conditions which we have called change inputs from without are the critical factors in the significant modification of organizations. Often the changes from without interact with internal strains to promote organizational revolution. The Marxian theory that change arises from basic internal contradictions that become aggravated as the system develops seems to us disproved by the facts of history. Systems develop many mechanisms for handling internal conflict. Though they change in this process, the change is slow and generally does not alter the basic character of the system. The highly developed capitalistic countries in which internal contradictions were to have led to revolution, according to Marx, have been able to compromise their internal conflicts and maintain their essential systemic character. On the other hand, the countries which have experienced revolutions are those which suffered changed inputs. The blows of the First World War destroyed the social structure of Tsarist Russia and only then were the revolutionists able to come to power. Similarly the Chinese regime of Chiang Kai-shek was weakened by years of assault from without before it was overcome by internal revolution. The overthrow of the ancient Manchu dynasty in the earlier years of this century illustrates the same pattern of decisive external defeat as the predecessor of internal revolution.

The basic hypothesis is that organizations and other social structures are open systems which attain stability through their authority structures, reward mechanisms and value systems, and which are changed primarily from without by means of some significant change in input. Some organizations, less open than most, may resist new inputs indefinitely and may perish rather than change. We would predict, however, that in the absence of external changes, organizations are likely to be reformed from within in limited ways. More drastic or revolutionary changes are initiated or made possible by external forces.

A large-scale business organization set up along hierarchical lines and pursuing a policy of profit maximization, will not become a producers' cooperative or some other kind of democratic collectivity unless it collides with important environmental obstacles and is subjected to new inputs. A trade union with protective policies for its own members, including discriminatory hiring practices and restrictive apprentice training, becomes more open and democratic primarily as it meets obstacles to its way of operating in the larger society. A university is transformed from a teaching institution into a research–teaching complex primarily because outside funds are made available for the research function.

Two qualifications to our emphasis on external events remain to be made. First, we recognize that every organization, as a unit in a sypersystem, not only is influenced by events in that supersystem but also contributes to those events. We have, for example, spoken of the ways in which American industry has been influenced by the spread of democratic doctrine and values in the larger culture. It is no less true that life within the organization feeds into that culture as members of the organization move back and forth across the organizational boundary. The contribution of any single organization may be impossible to trace, but the relation of the organization to the outside world is nevertheless a two-way transaction.

The second qualification has to do with the cumulative effects of small internal changes. Until we have evidence from longitudinal studies of a more ambitious kind than have yet been attempted, the profundity of such cumulative changes in organizations remains a subject of speculation. It seems a logical possibility that a succession of such internally generated changes might in time produce organizational transformations of great depth without the advent of external forces. Our reading of organizational history nevertheless argues the primary role of external forces in major organizational change.

Summary

The study and the accomplishment of organizational change has been handicapped by the tendency to disregard systemic properties of organizations and to confuse individual change with change in organizational variables. More specifically, scientists and practitioners have assumed too often that an individual change will produce a corresponding organizational change. This assumption seems to us indefensible. To clarify the issue this chapter analyses seven approaches to organizational change, and considers their characteristic strengths and weaknesses.

Information. The supplying of additional cognitive input has real but limited value as a way of creating organizational change. It can support other methods, give the rationale for proposed changes, and explain what will be expected of individuals. It is not, however, a source of motivation; other methods are required to provide the necessary motive force to change. Moreover, the target of information is necessarily the individual and not the organization.

Individual counseling and therapy. These methods represent attempts, in part successful, to avoid the limitations of mere information-giving and to bring about individual change at a deeper level. It is true that the production of new insight can lead to deeper and more enduring changes in attitudes, and therefore to tendencies toward altered behavior. The target of such attempts is still the individual, however, and the translation of his new insights to organizational change is left wholly to him.

Influence of the peer group. A third, and in many ways a more potent, approach to organizational change is through the influence of the peer group. It is based on the undeniable fact that peers do constitute strong influences on individual behavior, and that a process of change successfully initiated in a peer group may become self-energizing and self-reinforcing. A dilemma is encountered, however, in trying to maximize the relevance of the peer group approach to organizational change. If the peer group consists of strangers without a common organizational affiliation, they face the same problems of transferring their insights and individual changes that we have already noted for individual approaches. If, on the other hand, the peer group is taken intact from the organization, it is likely to be inhibited in its change efforts by the role and authority structure which characterize it in the organizational setting.

Sensitivity training. This technique is essentially an ingenious extension of the peer-group approach to individual and organizational change. The primary target of change remains the individual, although recent variations of this training technique deal specifically with the problem of adapting individual change to the organizational context.

Group therapy in organizations. This approach is best illustrated by the work of Jaques, and some of his colleagues in the Tavistock Institute. It has shown significant results, and represents an original and important fusion of individual therapy and the social psychology of organizations. Its most serious limitation is the assumption that organizational conflicts are primarily the expression of individual characteristics and neuroses, for the most part unrecognized by the individual.

Feedback. This approach to organizational change developed out of the attempt to make survey research results more usable by management. It has evolved into a well-defined procedure which relies on discussion of relevant findings by organizational families, each consisting of a supervisor and his immediate subordinates. The organization-wide use of feedback begins with the president and his executive vice-presidents, and works through the hierarchy of organizational families in order. The targets of this demonstrably effective technique are personal and role relations within the organizational family.

Systemic change. In our view this is the most powerful approach to changing human organizations. It requires the direct manipulation of organizational variables. One example of this approach is the work of Morse and Reimer, in which the target of change was the hierarchical distribution of decision-making power in a large clerical organization. Other examples are provided in the work of Trist and of Rice, in mining and textile industries respectively. The target of change in their work is the goodness of fit between the social and the technical systems which comprise the organization.

The concluding sections of this chapter deal with the broad issue of change and stability in organizations, and consider the relative significance of inputs from the environment and internal strains as sources of organizational change. The argument is made that changed inputs of various kinds are the most important sources of organizational change.

References

ARGYRIS, C. (1964) *Integrating the Individual and the Organization,* Wiley.
BLAKE, R. R., and MOUTON, J. S. (1964), *The Managerial Grid,* Gulf.
BRADFORD, L., GIBB, J. and BENNE, K. (eds.) (1964), *T-Group Theory and Laboratory Method: Innovation in Re-Education.* Wiley.

Brown, W. (1960) *Exploration in Management*, Heinemann.

Emery, F. E., and Trist, E. L. (1960), 'Socio-technical systems', in *Management Sciences Models and Techniques*, vol. 2, Pergamon Press.

Horwitz, M. (1954), 'The recall of interrupted group tasks: an experimental study of individual motivation in relation to group goals', *Human Relations*, vol. 7, pp. 3–38.

Jaques, E. (1951), *The Changing Culture of a Factory*, Tavistock Publications.

Lewis, H. B., and Franklin, M. (1944), 'An experimental study of the role of ego in work: the significance of task orientation in work, *Journal of Experimental Psychology*, vol. 34, pp. 195–215.

Lippitt, R., Watson, J. and Westley, B. (1958), *The Dynamics of Planned Change*, Harcourt, Brace & World.

Mann, F. C. (1957), 'Studying and creating change: a means to understanding social organization', *Research in Industrial Human Relations*, Industrial Relations Research Association, no. 17, pp. 146–67.

Morse, N., and Reimer, E. (1955), Mimeographed report on organizational change. Survey Research Center, University of Michigan.

Morse, N., and Reimer, E. (1956), 'The experimental change of a major organizational variable', *Journal of Abnormal and Social Psychology*, vol. 52, pp. 120–29.

Rice, A. K. (1958), *Productivity and Social Organization: The Ahmedabad Experiment*, Tavistock Publications.

Schein, E. H., and Bennis, W. G. (1965), *Personal and Organizational Change through Group Methods*, Wiley.

Trist, E. L., and Bamforth, K. W. (1951), 'Some social and psychological consequences of the long-wall method of coal-getting', *Human Relations*, vol. 4, pp. 3–38.

Trist, E. L., Higgin, G. W., Murray, H., and Pollock, A. B. (1963), *Organizational choice*, Tavistock Publications.

Zeigarnik, B. (1927), 'Das Behalten erledigter und unerledigter Handlungen, III. The memory of completed and uncompleted actions', *Psychologische Forschung*, vol. 9, pp. 1–85.

Part Five
Issues and Concepts in Organizational Conflict

Heretofore our primary concern has been the analysis of the process of planned change in organizations. Along the way two assumptions have been paramount:

1. As the viewpoint of Katz and Kahn quoted in the introduction to Part Four states, the main source of organizational change is the external environment of the organization and the 'revolutionary' social, technological, cultural and political forces contained therein. Hence, an awareness and understanding of these forces becomes increasingly critical for the contemporary manager.

2. We stress the interdependence of change and conflict, believing that the effective management of one is not possible without the effective management of the other.

We now turn our attention specifically to conceptual issues in the management of conflict. And in line with these two assumptions, it might be useful at this point to systematically relate several of the dimensions of change discussed previously to three models of organizational conflict developed by Pondy in Reading 13:

Environmental change	*Organizational conflict model (Pondy)*
1. Pressure to pursue more goals, to become 'multi-valued' according to Bolt (Part Two); increased pluralism in organization's constituencies (Bennis, Part One); growing inter-organizational complexity (Terreberry, Part Two); growing demands for power among interest groups affected by the organization	*Bargaining model:* the problem of competition – competing goals and scarce resources
2. V. Thompson's 'bureaupathology' – increased task specialization and competence in subordinates, growing authority by virtue of technical expertise; greater diversity of incentive structures and the types of rewards appealing to members (Wilson, Part Three); revolutionary forces of social change (Harman and Katz and Georgopoulos, Part One); increasing aspiration levels; growing complexity of motivational structures, the emergence of 'classes in the organization' according to Brzezinski.	*Bureaucratic model:* the problem of control – superior – subordinate, vertical conflict

3. Increased experimentation with matrix structures (Argyris, Part Two); increasing differentiation and problems of integration (Lorsch and Lawrence, Part Four); growing complexity of task structures (Wilson, Part Three); problems requiring more complex interdependencies; the problem of managing information and expertise; increased role conflict and role ambiguity (See Kahn *et al.*, Part Six)

Systems model: the problem of coordination; conflict between function and specialization

Reading 14 is a comparative analysis by Deutsch of what he terms productive *vs.* destructive conflict. The appearance of Lewis Coser's *The Functions of Social Conflict* (1956), did much to direct attention to the productive potential of conflict, if managed properly. As Deutsch points out 'productive' conflict can be growthful as a means of testing one's competence and capacities; and, because it demarcates groups from one another, can foster group and individual identity. To a considerable degree, social change occurs through a process whereby groups differentiate themselves – and view themselves in conflict with other groups. Deutsch's conceptualization of productive conflict resolution is based on a model of individual creative thinking. An appreciation of the potential contribution of conflict to change can be obtained if we visualize both these organizational problems as analogous to the processes of problem-solving and creativity.

Boulding's paper (Reading 15) takes up a new and increasingly significant dimension of organizational conflict – that among organizations (inter-organizational) and between the organization and its environment. A portion of his analysis defines the relationship between *intra-* and *inter*-organizational conflict. The latter can be a planned intervention aimed at decreasing the former – a planned change *vis-à-vis* the environment whose goal is the reintegration and stabilization of the organization.

Boulding's seminal concept, 'the image', demonstrates the importance of perceptual fields in a situation of conflict. According to Boulding: 'The clue to the character of any conflict system is the self-images of the parties.' The effective management of information and organizational intelligence is an important prescription for developing the right image (see Wilensky, 1967); it is a means by which the organization can develop what Boulding calls its *proprioceptive function*: the necessity of using valid information in order 'to give it an image of itself as well as an image of the environment.'

References

COSER, L. (1956), *The Functions of Social Conflict*, Free Press.
WILENSKY, H. (1967), *Organizational Intelligence*, Basic Books.

13 L. R. Pondy

Organizational Conflict: Concepts and Models

Excerpts from L. R. Pondy, 'Organizational conflict: concepts and models', *Administrative Science Quarterly*, September, 1967, vol. 12, no. 2, pp. 296–320.

A working definition of conflict

The term 'conflict' has been used at one time or another in the literature to describe: (a) *antecedent conditions* (for example, scarcity of resources, policy differences) of conflictful behavior, (b) *affective states* (e.g. stress, tension, hostility, anxiety, etc.) of the individuals involved, (c) *cognitive states* of individuals, i.e. their perception or awareness of conflictful situations, and (d) *conflictful behavior*, ranging from passive resistance to overt aggression. Attempts to decide which of these classes – conditions, attitude, cognition, or behavior – is really conflict is likely to result in an empty controversy. The problem is not to choose among these alternative conceptual definitions, since each may be a relevant stage in the development of a conflict episode, but to try to clarify their relationships.

Conflict may be more readily understood if it is considered a dynamic process. A conflict relationship between two or more individuals in an organization can be analysed as a sequence of conflict episodes. Each conflict episode begins with conditions characterized by certain conflict potentials. The parties to the relationship may not become aware of any basis of conflict, and they may not develop hostile affections for one another. Depending on a number of factors, their behavior may show a variety of conflictful traits. Each episode or encounter leaves an aftermath that affects the course of succeeding episodes. The entire relationship can then be characterized by certain stable aspects of conditions, affect, perception and behavior. It can also be characterized by trends in any of these characteristics.

This is roughly analogous to defining a 'decision' to include activities preliminary to and following choice, as well as the choice itself. In the same sense that a decision can be thought of as a process of gradual commitment to a course of action, a conflict episode can be thought of as a gradual escalation to a state of disorder. If choice is the climax of a decision, then by analogy, open war or aggression is the climax of a conflict episode.

This does not mean that every conflict episode necessarily passes through every stage to open aggression. A potential conflict may never be perceived by the parties to the conflict, or if perceived, the conflict may be resolved before hostilities break out. Several other alternative courses of development are possible. Both Coleman (1957) and Aubert (1963) make these points clearly in their treatments of the dynamics of conflict.

Just as some decisions become programmed or routinized, conflict management in an organization also becomes programmed or institutionalized sometimes. In fact, the institutionalization of means for dealing with recurrent conflict is one of the important aspects in any treatment of the topic. An organization's success hinges to a great extent on its ability to set up and operate appropriate mechanisms for dealing with a variety of conflict phenomena.

Five stages of a conflict episode are identified: (a) latent conflict (conditions), (b) perceived conflict (cognition), (c) felt conflict (affect), (d) manifest conflict (behavior), and (e) conflict aftermath (conditions). The elaboration of each of these stages of a conflict episode will provide the substance for a working definition. Which specific reactions take place at each stage of a conflict episode, and why, are the central questions to be answered in a theory of conflict. Only the framework within which those questions can be systematically investigated is developed here.

Latent conflict

A search of the literature has produced a long list of underlying sources of organizational conflict. These are condensed into three basic types of latent conflict: (a) competition for scarce resources, (b) drives for autonomy, and (c) divergence of sub-unit goals. Later in the paper each of these fundamental types of latent conflict is paired with one of the three conceptual models. Briefly, competition forms the basis for conflict when the aggregated demands of participants for resources exceed the resources available to the organization; autonomy needs form the basis of conflict when one party either seeks to exercise control over some activity that another party regards as his own province or seeks to insulate itself from such control; goal divergence is the source of conflict when two parties who must cooperate on some joint activity are unable to reach a consensus on concerted action. Two or more types of latent conflict may, of course, be present simultaneously.

An important form of latent conflict, which appears to be omitted from this list, is role conflict. The role conflict model treats the organization as a collection of role sets, each composed of the focal person and his role senders. Conflict is said to occur when the focal person receives incompatible role demands or expectations from the persons in his role set (Kahn *et al.*, 1964, pp. 11–35). This model has the drawback that it treats the focal person as merely a passive receiver rather than as an active participant in the relationship. It is argued here that the role conflict model does not postulate a distinct type of latent conflict. Instead, it defines a conceptual relationship, the role set, which may be useful for the analysis of all three forms of latent conflict described.

Perceived conflict

Conflict may sometimes be perceived when no conditions of latent conflict exist, and latent conflict conditions may be present in a relationship without any of the participants perceiving the conflict.

The case in which conflict is perceived when no latent conflict exists can be handled by the so-called 'semantic model' of conflict (Bernard, Pear, Aron and Angell, 1957). According to this explanation, conflict is said to result from the parties' misunderstanding of each other's true position. It is argued that such conflict can be resolved by improving communications between the parties. This model has been the basis of a wide variety of management techniques aimed at improving interpersonal relations. Of course, if the parties' true positions *are* in opposition, then more open communication may only exacerbate the conflict.

The more important case, that some latent conflicts fail to reach the level of awareness also requires explanation. Two important mechanisms that limit perception of conflict are the suppression mechanism and the attention-focus mechanism.[1] Individuals tend to block out of awareness conflicts that are only mildly threatening.[2] Conflicts become strong threats, and therefore must be acknowledged, when the conflicts relate to values central to the individual's personality. The suppression mechanism is applicable more to conflicts related to personal than to organizational values. The attention-focus mechanism, however, is related more to organizational behavior than to personal values. Organizations are characteristically faced with more conflicts than can be dealt with, given available time and capacities. The normal reaction is to focus attention on only a few of these, and these tend to be the conflicts for which short-run, routine solutions are available. For organizations successfully to confront the less programmed conflicts, it is frequently necessary to set up separate sub-units specifically to deal with such conflicts.

Felt conflict

There is an important distinction between perceiving conflict and feeling conflict. *A* may be aware that *B* and *A* are in serious disagreement over some policy, but it may not make *A* tense or anxious, and it may have no effect whatsoever on *A*'s affection towards *B*. The personalization of conflict is the mechanism which causes most students of organization to be concerned with the dysfunctions of conflict. There are two common explanations for the personalization of conflict.

One explanation is that the inconsistent demands of efficient organization and individual growth create anxieties within the individual (Argyris, 1957). Anxieties may also result from identity crises or from extra-organizational pressures. Individuals need to vent these anxieties in order to maintain internal equilibrium. Organizational conflicts of the three latent types described earlier provide defensible excuses for displacing these anxieties against suitable targets. This is essentially the so-called 'tension-model' (Bernard, Pear, Aron and Angell, 1957).

A second explanation is that conflict becomes personalized

1. These two mechanisms are instances of what Cyert and March (1963, pp. 117–18) call the 'quasi-resolution' of conflict.
2. Leavitt (1964, pp. 53–72).

when the whole personality of the individual is involved in the relationship. Hostile feelings are most common in the intimate relations that characterize total institutions, such as monasteries, residential colleges and families.[3] In order to dissipate accumulated hostilities, total institutions require certain safety-valve institutions such as athletic activities or norms that legitimize solitude and withdrawal, such as the noncommunication norms prevalent in religious orders.

Thus, felt conflict may arise from sources independent of the three types of latent conflict, but latent conflicts may provide appropriate targets (perhaps symbolic ones) for undirected tensions.

Manifest conflict

By manifest conflict is meant any of several varieties of conflictful behavior. The most obvious of these is open aggression, but such physical and verbal violence is usually strongly proscribed by organizational norms. Except for prison riots, political revolutions, and extreme labor unrest, violence as a form of manifest conflict in organizations is rare. The motivations toward violence may remain, but they tend to be expressed in less violent form. Dalton (1959) has documented the covert attempts to sabotage or block an opponent's plans through aggressive and defensive coalitions. Mechanic (1964, pp. 136–49) has described the tactics of conflict used by lower-level participants, such as apathy or rigid adherence to the rules, to resist mistreatment by the upper levels of the hierarchy.

How can one decide when a certain behavior or pattern of behavior is conflictful? One important factor is that the behavior must be interpreted in the context in which it takes place. If A does not interact with B, it may be either because A and B are not related in any organizational sense, or because A has withdrawn from a too stressful relationship, or because A is deliberately frustrating B by withdrawing support, or simply because A is

3. It should be emphasized that members of total institutions characteristically experience both strong positive *and* negative feelings for one another and toward the institution. It may be argued that this ambivalence of feeling is a primary cause of anxiety. See Coser (1956, pp. 61–5); and Etzioni and Taber (1963).

drawn away from the relationship by other competing demands upon his time. In other words, knowledge of the organizational requirements and of the expectations and motives of the participants appears to be necessary to characterize the behavior as conflictful. This suggests that behavior should be defined to be conflictful if, and only if, some or all of the participants perceive it to be conflictful.

Should the term manifest conflict be reserved for behavior which, in the eyes of the actor, is deliberately and consciously designed to frustrate another in the pursuit of his (the other's) overt or covert goals? But what of behavior which is not *intended* to frustrate, but does? Should not that behavior also be called conflictful? The most useful definition of manifest conflict seems to be that behavior which, in the mind of the actor, frustrates the goals of at least some of the other participants. In other words, a member of the organization is said to engage in conflictful behavior if he consciously, but not necessarily deliberately, blocks another member's goal achievement. He may engage in such behavior *deliberately* to frustrate another, or he may do so in spite of the fact that he frustrates another. To define manifest conflict in this way is to say that the following question is important: 'Under what conditions will a party to a relationship *knowingly* frustrate another party to the relationship?' Suppose A unknowingly blocks B's goals. This is not conflictful behavior. But suppose B informs A that he perceives A's behavior to be conflictful; if then A acknowledges the message and *persists* in the behavior, it is an instance of manifest conflict.

The interface between perceived conflict and manifest conflict and the interface between felt conflict and manifest conflict are the pressure points where most conflict resolution programs are applied. The object of such programs is to prevent conflicts which have reached the level of awareness or the level of affect from erupting into non-cooperative behavior. The availability of appropriate and effective administrative devices is a major factor in determining whether conflict becomes manifest. The collective bargaining apparatus of labor–management disputes and budgeting systems for internal resource allocation are administrative devices for the resolution of interest-group conflicts. Evan and Scott have described due process or appeal systems for resolving superior–subordinate conflicts (Evan, 1965; Scott, 1965).[4] Mechanisms for resolving lateral conflicts among the parties to a functional relationship are relatively undeveloped. Transfer-pricing systems constitute one of the few exceptions. Much more common are organizational arrangements designed to *prevent* lateral conflicts, e.g. plans, schedules and job descriptions which define and delimit sub-unit responsibilities. Another alternative is to reduce the interdependence between conflicting sub-units by introducing buffers, such as inventories, which reduce the need for sales and production departments in a business firm to act in perfect accord.

The mere availability of such administrative devices is not sufficient to prevent conflict from becoming manifest. If the parties to a relationship do not value the relationship, or if conflict is strategic in the pursuit of sub-unit goals, then conflictful behavior is likely. Furthermore, once conflict breaks out on some specific issue, then the conflict frequently widens and the initial specific conflict precipitates more general and more personal conflicts which had been suppressed in the interest of preserving the stability of the relationship.[5]

Conflict aftermath

Each conflict episode is but one of a sequence of such episodes that constitute the relationships among organization participants.[6] If the conflict is genuinely resolved to the satisfaction of all participants, the basis for a more cooperative relationship may be laid; or the participants, in their drive for a more ordered

4. It is useful to interpret recent developments in leadership and supervision (e.g. participative management, Theory Y, linking-pin functions) as devices for preventing superior–subordinate conflicts from arising, thus, hopefully, avoiding the problem of developing appeals systems in the first place.

5. See Coleman (1957, pp. 9–11) for an excellent analysis of this mechanism. A chemical analogue of this situation is the supersaturated solution, from which a large amount of chemical salts can be precipitated by the introduction of a single crystal.

6. The sequential dependence of conflict episodes also plays a major role in the analysis of role conflicts by Kahn *et al.* (1964, pp. 11–35). Pondy (1964) has used the concept of 'budget residues' to explain how precedents set in budgetary bargains guide and constrain succeeding budget proceedings.

relationship, may focus on latent conflicts not previously perceived and dealt with. On the other hand, if the conflict is merely suppressed but not resolved, the latent conditions of conflict may be aggravated and explode in more serious form until they are rectified or until the relationship dissolves. This legacy of a conflict episode is here called 'conflict aftermath' (Aubert, 1963).

However, the organization is not a closed system. The environment in which it is imbedded may become more benevolent and alleviate the conditions of latent conflict, for example, by making more resources available to the organization. But a more malevolent environment may precipitate new crises. The development of each conflict episode is determined by a complex combination of the effects of preceding episodes and the environmental milieu. The main ideas of this view of the dynamics of conflict are summarized in Figure 1.

Functions and dysfunctions of conflict

Few students of social and organizational behavior have treated conflict as a neutral phenomenon to be studied primarily because of scientific curiosity about its nature and form, its causes and its effects. Most frequently the study of conflict has been motivated by a desire to resolve it and to minimize its deleterious effects on the psychological health of organizational participants and the efficiency of organization performance. Although Kahn and others pay lip service to the opinion that, 'one might well make a case for interpreting some conflict as essential for the continued development of mature and competent human beings', the overriding bias of their report is with the 'personal costs of excessive emotional strain', and, they state, 'that common reactions to conflict and its associated tensions are often dysfunctional for the organization as an on-going social system and self-defeating for the person in the long run' (Kahn et al., 1964, p. 65). Boulding (1962, pp. 305–7) recognizes that some optimum level of conflict and associated personal stress and tension are necessary for progress and productivity, but he portrays conflict primarily as a personal and social cost. Baritz (1960, p. 203) argues that Elton Mayo has treated conflict as 'an evil, a symptom of the lack of social skills', and its alleged opposite, cooperation, as 'symptomatic of health'. Even as dispassionate a theory of organization as that of March and Simon (1958, p. 112)[7] defines conflict conceptually as a '*breakdown* in the standard mechanisms of decision making', i.e. as a malfunction of the system.

It has become fashionable to say that conflict may be either

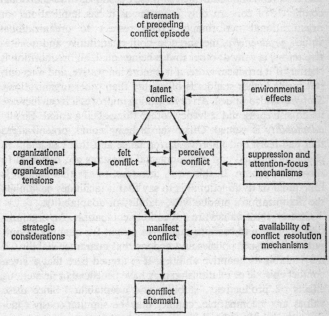

Figure 1 The dynamics of a conflict episode

functional or dysfunctional and is not necessarily either one. What this palliative leaves implicit is that the effects of conflict must be evaluated relative to some set of values. The argument with those who seek uniformly to abolish conflict is not so much with their *a priori* assertion that conflict is undesirable, as it is with their failure to make explicit the value system on which their assertion rests.

7. Italics mine. At least one author, however, argues that a 'harmony bias' permeates the entire March–Simon volume. It is argued that what March and Simon call conflicts are mere 'frictions' and 'differences that are not within a community of interests are ignored'. See Krupp (1961, pp. 140–67).

For the purposes of this research, the effects of organizational conflict on individual welfare are not of concern. Conflict may threaten the emotional well-being of individual persons; it may also be a positive factor in personal character development; but this research is not addressed to these questions. Intra-individual conflict is of concern only in so far as it has implications for organizational performance. With respect to organizational values, *productivity*, measured in both quantitative and qualitative terms, is valued; other things being equal, an organization is 'better' if it produces more, if it is more innovative, and if its output meets higher standards of quality than other organizations. *Stability* is also valued. An organization improves if it can increase its cohesiveness and solvency, other things being equal. Finally *adaptability* is valued. Other things being equal, organizations that can learn and improve performance and that can adapt to changing internal and environmental pressures are preferred to those that cannot. In this view, therefore, to say that conflict is functional or dysfunctional is to say that it facilitates or inhibits the organization's productivity, stability or adaptability.

Clearly, these values are not entirely compatible. An organization may have to sacrifice quality of output for quantity of output; if it pursues policies and actions that guarantee stability, it may inhibit its adaptive abilities. It is argued here that a given conflict episode or relationship may have beneficial or deleterious effects on productivity, stability and adaptability. Since these values are incompatible, conflict may be simultaneously functional and dysfunctional for the organization.

A detailed examination of the functional and dysfunctional effects of conflict is more effectively made in the context of the three conceptual models. Underlying that analysis is the notion that conflict disturbs the 'equilibrium' of the organization, and that the reaction of the organization to disequilibrium is the mechanism by which conflict affects productivity, stability and adaptability.

Conflict and equilibrium

One way of viewing an organization is to think of each participant as making contributions, such as work, capital and raw materials, in return for certain inducements, such as salary, interest and finished goods. The organization is said to be in 'equilibrium' if inducements exceed contributions (subjectively valued) for every participant, and in 'disequilibrium' if contributions exceed inducements for some or all of the participants. Participants will be motivated to restore equilibrium either by leaving the organization for greener pastures, when the disequilibrium is said to be 'unstable', or by attempting to achieve a favorable balance between inducements and contributions within the organization, when it is considered 'stable'. Since changing organizational affiliation frequently involves sizable costs, disequilibria tend to be stable.

If we assume conflict to be a cost of participation, this inducements–contributions balance theory may help in understanding organizational reactions to conflict. It suggests that the perception of conflict by the participants will motivate them to reduce conflict either by withdrawing from the relationship, or by resolving the conflict within the context of the relationship, or by securing increased inducements to compensate for the conflict.

The assumption that conflict creates a disequilibrium is implicit in nearly all studies of organizational conflict. For example, March and Simon (1958, pp. 115, 129) assume that 'where conflict is perceived, motivation to reduce conflict is generated', and conscious efforts to resolve conflict are made. Not all treatments of the subject make this assumption, however. Harrison White (1961) attacks the March–Simon assumption of the disequilibrium of conflict as 'naive'. He bases his assertion on his observation of chronic, continuous, high-level conflict in administrative settings. This, of course, raises the question, 'Under what conditions *does* conflict represent a disequilibrium?'

To say that (perceived) conflict represents a state of disequilibrium and generates pressures for conflict resolution, is to say three things: (a) that perceived conflict is a *cost* of participation; (b) that the conflict disturbs the inducements–contributions balance; and (c) that organization members react to perceptions of conflict by attempting to resolve the conflict, *in preference to* (although this is not made explicit in the March–Simon treatment) other reactions such as withdrawing from the relationship or attempting to gain added inducements to compensate for the conflict.

Conflict as a cost. Conflict is not necessarily a cost for the individual. Some participants may actually enjoy the 'heat of battle'. As Hans Hoffman argues, 'The unique function of man is to live in close creative touch with chaos and thereby experience the birth of order.'[8]

Conflict may also be instrumental in the achievement of other goals. One of the tactics of successful executives in the modern business enterprise is to create confusion as a cover for the expansion of their particular empire (Dalton, 1959), or, as Sorensen (1963, p. 15) observes, deliberately to create dissent and competition among one's subordinates in order to ensure that he will be brought into the relationship as an arbiter at critical times, as Franklin D. Roosevelt did.[9] Or, conflict with an out-group may be desirable to maintain stability within the in-group.

In general, however, conflict can be expected to be negatively valued; particularly if conflict becomes manifest, and sub-unit goals and actions are blocked and frustrated. Latency or perception of conflict should be treated as a cost only if harmony and uniformity are highly valued. Tolerance of divergence is not generally a value widely shared in contemporary organizations, and under these conditions latent and perceived conflict are also likely to be treated as costly.

Conflict as a source of disequilibrium. White's (1961) observation of *chronic* conflict creates doubt as to whether conflict represents a disequilibrium. He argues that if conflict *were* an unstable state for the system, then only transient conflict or conflict over shifting foci would be observable. Even if organizational participants treat conflict as a cost, they may still endure intense, chronic conflict, if there are compensating inducements from the organization in the form of high salary, opportunities for advancement and others. To say that a participant will endure chronic conflict is not to deny that he will be motivated to reduce it; it is merely to say that if the organization member is unsuccessful in reducing conflict, he may still continue to participate if the inducements offered to him exceed the contributions he makes in return.

8. Quoted in Leavitt and Pondy (1964), p. 58.
9. This latter tactic, of course, is predicated on the fact that, *for the subordinates,* conflict is indeed a cost!

Although conflict may be one of several sources of disequilibrium, it is neither a necessary nor a sufficient condition of disequilibrium. But, as will be shown, equilibrium nevertheless plays an important role in organizational reactions to conflict.[10]

Resolution pressures a necessary consequence of conflict. If conflicts are relatively small, and the inducements and contributions remain in equilibrium, then the participants are likely to try to resolve the conflict within the context of the existing relationship.[11] On the other hand, when contributions exceed inducements, or when conflict is intense enough to destroy the inducements–contributions balance and there is no prospect for the re-establishment of equilibrium, then conflict is likely to be reduced by dissolving the relationship. Temporary imbalances, of course, may be tolerated; i.e. the relationship will not dissolve if the participants perceive the conflicts to be resolvable in the near future.

What is the effect of conflict on the interaction rate among participants? It depends on the stability of the relationship. If the participants receive inducements in sufficient amounts to balance contributions, then perception of conflict is likely to generate pressures for *increased* interaction, and the content of the interaction is likely to deal with resolution procedures. On the other hand, if conflict represents a cost to the participant and this cost

10. Conflict may actually be a source of equilibrium and stability, as Coser (1956, p. 159), points out. A multiplicity of conflicts internal to a group, Coser argues, may breed solidarity, provided that the conflicts do not divide the group along the same axis, because the multiplicity of coalitions and associations provide a web of affiliation for the exchange of dissenting viewpoints. The essence of his argument is that some conflict is inevitable, and that it is better to foster frequent minor conflicts of interest, and thereby gradually adjust the system, and so forestall the accumulation of latent antagonisms which might eventually disrupt the organization. Frequent minor conflicts also serve to keep the antagonists accurately informed of each other's relative strength, thereby preventing a serious miscalculation of the chances of a successful major conflagration and promoting the continual and gradual readjustment of structure to coincide with true relative power.

11. For example, labor unions, while they wish to win the economic conflict with management, have no interest in seeing the relationship destroyed altogether. They may, however, choose to threaten such disruptive conflict as a matter of strategy.

is not compensated by added inducements, then conflict is likely to lead to *decreased* interaction or withdrawal from the relationship.

To summarize, conflict is frequently, but not always, negatively valued by organization members. To the extent that conflict *is* valued negatively, minor conflicts generate pressures towards resolution without altering the relationship; and major conflicts generate pressures to alter the form of the relationship or to dissolve it altogether. If inducements for participation are sufficiently high, there is the possibility of chronic conflict in the context of a stable relationship.

Three conceptual models of organizational conflict

As Ephron (1961, p. 55) points out, only a very abstract model is likely to be applicable to the study of all organizational conflict phenomena. To be useful in the analysis of real situations, a general theoretical framework must at least fit several broad classes of conflict, some or all of which may occur within the same organization. This suggests that different ways of abstracting or conceptualizing a given organization are required, depending on what phenomena are to be studied. The three models of organization described at the beginning of this paper are the basis of the general theory of conflict presented here.

Bargaining model

A reasonable measure of the potential conflict among a set of interest groups is the discrepancy between aggregated demands of the competing parties and the available resources. Attempts at conflict resolution usually center around attempting either to increase the pool of available resources or to decrease the demands of the parties to the conflict. Because market mechanisms or elaborate administrative mechanisms have usually evolved to guarantee orderly allocation of scarce resources, bargaining conflicts rarely escalate to the manifest level, except as strategic maneuvers.[12] Walton and McKersie (1965) describe such con-

12. However, the Negro demonstrations of the 1960s and the labor riots of the early twentieth century testify to the futility of managing interest-group conflicts when mechanisms for resolution are not available or when the parties in power refuse to create such mechanisms.

flicts as complex relationships which involve both integrative (cooperative) and distributive (competitive) sub-processes. Each party to the conflict has an interest in making the total resources as large as possible, but also in securing as large a share of them as possible for itself. The integrative sub-process is largely concerned with joint problem solving, and the distributive sub-process with strategic bargaining. A major element of strategy in strategic bargaining is that of attitudinal structuring, whereby each party attempts to secure the moral backing of relevant third parties (for example, the public or the government).

An important characteristic of interest-group conflicts is that negotiation is frequently done by representatives who face the dual problems of (a) securing consensus for the negotiated solution among respective group members, and (b) compromising between the demands for flexibility by his opposite number and the demands for rigidity by his own group.[13] The level of perceived conflict will increase as the deadline for a solution approaches; and interest-group conflicts are invariably characterized by deadline pressures.

Most of Walton and McKersie's framework has been developed and applied within the context of labor–management relations. But the interest-group model is not limited to this sphere of activity. Pondy has described the process of capital budgeting as a process of conflict resolution among departments competing for investment funds (1964). Wildavsky (1964) has described government budgeting as a political process involving the paraphernalia of bargaining among legislative and executive interest groups. Just as past labor agreements set precedents for current labor agreements, budgeting is an incremental process that builds on the residues of previous budgetary conflicts. But, whereas the visible procedures of bargaining are an accepted part of labor–management relations, there are strong pressures in budgeting (particularly *business* budgeting) to conceal the bargaining that goes on and to attempt to cloak all decisions in the guise of rationality (March and Simon, 1958, p. 131).

13. These two negotiator problems are termed 'factional conflict' and 'boundary conflict' by Walton and McKersie (1965), p. 283 *et seq*.

Bureaucratic model

The bureaucratic model (roughly equivalent to Ephron's 'political' model) is appropriate for the analysis of conflicts along the *vertical* dimension of a hierarchy, that is, conflicts among the parties to an authority relation. Vertical conflicts in an organization usually arise because superiors attempt to control the behavior of subordinates, and subordinates resist such control. The authority relation is defined by the set of subordinate activities over which the subordinate has surrendered to a superior the legitimacy to exercise discretion.[14] The potential for conflict is thus present when the superior and subordinate have different expectations about the zone of indifference. The subordinate is likely to perceive conflict when the superior attempts to exercise control over activities outside the zone of indifference; and the superior perceives conflict when his attempts at control are thwarted. Superiors are likely to interpret subordinate resistance as due to resentment of the exercise of *personal* power. A typical bureaucratic reaction to subordinate resistance is therefore the substitution of impersonal rules for personal control. As numerous students of bureaucracy are quick to point out, however, the unanticipated reaction to rules is more conflict, not less. The usual reasoning goes as follows: The imposition of rules defines the authority relation more clearly and robs the subordinate of the autonomy provided by ambiguity. Replacing supervision with control by rules invariably narrows the subordinate's freedom of action, makes his behavior more predictable to others, and thus weakens his power position in the organization. Control over the conditions of one's own existence, if not over others', is highly valued in organizations, particularly in large organizations. The subordinate therefore perceives himself to be threatened by and in conflict with his superiors, who are attempting to decrease his autonomy.

But why should autonomy be so important? What is the drawback to being subject to a benevolent autocrat? The answer, of course, is that autocrats seldom are or seldom remain benevolent.

14. This set of activities is usually called the 'zone of indifference' or 'zone of acceptance'. See Barnard (1960, pp. 168–70) and Simon (1960, pp. 11–13).

There is no assurance that the superior's (the organization's) goals, interests, or needs will be compatible with those of the subordinate, especially when: (a) organizations are so large that the leaders cannot identify personally with the rank and file; (b) responsibilities are delegated to organizational sub-units, and sub-unit goals, values, etc., become differentiated from those of the hierarchy; and (c) procedures are formalized, and the organization leaders tend to treat rank and file members as mere instrumentalities or executors of the procedures.

In short, numerous factors influence goals and values along the vertical dimension of an organization; therefore, because subordinates to an authority relation cannot rely on superiors to identify with their goals, autonomy becomes important. This leads to resistance by subordinates to attempts by superiors to control them, which in turn generates pressures toward routinization of activities and the institution of impersonal rules. This may lead to relatively predictable, conflict-free behavior, but behavior which is rigid and largely immune to personal persuasion. It is ironic that these very factors provide the potential for conflict when the organization must adapt to a changing environment. Rigidity of behavior, which minimizes conflict in a stable environment, is a major source of conflict when adaptability is required.

Research on leadership and on role conflict also provides important insights into vertical conflict. Whereas bureaucratic developments have sought to minimize conflict by altering the *fact* of supervision (for example, the use of impersonal rules and emphasis on procedure), leadership developments have sought to alter the *style* of supervision (for example, Likert's 'linking-pin' proposal and the various techniques of participative management).[15] Instead of minimizing dependence and increasing autonomy, leadership theorists have proposed minimizing conflict by using personal persuasion and group pressures to bring subordinate goals more closely into line with the legitimate goals of the organization. They have prescribed solutions which decrease autonomy and increase dependence. By heightening the individual's involvement in the organization's activities, they have actually provided the basis for the intense personal conflict that characterizes intimate relations (Coser, 1956, pp. 67–72).

15. Likert (1961). See, for example, Argyris (1962) or McGregor (1960).

Both the bureaucratic and the leadership approaches to vertical conflict, as discussed here, take the superior–subordinate dyad as the unit of analysis. The role-conflict approach opens up the possibility of examining the conflicts faced by a man-in-the-middle between the demands of his subordinates and the demands of his superiors. Blau and Scott (1962, pp. 162–3) have suggested that effective leadership can occur only on alternative levels of a hierarchy. The 'man-in-the-middle' must align himself with the interests of either his superior or his subordinate, and in so doing he alienates the other. Of the three conceptual models of conflict, the bureaucratic model has probably received the most attention from researchers from a wide variety of disciplines. Partly because of this diversity, and partly because of the ease with which researchers identify with values of efficiency or democracy, this model is the least straightforward of the three.

Systems model

The systems model, like Ephron's 'administrative' model, derives largely from the March–Simon treatment of organizational conflict (March and Simon, 1958, pp. 112–35). It is appropriate for the analysis of conflicts among the parties to a functional relationship. Or, to use Walton's terminology, the systems model is concerned with 'lateral' conflicts or conflicts among persons at the same hierarchical level (Walton, 1964). Whereas the authority-structure model is about problems of control, and the interest-group model is about problems of competition, the systems model is about problems of coordination.

The dyad is taken as the basic building block of the conceptual system. Consider two individuals, each occupying some formal position in an organization and playing some formal role with respect to the other. For example, *A* is the production manager and *B* the marketing manager of the *XYZ* company. The production manager's position is defined by the responsibility to use resources at his disposal (for example, raw materials, workers, machines) to manufacture specified products within certain constraints of quantity, quality, cost, time and perhaps procedure. The marketing manager's position is defined by the responsibility to use resources at his disposal (for example, promotional media, salesmen, saleable goods) to market and sell the company's products within certain constraints of product mix, cost, profitability, customer satisfaction, and so on. The constraints under which each manager operates and the resources at his disposal may be set for him by himself, by the other manager, or by someone else either in or outside of the company. The role of each with respect to the other is specified by the set of directions, requests, information and goods which he minimally must or maximally may give to or receive from the other manager. The roles may also specify instances of and procedures for joint selection of product mix, schedules and so on. These *formal* specifications of position and role are frequently described in written job descriptions, but may also form part of a set of unwritten, stable, widely shared expectations legitimized by the appropriate hierarchical authorities. If certain responsibilities and activities are exercised without legitimization, that is, without the conscious, deliberate recognition and approval of the appropriate authorities, then they constitute *informal* positions and roles. Such expectations may still be widely shared, and are not necessarily illegitimate, i.e. specifically proscribed by the hierarchical authorities.

The fundamental source of conflict in such a system arises out of the pressures toward sub-optimization. Assume first that the organization is goal-oriented rather than procedure-oriented. The sub-units in a goal-oriented system will, for various reasons, have different sets of active goals,[16] or different preference orderings for the same set of goals. If in turn, two sub-units having differentiated goals are functionally interdependent, then conditions exist for conflict. Important types of interdependence matter are: (a) common usage of some service or facility, (b) sequences of work or information flow prescribed by task or hierarchy, and (c) rules of unanimity or consensus about joint activity.

Two ways of reducing conflict in lateral relationships, if it be desirable to do so, therefore, are to reduce goal differentiation by modified incentive systems, or by proper selection, training, or assignment procedures; and to reduce functional interdependence. Functional interdependence is reduced by (a) reducing dependence on common resources; (b) loosening up schedules or introducing buffers, such as inventories or contingency funds; and (c)

16. Following Simon, we treat a goal as any criterion of decision. Thus, both purposes and constraints are taken to be goals. See Simon (1964).

reducing pressures for consensus. These techniques of preventing conflict may be costly in both direct and indirect costs. Interpersonal friction is one of the costs of 'running a tight ship'.

If the parties to the conflict are flexible in their demands and desires,[17] the conflict is likely to be perceived only as a transient disturbance. Furthermore, the conflict may not be perceived, if alternative relationships for satisfying needs are available. This is one of the persuasive arguments for building in redundant channels of work and information flow.

Some relationships may be traditionally conflictful (e.g administration–faculty, sales–production and others). The parties to such a relationship have a set to expect conflict, and therefore may perceive conflict when none exists.

As to the forms of manifested conflict, it is extremely unlikely that any violent or aggressive actions will occur. First, strongly held norms proscribe such behavior. Secondly, the reaction of other parties to the relationship is likely to be that of withdrawing all cooperation. A much more common reaction to perceived conflict is the adoption of a joint decision process characterized by bargaining rather than problem solving. Walton, Dutton and Fitch (1964) have described some of the characteristics of a bargaining style: careful rationing of information and its deliberate distortion; rigid, formal and circumscribed relations; suspicion, hostility, and disassociation among the sub-units. These rigidities and negative attitudes, of course, provide the potential for conflict over other issues in future episodes of the relationship.

Summary

It has been argued that conflict within an organization can be best understood as a dynamic process underlying a wide variety of organizational behaviors. The term conflict refers neither to its antecedent conditions, nor individual awareness of it, nor certain affective states, nor its overt manifestations, nor its residues of feeling, precedent, or structure, but to all of these taken together as the history of a conflict episode.

Conflict is not necessarily bad or good, but must be evaluated

17. Such flexibility is one of the characteristics of a problem-solving relationship. Conversely, a bargaining relationship is characterized by rigidity of demands and desires.

in terms of its individual and organizational functions and dysfunctions. In general, conflict generates pressures to reduce conflict, but chronic conflict persists and is endured under certain conditions, and consciously created and managed by the politically astute administrator.

Conflict resolution techniques may be applied at any of several pressure points. Their effectiveness and appropriateness depends on the nature of the conflict and on the administrator's philosophy of management. The tension model leads to creation of safety-valve institutions and the semantic model to the promotion of open communication. Although these may be perfectly appropriate for certain forms of imagined conflict, their application to real conflict may only exacerbate the conflict.

A general theory of conflict has been elaborated in the context of each of three conceptual models: (a) a bargaining model, which deals with interest groups in competition for resources; (b) a bureaucratic model, which deals with authority relations and the need to control; and (c) a systems model, which deals with functional relations and the need to coordinate.

References

ARGYRIS, C. (1957), *Personality and Organization: The Conflict Between the System and the Individual*, Harper.

ARGYRIS, C. (1962), *Interpersonal Competence and Organizational Effectiveness*, Dorsey.

AUBERT, V. (1963), 'Competition and dissensus: two types of conflict and conflict resolution', *Journal of Conflict Resolution*, vol. 7, March, pp. 26–42.

BARITZ, L. (1960), *The Servants of Power*, Wesleyan University Press.

BERNARD, C. (1960), *The Functions of the Executive*, Harvard University Press.

BERNARD, J., PEAR, T. H., ARON, R., and ANGELL, R. C. (1957), *The Nature of Conflict*, UNESCO.

BLAU, P., and SCOTT, R. (1962), *Formal Organizations*, Chandler.

BOULDING, K. (1962), *Conflict and Defense*, Harper.

COLEMAN, J. S. (1957), *Community Conflict*, Free Press.

COSER, L. (1956), *The Functions of Social Conflict*, Free Press.

CYERT, R. M., and MARCH, J. G. (1963), *A Behavioral Theory of the Firm*, Prentice-Hall.

DALTON, M. (1959), *Men Who Manage*, Wiley.

EPHRON, L. R. (1961), 'Group conflict in organizations: a critical appraisal of recent theories', *Berkeley Journal of Sociology*, vol. 6, Spring, pp. 53–72.

ETZIONI, A., and TABER, W. R. (1963), 'Scope, pervasiveness and tension management in complex organizations', *Social Research*, vol. 30, Summer, pp. 220–38.

EVAN, W. (1965), 'Superior–subordinate conflict in research organizations', *Administrative Science Quarterly*, vol. 10, June, pp. 52–64.

KAHN, R. L., *et al.* (1964), *Studies in Organizational Stress*, Wiley.

KRUPP, S. (1961), *Pattern in Organization Analysis*, Holt, Rinehart & Winston.

LEAVITT, H. J. (1964) ,*Managerial Psychology*, University of Chicago Press.

LEAVITT, H. J., and PONDY, L. R. (1964), *Readings in Managerial Psychology*, University of Chicago Press.

LIKERT, R. (1961), *New Patterns of Management*, McGraw-Hill.

MARCH, J. G., and SIMON, H. A. (1958), *Organizations*, Wiley.

MCGREGOR, D. (1960), *The Human Side of Enterprise*, McGraw-Hill.

MECHANIC, D. (1964), 'Sources of power of lower participants in complex organizations' in W. W. Cooper, H. J. Leavitt, and M. W. Shelley (eds.), *New Perspectives in Organization Research*, Wiley.

PONDY, L. R. (1964), 'Budgeting and inter-group conflict in organizations', *Pittsburgh Business Review*, vol. 34, April, pp. 1–3.

SCOTT, W. G. (1965), *The Management of Conflict: Appeals Systems in Organizations*, Irwin.

SIMON, H. A. (1960), *Administrative Behavior*, Macmillan.

SIMON, H. A. (1964), 'On the concept of organizational goal', *Administrative Science Quarterly*, vol. 9, June, pp. 1–22.

SORENSON, T. (1963), *Decision Making in the White House*, Columbia University Press.

WALTON, R. E. (1964), 'Theory of conflict in lateral organizational relationships', Institute Paper, no. 85, *Purdue University*.

WALTON, R. E., DUTTON, J. M., and FITCH, H. G. (1964), 'A study of conflict in the process, structure and attitudes of lateral relationships', Institute Paper no. 93, *Purdue University*.

WALTON, R. E., and MCKERSIE, R. B. (1965), *A Behavioral Theory of Labor Negotiations*, McGraw-Hill.

WHITE, H. (1961), 'Management conflict and sociometric structure', *American Journal of Sociology*, vol. 67, September, pp. 185–99.

WILDAVSKY, A. (1964), *The Politics of the Budgetary Process*, Little, Brown.

14 M. Deutsch

Productive and Destructive Conflict

Excerpts from M. Deutsch, 'Productive and destructive conflict'
Journal of Social Issues, January, 1969, vol. 25, no. 1, pp. 7–42.

Productive conflict

It has been long recognized that conflict is not inherently pathological or destructive. Its very pervasiveness suggests that it has
many positive functions. It prevents stagnation, it stimulates
interest and curiosity, it is the medium through which problems
can be aired and solutions arrived at; it is the root of personal
and social change. Conflict is often part of the process of testing
and assessing oneself and, as such, may be highly enjoyable as one
experiences the pleasure of the full and active use of one's
capacities. Conflict, in addition, demarcates groups from one
another and, thus, helps to establish group and personal identi-
ties; external conflict often fosters internal cohesiveness. Moreover, as Coser (1956) has indicated:

In loosely-structured groups and open societies, conflict, which aims
at a resolution of tension between antagonists, is likely to have stabilizing and integrative functions for the relationship. By permitting immediate and direct expression of rival claims, such social systems are
able to readjust their structures by eliminating the sources of dissatisfaction. The multiple conflicts which they experience may serve to
eliminate the causes for dissociation and to re-establish unity. These
systems avail themselves, through the toleration and institutionalization of conflict, of an important stabilizing mechanism (p. 154).

I stress the positive functions of conflict, and I have by no
means provided an exhaustive listing, because many discussions
of conflict cast it in the role of the villain as though conflict *per se*
were the cause of psychopathology, social disorder, war. The
question I wish to raise now is whether there are any distinguishing features in the process of resolving conflict which lead to the
constructive outcomes? Do lively, productive controversies have

common patterns that are distinctive from those characterizing deadly quarrels? [. . .]

My own predilections have led me to the hunch that the major features of the productive conflict resolution are likely to be similar, at the individual level, to the processes involved in creative thinking and, at the social level, to the processes involved in cooperative group problem-solving. Let me first turn to the process involved in creative thinking. For an incisive, critical survey of the existing literature I am indebted to Stein (1968).

Creative thinking

The creative process has been described as consisting of several overlapping phases. Although various authors differ slightly in characterizing the phases, they all suggest some sequence such as the following:

1. An initial period which leads to the experiencing and recognition of a problem which is sufficiently arousing to motivate efforts to solve it.

2. Second, a period of concentrated effort to solve the problem through routine, readily available, or habitual actions.

3. Then, with the failure of customary processes to solve the problem, there is an experience of frustration, tension and discomfort which leads to a temporary withdrawal from the problem.

4. During this incubation period of withdrawal and distancing from the problem it is perceived from a different perspective and is reformulated in a way which permits new orientations to a solution to emerge.

5. Next, a tentative solution appears in a moment of insight often accompanied by a sense of exhilaration.

6. Then, the solution is elaborated and detailed and tested against reality.

7. And finally, the solution is communicated to relevant audiences.

There are three key psychological elements in this process:

1. The arousal of an appropriate level of motivation to solve the problem.

2. The development of the conditions which permit the re-formulation of the problem once an impasse has been reached.

3. And the concurrent availability of diverse ideas which can be flexibly combined into novel and varied patterns.

Each of these key elements are subject to influence from social conditions and the personalities of the problem-solvers.

The arousal of the optimal level of motivation

Consider the arousal of an optimal level of motivation, a level sufficient to sustain problem-solving efforts despite frustrations and impasses and yet not so intense that it overwhelms or that it prevents distancing from the problem. Neither undue smugness nor satisfaction with things as they are, nor a sense of helplessness, terror or rage are likely to lead to an optimal motivation to recognize and face a problem or conflict. Nor will a passive readiness to acquiesce to the demands of the environment; nor will the willingness to fit oneself into the environment no matter how poorly it fits oneself. Optimal motivation, rather, pre-supposes an alert readiness to be dissatisfied with things as they are and a freedom to confront one's environment without excessive fear, combined with a confidence in one's capacities to persist in the face of obstacles. The intensity of motivation that is optimal will vary with the effectiveness with which it can be controlled: the more effective the controls, the more intense the motivation can be without its having disruptive consequences.

Thus, one of the creative functions of conflict resides in its ability to arouse motivation to solve a problem which might otherwise go unattended. A scholar who exposes his theories and research to the scrutiny of his peers may be stimulated to a deeper analysis when he is confronted with conflicting data and theoretical analysis by a colleague. Similarly, individuals and groups who have authority and power and who are satisfied with the status quo may be aroused to recognize problems and be motivated to work on them as opposition from the dissatisfied makes the customary relations and arrangements unworkable and unrewarding. They may be motivated also by being helped to perceive the possibilities of more satisfying relations and arrangements. Acceptance of the necessity of a change in the status quo rather than a rigid, defensive adherence to previously existing positions is most likely, however, when the circumstances arousing new motivations suggest courses of action that contain minimal threat to the social or self-esteem of those who must change.

Threats induce defensiveness

Thus, although acute dissatisfaction with things as they are, on the one hand, and the motivation to recognize and work at problems on the other, are necessary for creative solutions, they are not sufficient. The circumstances conducive to creativity are varied but they have in common that 'they provide the individual with an environment in which he does not feel threatened and in which he does not feel under pressure. He is relaxed but alert' (Stein, 1968). Threat induces defensiveness and reduces the tolerance of ambiguity as well as openness to the new and unfamiliar; excessive tension leads to a primitivization and stereotyping of thought processes. As Rokeach (1960) has pointed out, threat and excessive tension leads to the 'closed' rather than 'open' mind. To entertain novel ideas which may at first seem wild and implausible, to question initial assumptions or the framework within which the problem or conflict occurs, the individual needs the freedom or courage to express himself without fear of censure. In addition, he needs to become sufficiently detached from his original viewpoints to be able to see the conflict from new perspectives.

Although an unpressured and unthreatening environment facilitates the restructuring of a problem or conflict, and, by so doing, makes it more amenable to solution, the ability to reformulate a problem and to develop solutions is, in turn, dependent upon the availability of cognitive resources. Ideas *are* important for the creative resolution of conflict and any factor which broadens the range of ideas and alternatives cognitively available to the participants in a conflict will be useful. Intelligence, the exposure to diverse experiences, an interest in ideas, a preference for the novel and complex, a receptivity to metaphors and analogies, the capacity to make remote associations, independence in judgement, the ability to play with ideas are some of the personal factors which characterize creative problem-solvers. The availability of ideas is also dependent upon social conditions such as the opportunity to communicate with and be exposed to other people who may have relevant and unfamiliar ideas (i.e. experts, impartial outsiders, people with similar or analogous situations), a social atmosphere which values innovation and originality and which encourages the exchange of ideas, and a social tradition which fosters the optimistic view that, with effort and time, constructive solutions can be discovered or invented to problems which seem initially intractable.

Let me note that in my view the application of full cognitive resources to the discovery and invention of constructive solutions of conflict is relatively rare. Resources are much more available for the waging of conflict. The research and development expenditures on techniques of conflict-waging or conflict suppression, as well as the actual expenditures on conflict-waging, dwarf the expenditures for peace-building. This is obviously true at the national level where military expenditures dominate our national budget. I would contend that this is also true at the interpersonal and intergroup levels. At the interpersonal level, most of us receive considerable training in waging or suppressing conflict and we have elaborate institutions for dealing with adversary relations and for custodial care of the psychological casualties of interpersonal conflict. In contrast, there is little formal training in techniques of constructive conflict resolution, and the institutional resources for helping people to resolve conflicts are meager indeed. [. . .]

Controlled competitive conflict

So far my discussion has centered on unregulated conflict. I have considered characteristics of a destructive competitive process in which the outcomes are determined by a power struggle and also those of a cooperative process in which the outcomes are determined by joint problem-solving. However, it is evident that competitive conflict, because of its destructive potential, is rarely unregulated. It is limited and controlled by institutional forms (e.g. collective bargaining, the judicial system), social roles (mediators, conciliators, referees, judges, policemen), social norms ('fairness' 'justice', 'equality', 'nonviolence', 'integrity of communication', etc.), rules for conducting negotiations (when to initiate and terminate negotiations, how to set an agenda, how to present demands, etc.) and specific procedures ('hinting' versus 'explicit' communication, public versus private sessions, etc.). These societal forms may be aimed at regulating how force may be employed (as in the code of a duel of honor or in certain rules of warfare), or it may be an attempt to ascertain the basic power relations of the disputants without resort to a power struggle (as is often the case in the negotiations of collective bargaining and international relations), or it may be oriented toward removing power as the basis for determining the outcome of conflict (as is often the case in judicial processes).

With regard to regulated conflict, it is pertinent to ask what are the conditions which make it likely that the regulations will be adhered to by the parties in conflict? In a duel of honor, when would a duelist prefer to die rather than cheat? These questions, if pursued along relevant intellectual lines, would lead to an examination of different forms of rule violation and social deviance, their genesis and control. Such an investigation is beyond the scope of this paper. However, it seems reasonable to assert that adherence to the rules is more likely when: (a) the rules are known, unambiguous, consistent and unbiased; (b) the other adheres to the rules; (c) violations are quickly known by significant others; (d) there is significant social approval for adherence and significant social disapproval for violation; (e) adherence to the rules has been rewarding while uncontrolled conflict has been costly in the past; and (f) one would like to be able to employ the rules in future conflicts. Undoubtedly, the most critical influence serving to encapsulate and control competitive conflict is the existence of common membership in a community which is strong enough to evoke habitual compliance to its values and procedures and also confident enough of its strength to tolerate internal struggles.

There are several productive possibilities which inhere in regulated conflict. It provides a basis for resolving a conflict when no other basis for agreement can be reached: 'first choice' goes to the winner of the contest. However, the winner is not necessarily the sole survivor as may be the case in an uncontrolled test of power. The values and procedures regulating the conflict may select the winner on some other basis than the relative combat strength of the contestants. A conflict between husband and wife or between the United States and one of its citizens may be settled by a judicial process which permits the contestant with a stronger legal claim to win even though his physical prowess may be weaker. Or, the rules may make the contest one of intellectual rather than physical power. Thus, by the regulation of conflict a society may encourage the survival of certain values and the extinction of others because the rules for conducting conflict reflect the values of the society.

Also, insofar as a framework for limiting a conflict exists it may encourage the development of the conflict sufficiently to prevent 'premature cooperation'. The fear of the consequences of unrestrained conflict may lead to a superficial, unsatisfying and unstable agreement before the underlying issues in the conflict have been worked through. The freedom to push deeper into a conflict because some of its potential dangers have been eliminated is, of course, one of the characteristics of creative conflict resolution. However, for the conflict to be contained as it deepens, there must be a community which is strong enough to bind the conflicting parties to the values and procedures regulating conflict. If the direct or mediated cooperative interests of the conflicting parties are weak, the control process is likely to fail or be subverted; the agreements arrived at will be challenged and undermined; conflict will escalate and take a destructive turn. Effective regulation presupposes a firm basis of confidence in the mutual allegiance to the procedures limiting conflict.

Conditions which influence the course of conflict resolution

I now turn to a consideration of the factors which tend to elicit one or the other process of conflict resolution. First, I shall consider the question: What gives rise to a destructive or constructive course of conflict? Next, I shall consider the more difficult question: What can be done to change a destructive conflict into a constructive one?

Factors determining the course of conflict

There are innumerable specific factors which may influence the course which a conflict takes. It is useful to have some simplifying outline that highlights central determinants and permits a proliferation of detail as this becomes necessary.

Process

In the preceding sections, I have indicated that the characteristic strategies and tactics elicited by cooperative and competitive processes tend to be self-confirming and self-perpetuating. The strategy of power and the tactics of coercion, threat and deception result from and result in a competitive orientation. Similarly, the strategy of mutual problem-solving and the tactics of persuasion, openness and sharing elicit and are elicited by a cooperative orientation. However, cooperation which is reciprocated by competition is more likely to end up as mutual competition than mutual cooperation.

Prior relationship

The stronger and the more salient the existing cooperative as compared with the competitive bonds linking the conflicting parties, the more likely it is that a conflict will be resolved co-operatively. The total strength of the cooperative bonds is a function of their importance as well as their number. There are obviously many different types of bonds that could be enumerated: superordinate goals, mutually facilitating interests, common allegiances and values, linkages to a common community, and the like. These bonds are important to the extent that they serve significant needs successfully. Thus, experiences of successful prior cooperative relationships together enhance the likelihood of present cooperation; experiences of failure and disillusionment in attempts to cooperate make it unlikely. On the other hand, the past experience of costly competitive conflict does not necessarily enhance the probability of cooperation, although this is a possible result.

The nature of the conflict

Here I wish to highlight several major dimensions of conflict: the size (scope, importance, centrality), rigidity and interconnectedness of the issues in conflict.

Roger Fisher (1964), in a brilliant paper entitled 'Fractionating conflict', has pointed out that 'issue control' may be as important as 'arms control' in the management of conflict. His thesis is the familiar one that small conflicts are easier to resolve than larger ones. However, he also points out that the participants may have a choice in defining the conflict as a large or small one. Conflict is enlarged by dealing with it as a conflict between large rather than small units (as a conflict between two individuals of different races or as a racial conflict), as a conflict over a large substantive issue rather than a small one (over 'being treated fairly' or 'being treated unfairly at a particular occasion'), as a conflict over a principle rather than the application of a principle, as a conflict whose solution establishes large rather than small substantive or procedural precedents. Many other determinants of conflict size could be listed. For example, an issue which bears upon self-esteem or change in power or status is likely to be more important than an issue which does not. Illegitimate threat or attempts to coerce are likely to increase the size of the conflict and thus increase the likelihood of a competitive process.

'Issue rigidity' refers to the availability of satisfactory alternatives or substitutes for the outcomes initially at stake in the conflict. Although motivational and intellectual rigidity may lead the parties in conflict to perceive issues more rigidly than reality dictates, it is also evident that certain issues are less conducive to cooperative resolution than others. 'Greater power over the other', 'victory over the other', 'having more status than the other' are rigid definitions of conflict, since it is impossible on any given issue for both parties in conflict to have outcomes which are superior to the other's.

Many conflicts do not, of course, center on only one issue. If the issues are separable or sufficiently uncorrelated, it is possible for one side to gain on one issue and the other side to find satisfaction in another issue. This possibility is enhanced if the parties do not have the same evaluations: if issue A is important to one and not the other, while the reverse is true for issue B.

The characteristics of the parties in conflict

Ideology, personality and position may lead to a more favorable evaluation of one process than the other. The strategy and tactics associated with competitive struggle may seem more manly or intriguing than those associated with cooperation: consider the contrasting popular images of the soldier and of the diplomat. Similarly, the characteristics of the individual parties to a conflict will help determine the size and rigidity of the issues that they perceive to be in conflict and also their skill and available resources for handling conflict one way or another.

In addition, conflict and dissension within each party may affect the course of conflict between them. Internal conflict will often either increase external belligerence as a tactic to increase internal cohesiveness or lead to external weakness and possibly tempt the other side to obtain a competitive advantage. Internal instability also interferes with cooperative conflict resolution by making it difficult to work out a durable, dependable agreement.

Estimations of success

Many conflicts have an unplanned, expressive character in which the course of action taken is an expression both of the quality of the relationship between the participants and of the characteristics of the individual participants. Other conflicts are guided by an instrumental orientation in which courses of action are consciously evaluated and chosen in terms of how likely they are to lead to satisfying outcomes. Many factors influencing the estimations of success of the different processes of conflict resolution could be listed. Those who perceive themselves to have a clear superiority in power are likely to favor an unregulated competitive process; those who perceive themselves as having a legal superiority in 'rights' are likely to favor adversary relations that are regulated by legal institutions; those who are concerned with the long-range relationships, with the ability to work together in the future are more likely to favor a cooperative process. Similarly, those who have been excluded from the cooperative process and expect the regulations to be stacked against them may think of the competitive process as the only one offering any potential of satisfaction.

Third parties

The attitudes, strength and resources of interested third parties are often crucial determinants. Thus, a conflict is more likely to be resolved cooperatively if powerful and prestigeful third parties encourage such a resolution and help to provide problem-solving resources (institutions, facilities, personnel, social norms and procedures) to expedite discovery of a mutually satisfactory solution [. . .]

What action induces cooperation?

I have, so far, outlined what one should *not* do if one wants to elicit authentic cooperative conflict resolution. Let me turn now to the question of what courses of action can be taken which are likely to induce cooperation. In so doing, I wish to focus on a particularly important kind of conflict: conflict between those groups who have considerable authority to make decisions and relatively high control over the conventional means of social and political influence and those groups who have little decision-making authority and relatively little control over the conventional means of influence.

Although there have always been conflicts between the ruler and the ruled, between parents and children, and between employers and employees, I suggest that this is the characteristic conflict of our time. It arises from the increasing demand for more power and prosperity from those who have been largely excluded from the processes of decision-making, usually to their economic, social, psychological and physical disadvantage. The racial crisis in the United States, the student upheavals throughout the world, the revolutionary struggles in the underdeveloped areas, the controversies within and between nations in Eastern Europe, and the civil war in South Vietnam: all of these conflicts partly express the growing recognition at all levels of social life that social change is possible, that things do not have to remain as they are, that one can participate in the shaping of one's environment and improve one's lot.

Role satisfaction

It is evident that those who are satisfied with their roles in, and the outcomes of, the decision-making process may develop both a vested interest in preserving the existing arrangements and appropriate rationales to justify their positions. These rationales generally take the form of attributing superior competence (more ability, knowledge, skill) and/or superior moral value (greater initiative, drive, sense of responsibility, self-control) to oneself compared to those of lower status. From the point of view of those in power, lack of power and affluence is 'little enough punishment' for people so incapable and so deficient in morality and maturity that they have failed to make their way in society. The rationales supporting the status quo are usually accompanied by corresponding sentiments which lead their possessors to react with disapproval and resistance to attempts to change the power relations and with apprehension and defensiveness to the possibility that these attempts will succeed. The apprehension is often a response to the expectation that the change will leave one in a powerless position under the control of those who are incompetent and irresponsible or at the mercy of those seeking revenge for past injustices.

If such rationales, sentiments and expectations have been developed, those in power are likely to employ one or more defense mechanisms in dealing with the conflict-inducing dissatisfactions of the subordinated group: *denial*, which is expressed in a blindness and insensitivity to the dissatisfactions and often results in an unexpected revolt; *repression*, which pushes the dissatisfactions underground and often eventuates in a guerrilla-type warfare; *aggression*, which may lead to a masochistic sham co-operation or escalated counter-aggression; *displacement*, which attempts to divert the responsibility for the dissatisfactions into other groups and, if successful, averts the conflict temporarily; *reaction-formation*, which allows expressions of concern and guilt to serve as substitutes for action to relieve the dissatisfaction of the underprivileged and, in so doing, may temporarily confuse and mislead those who are dissatisfied; *sublimation*, which attempts to find substitute solutions – e.g. instead of increasing the decision-making power of Harlem residents over their schools, provide more facilities for the Harlem schools. [. . .]

Attention, comprehension, acceptance

But given the resistance and defensiveness of those in high power, what can we recommend to those in low power as a strategy of persuasion? As Hovland, Janis and Kelley (1953) have pointed out, the process of persuasion involves obtaining the other's *attention*, *comprehension* and *acceptance* of the message that one is communicating. The process of persuasion, however, starts with the communicator having a message that he wants to get across to the other. He must have an objective if he is to be able to articulate a clear and compelling message. Further, in formulating and communicating his message, it is important to recognize that it will be heard not only by the other, but also by one's own group and by other interested audiences. The desirable effects of a message on its intended audience may be negated by its unanticipated effects on those for whom it was not intended. I suggest that the following generalized message contains the basic elements of what Acme must communicate to Bolt to change him and, in addition, it is a message which can be overheard by other audiences without harmful consequences. Admittedly, it must be communicated in a way which elicits Bolt's attention, comprehension and acceptance of its credibility rather than in the abstract, intellectualized form in which it is presented below. And, of course, the generalized objective of equality must be detailed in terms of specific relations in specific contexts.

I am dissatisfied with our relationship and the effects it has. I think it can be improved in ways which will benefit you as well as me. I am sufficiently discontent that I can no longer continue in any relationship with you in which I do not participate as an equal in making the decisions which affect me as well as you, except as a temporary measure while we move toward equality. This may upset and discomfort you but I have no alternative other than to disengage myself from all forms of inauthentic cooperation: my dignity as well as pressure from my group will no longer allow me to engage in this self-deception and self-abasement. Neither coercion nor bribery will be effective; my self-respect and my group will force me to resist them. I remain prepared to cooperate with you as an equal in working on joint problems, including the problems involved in redefining our relationship to one another. I expect that changing our relationship will not be without its initial difficulties for both of us; we will be uncertain and perhaps suspicious, we will misunderstand and disagree and regress to old habits from time to time. I am willing to face these difficulties. I invite you to join with me to work toward improving our relationship, to overcome your dissatisfactions as well as mine. I believe that we both will feel more self-fulfilled in a relationship that is not burdened by inauthenticity.

It would take too long to detail all of the elements in this message and their rationales. But essentially the message commits Acme irreversibly to his objective, self-esteem and social esteem are at stake; he will be able to live neither with himself nor his group if he accepts an inferior status. This is done not only in words but also by the style of communicating which expresses a self-confident equality and competence. It provides Bolt with the prospect of positive incentives for changing and negative ones for not changing; Acme maintains a cooperative stance throughout and develops in action the possibility of a true mutual exchange by expressing the awareness that dissatisfactions are not one-sided. It also inoculates against some of the expected difficulties involved in change. It should be noted that Acme's statements of the threats faced by Bolt if change is not forthcoming (the instrumental threat of non-cooperation, the moral threat that the status quo violates important social norms concerning human dignity and authenticity, the threat of resistance to coercion) are neither arbitrary, illegitimate, coercive nor demanding to Bolt – i.e. they are not strongly alienating. [. . .]

Authentic cooperation

Thus, the ability to offer and engage in authentic cooperation presupposes an awareness that one is neither helpless nor power-less, even though one is at a relative disadvantage. Not only independent action but also cooperative action requires a recognition and confirmation of one's capacity to 'go it alone' if necessary. Unless one has the freedom to choose not to co-operate, there can be no free choice to cooperate. 'Black power' is, thus, a necessity for black cooperation: of black cooperation with blacks as well as with whites. Powerlessness and the associated lack of self and group esteem are not conducive either to internal group cohesiveness or to external cooperation. 'Black power' does not, however, necessarily lead to white cooperation. This is partly because, in its origin and rhetoric, 'black power' may be oriented against 'white power' and thus is likely to intensify the defensiveness of those with high power. When 'black power' is primarily directed against 'whitey' rather than for 'blacks' it is, of course, to be expected that 'whitey' will retaliate. The resulting course of events may provide some grim satisfaction to those despairing blacks who prefer to wield even short-lived destructive power rather than to be ineffectual and to those whites who prefer to be ruthless oppressors rather than to yield the psychic gains of pseudo-superiority.

However, even if 'power' is 'for' rather than 'against' and provides a basis for authentic cooperation, cooperation may not occur because it is of little import to the high power group. It may be unaffected by the positive or negative incentives that the low power group control; it does not need their compliance. Universities can obtain new students; the affluent nations no longer are so dependent upon the raw materials produced in the underdeveloped nations; the white industrial society does not need many unskilled Negro workers.

What can the group do for itself?

What can the low power group do in such situations? First of all, theoretically it may be possible to 'opt out' more or less completely – to withdraw, to migrate, to separate so that one is no longer in the relationship. However, as the world and the societies composing it become more tightly knit, this option becomes less and less available in its extreme forms. Black communities can organize their own industries, schools, hospitals, shopping centers, consumer cooperatives and the rest, but only if they have resources, and these resources would be sharply curtailed if their relationship with the broader society were completely disrupted. Similarly, students can organize their own seminars, their own living communes, their own bookstores, but it would be difficult for them to become proficient in many of the sciences and professions without using the resources available in the broader academic community. Self-imposed 'apartheid' is self-defeating. 'Build baby build' is a more useful slogan than 'out baby out' or 'burn baby burn'.

Through building its own institutions and developing its own resources a low power group makes itself less vulnerable to exploitation and also augments its power by providing itself with alternatives to inauthentic cooperation. In so doing, it increases the likelihood that those in high power will be responsive to a change: the positive incentives for changing and the negative incentives for not changing take on greater value. Moreover, such self-constructive action may help to reduce the fears and stereotypes which underlie much of the defensiveness of high power groups.

In addition to the strategy of developing one's own resources and building one's own institutions, there are still other strategies that can be followed by a low power group in the attempt to influence a reluctant or disinterested high power group. The various strategies are not incompatible with one another. I list several of the major ones: (a) augment its power by collecting or activating subgroups within the high power group or third parties as allies; (b) search for other kinds of connections with the high power group which, if made more salient, could increase its affective or instrumental dependence upon the low power group and thus change the power balance; (c) attempt to change the attitudes of those in high power through education and moral persuasion; (d) use existing legal procedures to bring pressures for change; and (e) use harassment techniques to increase the other's costs of adhering to the status quo.

The effectiveness of any strategy of influence is undoubtedly much determined by the particular circumstances so that no strategy can be considered to be unconditionally effective or ineffective. Nevertheless, it is reasonable to assume that low power groups can rarely afford to be without allies. By definition, a low power group is unlikely to achieve many of its objectives unless it can find allies among significant elements within the high power group or unless it can obtain support from other ('third party') groups that can exert influence on the high power group. There is considerable reason to expect that allies are most likely to be obtained if: (a) they are sought out rather than ignored or rejected; (b) superordinate goals, common values and common interests can be identified which could serve as a basis for the formation of cooperative bonds; (c) reasonably full communication is maintained with the potential allies; (d) one's objectives and methods are readily perceived as legitimate and feasible; (e) one's tactics dramatize one's objectives and require the potential allies to choose between acting 'for' or 'against' these objectives and, thus, to commit themselves to taking a position; and (f) those in high power employ tactics, as a counter-response, which are widely viewed as 'unfitting' and thus produce considerable sympathy for the low power group. [. . .]

Conclusion

[. . .] As social scientists we have rarely directed our attention to the defensiveness and resistance of the strong and powerful in the face of the need for social change. We have not considered what strategies and tactics are available to low power groups and which of these are likely to lead to a productive rather than destructive process of conflict resolution. We have focused too much on the turmoil and handicaps of those in low power and not enough on the defensiveness and resistance of the powerful; the former will be overcome as the latter is overcome.

Is it not obvious that with the great disparities in power and affluence within nations and between nations that there will be continuing pressures for social change? And is it not also obvious that the processes of social change will be disorderly and destructive unless those in power are able or enabled to lower their defensiveness and resistance to a change in their relative status? Let us refocus our efforts so that we will have something useful to say to those who are seeking radical but peaceful social change. Too often in the past significant social change in the distribution of power has been achieved at the cost of peace; this is a luxury that the world is no longer able to afford.

References

COLEMAN, J. S. (1957), *Community Conflict*, Free Press.

COSER, L. (1956), *The Functions of Social Conflict*, Free Press.

DEUTSCH, M. (1962a), 'Cooperation and trust: some theoretical notes', in M. R. Jones (ed.), *Nebraska Symposium on Motivation*, University of Nebraska Press.

DEUTSCH, M. (1962b), 'A psychological basis for peace', in Q. Wright, W. M. Evan and M. Deutsch (eds.), *Preventing World War III: Some Proposals*, Simon & Schuster.

DEUTSCH, M. (1965a), 'Conflict and its resolution', Presidential address before the Division of Personality and Social Psychology of *The American Psychological Association*, September 5.

DEUTSCH, M. (1965b), 'A psychological approach to international conflict', in G. Sperrazzo (ed.), *Psychology and International Relations*, Georgetown University Press.

DEUTSCH, M. (1966), 'Vietnam and the start of World War III: some psychological parallels', Presidential address before the *New York State Psychological Association*, May 6.

DEUTSCH, M. (1969), *The Resolution of Conflict*, Yale University Press.

FESTINGER, L. (1961), 'The psychological effects of insufficient reward', *American Psychologist*, vol. 16, pp. 1–11.

FISHER, R. (1964), 'Fractionating conflict', in R. Fisher (ed.), *International Conflict and Behavioral Science: The Craigville Papers*, Basic Books.

HOVLAND, C. I., JANIS, I. L., and KELLEY, H. H. (1953), *Communication and Persuasion*, Yale University Press.
ROKEACH, M. (1960), *The Open and Closed Mind*, Basic Books.
STEIN, M. I. (1968), *The Creative Individual*, in manuscript.
TOMKINS, S. S., IZARD, C. C. (eds.) (1965), *Affect, Cognition and Personality*, Springer.

15 K. Boulding

The Organization as a Party to Conflict

K. Boulding, 'The organization as a party to conflict', *Conflict and Defense*, Harper & Row, 1963, pp. 145–65.

There is a strong tendency in human society for the unorganized group to develop organization and for organizations to develop even where there has been no consciousness of a group previously, in which case the organization itself creates the group that it expresses and embodies. Consequently, group conflict tends easily to pass over into organizational conflict, and the growth of organizations themselves may create conflict where no previous consciousness of conflict existed. Furthermore, the perception of conflict with other organizations is frequently an important and sometimes a dominating factor in determining the behavior of a particular organization. Organizations frequently organize themselves against something, and, in the absence of a perception of conflict, their reason for existence is weakened or disappears, and they suffer from internal disorganization or even dissolution. Conversely, the perception of conflict is frequently heightened by the existence of organizations that are specialized for conflict. The existence of weapons predisposes both animals and men to fight, the existence of specialized conflict agencies such as armed forces predisposes nations to war, and whereas one would not want to accuse the profession of law of promoting litigation, there can be no doubt that familiarity with the law promotes litigiousness. By far the most impressive conflicts are those of organizations. Duels are less impressive than war, private lawsuits are less impressive than legislative struggles between parties or organized pressure groups, and a debate between two individuals is less impressive than the mighty clash of conflicting (and organized) ideologies or religions. I use the word 'impressive' rather than 'important' because I am not sure how to evaluate the importance of a conflict, but there can be little doubt that, by and large, the conflict of organizations makes more impression on the world than merely private quarrels.

Group conflicts either tend to be below the surface of consciousness, in which case they approach the condition that we have called competition rather than explicit conflict, or if they do rise to the surface of consciousness, they frequently produce organizations and, hence, transform themselves into organizational conflicts. These organizations may be temporary, like the informal organization of a mob under a leader or of industrial conflict among unorganized workers. There is a tendency, however, for groups to develop more formal organization, as we see it, for instance, in the development of churches out of religious movements, trade unions out of a labor force, or corporations out of informal partnerships and of nation-states out of national groups. We shall not go far wrong, then, in supposing that organizational conflict is the dominant form. Before examining its properties, however, we must take a brief look at the nature of organization and organizational behavior.

An organization is a structure of units that are called *roles*, a role being that part of a person's behavior and potential behavior that is relevant to the organization. These roles – more exactly, the persons who occupy the roles in their capacity as an occupant – are connected by lines of communication and by mutual compatibility of expectations. Thus, in a business enterprise, we have the roles of president, vice-president, controller, accountant, general manager, plant manager, sales manager, production engineer, foreman, operative, janitor and so on. The role is a job; the nature of the job to be done, to a very large extent, governs the behavior of the person doing it. We expect a manager to behave like a manager and a janitor like a janitor, no matter who occupies the role. It is true, of course, that the personality of the occupant makes some impression on the role itself. This is particularly true of the higher and more responsible roles. Nevertheless, for most roles and for most occupants, the nature of the role itself exerts a predominant influence on the behavior of the occupant in the role.

Roles may be classified according to a hierarchical, or *line*, classification or according to a division of labor, or *staff*, classification. Any organization will have some kind of hierarchy, formal or informal. There will be some communications within it that take the form of orders or instructions, and these invariably pass from higher to lower members of the hierarchy. The familiar rankings of pope, cardinals, archbishops, bishops, priests, or commander-in-chief, generals, colonels, majors, captains, lieutenants, sergeants, corporals, privates, or president, vice-president, dean, department chairman, professor, or president, general manager, branch manager, superintendent, foreman, operative are all examples of the universal pattern of line organization. Each role in a hierarchy, except the highest and the lowest, will have a number of roles beneath it to which it issues instructions and will be a member of a group of roles of equal status that receives instructions from a higher role.

Not only instructions, however, but information passes both up and down the hierarchy. A *decision* in any role is made as a result of information received as well as instructions. Instructions always have to be more general than the situations in which they have to be carried out. They set limits for the behavior of those who receive them but do not prescribe the exact behavior to be employed in all circumstances. To try to do this would be to destroy the whole purpose of organization, which is to enable the higher members of the hierarchy to control broad lines of behavior without having to channel through their minds the enormous amount of information that would be necessary to prescribe behavior in detail. The hierarchy, therefore, operates as an information filter upward, with each level of the hierarchy only passing up to the next such information as is considered relevant. The president of the corporation does not want to know that a particular machine in plant X needs oiling; the pope does not want to know the troubles of a particular parish priest in Bolivia; the general does not want to know the feelings of a particular private. The organization is thus an apparatus mainly set up to shield the executive from information. Similarly, on the downward flow of instructions, the higher the level, the more general the instructions. The president of the corporation does not want to tell a particular operative what to do with his machine; the pope does not pass on the plans for a new church building in the Philippines; the general does not set the menu for Thursday's dinner in camp X.

The simple hierarchical model is rarely adequate to describe an organization. In addition to the line organization, there is almost always a staff that is auxiliary to a particular position in the hierarchy or to some group within the organization. The main task of the staff is to collect and transmit information outside the line channels, which will give the executive in the upper ranks of the hierarchy some independent check on the general state of the organization. This is the main function of accountants, statisticians, market research men, spies, intelligence officers, stool pigeons, secret police, papal legates, ambassadors and so on. The need for these staff sources of information is twofold. In the first place, there is need for information about the environment of the organization beyond what is received by members at the end of the line. It is usually by its humblest members that an organization directly touches its external environment, for these members constitute the social surface or the extremities of the organization. Thus it is the sales-clerks who are the contacts with the selling-market environment of a great department or chain store; it is the parish priest who is the chief contact of the Roman Catholic Church with its parishioners; it is the private soldier who is most likely to come into contact with the enemy. These sources of information may be likened to the touch receptors of the body: they inform the executives or upper members of the hierarchy about its immediate environment, or the conditions at the surface. They do not, however, bear much information about the larger environment, or conditions away from the surface. Just as the body has developed information sources in the eyes and ears that inform the 'central agent' about matters at a distance through utilizing the wave motions of sound and light as information carriers, so organizations develop information sources in the staff to inform the central executive about matters at a distance. The image that the executive has of the organization and its environment, then, is built up from two sources of information: information that is filtered up the line from the lower members of the hierarchy at the surface of the organization, and information that is funneled through a staff organization specialized in the detection of conditions at a greater distance.

The second function of staff organization is to check on the information received up the filter of the hierarchy. One of the difficulties of hierarchical organization is the dependency of the lower members of the hierarchy on the upper members. This dependency almost inevitably tends to distort the information that passes from lower to higher members of the hierarchy. The lower members tend to tell the higher members what they think will be acceptable rather than what they know to be true. This is particularly likely where the upper members are domineering, aristocratic, or proud and look down on the lower members as inferiors. Such executives, whether they are monarchs, barons, dictators, or movie magnates, tend to surround themselves with yes men. Their information systems, therefore, are subject to distortion, even to the point where a totally false image of the organization and its environment is created. These false images not infrequently result in disastrous policy decisions. The greater independence of a staff organization reduces the probability of distortions of information due to dependent personal relations, especially where the staff participates in a larger professional community and develops professional, peer-judged standards of conduct. Even in the case of staff organizations, however, the problem of dependence arises. One solution of this problem is the development of independent staff organizations that sell their services to many different clients, thus ensuring themselves and the clients against undue dependency on any one of them. Thus, the auditor is an independent check on the accountant and the management consultant on the junior executives and the research staff. Similarly, the Willmark operative checks up on the salesclerks of a store, and private detectives have frequently been employed to detect disaffection among employees. The United Nations secretariat performs something of this function of an independent outside agency in the information processes of its constituent states. This function, using again an analogy from the biological organism, might be called the *proprioceptive function*. Just as the body has information receptors that inform it directly as to the position of the limbs, so an organization needs information sources to give it an image of itself as well as an image of the environment.

The fundamental principle of behavior is much the same whether we are considering an individual acting on his own behalf or a person acting in an organizational role. In each case, the behavior unit has some image of the state of things, of himself, and his environment and especially some image of the possible alternative situations or positions that this state might take under various possible lines of behavior. A decision consists of a choice among alternative states. Involved in any decision, then, are two properties of the image. There must be a set of alternatives; that is, there must be some distinction between possible and impossible states of the relevant universe in the mind of the decider. Then there must also be an ordering of these possible states at least adequate to permit identification of the state at the top of the ordering. This best state is, of course, the one that is selected. This is frequently regarded as if it were a theory of rational behavior only. This, however, is too narrow a view. All behavior, in so far as the very concept of behavior implies doing one thing rather than another and, therefore, choosing one state rather than another, falls into the above pattern, even the behavior of the lunatic and the irrational or irresponsible and erratic person. The distinction between rational and irrational behavior lies in the degree of self-consciousness and the stability of the images involved rather than in any distinction of the principle of the optimum. We must not suppose that it is only the self-conscious parts of the image that govern behavior. The image both of the state of things, of the alternatives, and of the value ordering lies partly in the conscious and partly in the unconscious. Even the most stupid and irrational behavior always involves some kind of image of the state of affairs, and the behavior that is selected is that which seems best at the moment. Thus, the difference between rational and irrational behavior must be found in the broader, more consistent, and truer images of the rational behavior rather than in any difference in the principle of behavior itself. The rational person builds up an image of the relevant state of the universe that is reasonably consistent, responsive to suitable modifications from information received, organized with the information receptors into a coherent system, and valued according to a consistent though not rigid value ordering. The irrational person has a view of the relevant universe which is partial and incomplete, or false in the sense that behavior according to this view leads to unexpected results, but which also may be rigid, not subject to modification by information received and valued by inconsistent and constantly shifting orderings, so that one state is preferred at one moment and a contrary state at another.

With this very brief sketch of a theory of organization and behavior, let us now return to the main theme of conflict, and consider the nature of a conflict system between organizations. For conflict to exist between two organizations, the following conditions must be fulfilled. First, each of the organizations must be present in the image of the responsible decision makers of the other. For simplicity, let us suppose that each organization has a single responsible decision maker, whom we will call the executive, whose decisions govern the role behavior of every member of his organization. In the minds of each of the executives, then, there must be an image of his own and of the other organization both as to their respective states and as to the value ordering that is imposed on relevant alternative states. Two organizations that are quite ignorant of each other obviously cannot be in conflict, though they might be in competition, in the sense that the actions of one might unknowingly affect the state of the other in a direction that it would value as worse. The second condition of conflict is that a decision on the part of either executive must affect the state of both organizations in value-significant directions. Two organizations that do not affect each other cannot be in competition and, therefore, cannot be in conflict. The third condition is that a decision on the part of either executive must affect the image of the state of the other in a direction that he regards as unfavorable. If every decision on the part of one produces a change in the state of the system that the other regards as favorable, that is, higher on his value scale, then there is no conflict between them.

The concept of the relevant state of the universe in the image of each organization is, of course, a complex one. It will include an image of the *extent* of both organizations and also probably an image of the power, or potential extent, of each organization. It also includes a dimension of hostility or friendliness or identification of each with the other. When two organizations, A and B, are hostile, then a movement to a state that A regards as worse for B is regarded as better by A, simply because it is thought to be worse for B.[1] It should be observed that hostility is related to the image of the other in each organization, not to the self-images. Thus it is possible for A to like a certain move because A thinks that this injures B, whereas B might regard the move as beneficia to him. This would still indicate hostility.

In all cases of conflict, we have identified the field of conflict as that set of relevant variables within which conflict movements may occur that make one party worse off and one better off in their own estimation. In the case of the organization, a very important aspect of the field of conflict is the extent of the organization. The extent of an organization may have dimensions; it may be measured, for instance, by membership, or by income, or by territory. Wherever two organizations are expanding into a common field, so that possession of part of the field by one excludes the other, conflict is possible. Thus, two churches or two trade unions may be competing for members; two nations may be competing for territory; two corporations may be competing for sales and income. As long as both organizations wish to expand into the same field, conflict is almost inevitable. Much depends here, however, on the self-image of each organization. The existence of potential conflict in a field of expansion does not necessarily involve actual conflict, if the self-images of the organizations make them content with the existing situation. Thus, two

---

1. We should perhaps distinguish between malevolent and nonmalevolent hostility. Malevolent hostility exists when A values positively his image of the worsening of B's position, simply because it is a worsening of B's position, without regard of its subsequent effects on A himself. Nonmalevolent hostility exists when A values positively a worsening of B's position, but only because of A's image of the consequences of this for A's own position; that is, the worsening of B's position is valued only because it leads directly to a bettering of A's absolute or relative position. In the case of malevolent hostility, A may move to a position that weakens or injures himself, as long as it weakens and injures B sufficiently. In nonmalevolent hostility, A will never move to a position that weakens or injures himself, though he may move to positions that weaken or injure B. Hitler's attitude toward the Jews could almost certainly be described as malevolent hostility; two firms in competition are usually in nonmalevolent hostility, for neither desires injury to the other as such but only as a means to some other end. We might even push farther up the scale and notice the possibility of *benevolent hostility*, a situation where 'this hurts me more than it hurts you'; A is forced to be hostile to B regretfully because of B's impact on A.

nations may be content with their common boundary, like the United States and Canada, even though each could only expand across this boundary at the expense of the other. Similarly, two trade unions may be content with their respective jurisdictions, even though each might possibly expand into the jurisdiction claimed by the other. Similarly, an employer and a union may stake out a boundary of rights and responsibilities that neither wishes to invade.

The condition that turns potential conflict into actual conflict might be described as *expansion pressure*; where the self-image of the organization attaches a high value to its expansion, or increase in extent in some field, whether membership, income, or territory, the possibilities of conflict are high. We can measure the expansion pressure by some desired or homeostatic rate of growth of the organization; that is, we suppose that there is some rate of growth that satisfies the self-image of the organization. If the rate of growth is below this ideal, the organization will be dissatisfied and will seek to expand faster; if it is above the ideal, the organization will slacken its efforts and not try to expand so fast. We can now make a weighted sum of the ideal rates of growth of all the organizations in a field. This we may call the no-conflict rate of growth for the whole field. If the field itself is growing at this rate, all organizations in it can achieve their ideal rates of growth, and there will be no conflict among them, at least, no conflict due to expansion competition. This assumes that the field is homogeneous and that each organization can expand into any part of it. In the case of spatial expansion, this is not so; each organization can usually expand only into that portion of space that is contiguous or at least convenient to it. This modification, however, does not affect the fundamental principle.

If, then, the rate of growth of the whole field is less than the no-conflict rate, there will inevitably be conflict among the competing organizations, in the sense that all of them together cannot satisfy their ideal rates of growth, and, therefore, if one attains or moves toward its ideal rate, this can only be done at the cost of preventing some other organization or organizations from expanding at their ideal rates. The success of one, in this case, means failure of another. If, on the other hand, the growth of the field equals or exceeds the no-conflict rate, each organization can expand at its ideal rate, and the expansion is no occasion for conflict.

There are many historical occasions that at least have the appearance of being illustrations of the above principle. Thus, when the labor movement is expanding in total membership into the field of the unorganized, the intensity of jurisdictional disputes between unions is observed to decline, for each union can expand by organizing the unorganized rather than by trying to obtain jurisdiction over the members of another union. On the other hand, in periods like the 1920s, when total union membership was stationary or declining, the intensity of jurisdictional disputes was high, for the expansion of one union frequently took place at the expense of others. It is tempting also to attribute the relative peace in Europe between 1815 and 1914 to the fact that the more aggressive European powers were busy carving themselves empires in other parts of the world and so were able to expand at the expense of the weak non-European powers rather than at the expense of each other. By 1914, however, this process had come to an end, partly because the process of exploration and seizure of the unorganized parts of the world was almost complete and partly because of the rise of non-European powers like Japan and the United States. The belligerency of the twentieth century in Europe by contrast with the nineteenth may in part be due to this cessation in the expansion of the field. The diminution in religious strife in Christendom in the nineteenth century may also in part be attributed to the fact that a great part of the energy of the more belligerent and expansion-minded sects was diverted into the task of missionary activity in non-Christian areas (organizing the unorganized) rather than to mutual competition for members at home.

We must be careful, of course, not to erect what is at best an insight, or a partial model, into a universal principle. It is not always true that an expansion of the field leads to a diminution of conflict among the organizations that seek to occupy it. The ideal rate of growth of an organization is not a stationary magnitude; it can and does vary with the history of the organization. Frequently, a dangerously unstable situation arises because the experience of a little growth whets the appetite for more. Thus, a situation in which the field has been stationary for a considerable period and in which the organizations in it have adjusted themselves to zero or to very small rates of growth may be disturbed by a sudden expansion in the field, so that organizations now revise their ideal rates of growth sharply upward and may collectively overestimate the potential growth of the field, so that an acute conflict situation may develop from what originally was an expansion of the field, which normally one would expect to diminish conflict.

It is clear that the problem of the determinants of the self-image of organizations and especially the determinants of their image of the ideal rate of growth is quite critical for the theory of organizational conflict. Unfortunately, this is a vast and little-explored field, and only a few tentative suggestions can be made at this point. Reverting to our skeleton theory of the organization itself, we can postulate that the contrast between a conservative, timid organization with a low ideal rate of growth and little expansion pressure and an aggressive, expansion-minded organization with a high ideal rate of growth depends to a considerable extent on the nature of the persons who occupy the critical executive roles; that is, this is a characteristic that is person-determined rather than role-determined. The higher we go in the hierarchy of an organization, the more important become the person-determined aspects of behavior relative to the role-determined aspects. The operative or the private soldier has little opportunity for stepping outside his prescribed role, that is, for the exercise of individuality and initiative. The leader of a great state, the president of a university, or the head of a church has a less clearly prescribed role, even though the extent of his freedom to mold the role can easily be exaggerated. Consequently, the inevitable succession of persons in the top roles brings changes to the character of an organization that are the result of the personality of the occupant rather than that of the role structure itself. In looking at the larger dynamics of an organization, then, we must look carefully at the processes by which the top roles are filled. Where the occupants of top roles are drawn from a small, self-perpetuating oligarchy, the character of the organization is likely to be fairly stable, because as each place in the group falls vacant, say, by death or retirement, the surviving members are likely to select a new occupant who has characteristics much like the old. Where, however, the occupants of top roles are selected by processes in which chance plays a large role, it is quite possible for the role to be occupied by a succession of very different personality types, each of which will give his distinctive stamp to the role and, therefore, to the whole organization. The self-image of the organization, therefore, depending, as it does, to no small extent on the personality of the occupant of the dominant role or roles, may undergo radical shifts, from, say, passive to active or peaceable to aggressive, as chance places aggressive or peaceable individuals in the key roles.

Two highly contrasting processes of selection of the occupants of upper roles have this common property of having a large element of chance. One is the hereditary principle, and the other is democratic election. In neither of these, of course, is the selection of the occupant of the upper role a matter of pure chance, as it almost seems to have been in those Greek republics which chose their officials by lot. The eldest son is likely to inherit at least some of the qualities of his father and will certainly receive an important cultural inheritance to build him up into the role that he is to occupy. Nevertheless, in the accidents of human heredity, chance plays an important part, and cases have been numerous where strong, vigorous fathers have been succeeded by weak, timorous sons and, perhaps somewhat less numerous but still not uncommon, where weak fathers have produced strong sons. In democratic election, likewise, the process is not one of pure chance, less so, in fact, than when the succession of role occupants is determined by the hereditary principle. Nevertheless, it must be admitted that chance factors are important both in the selection of candidates and in the final election. In both the hereditary monarchy and the representative democracy, a certain principle of alternation may frequently be observed. A vigorous and aggressive king is succeeded by a son who has grown up under that shadow of his father and who reacts by contrast to become a less aggressive character. Similarly, in democratic states, an aggressive and militaristic government is often succeeded by a quiet and peaceable one, and vice versa, as the policies of one lead to exhaustion or of the other to apparent weakness or to a humbling of national pride.

We have looked here at the impact of the occupant on the role;

we must not neglect, however, the equally important, perhaps more important, impact of the role on the occupant. We have noticed that this impact is likely to be stronger, the further down the hierarchy we go. Nevertheless, it is frequently very strong even at the upper levels. This is especially true in large organizations where each of the upper roles is the nucleus of a large inner organization of staff. To a very large extent, the staff creates the role that it serves, because of its control over the information that reaches the occupant of the role and especially because of the atmosphere of valuation that it creates. If no man is a hero to his valet, still less is he a hero to his staff, and, by subtle and often not so subtle judgements on the decisions of a boss, the staff molds his image of the role to its own. This provides continuity even in those roles where chance plays a large part in the selection of the occupant. We see this, for instance, in the basic continuity that guides the policies of great nations in spite of wide divergence in character and even in the overt policies of the occupiers of the top roles. This continuity comes in very large part from the staff – the civil service, the career diplomats, and the foreign office or department of state, which act in many ways as self-perpetuating oligarchies.

The staff may provide continuity, but what determines the nature of these continuous policies? This is a difficult question to answer, for the basic character of an organization is a product of its whole history. Nevertheless, the influence of the environment of the organization is powerful, especially the influence of the other organizations that form usually so important a part of that environment. Frequently, indeed, the character of an organization is determined by the nature of its enemies, for its enemies are the most important part of its environment. Thus we often find that corrupt or aggressive unions face corrupt or aggressive employers, that aggressiveness in one nation produces aggressiveness in its neighbors, or even that one hostile or aggressive family in a neighborhood can set the whole neighborhood to quarrelsomeness. The more cheerful converse of this gloomy picture is that generous and responsible attitudes on the part of employers and unions reinforce each other and that nations, like Canada and the United States, frequently are able to live together for long periods in mutual trust and security. We do not explain much, of course, by saying that the character of an organization is determined by its environment, especially by the other organizations that surround it, unless we know what determines the character of these other organizations. There is danger of being involved in circular reasoning here. Nevertheless, we can appeal to something like a generalized Richardson process of character action and reaction that moves a group of interacting organizations either toward aggressive and corrupt characters as each reacts to the other or toward peaceable and responsible characters. As in all these dynamic processes, it may frequently be a hairbreadth at the beginning of the process that determines whether the end product will be good or bad; this is the watershed principle that we have noticed earlier. In this characterological dynamics, the influence of the saints and the devils may be of importance. The saints are those organizations which react to bad characteristics of their surrounding organizations in such a way as to improve them. Similarly, the devils react to good characteristics of the surrounding organizations in such a way as to worsen them. Because of the watershed principle, a few saints or devils may at times exercise a quite disproportionate influence on the final result.

Beside the external influences on the character or self-image of an organization, there are also important influences that arise out of the internal structure of an organization. One of the most acute problems in the perpetuation of an organization is that of maintaining internal cohesion. The larger an organization grows, the more tendency there is for factions and dissident elements to grow within it and for the organization ultimately to split or to fall apart. We see this happening in a perfectly regular and creative way in the splitting of the cell. We see it happening in irregular and disorderly ways in civil war and wars of independence, in religious schisms, in trade-union splits and so on. The problem here is that of maintaining a consistent structure of roles that can be filled by reasonably satisfied occupants. If the organization consists of a structure of roles which nobody can be found to fill or for which only dissatisfied occupants can be found, then it is in grave danger of dissolution. We may distinguish perhaps between a situation of factionalism, where there is competition for the top roles among those who occupy the roles immediately below the top, and the revolutionary situation, in which there is dissatisfaction among those who occupy the lower roles sufficient to disrupt the organization or to displace those who occupy all the higher places in the hierarchy.

The problem of internal stability in an organization thus resolves itself into that of the rewards of the role: generally speaking, an organization with rewarding roles will be internally stable; one with unrewarding roles will be internally unstable. The rewards of a role may in turn be of two kinds: external rewards, such as wages or salaries or other perquisites, which are granted to the individual as an inducement to occupy the role, and internal rewards, which consist in the satisfaction derived from the performance of the role itself. Some roles, like that of the honorary secretary, are so rewarding internally that they need no external inducements; most jobs, however, need external rewards before incumbents can be found to occupy them. Practically all roles involve a mixture of both internal and external inducements: by and large, the greater the one, the smaller need be the other.

The power of an organization to offer external rewards to its role occupants depends mainly on its ability to attract revenue of some kind. This it may do by producing and selling goods and services, like a business firm, or by attracting voluntary contributions, like a church or charitable institution, or by being able to exact involuntary contributions (taxes), like the state. Its power to offer internal rewards depends to a great extent on the significance for the value systems of the participants of the overall task and function of the organization and on the extent to which the roles themselves are felt to be significant in the larger purposes of the occupants. An organization that is felt to have mean and unworthy purposes will find it hard to offer internal rewards, and if this is to survive, it must, therefore, find itself in a position where it can attract sufficient revenue to pay the necessary external rewards. An organization, on the other hand, that is felt to have noble purposes with which the participant wishes to be identified can offer large internal rewards. The ability of states, churches, armies and religious orders to attract devoted service with very little in the way of external reward is an important factor in the survival and in the competitive strength of these organizations.

An important element in the internal strength of large organizations is their ability to capitalize on loyalties that are generated toward smaller groups within the organization. It is often the small face-to-face group that commands the deepest loyalties, especially in difficult or dangerous situations. A man dies for his buddies rather than for his country, and the large internal rewards that have to be generated by states at war are frequently aroused by exploiting for the benefit of the larger group loyalties that are generated by putting small groups to difficult or concentrated tasks, in which success or failure is easily measured. One of the problems of large organizations is that it is difficult to keep large purposes before the minds of small people. Consequently, organizations frequently devise a system of minor goals for individuals and smaller groups which altogether may fit into the larger purpose but which are close enough to the individual and to his levels of aspiration to be powerful as motivators. So we have courses and grades in school and college as aids to the broader objective of the increase in knowledge, we have production quotas and group productivity tests in both socialized and in private industry as aids to the larger ends of the organizations, and so on. Degrees, titles, orders, medals, citations and suchlike claptrap of life are part of the same process.

It seems to be a fact that most organizations can increase the internal rewards of their role occupants by putting the organization in a situation of strain or conflict. There are several possible reasons for this. One is that a situation of conflict heightens the sense of the larger purpose of the organization and so augments the internal rewards that come from a feeling of participation in these larger purposes. A conflict usually simplifies the purposes of an organization, simply because the objective of winning or surviving the conflict comes to dominate over all others. Thus, a nation in peacetime has a diversity of purposes and objectives. It is harder to achieve a sense of national unity under these conditions, and factions and diverse interests within the nation tend to pull it apart. A strong enemy, however, is a great unifying force; in the face of a common threat and the overriding common purpose of victory or survival, the diverse ends and conflicting interests of the population fall into the background and are swallowed up into the single, measurable, overriding end of winning the conflict. We see this principle operating most clearly in alliances: the threat of Hitler, for instance, produced an alliance between the Western powers and Russia that fell apart as soon as the common threat disappeared. In many ways, organizations are creations of their enemies, and it is through a common hatred of the enemy that they establish their internal unity. We see this not only in nations – where George III's England created the United States, Napoleon's France created Germany, and so on – but in labor unions, where the enmity of the employer frequently creates a solidarity of feeling that no mere common interest could create, and even in churches, where a sect often establishes its internal unity by battles against the heretic and the unbeliever.

It is, therefore, a very serious question for the theory of conflict whether there are circumstances under which conflict is necessary for the internal stability of organizations. We need perhaps to distinguish three cases. Case 1 is where we have organizations existing in contact but without conflict, or at least without serious and organized conflict, because neither their internal stability requires an enemy nor are their self-images inconsistent with the maintenance of the *status quo*. Case 2 is where we have organizations existing in stable conflict, where either because of the requirements of internal stability or because of the incompatible self-images of the organizations, conflict is a necessary part of the system but does not proceed to the extinction of the organizations or of the system. There is just enough conflict to maintain the internal unity of the organizations and not enough to destroy them. Perhaps the best example of such a system is an athletic league. The whole purpose and internal unity of the teams would disappear if there were no conflict, for conflict with other teams is almost the sole purpose of the organization. Nevertheless, the conflict is limited by a larger organization and by a set of rules that prevents or at least limits the destruction of the constituent organizations. Case 3 is that of unstable conflict, where conflict is a necessary part of the system for much the same reasons that prevail in case 2 but where the absence of an overall organization, or any limits on the conflict, or mutual viability of the constituent organizations makes the system unstable, so that some or all of the organizations are destroyed and the system disintegrates. Examples of all three cases can be found in history. Thus, in international relations, the United States and Canada, at least since the mid-nineteenth century, are an example of case 1. Enmity toward Canada is in no sense necessary to the internal unity of the United States; a somewhat covert enmity toward the United States is of more importance in the national unity of Canada, but it apparently is sufficient for this enmity to remain covert. The self-images of the two nations are compatible: Canada does not have the power and the United States does not have the will to upset the present arrangement of frontiers and the existing mutual disarmament. The international system of, say, the eighteenth and nineteenth centuries approximates case 2: the self-images, for instance, of Britain and France were inconsistent over most of the period, and rising nations like the United States and Germany needed wars to create their internal national unity. The system as a whole, however, was fairly stable; the various nations were probably mutually viable, and the conventions of limited war for the most part prevailed. International relations in the twentieth century probably illustrate case 3: nations are neither mutually viable, nor do they have consistent self-images; and a desperate state of peril results.

One of the phenomena observed in organizational conflict is the possibility of sudden shifts in the character of one or more of the parties as new occupants get into top roles, as new factions within an organization rise to dominance, or as old bosses get new ideas. The character of organizations is probably much less stable than the character of persons, and an important element in organizational conflict consists in attempts by one organization to change the character of another in a direction that the former regards as favorable. Communists, for instance, indulge in a good deal of boring from within in the attempt to remake the character of organizations with which they are in potential conflict. It is not unknown for one nation to foment a revolution in another. This technique is rare in the case of conflict among corporations or firms, unless we interpret the merger movement along these lines. The whole vast art of persuasion, however, whether expressed in advertising, missionary work, government propaganda, or political-party campaigning, can be interpreted as attempts on the part of some organizations to affect the behavior of other organizations favorably to the first, even though these organizations are not necessarily in conflict. A constant source of error and ineptitude in conflict situations is a result of an *image-lag*, the failure to recognize changes in the nature of the enemy or even of the friend. We build up our images slowly and often painfully, and it is painful to change them: contradictory evidence is at first rejected or may even be twisted to support the image, as every act of the outside world, for instance, no matter how friendly, is interpreted by the paranoic as hostile.

We are now perhaps in a position to evaluate more carefully the similarities and differences between individuals and organizational conflict. In spite of the greater complexities of organizational conflict, the similarities bulk larger than the differences. The clue to the character of any conflict system is the self-images of the parties. In the case of an individual, this may be a fairly simple, unified image; in the case of an organization, we must consider the images of its many participant members, and the chain by which information reaches these members and modifies the images is longer, more diffuse, and correspondingly more capable of false transmissions. Even in the case of large organizations, however, the image of certain key persons occupying top roles is of dominating importance, and even though the processes by which these images are created and modified is more complex, it is not essentially different from that by which the image of an individual is created and modified. Whereas we must be careful to avoid a certain oversimplification that is involved in the personification of organizations, it is not inappropriate to regard such broad concepts as character and personality as having applicability both to persons and to organizations. Much of the theory of conflicting organizations, therefore, applies equally well either to organizations or to persons. The main difference lies in the greater capacity of organizations for growth and, therefore, for incompatability in their self-images. Persons are sharply limited in extent by their biological structure; organizations are much less limited in this way, though, even here, the biological limits on the capacity for the receipt of information and for the elaboration of images may be important. For this reason, organizational conflict is likely to be more extensive, more diffuse, and perhaps more dangerous than the conflict of persons. It is not, however, an essentially different system.

Part Six
The Management of Conflict

Under conditions of conflict, we often have an image that we
are making strategic moves which enhance our own values,
when in fact we are not. Boulding has coined an important
concept – *long-sightedness* – to describe the existence of valid
'realistic images' in such situations, and in a recent essay he
offers a prescription for developing this capability:

Conflict management is something which does not necessarily arise
out of the conduct of conflict itself. It has to be fed into it from
outside. That is to say, it is when conflict exists in a social matrix
and also an organizational matrix which can lead to a lot of input
into the system from outside parties that it is most likely to result in
constructive learning and benign processes (Boulding, 1966, pp.
246–7).

Reading 16, the summary chapter of Kahn *et al.*'s book
Organizational Stress, provides an original and useful
'organizational matrix' within which to analyse conflict.
This study conceives of an organization as a system of
overlapping role sets – organization positions manned by
individuals who send and receive expectations, which can be
highly conflicting and ambiguous. The empirical analysis
conducted by Kahn *et al.* found that role conflict is related to
job tension; hence, an understanding of this unique form of
conflict seems critically important.

Reading 17, by Gamson, is based upon a perspective that
the exercise of power in organizations should be analysed in
two ways: (a) as generated by 'potential partisans' attempting
to influence the choices of authorities; and (b) as the process
by which authorities maintain social control in attempting to
achieve certain collective goals. This two-way perspective is
important because a major problem of contemporary change

for organizations is managing the crisis of legitimacy generated by partisans who do not necessarily consider themselves, in Gamson's terminology, 'agents of the social system'. The problem for those in authority is how to respond to the conflict generated by such discontent. This task becomes rather awesome as a leader must have the potential for meaningful change in influence attempts, yet, also be cognizant of the potential major breakdown in social control inherent in the dynamics of this process.

Gamson examines strategies which can enable authorities to contain the bounds of excessive attempts at influence by partisans. We would argue that the effectiveness of these strategies – where effectiveness includes a capacity to accept significant change as well as maintain needed social control – depends on the ability of the leader to empathize with both of Gamson's perspectives on power. The reader should attempt to empathize with both roles – as one in authority and as a discontented 'partisan'.

The last paper in this closing section (Reading 18) also relates the management of conflict to the problem of effecting change. Richard Walton's paper analyses the conflict processes inherent in two approaches to social change: one based upon power strategies, the second based on attitude-change strategies. If a power strategy is adopted, the manager then requires a compatible paradigm of conflict management – one based upon such concepts as game theory, bargaining and so on. The attitude-change approach assumes that the most meaningful change will occur if a paradigm is utilized which involves reducing inter-group hostilities, developing trust, empathy, minimizing perceived differences. Walton's analysis raises the intriguing possibility that a major problem in planned organizational change may not be the change *per se* or resistance to it, but rather the differing assumptions made by individuals and groups about how to manage the conflict which invariably accompanies it.

Reference

BOULDING, K. (1966), 'Conflict management as a learning process', in A. de Reuck (ed.), *Conflict in Society*, Little, Brown.

16 R. L. Kahn *et al.*

The Management of Organizational Stress

R. L. Kahn *et al.*, 'The management of organizational stress', from
Organizational Stress, Wiley, 1964, chapter 19, pp. 375–98.

This has been a study of organizations and some of their unintended effects on the people who work in them. Organizations
were not invented, of course, to damage their members, and they
are not run for that purpose. As one executive murmured regretfully, 'It just comes out that way'. It does indeed come out that
way for many people; the nature, the extent and some of the
reasons for this costly form of industrial accident were the subject
of our research.

In concentrating on such side effects of organization, however,
it is easy to fall into the trap so often occupied by those who deal
with illness rather than health. If one focuses only on people's
troubles, the whole world appears disease-ridden.

We reject this tendency. We recognize the positive contributions of work and organizational membership, not only to standards of consumption but to the meaningfulness and enjoyment
of life. Four out of five men claim that they would continue working even if they inherited enough money to make work economically unnecessary. Moreover, in explaining this widespread view
most of them emphasize the contribution of work to the content
of their lives. They speak, on the positive side, of the need to keep
occupied and interested, and on the negative side of feeling lost
and directionless without work. When asked to think of the
things they would miss most if they were not allowed to work,
more mention friends, 'the people I know', than any other single
factor (Morse and Weiss, 1955; Weiss and Kahn, 1960).

These attitudes reflect a recognition of the positive functions of
work and organizational membership; they do not imply, however, an idealization of particular conditions of employment. The
majority of men would like to continue working – but not at the

same job! People who are bound tightly into large organizations (especially their lower echelons) are most emphatic in stating that, were they to work without economic need, they would do so in a different job. The people who are most certain that they would continue in their present jobs come from the least bureaucratized occupations – the professions and farming. These responses are consistent with the idea that work is important scarcely less for the experience of working than for the sake of consuming the products of work.

Our assertions about organizational conflict and ambiguity are best assessed against this background. The positions under study in our intensive research design were not selected for unusual stressfulness, and the respondents in the national survey were chosen for representativeness, not to dramatize the problems of organizational conflict and ambiguity. These problems are by no means universal in organizations; there are organizations and positions in which harmony and clarity are the dominant conditions. We have treated conflict and ambiguity as dimensions for the study of organizational roles, not as unvarying attributes of organization. We do assert, however, that conflict and ambiguity as conditions of organizational life are commonly encountered, that they express deep trends in contemporary social organization, and that they are in opposition to still deeper needs of individuals.

We assert also that the difficulties people have with their organizational roles increase as conflict and ambiguity increase, and that these difficulties are expressed in performance, not necessarily in the role in which the stress was experienced, but somewhere in the array of roles which constitute the social and affiliative life of the person – as husband and father, as worker, as friend and as citizen. Where these expressions will occur, what forms they will take, after what intervals of time and silent pain they will become manifest, our research and theory knows little. About these things we have much to learn.

This has been not only a study of organizations, however; it has been also a study of health, in the sense of psychological well-being. In this context role conflict and ambiguity constitute two stressor conditions out of many which might be investigated in and outside of organizations. In other studies related to this research, additional stressors are being considered. These include status and status incongruence, as when a highly trained and formally educated person is employed in an unskilled position. They also include temporal discontinuities imposed on individuals and groups, as among industrial workers and their families who are subjected to recurring changes in shift. Another environmental stress being studied currently is technological obsolescence, and the resulting experience of discovering that a laboriously acquired and highly valued skill, around which there has been investment of self and the development of self-identity, is becoming de-valued in one's organization and in the larger society. We are interested also in the effects on the person of negative feedback about the self, as for example when a hierarchical superior in the course of an appraisal interview states that performance is unsatisfactory.

All these researches share an orientation toward a few key questions: To what extent are individual well-being and performance similarly affected by stressors of various kinds, and to what extent do their effects appear to be distinct? What are the social and organizational conditions which give rise to the immediate stressors, and what qualities of personality and interpersonal relations mitigate the effects of stress?

Finally, the present research is a study in organizational theory or, more properly, in the organizational application of role theory. We have attempted to bring into the same theoretical schema the organization as an ongoing system, the work group and the individual. The key concept in this attempt has been *role expectations*, those cognitions of relevant other people about what the occupant of a certain organizational office should and should not do. In these terms, the influential communication of role expectations begins the basic cycle by which organizational performance is ensured; in the communication of expectations also we have discerned the immediate origins of role conflict and ambiguity.

We have regarded an organization as made up of an array of overlapping role sets, each consisting of the individual occupant of a certain position and those other persons whose behaviors must interact with his in the creation of the organizational product. We have been interested in the process of influence from role senders to focal person, in the clarity or ambiguity of the expectations transmitted, and the harmony or conflict in the total pattern of expectations communicated to any single position. We have been interested in the consequences of such differing patterns, and in the bases of power by which the expectations of one person have effects on another. We have wanted also to learn something of the prevalence and location of conflict and ambiguity in the society as a whole.

The theoretical model for this research began with a discussion and diagram of a role episode (Chapter 2), that is, a cycle of events which can be regarded as initiated by the communication of a set of expectations to a person from others whose activities are interdependent with his (focal person and role senders). The role episode ends with some response on the part of the person who is the target of these influence attempts (communicated expectations). His response, and especially the degree of compliance which it signifies, is observed by the members of his role set, who decide in turn how to respond, and thus another cycle begins. The schema is equally appropriate for illustrating ongoing stable states (for example, states of clarity or ambiguity, conflict or harmony) which characterize a series of such cycles over some stated period of time.

In addition to these categories of variables, which include the main causal sequences about which we have formulated hypotheses, we are interested in three additional classes of variables that refine and extend our basic hypotheses about role conflict and ambiguity. One is the class of organizational variables, which can be thought of as the breeding ground for role expectations. Another is the category of personality variables, which we think of as modifying and extending the basic relationships in several ways: by mediating the perception of conflict and ambiguity, by mediating the effects and responses of a person to conflict and ambiguity, and by influencing directly the perceptions and therefore the actions of one's co-workers. The third class of variables by which we extend our basic findings is made up of interpersonal dimensions, and these enter into our theoretical schema in much the same way as personality factors: as potential mediators of the relationship between objective and experienced conditions, as mediators of the relationship between experienced conditions and

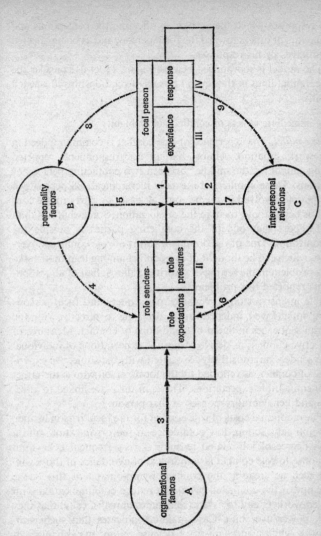

Figure 1 A theoretical model of factors involved in adjustment to role conflict and ambiguity

the responses which they evoke, as affecting the perceptions and behaviors of others toward the focal person, and as being affected themselves by his responses.

The model is reproduced here as Figure 1; let us consider the research findings in the several classes of relationships illustrated by it.

The immediate effects of conflict and ambiguity

Role conflict. The experience of role conflict is common indeed in the work situation. Almost half of our respondents reported being caught 'in the middle' between two conflicting persons or factions. These conflicts are usually hierarchical; 88 per cent of the people involved in them report at least one party to the conflict as being above them in the organization. Somewhat less than half report that one of the conflicting parties is outside the organization. One of the dominant forms of role conflict is overload, which can be thought of as a conflict among legitimate tasks or a problem in the setting of priorities; almost half of all respondents reported this problem.

The intensive study, in which role senders and focal persons were interviewed independently, deals more directly with the causal sequences initiated by conditions of conflict. Measures of objective conflict, as derived from the expectations of individual role senders, are positively associated with the subjective experience of conflict, as reported by the focal person who is the target of incompatible expectations. These, in turn, are linked to affective and behavioral responses of that person.

The emotional costs of role conflict for the focal person include low job satisfaction, low confidence in the organization, and a high degree of job-related tension. A very frequent behavioral response to role conflict is withdrawal or avoidance of those who are seen as creating the conflict. Symptomatic of this is the attempt of the conflicted person to reduce communication with his co-workers and to assert (sometimes unrealistically) that they lack power over him. Case material indicates that such withdrawal, while a mechanism of defense, is not a mechanism of solution. It appears to reduce the possibility of subsequent collaborative solutions to role conflict.

Role ambiguity. The prevalence of role ambiguity is comparable to that of role conflict. Four specific subjects of ambiguity are cited as disturbing and troublesome in approximately equal numbers by respondents. These include uncertainty about the way in which one's supervisor evaluates one's work, about opportunities for advancement, about scope of responsibility, and about the expectations of others regarding one's performance. Each of these areas of ambiguity was mentioned by approximately one third of the respondents. In all, about two persons out of five considered that they were given insufficient information to perform their jobs adequately.

Among the major sources of role ambiguity about which we speculated were complexity of task and technology, rapidity of organizational change, interconnectedness of organizational positions, and that managerial philosophy which advocates restriction of information on the assumption that the division of labor makes broad information unnecessary for most positions.

The individual consequences of ambiguity are in general comparable to the individual effects of role conflict. These include, for ambiguity: low job satisfaction, low self-confidence, a high sense of futility and a high score on the tension index. There is evidence, however, that the response of the person to ambiguity is selective. For example, ambiguity regarding the evaluations of others does not decrease the intrinsic satisfaction of the employee with the job, although it does decrease his self-confidence and weaken his positive affect for co-workers.

Organizational determinants of conflict and ambiguity

The major organizational determinants of conflict and ambiguity include three kinds of role requirements: the requirement for crossing organizational boundaries, the requirement for producing innovative solutions to nonroutine problems, and the requirement for being responsible for the work of others (arrow 3 in Figure 1).

Let us consider first the requirement for crossing a company boundary. Both the frequency and the importance of making contacts outside one's company are associated with the experience of role conflict. Crossing the company boundary is associated also with experienced tension, but the relationship is curvilinear;

greatest tension is experienced by those who have discontinuous contacts outside the organization. We propose the hypothesis that in positions which require extracompany contacts on a continuous basis, there are special facilities or some other organizational acknowledgment of boundary difficulties which renders them less painful.

Hypothetical explanations for the stressfulness of boundary crossing are available primarily from case materials. It appears that the person who must frequently deal with people outside the company usually has limited control over these outsiders. He cannot strongly influence their demands and the resources which they supply to him. Moreover, a person in a boundary position is likely to be blamed by people in his own company for what his outside contacts do or fail to do. They in turn may blame him for shortcomings in his own company. The difficulties of living at the boundary of an organization are intensified when the boundary dweller must coordinate his extra-organizational activities with people in other departments within the company.

In general, living near a departmental or other intra-organizational boundary has effects very like those just remarked for boundaries of the organization itself. Nearness to a departmental boundary and frequency of dealing across such boundaries are associated with felt conflict and with experienced tension.

Roles which demand innovative problem solving are associated with high role conflict and with tension. The occupants of such roles appear to become engaged in conflict primarily with the organizational old guard – men of greater age and power, who want to maintain the status quo. Among the major role conflicts which persons in innovative jobs complain of is the conflict of priority between the nonroutine activities which are at the core of the creative job and the routine activities of administration or paper work. These latter, according to the people who fill innovative positions, are unduly time consuming, disrupt the continuity of their creative work and are generally unpalatable.

There is considerable evidence that organizations exercise selective effort in choosing people for innovative positions. People in such positions tend to be characterized by high self-confidence, high mobility aspirations, high job involvement and a tendency to rate the importance of a job extremely high compared to the importance of other areas of their lives.

Supervisory responsibility emerges as a major organizational determinant of role conflict. Either the supervision of rank and file employees or the supervision of people who are themselves supervisors appears to have substantial effects on the degree of role conflict and the amount of experienced tension. In combination direct and indirect supervisory responsibility produce very substantial role conflict and tension.

There is a systematic relationship also between rank and role conflict, as there is between rank and tension. The often heard assertion that the lowest levels of supervision are subjected to the greatest conflict is not borne out by these data. Rather, there is a curvilinear relationship in which the maximum of conflict occurs at what might be called the upper middle levels of management. We interpret this in part as a consequence of the still unfulfilled mobility aspirations of middle management, in contrast to the better actualized aspirations of top management people.

The significance of interpersonal relations

The sources of pressure and conflict for a person can be expressed rather fully in terms of his interpersonal relations with these pressure sources (arrow 6 in Figure 1). The greatest pressure is directed to a person from other people who are in the same department as he is, who are his superiors in the hierarchy, and who are sufficiently dependent on his performance to care about his adequacy without being so completely dependent as to be inhibited in making their demands known. The people who are least likely to apply such pressures are a person's peers and role senders outside his own department.

The kinds of influence techniques which people are prepared to apply, as well as the degree of pressure they exert, vary with their formal relationship to the potential target of their pressures. To a considerable degree the actual power structure of organizations follows the lines of formal authority. Legitimate power, rewards and coercive power over an organizational member are largely in the hands of his direct organizational superiors. Although a supervisor has coercive power available to him as a basis for influencing his subordinates, he is likely to refrain from using it where it might impede the performance of these subordinates and perhaps reflect upon the supervisor himself. On the other hand, the techniques used by subordinates to apply coercive power are precisely those which threaten the efficiency of the organization. They include the withholding of aid and information.

The deleterious effects of role conflict are most severe where the network of an individual's organizational relations binds him closely to members of his role set (arrow 7 in Figure 1). When a person must deal with others who are highly dependent on him, who have high power over him, and who exert high pressure on him, his response is typically one of apathy and withdrawal – psychological if not behavioral. Under such circumstances the experience of role conflict is intense and job satisfaction correspondingly low. Emotionally, the focal person experiences a sense of futility, and he attempts a hopeless withdrawal from his co-workers. Likewise, the costs of role conflict upon the focal person are most dear where there is a generally high level of communication between the focal person and his role senders.

Since close ties to role senders with regard to functional dependence, power and communication intensify the effects of an existing conflict, an obvious means of coping with conflict is to sever ties with one's role senders. Symptomatic of this pattern of withdrawal in the face of conflict is the tendency of an individual experiencing role conflict to reduce the amount of communication with his role senders, to derogate the power these senders have over him, and to weaken his affective bonds with these senders (arrow 9 in Figure 1). Although this pattern of coping with stress is common, its logic is questionable. Withdrawal may be successful in alleviating the effects of stress for a time; in the longer run it is likely to prove self-defeating. Withdrawal may not only leave the initial conflict unresolved, but may in addition set off a chain reaction of derivative conflicts.

The significance of personality variables

Several personality dimensions mediate significantly the degree to which a given intensity of objective conflict is experienced as strain by the focal person (arrow 5 in Figure 1). These personality dimensions include emotional sensitivity, introversion–extroversion, flexibility–rigidity and need for career achievement. For example, the effects of objective role conflict on interpersonal bonds and on tension are more pronounced for introverts. The introverts develop social relations which, while sometimes congenial and trusting, are easily undermined by conditions of stress. The preference of such people for autonomy becomes manifest primarily when social contacts are stressful, that is, when others are exerting strong pressures and thereby creating conflict for them. In similar fashion, emotional sensitivity mediates the relationship between objective conflict and tension, with emotionally sensitive persons showing substantially higher tension scores for any given degree of objective conflict. An individual who is strongly achievement oriented exhibits a high degree of personal involvement with his job, and the adverse effects of role conflict are more pronounced for him than for those who are less involved.

There is also a tendency for people of different personality characteristics to be exposed by their role senders to differing degrees of objective conflict (arrow 4 in Figure 1). Thus people who are relatively flexible are subjected to stronger pressures than those who have already demonstrated by their rigidity the futility of applying such pressures. Likewise, one who is highly achievement oriented, particularly where such orientation takes on a neurotic cast, is more likely than others to alienate his role senders and to evoke from these role senders increased pressures to change his personal style of behavior.

The identification of coping responses

How, then, do individuals confronted by a stressful situation attempt to cope with this situation? Our theoretical model of reactions to role stress should indicate that this question so phrased cannot be answered. This model suggests that no coping response to organizational stress can be fully understood without considering the type of stress involved, the organizational conditions creating the stress, the personality of the individual experiencing the stress, and the network of interpersonal relations binding the individual to his role senders. But even a specification of all such variables gives an incomplete picture of a particular stressful episode, since such an episode may take place against a backdrop of many other stressful episodes both past and present. A penetrating study of coping responses in stressful situations cannot therefore be a study of neat, self-contained episodes and one-to-one relationships. If at times in the preceding chapters we have postulated such relationships, we have done so in full realization that we were thereby oversimplifying an exquisitely complex problem. We attempted to emphasize this complexity in Chapter 18, in which our analyses of coping behavior took the form of six detailed case studies. The importance of these case analyses lies partly in their integration of the findings of earlier chapters and partly in what they may suggest in the way of specific hypotheses for future studies of coping behavior; their primary importance, however, stems from the general guidelines they set for such research. We feel that analyses of coping responses to a stress episode – be this episode one of conflict, ambiguity, or some other stress – should be guided by the following considerations:

1. The study of coping behavior should include failures as well as coping mechanisms which are successful. The concept of coping is defined by the behaviors subsumed under it, not by the success of these behaviors. It may even prove profitable to concentrate upon those behaviors which are intended to cope with stress but which fail to do so. The psychoanalytic study of defense mechanisms would have been seriously retarded had it confined itself to the observation of conspicuously successful defenses. It is often in situations of failure where the ramifications of a particular coping mechanism or defense can be seen most vividly.

2. The analysis of a stressful role episode should distinguish between core problems (the initial stress which persists either manifestly or latently) and derivative problems (those problems created by an individual's attempts to cope with the core problem). Our case analyses indicate that individuals with similar core problems may currently be experiencing stress because of quite dissimilar derivative problems, and that individuals whose observable derivative problems are dissimilar may be coping with similar core problems.

3. The success of coping behavior should be evaluated with reference to a designated time period. An individual may be confronted

with a job-related problem this morning and completely avoid the problem this afternoon. He may go home unconcerned this evening only to return to find the problem intensified tomorrow. Our data indicate that one who is faced with conflict or ambiguity often tries to withdraw from his various attachments to his role senders. Although such a detachment may temporarily alleviate problems of conflict or ambiguity, are such problems thereby resolved? Does restriction of communication with role senders help alter their incompatible or overdemanding role expectations and thereby resolve role conflict? Can such restriction of communication with role senders eliminate role ambiguity, which itself seems to be a problem of inadequate communication?

4. The cost of a coping maneuver should be reckoned with reference to all affected systems. The designation of coping behavior as successful or unsuccessful has little meaning unless one asks 'successful for whom?' This designation is particularly critical in studies of coping behavior in organizations, for what is good for an individual is not necessarily good for his role set. And what is good for the individual and his role set need not be consonant with the goals of the organizational system. Our case analyses of coping behavior suggest that those who pay the piper are not always those who have called his tune.

Implications for human organization

The research on which this book is based is in part descriptive, attempting to set out something of the prevalence and distribution of two common conditions of organizational life: role conflict and role ambiguity. Our major emphasis, however, has been on explanation – on showing the organizational origins, the immediate causes, and some of the consequences of these two conditions. The practitioner who reads these pages will do so with still a third consideration dominant in his mind: what can be done to reduce the incidence of role conflict and ambiguity, and to make the effects of these conditions (when they cannot be avoided) minimally damaging to the person and to the organization?

We address ourselves gladly to these questions, partly out of a sense of just obligation to the practitioner and partly because we are not neutral with respect to the issues they raise. We can imagine organizations more sensitive to human needs and more nurturant of human potentialities, and we are interested in contributing to the development of such organizations.

Let us begin by acknowledging a degree of inevitability in the occurrence of role conflict and ambiguity in complex organizations. Human behavior in organizations is patterned, influenced by organizational circumstances; it is, in short, behavior which would not otherwise have occurred. This very definition implies that some forces are being overcome in order to produce the required behavior. These may be forces generated by enduring properties of the individual himself, or they may stem from various external sources. In either case, they imply conflict, at least in the limited sense of relinquishing alternatives. The individual foregoes something for the sake of performing the organizational role.

Some measure of ambiguity is no less inevitable in organizations. To attempt the creation of a complete organizational blueprint, in which every task would be specified, every method prescribed, and every contingency foreseen would be a self-defeating effort. It would be impossibly costly; it would be constantly upset by changes in the organizational environment. Moreover, it would be most unwelcome; to work under conditions of absolute and unrelieved specificity does not suit the human organism.

The issue, then, is not the elimination of conflict and ambiguity from organizational life; it is the containment of these conditions at levels and in forms which are at least humane, tolerable and low in cost, and which at best might be positive in contribution to individual and organization. The present research implies four ways in which this goal might be approached: by introducing direct structural changes into organizations, by introducing new criteria of selection and placement, by increasing the tolerance and coping abilities of individuals, and by strengthening the interpersonal bonds among organizational members. The research suggests also that all four of these approaches will be facilitated by a substantial revision of conventional views of organizational structure and by the direct utilization of the role set in bringing about organizational change.

A new view of the organization

We would urge that an organizational leader bent on reducing conflict and ambiguity to optimal levels begin by asking himself some old questions about organization and refusing to be content with the old answers. What is an organization? Wherein lies organizational structure? Our research argues that the answers to these questions should not be given merely in terms of buildings and equipment; they are empty and inanimate; they may remain after the business fails or the organization dissolves. Nor is it satisfactory to define the organization by naming its officers or enumerating its membership; they change or leave the organization entirely, and yet it persists and is recognizable as somehow the same organization. Deprived of these conventional means of identification, the company president or union leader might next point to the organization chart as the defining document. In so doing he might come close to reality or not, depending on the accuracy of the chart; he would at best, however, be pointing to a representation of the organization rather than to the thing itself. At worst, he would be designating a nonrepresentation of the organization, a piece of abstract art which can claim neither fidelity to life nor insight-giving distortions of it. We have proposed a different definition: The organization is an open system, a system of roles; it consists of continuing, interdependent cycles of behavior, related in terms of their contribution to a joint product.

What does this definition imply for conventional ways of looking at and representing organizations? It implies immediately that the organization chart is inadequate; such charts show the lines of authority from supervisors to subordinates; all other bonds, all other forms of interdependency are neglected. More recently, Likert (1961) has proposed a revision of the typical organization chart and the style of administration which it allegedly reflects. Likert's theory and representation of organizational structure emphasizes the group (the supervisor and his immediate subordinates) – rather than the dyad (supervisor and each subordinate taken one at a time). This is an important revision, because it adds two ideas to conventional representations of organization: interdependence among subordinates who report to the same supervisor, and the interlocking of such groups throughout the organization, by means of the 'linking-pin' functions of formal supervisors.

The implications of our research suggest a further revision. If the organization is a network of interrelated roles (or, more precisely, of role behaviors), it follows that the bonds which connect one role to another may be of many kinds, not of formal authority alone. Two roles may be related in terms of authority, to be sure, but they may also be related because of the sequence of work flow, or of information, or because of the liking which one person has for another, or because of expertise. All these bonds have in common the properties of expectation and influence; they imply that the occupant of one role is concerned with the behavior of another, is in some fashion dependent on that behavior, has ideas about what constitutes acceptable performance in terms of his own needs, and acts to influence the other person toward such performance. The organization is a complex network of roles connected by such bonds of expectation and influence, some of them reciprocal, some asymmetrical. Thus, no role in an organization is intact or fully separable from others. Each is defined in terms of expectations which stem from others, and in terms of behaviors which relate to the behavior of others.

We may wish to deal with a single role, and for that purpose we figuratively pluck it out of the network of other roles to which it is connected. When we do so, we find that what we have in hand is an assortment of duties and obligations, expectations and rights which state relationships between this role and various others. These relational statements dangle from the role like strands from a knot which has been cut out of a larger net of which it was a part. And if we try to eliminate those bonds and define the role without mentioning its connections to any other, we make a startling discovery: there is virtually nothing left. The role is defined in terms of its relationships to others, just as the knot in a net is no more than the intersection of bonds and disappears if we try to trim too closely.

The implications of this view of organization are not only distant and theoretical; they are immediate and practical:

1. To understand and predict a man's behavior on the job, we

must ask to what other jobs his is connected (to what other persons he is connected) and what is the nature of the connecting bonds (formal authority, personal liking, task interdependence, and the like).

2. To change the behavior of an individual or the content of a job involves complementary change on the part of all the 'bond-holders', the people to whom he is directly connected in the organization and who constitute his role set (Chapter 2). Unless such complementary changes are carried through, there will be conditions of conflict or of ambiguity between the individual and the members of his role set.

3. It follows that management should recognize the individual and the role set as the basic unit of which organizations are constructed. This is the minimum relevant group for decision making involving changes in the duties of any position in the organization. It follows also that each member of an organization should have the legitimate authority to convene the members of his role set to reach understanding and agreement regarding his duties (their role expectations of him) and his performance on the job (his role behavior). In doing these things, management would recognize formally the importance of the role set, and acknowledge the organization as made up of an array of such sets, one associated with each position in the organization, each set typically overlapping several others. In Figure 2 three views of organizational structure are contrasted – conventional management theory, the Likert revision as proposed in *New Patterns of Management* (1961), and the present version of role theory.

In this figure two revised views of organizational structure have been superimposed on a conventional organizational chart: the overlapping groups of the Likert theory are shown by dotted lines; the role set for position *C*-6 is enclosed with a heavy solid line. To make clear the different implications of these several views, let us assume that an issue has arisen which involves the performance and task requirements for position *C*-6, one of sixteen jobs at the first level of supervision in the organization. Conventional approaches to management would regard this issue as a matter to be settled between the immediate supervisor and the subordinate whose job is at issue – that is, between *B*-2 and

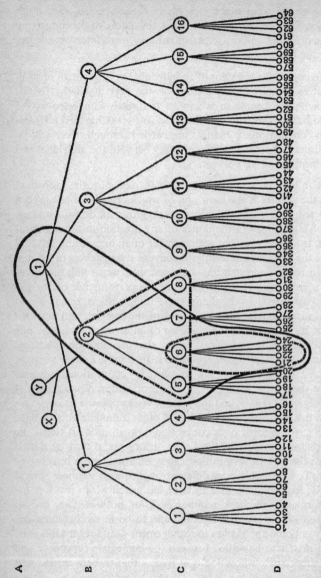

Figure 2 Three views of organizational structure

C-6. The theory of overlapping group structure (Likert, 1961) would see the issue as appropriately settled within two 'organizational families', primarily within the group consisting of supervisor *B*-2 and subordinates *C*-5, 6, 7, and 8; secondarily between *C*-6 and his own immediate subordinates, *D*-21, 22, 23 and 24.

To approach the same problem in terms of the role set, we would begin by identifying the role set for position *C*-6. To do this precisely would require us to determine those other positions in the organization to which *C*-6 is directly linked; that is, positions whose occupants have specific expectations regarding what the occupant of *C*-6 shall and shall not do, and who communicate these expectations in some fashion to him. The role set as drawn in Figure 2 is typical, however; it includes for position *C*-6 the immediate superior (*B*-2), the superior once removed (*A*-1), those peers who are adjacent in the workflow system (*C*-5 and *C*-7), all immediate subordinates (*D*-21, 22, 23, 24), and two persons whose importance for *C*-6 is determined by personal bonds rather than the formal facts of authority or flow of work (*X* and *Y*).

There is no implication that this set of people ought to be convened to consider all problems relating to position *C*-6. Such a procedure would be costly, frequently unnecessary, and sometimes ridiculous. We do argue that the behavior of *C*-6 is of direct concern to the others in his role set and is substantially determined by their behavior toward him, that any change in his behavior will require some complementary changes on their part, and that the success of such a proposed change in the behavior of *C*-6 will depend in large part upon their acceptance and reinforcement of it. It follows that the expectations of these role senders ought to be taken into account in any process of evaluating and attempting to change the behavior of *C*-6. Whether a meeting of the entire set, consultation with subsets, or mere information will suffice depends upon the significance of the proposed action for their own needs and behavior.

Stress and structure

Another broad implication of the present research has to do with the importance of organizational structure, the formalities and architecture of organization. It is perhaps unnecessary to remind most leaders of organizations that structure is important; they tend to be aware of the fact. Nevertheless, the human relations emphasis of the past twenty years, in the hands of some of its enthusiasts, has de-emphasized questions of formal structure. The very term human relations suggests that the causes of organizational health or illness will be sought in the area of personal and interpersonal style. Our research concurs in the importance of personality and interpersonal relations, but in a context which begins with the structural facts of organization.

It is not easy, however, to extrapolate from the research findings on organizational structure to specific organizational advice. For example, we have found that liaison positions, rank, supervisory responsibility, innovative roles, and functional interdependence are significant sources of stress in organizations. Shall we then eliminate them, and construct an organization which is unconnected and therefore unresponsive to the outside world, which is without supervisory responsibilities and therefore without supervision, without innovative roles and therefore perhaps lacking in innovation, without functional interdependence and therefore no organization at all? Obviously not; we must attempt to construct human organizations which incorporate optimal compromise solutions to certain persisting organizational dilemmas.

One such dilemma is the balance between stress and performance. Although measures of organizational performance were not available in the present research, it is clear that the direct elimination of some sources of stress would be possible but that the effects on performance might be serious.

Another is the dilemma of containment versus allocation of stress. In every organization some compromise must be reached between sharing out stressful attributes with absolute equality among all positions and concentrating the stressful requirements in a single, heroic task. Moreover, solutions which favor either alternative carry with them their own derivative problems. Concentrating the functions of organizational liaison on a very few positions, for example, risks much in a few hands, forces a search for champions to fill the crucial positions, and is likely to create intraorganizational stresses as different parts of the organization struggle to insure that their interests will be well-represented by the overworked representative.

A third persisting dilemma in moving from research findings to specific recommendations about structure involves the choice between stress and stress. The elimination of a source of stress often brings side effects in the form of new and still stressful imbalances. For example, innovative roles have been found to be stressful, but it does not follow that a highly creative person will be happier and healthier if he is assigned to more routine tasks. The lack of self-actualization in such a role might subject such a person to greater strain than he experienced as an innovator, fighting the battles of innovation against the old guard.

With these dilemmas before us, reminding us of the tentative quality of our recommendations, we offer the following proposals as worth consideration by those architects of organizations who wish to create less stressful structure:

With respect to the liaison of the organization with the outside world, create specialized positions for which liaison is the major and continuing function. Provide strong support for such positions, in terms of power, ancillary services, and organizational recognition. Establish multiple rather than single liaison arrangements whenever the work load justifies; all truth is seldom contained in one channel. Build into the organization formal procedures for maintaining agreement and understanding between the boundary dwellers and those who are oriented inward.

This latter suggestion will require the creation of opportunities and indeed responsibilities for each person in a boundary position to see first hand the problems and circumstances of those whom he represents, to learn the ways in which his liaison activities affect them. It is no less important, of course, to provide for the occasional exposure of people deep within the organization to the forces encountered daily by the liaison person.

The means for doing these things are not mysterious, given acceptance of the principle. They include the rotation of persons from boundary to inside positions, such as brief tours of duty of salesmen in manufacturing, for example, or line supervisors into personnel or labor relations. In some situations it may be feasible and valuable to arrange meetings at which outsiders are imported expressly for the purpose of communicating directly the needs and preferences which ordinarily reach the organization only through the liaison person.

A second proposal for minimizing stress in the structural design of organizations has to do with size, shape, and requirements for coordination among positions and subunits of the organization. Americans are accustomed to thinking of growth as synonymous with organizational life, and of large size as a condition for maximum efficiency. Against these assertions must be placed the finding that stress and organizational size are substantially related. The curve of stress begins to rise as we turn from tiny organizations to those of fifty or 100 persons, and the rising curve continues until we encounter the organizational giants. Only for organizations of more than 5000 persons does the curve of stress level off – perhaps because an organization so large represents some kind of psychological infinity and further increases are unfelt.

We interpret this finding as urging changes in structure, however, rather than gross changes in size; the economic consequences of shrinking down to stress-free organizations of a dozen or so members would be tragic. The stressfulness of size, we believe, stems in considerable part from increased requirements for coordination. All coordination involves costs; to require that even two persons somehow synchronize their activities takes time, effort and some psychological costs of accommodation. Moreover, each additional person who is introduced into such an interdependent set adds disproportionately to the total number of coordinative bonds. To be precise, each new person with whom the others must coordinate adds $(N - 1)$ to the total number of bonds. Thus, for two persons, there is only one bond; for three persons, three bonds; four persons, six bonds; five persons, ten bonds; and so on up the curve of strain and confusion.

The implications for builders and leaders of organizations can be summed up in these terms: Minimize the requirements for coordination between positions and groups; in other words, treat every coordinative requirement as a cost, which it is. For each functional unit of the organization, ask how independent it can be of others and of top management. For each position, ask how autonomous it can be made, what is the minimum number of other positions with which it must be connected, and for what activities and purposes the connections are essential. For each coordinative bond which must be established between positions and units, seek the minimum number of activities which must be coordinated in order to avoid undue organizational risks. The basic justification for coordination becomes functional interdependence, the requirement which stems directly from the productive process. Examples would include the feeder lines which support the assembly line, or the use of a common unique facility like a computer installation by several producing units. The safety of the total system would of course constitute another undeniable basis for coordination; no one proposes that the final inspection unit in aircraft maintenance should be uncoordinated with other units, including the mechanics and pilots.

The advocacy of minimal coordination contrasts sharply with the notions of centralized leadership, with the idea that ultimate and maximum control must originate from a central source and maximum information return to that source. Coordination only when justified by functional requirements or systemic risk also points up a common fault of management, a preoccupation with organizational symmetry and aesthetics, and an emphasis on the regularities and beauties of the organizational chart. The organization which follows this principle of coordinative economy would not necessarily be small, but it would not have grown haphazardly and it would not regard size as an unmixed blessing. It would be decentralized, flat and lean, a federated rather than a lofty hierarchical structure.

Advice to reduce the coordinative requirements of organization is unlikely to arouse much managerial enthusiasm, especially among those who see only the alternatives of close coordination by authority and absolute anarchic diversity. There are, however, other means than authority for infusing order into organizational life and insuring behavior in the service of organizational objectives. One vital means, often neglected and still more often misused, is the reward structure of the organization. Deutsch (1960) distinguishes between two kinds of interdependence – promotive and contrient. Two persons or groups are promotively interdependent when the success of one facilitates the success of the other. The members of a football team, for example, are promotively interdependent; the joys and rewards of victory (individual records aside for the moment) can come only through collaborative effort and exist for all members of the team or for none. On the other hand, opponents in a boxing match are contriently interdependent; there can be a match only if they collaborate to make one, but either of them can win only if the other loses.

The principle of promotive interdependence exemplified in the reward structure of an organization would require that rewards to individual members would be maximized under the same conditions, that is, when the attainment of organizational objectives was maximized. To the extent that coordination of effort would contribute to those objectives, the extrinsic rewards of the organization at least would be utilized to motivate such coordination. Workers under an individual incentive plan must sometimes be ordered into coordination; salesmen on commission must sometimes be ordered out of intramural competition. In these instances management tries to achieve by fiat a necessary collaboration which is explicitly discouraged by the emphasis of the reward system on individual achievement only. Far more appropriate would be the gearing of rewards to the success of those forms of collaboration which maximize the attainment of organizational objectives. The Scanlon Plan (McGregor, 1960; Lesieur, 1958; Krulee, 1955) is perhaps the best example available to American industry of the use of a reward system which creates promotive interdependence among factory workers. The significance of the example for our present discussion of coordination is that the Scanlon Plan has achieved in a number of companies a degree of collaboration and mutual assistance in the service of organizational objectives which authoritative demands for diligence and coordination had not been able to attain. Such a use of extrinsic rewards can strengthen greatly the relatively autonomous structure of organization which we advocate.

Organizational change

The last of the aspects of organizational life about which we will hazard advice is the accomplishment of change. The leadership of any organization is forever engaged in efforts to promote some kinds of change and prevent others. The tools of change are many, including exhortation, publication, training programs, and demonstrations. Orders and memoranda without number daily demand or implore change, yet every manager knows how partial and infrequent are his successes in creating change. We propose that these difficulties are due in part to the persistent utilization of the wrong unit for achieving change; the concentration has been on the individual when it should be on the role set, focal person and role senders.

To produce a change in the way in which Person A performs his role, there must be an acknowledgment of the change by the members of his role set; more, they must themselves change in complementary fashion. If he attempts to change and they refuse to do so, Person A is in a state of imbalance or conflict; he no longer conforms to the expectations of his role set. We can predict that he will experience the role conflict as unpleasant, and that he will do various things to reduce or avoid it. In the circumstances of this example, his most obvious and most likely course of action is to revert to his earlier pattern of performance, assuming that it gave reasonable satisfaction to the members of his role set. And when he has so reverted, the man who gave the lecture, wrote the memorandum, or conducted the training program says sorrowfully that 'you can't change Mr A'.

To remove a person from his role set, tell him in a training program or executive interview that he should change his behavior, and then return him to the unchanged set burdens him with a double responsibility. He must not only change his own behavior; he must effect complementary changes in the expectations and behavior of his role senders. This is the characteristic and crucial weakness shared by conventional programs of training, communications, and executive exhortation.

Yet the evidence in favor of using the natural group to carry through such behavioral changes is great, and continues to grow. The well-known industrial experiment of Coch and French (1948) in overcoming resistance to change can be interpreted as demonstrating the potency of the role set, and so in part can the work of Mann and his colleagues (1957) in introducing research data into organizational families of supervisor and immediate subordinates at successive echelons of an organization. The power of 'laboratory' or 'T-group' training (Bradford *et al.*, 1964) also illustrates the importance of the role set in achieving change, since the purposeful isolation of the T-group creates a situation in which for a time each member has for his role senders only other members of the group. It is in keeping with this interpretation that current extensions of the T-group technique emphasize the use of 'natural groups' (organizational role sets and parts of role sets) as appropriate units for training.

New trends in therapy also show a turning away from the classic solitude of patient and analyst, in favor of utilizing the family as the unit within which the health of the patient is determined (Ackerman, 1958). We urge acceptance of the role set by leaders of organization as the key unit for the achievement of change. The role set is not neutral to attempts at changing the behavior of an individual; it characteristically opposes or reinforces those efforts. Its proper utilization in the change process can not only increase the probability that real change will be achieved; it can also make the process relatively conflict-free, and bring the organization closer to meeting that relentless demand on all open systems: to change appropriately in response to environmental demands for change.

We have interpreted our research data on organizational stress as urging on practitioners of organization the importance of the key concept which has informed the research: the idea of the focal person and role set. We have argued that from this idea stems a new view of the organization, a fuller appreciation of organizational structure, and a more powerful approach to creating individual and organizational change. In urging our views on practitioners with such seeming confidence, we are nevertheless painfully aware that knowledge of human organizations is still fragmentary; that knowledge can best be advanced by research which attempts to deal simultaneously with data at different levels of abstraction – individual, group and organization. This is a difficult task, and the outcome is not uniformly satisfactory. It is, nevertheless, a core requirement for understanding human organizations. Organizations are reducible to individual human acts; yet they are lawful and in part understandable only at the level of collective behavior. This duality of level, which is the essence of human organization as it is of social psychology, we have attempted to recognize in our theoretical model and in our research design. Our hope is that the effort and its product may contribute to the understanding of organized human behavior. We know of no more urgent problem.

References

ACKERMAN, N., (1958), *The Psychodynamics of Family Life*, Basic Books.

BRADFORD, L., GIBB, J., and BENNE, K. (eds.), (1964), *T-Group Theory and Laboratory Method*, Wiley, 1964.

COCH, L., and FRENCH, J., (1948), 'Overcoming resistance to change', *Hum. Rel.*, vol. 1, pp. 512–32.

DEUTSCH, M. (1960), 'The effects of cooperation and competition on group process', in D. Cartwright and A. Zander (eds.), *Group dynamics, research and theory*, 2nd edn., Harper & Row.

KRULEE, G., (1955), 'The Scanlon plan: cooperation through participation', *J. Business*, vol. 28, no. 2.

LESIEUR, F. (ed.), (1958), *The Scanlon Plan*, Technology Press and Wiley.

LIKERT, R. (1961), *New Patterns of Management*, McGraw-Hill.

McGREGOR, D. (1960), *The Human Side of Enterprise*, McGraw-Hill.

MANN, F. (1957), 'Changing interpersonal relations through training supervisors', in C. Arensberg *et al.* (eds.), *Research in industrial human relations*, Harper & Row.

MORSE, N., and WEISS, R. (1955), 'The function and meaning of work and the job, *Amer. sociol. Rev.*, vol. 20, no. 2, pp. 191–8.

WEISS, R., and KAHN, R. (1960), 'Definitions of work and occupation', *J. soc. Problems*, vol. 8, no. 2, pp. 142–51.

17 W. Gamson

The Management of Discontent

W. Gamson, 'The management of discontent', *Power and Discontent*,
Dorsey Press, 1968, chapter 6, pp. 111–43.

In exploring influence, we have taken the perspective of potential
partisans affecting the choices of authorities. From the standpoint of authorities, another set of questions emerges. By their
very nature, many choices will affect potential partisan groups in
different ways. Authorities will inevitably satisfy some groups
more than others. Only rarely will their choices be free of some
element of conflict, that is, only rarely will there exist an alternative that is the first choice of all groups. This basic fact of
conflict confronts authorities with the problem of managing
discontent and containing influence.

From their perspective, the basic question is 'how does one
prevent those potential partisans who are injured or neglected
by political decisions from trying to change the nature of the
decisions, the authorities, or the political system within which
decisions are made?' Authorities, I assume, wish to remain free
from the pressure of external limits, free of influence attempts
which more or less successfully tie their hands. If this sounds
cynical, it need not be. For example, Arthur M. Schlesinger, Jr.
(1965, p. 120) writes of the interregnum period following Kennedy's election as a test of the President-elect's 'executive
instincts and, in particular, of his skill in defending his personal
authority against people striving, always for the best of motives,
to contract his scope for choice.'

The authorities in question may be operating to the best of
their ability to satisfy the needs of as many potential partisans
as possible. They may operate as justly as they possibly can in
situations involving conflicts of interest. They may conscien-
tiously seek information from potential partisans so that they
can meet these objectives. But, in the end, such authorities, no

less than self-interested or tyrannical ones, experience attempts to influence them as a limitation on their freedom of action. There are exceptions to this generalization – for example, in situations in which authorities may wish to stimulate pressure from one source to free themselves from some opposing source. But even this exception is governed by the desire to contain influence and thus remain free of its limits.

Perhaps it would be more accurate to say that authorities *qua* authorities desire limitations on the ability of potential partisans to exercise influence. Individuals occupying positions of authority may frequently desire great personal discretion in how they may use this authority because such discretion allows them to use their authority as a resource. Even if such discretion invites influence from others, at the same time it enhances their ability to influence others. Thus, those in authority may welcome freedom from public surveillance and accountability which act as control devices on both potential partisans and themselves. Such desires are an outgrowth of their potential partisan role, not their authority role. From the standpoint of that collectivity for which they serve as agent, the increased opportunity for influence creates control problems; there is less guarantee in such situations that those with authority will function as agents instead of as independent operators. The demands of flexibility and adequate task performance may require that authorities be given some leeway, but the more that considerations of control are relevant, the more such leeway will be reduced.

Responses to influence pressure

Potential partisans who are discontented with the choices of authorities must be handled in some fashion. The most basic distinction in how such discontent may be handled is between some modification of the content of the decision and some effort to control the potential partisan. The former response deals with the object of discontent by modifying the outcome in some way; the latter deals with the source of the pressure. These responses to discontent have something in common.[1] Both aim at removing the pressure that potential partisans are likely to

1. This argument is developed in Gamson (1964).

put on authorities, one by yielding ground and the other by directing counter-influence.

Why call such counter-influence social control instead of simply encompassing it under the previous discussion of influence? The answer is that the agents of such counter-influence are acting *as agents of the social system*. We separate their actions in such a role from their actions in pursuit of personal values and interests in which they may use resources to affect the decisions of others. When they act upon potential partisans in some manner to prevent or lessen the likelihood of influence over an area in which they make binding decisions, they are acting in the role of authorities.

Altering the outcome of decisions

The distinction has been made between the efficiency of the political system in achieving collective goals and its bias in handling conflicts of interest. Potential partisans may be unhappy on either account. These who are dissatisfied with the efficiency of the system feel that more effective leadership or institutions are needed. Government may be criticized as 'wasteful' or 'inefficient'. Such dissatisfaction assumes a basic consensus within which decisions are made.

Discontent about the equity of the political system is more difficult to deal with because conflict is inherent in the nature of some decisions. It is impossible in such cases, even if they have some collective aspects, to meet the desires and interests of all potential partisans. When the problem is one of ineffective leadership on collective goals, then by 'wiser' or 'better' choices, the discontent of potential partisans can be assuaged. When it involves the handling of conflicts, such notions as 'better' invariably raise the question, 'better for whom?'

Altering the outcome of decisions is one approach to the problem of discontent. The collective aspects of decisions present few problems for authorities that cannot be met by simply choosing different alternatives. As members of the same collectivity as the partisans, the authorities will presumably be easily susceptible to persuasion or education since the partisans and the authorities will benefit by the same alternative.

Discontent over the handling of conflict can also be treated by outcome modification although this has the effect of redistributing discontent rather than alleviating it. Nevertheless, there may be many reasons why authorities would prefer to see some groups more contented than others. They may share the values and interests of one group and prefer to satisfy them for that reason. Or, some may have more resources or access than others and they may relieve pressure by yielding ground to the most powerful among the potential partisans. *The greater the inverse relation between the amount of resources controlled and the amount of discontent among potential partisans, the freer the authorities are from influence.* In short, they are most free when those with the most discontent have the least ability to influence. To contain influence, outcome modification will move in this direction.

Finally, outcome modification may be a way of undercutting the mobilization of a partisan group which is in the process of converting dissatisfaction into a force for influence. By giving a little at the right time, authorities may prevent later, more important outcome modifications. 'An astute set of authorities,' Easton (1965, p. 408) suggests, 'in Machiavellian fashion, often meets just enough [demands], at least so as to still any critical accumulation of discontent. In the language of practical politics, this involves offering sops or conciliatory outputs at just the right moment to head off any brewing storm of dissatisfactions.' Social movements may falter on partial success, winning small victories which, while leaving basic dissatisfactions untouched, hamper the members in their ability to mobilize resources for further influence.

Social control

The alternative to outcome modification is social control. If such control is successful, then there will be little influence and, hence, no need for outcome modification. The authorities will maximize their room for maneuverability and such maneuverability has three virtues.

1. It allows the incumbent authority to exercise his own personal preference. He is free to act as he pleases and to do what he thinks best, within the limits of his role but without the additional limits imposed by influence.

2. If he has no particular preferences, the freedom from influence on a given issue enables him to use his authority as a resource to influence other decisions on which he has a partisan interest. In other words, successful social control increases the resources of authorities by allowing them discretion in the areas in which they exercise authority; such freedom allows them to use their authority as an inducement or constraint on other authorities whom they would influence. They could not use their authority as a resource if their hands were tied by pressure from partisans just as they would be similarly hampered by structural limitations on their freedom to use their authority.

3. Effective social control increases slack resources. This means that influence is cheaper. 'Slack resources provide the political entrepreneur with his dazzling opportunity, . . .' Dahl writes (1961, p. 309). He can influence at bargain rates when the competition has been removed by effective social control.

The tendency for outcome modification and social control to be competing alternatives is nicely illustrated in a study of the impact of students on the operation of an experimental college (Gamson, 1966). Within the college, two faculty subdivisions existed with differing orientations toward students, described by the author as 'utilitarian' and 'normative'. The utilitarian orientation emphasized cognitive effects on students, was less concerned about developing high student commitment to the college and encouraged faculty to maintain some distance from students. The normative orientation emphasized reaching students personally as well as intellectually, encouraged high student commitment and promoted close, egalitarian relationships with students. The author discovered an apparent paradox – those groups within the faculty with the most intense and diffuse concern with students were less responsive to particular student demands than those with a more specific and contractual relationship.

The paradox, of course, was only apparent. While each social control orientation had its own characteristic strains, for a variety of reasons the utilitarian orientation was less successful in forestalling pressures for modification of curriculum decisions. As a result, the pressures for change were greater and the resultant modifications were more frequent and radical in the division with the utilitarian orientation. The normative orientation, while it produced problems of a different sort, proved a stronger fortress against pressures for curriculum change. Thus, student influence was greater where student-faculty relationships were more distant because the closer relationship in one case produced more potent social control and less outcome modification.

Types of social control

There are three general ways in which authorities can contain the influence of potential partisans at its source. They can (a) regulate the access of potential partisans to resources and their ability to bring these resources to bear on decision makers, (b) affect the situation of potential partisans by making rewards or punishments contingent on attempts at influence, or (c) change the desire of potential partisans to influence by altering their attitudes toward political objects.

Insulation

An extremely important set of controls operates by giving potential partisans differential access to authorities and to positions which involve the control of resources that can be brought to bear on authorities. Such selectivity operates at two points – entry and exit.

Selective entry. Not all social organizations can control who is let in but many exercise considerable selectivity. A society cannot, of course, control the characteristics of the infants born into it – at least not until the Brave New World arrives. This absence of selectivity makes the control problems more severe than those encountered by an organization that can control entry.

However, most societies do exercise control over entry through immigration. Normally, they do not ask others for their tired and poor and huddled masses yearning to be free. Once the demand for large quantities of unskilled labor has been met, they are more likely to request doctors and engineers and huddled intellectuals yearning to be rich. Those who are presumed to offer particularly acute control problems are not welcomed. This includes both those who are likely to commit a variety of individual acts of deviance and those who are likely to organize themselves or others into groups that threaten the existing social order. Societies, like other forms of social organization, try to simplify their subsequent control problems by refusing entry to those elements most likely to aggravate such problems.

Most complex organizations are able to exercise some degree of selectivity in entry although there is wide variability in this regard. A corporation about to hire an executive is interested in a wide variety of characteristics not directly relevant to job performance. These other characteristics are frequently relevant to control problems. Those who are highly independent or erratic or in other ways seem likely to use the resources of their position in a free wheeling manner are generally regarded with caution. Of course, extraordinary ability or an extraordinary situation may convince an organization that it ought to take risks, but this does involve the assumption of greater problems of subsequent control. In short, I am not asserting that the reduction of control problems alone determines who will be allowed access to important positions, but such considerations are one factor and the problems are minimized by admitting only orthodox people.

Organizations which have little control over whom they let in are confronted with more control problems than those organizations which can select. Prisons, state mental hospitals, public schools and other organizations that have large numbers of their members determined for them by other organizations in their environment have control problems which private mental hospitals and private schools do not have. State universities should, by the same token, have greater control problems than private colleges which exercise high selectivity.

An important aspect of selective entry is *self-selection*. Many voluntary organizations reduce their control problems inadvertently by attracting as members those who will 'fit well' and will offer few control problems and by repelling those who are likely to be discontented. In such cases, selective entry occurs not by the organization refusing admittance to potentially difficult individuals but by such individuals removing themselves by not seeking entry.

Self-selection is influenced by the organization's image. *An organization's efforts to project an image which will differentiate it from others can be viewed as a social control device.* The manipulation of organizational image has other purposes as well, the major one of which is to increase the organization's attractiveness, thereby increasing its ability to compete for desirable members, clients or customers. But the effects of selectivity can be distinguished from the effects of increased attractiveness. In the latter case, we would expect there to be a tendency for members of *all* subgroups in the organization's environment to show approximately the same degree of increase in numbers seeking entry.[2]

However, if the image is serving a function of differentiation rather than increased attraction, this will not be so. Instead, the numbers seeking entry will increase in some groups while decreasing in others, i.e. while the organization is becoming more attractive to some, it is becoming less attractive to others. When an organization's image serves such a process of differentiation we may think of it as serving a social control function; it is increasing selective entry through a process of self-selection among potential members.

Entry is not an all or nothing state. Once in, members may have differential access to resources and communication opportunities. All members of the House of Representatives cannot be members of the Rules Committee or of other committees which command large amounts of resources. One may regard most social systems as possessing a series of entry points each of which offers control opportunities by denying further access to certain categories of potential partisans. In fact, if the population arriving at each gate were sufficiently endowed with the 'right' kind of individuals and the process of selection were infallible and produced no errors, there would be no need for any other kind of

2. This does not imply that the organization is equally attractive to all subgroups but only that there is a relative increase in attractiveness across the board. For example, Eisenhower received a relatively high Republican voting percentage from *both* businessmen and workers but the absolute percentage of each group that voted for him was quite disparate.

control. Neither of the conditions above is usually met so that other forms of control must come into play.

Besides denying some potential partisans access to positions that control resources, they may also be denied access to resources in other ways. They may be prevented from acquiring sufficient skill and knowledge for access. Daniel Lerner (1958), for example, describes the Ottoman Imperium as 'not merely a variety of illiterate populations but an antiliterate elite, who regulated the daily round of public life by maintaining exclusive control over key points of contact between individuals and their larger environment' (p. 113). A communication system which carried the news orally from the Ottoman center to scattered villages served 'as an administrative technique of social control, not as an instrument for shaping enlightened public opinion'. Preventing the acquisition of communication skills in a population of potential partisans with serious discontent is an aid in controlling such a population. Keeping such a population physically separated so that no sense of common interest or solidarity can easily develop may also be regarded as a way of preventing potential partisans from organizing and mobilizing potential resources for influence.

Subsequently, the lack of requisite skill and training may serve to justify the denial of access should such disadvantaged groups press for it. Members of such a group might be advised that giving them access in the absence of 'proper qualifications' constitutes preferential treatment. Thus, the selective entry may be justified on highly legitimate and widely accepted criteria and this control device may be preserved from becoming the target of pressure *itself*.

Selective exit. Most of the above discussion of selective entry is applicable to selective exit as well. There are some differences worth noting. While some social organizations have small control over whom they let in as members, all have means of removing access. Societies may imprison, exile, or put to death members that prove too troublesome to be handled by other control techniques. Even prisons and state mental hospitals isolate some members from the rest; public schools can expel hard-core control problem students.

There is probably some tendency for selectivity in entry and exit to be inversely correlated. *Those organizations which exercise a great deal of control at entry should be less likely to use expulsion as a control device than those organizations which have little control over who gets in.* If they use care in selection and a 'low-risk' policy of entry, they can afford to be more lenient in subsequent actions, and should need to rely less on such drastic measures as expulsion. Those with little control at the point of entry are likely to have a higher frequency of difficult cases that cannot be handled by other control techniques.

Examples of insulation through exit devices are numerous and for the most part obvious. A particularly striking case occurred in the winter following the US military intervention in the Dominican Republic. The provisional government, buffeted by the continuing struggle among powerful partisan groups, attempted to relieve the pressure by requesting the voluntary exile of a number of army officers who were leaders of these groups. The unusual and striking thing in this instance is that the officers were themselves rivals and political enemies; thus, the meaning of the act as an attempt to contain influence is unusually clear. More typically, such actions are aimed at removing influence from a particular source and are not as readily recognizable as an act of social control.

The removal of access as a social control device is not without its own set of problems. Goffman (1964) has helped call attention to the fact that the use of such devices generates its own necessity for control. The removal of access tends to be regarded by the individuals involved as a mark of failure or repression and is consequently resented. This resentment may lead to action on the part of the victim. In the confidence game example from which Goffman draws his terminology, the 'mark' may decide to complain to the police or 'squawk'. In our more drab terminology, the person who has been removed from access may translate his resentment into influence unless it is dealt with in some way. The devices which a social system uses to help a victim accept his failure quietly are now generally called, following Goffman's provocative article, 'cooling-out mechanisms'. We should expect any organization which makes widespread use of the removal of access as a control device to employ such mechanisms. For example, the device of 'kicking upstairs' involves the removal from access to a position which commands significant resources while assuaging the resultant discontent by an accretion in status. Compulsory retirement at a given age is another device which removes access without creating the danger that the victim will squawk. As with discrimination in entry, discrimination in exit is most effective when it can be accomplished using accepted, universalistic criteria.

Sanctions

Social organizations maintain systems of sanctions to reward the 'responsible' and to punish the 'irresponsible' or 'deviant'. If these words carry with them the connotation of desirability and undesirability, it is because we are accustomed to assuming a social control perspective. Whether being responsible is desirable depends on the nature of the social organization to which one is being responsible. Adolph Eichmann was clearly acting responsibly from the standpoint of Hitler's Germany. There may be a conflict between loyalty to one's friends, constituents, or one's personal values and one's responsibility as agent of the social system. A person's loyalties and convictions may impel him to use the resources of his position in an attempt to bring about decisions that he believes are desirable. But in using his authority as a resource, an individual is acting in the role of potential partisan rather than authority and issues of control are created thereby.

Sanctions will follow what is considered to be the misuse of authority. The limits which these sanctions impose on freedom of action may not be desired by those who exercise authority for it places limits on their ability to influence. Such sanctions act as a control on both potential partisans and authorities who would be potential partisans at other times. Thus, partisans are typically prevented from openly bribing officials and penalties exist both for attempting and for accepting such illicit influence. Specified channels for 'proper' influence are frequently provided – for example, petitioning or testifying at open hearings. Such channels contain a double restriction. On the one hand, they restrict the use of resources by potential partisans by subjecting their influence attempts to public surveillance and accountability.

On the other hand, they restrict the opportunity of the target of influence to use his authority as a resource which he can exchange in some transaction with potential partisans. From the standpoint of both parties, ex parte presentations may be tempting, allowing as they do for the freer use of reciprocal influence. From a social control perspective, such off-the-record contacts between potential partisans and authorities offer less assurance that the latter are operating as agents of the social system rather than exercising personal influence.

The bestowal and withdrawal of effective authority is an important sanction. Losing effective authority over an area is a double loss: it means that the loser now must spend resources to influence decisions where formerly he could simply exercise authority. Moreover, he has lost an important resource which he previously was able to use in influencing the decisions of other authorities. He is, thus, put in a position in which he has both lost resources and at the same time needs them more. The threat of withdrawing effective authority is, for these reasons, an important form of control on the 'abuse' of such authority.

Social, structural and normative limits exist on every authority which circumscribe his ability to use his powers as a resource and, hence, operate as a social control. If the limits are sufficiently great and remove from him any discretion in how he may use his authority, then he has no resource at all stemming from his position. Usually, he is left some area of discretion bounded by some set of limits, the violation of which will result in sanctions. If selection mechanisms have failed to prevent an 'irresponsible' person from gaining access to resources, sanctions are an additional control that may keep him in line. If he is unmoved by such sanctions, he may be removed from his position. Short of removal, there are a wide variety of sanctions available. One may be passed over for promotion, denied salary increases, given less helpful and prestigeful facilities, and so forth. Daily life can be made exceedingly unpleasant by the noncooperation of associates on whom one is dependent for the performance of one's job. And the threat that one will not be given any benefit of the doubt in the decisions of others can be a powerful deterrent.

Social control is *not* the only consideration in the distribution of inducements and constraints in a social system. Individuals may be rewarded for outstanding performance or for being the son of the company president; they may be punished for their religion or their incompetence. Control is simply one aspect and in many cases may be far from the dominant one. It should be emphasized that this discussion is not intended as a complete explanation of why individuals are given access to resources or are rewarded; rather, it is an attempt to describe the manner in which such things can be and are used for social control, in addition to whatever other uses they may have.

Promotion within an organization has elements of both insulation and sanctions. It is likely to mean some change in access to resources while at the same time it contains certain rewards. The distinction here is an analytic one which is difficult to make in practice. A man who has just been made president of a major corporation now has authority over areas which affect large numbers of people in important ways. Furthermore, he is likely to have wide latitude in the use of this authority. Thus he has gained access to important new resources. On the other hand, there are many things which are personally rewarding to him in the promotion – the greater status, the greater pay, the challenge and difficulty of the job, and the additional resources which he has gained. To the extent that control elements are relevant to his promotion, they operate in a dual fashion. Perhaps he is allowed access to the new resources because he appears more likely than someone else of equal ability and qualifications to act strictly as an agent of the organization. He is given the rewards of the new position because as vice president of the company he has, even at some personal sacrifice, demonstrated his willingness to act as agent of the organization. In this case, access and sanctions amount to essentially the same thing and the distinction is artificial; however, in many other cases, the two processes of control are quite separate and distinguishing them alerts one to different features of the organization.

Persuasion

Persuasion attempts to control the desire rather than the ability to influence. Potential partisans may be persuaded in a variety of ways either that their interest is well served by political decisions or, if not served on a particular occasion, that the procedures by which decisions are made serve their larger interest. Such persuasion may involve emphasizing the collective aspects of decisions, making those aspects which involve conflict appear less salient or important. Thus, potential partisans may be persuaded that the authorities are operating in the interests of the larger collectivity to which both parties belong even if some *relative* disadvantage is involved for their own subgroup. If potential partisans are convinced that the overall system of decision making is unbiased, they will be more willing to accept temporary setbacks in the belief that 'things will even out in the long run'.

There is an interesting variety of words used to describe this social control technique – some of them highly pejorative and others complimentary. The approving words include education, persuasion, therapy, rehabilitation, and, perhaps more neutrally, socialization. The disapproving words include indoctrination, manipulation, propaganda, and 'brainwashing'. The choice of words is merely a reflection of the speaker's attitude toward the social system and its agents. If one believes the authorities are faithful agents of a social system which is accorded legitimacy, then they are 'socializing' potential partisans when they exercise social control. If one sides with the potential partisans and identifies with their grievances against the authorities, then this latter group is using 'manipulation' as a form of control. The behavioral referent, of course, may be identical in both cases; the choice of word reflects two different perspectives on the same relation.

As in the earlier chapters on influence, the word 'persuasion' is used in the broadest possible sense to include any technique which controls the orientation of the potential partisan *without* altering his situation by adding advantages or disadvantages. Some examples may help to make this breadth clear. The withholding of information from potential partisans about adverse effects of decisions is a use of persuasion as a means of social control. The withholding of information on fallout from atomic tests in Nevada during the period prior to the nuclear test-ban treaty was apparently done to avoid increasing public pressure for the cessation of such tests. Similarly, almost all social systems try to keep knowledge of their failures from circulating lest it generate pressure for change. Potential partisans who acquire such information (perhaps from allies among the authorities) publicize it for exactly the opposite reason – in the hope that it will mobilize their constituency to action. The selective withholding of information, then, is a technique of social control through persuasion.

Surrounding authorities with trappings of omniscience is another case of this control technique. If the authorities are viewed as distant, awe-inspiring figures possessed of tremendous intelligence and prescience plus access to privileged information that is essential for forming judgements, then the potential partisan may hesitate to challenge a decision even when he feels adversely affected by it.

There is, however, a contrasting technique which *minimizes* social distance between potential partisans and authorities. By personal contact and the 'humanization' of authorities, potential partisans may be encouraged to identify with them; this identification, in turn, produces a trust which makes influence appear less necessary. If the people making the decisions are just like me, then I need not bother to influence them; they may be trusted to carry out my wishes in the absence of influence.

Judged strictly as a social control device, awe offers certain protections that the humanization of authority does not. Minimizing the distance between authorities and potential partisans may encourage the development of trust but it also tends to increase access and allow greater opportunities for influence. The control gained by reducing the desire for influence may be offset by the control lost in increasing the capability of influence. Oracular authorities offer no such danger and usually require a minimum of access.

Doing one's duty. A particularly important use of persuasion as a source of control involves the activation of commitments or obligations to the social system. Potential partisans can be persuaded to refrain from trying to change or subvert those decisions that have unpleasant consequences for them by convincing them that they have a 'duty' to honor such decisions. The importance of legitimacy for a political system comes from its connection with this control technique. If legitimacy is high, then there is a high potential for activating commitments and other, more costly forms of control may be avoided. For example, if 'patriotism' and 'the duty to serve one's country' are sufficiently strong, then there is no need for conscription; a voluntary army can be counted on. However, if legitimacy is weak and alienation toward the political system is prevalent, then the call to duty may sound hollow.

Not everyone is as committed to duty as the young hero of *The Pirates of Penzance* who insists on fulfilling his obligation to the pirates to whom he was mistakenly bound in childhood in spite of his strenuous disapproval of their profession. Still, a wide variety of unpleasant commitments may be accepted with good grace when there is a surplus of political trust. A good illustration of the dependence on such trust may be found in the relatively sudden increase in opposition to the Selective Service System. Students who were able to reach graduate school were, for many years, given *de facto* exemptions from compulsory service. As long as American foreign policy was generally supported, the unequal sacrifices demanded from different groups in the society did not become an issue. However, with the erosion of confidence stemming from American policy in Vietnam, not only the bases of deferment but conscription itself has been seriously challenged. In the Second World War, appeals to duty activated many to enlist voluntarily and those who didn't were quiet about it. During the Vietnam War, the threat of severe sanctions has not deterred open and organized opposition to the draft. In fact, some student groups have themselves attempted to activate commitments to 'higher' values by urging the duty *not* to serve. The price authorities pay for losing political confidence is a loss in their ability to activate commitments and the necessity of relying on more costly types of social control.

The activation of commitments, then, depends on the existence of political trust but it becomes an even more powerful control when it is mediated by face-to-face interaction. This point is best demonstrated by a series of social psychological experiments going back to the early 1940s. These experiments, particularly the later ones in the series, have shocked and outraged many people and have stimulated a vigorous debate among social psychologists on the proper ethics in experimenting with human subjects. But whether or not such experiments *should* have been conducted, the fact is that they *have* been and their results are both surprising and instructive.

Jerome Frank (1944) designed a series of experiments aimed at exploring the conditions under which subjects would refuse to continue disagreeable or nonsensical tasks. Under some conditions, the experimenter simply told the subject what he was expected to do and this was sufficient to ensure performance. For example, some subjects were asked to perform the task of balancing a marble on a small steel ball; almost all of them continued to pursue this manifestly impossible task for a full hour with no overt resistance in spite of inward annoyance. Frank quotes one subject: 'I was griped all the way through . . . [but] I promised a man I'd help him out and I couldn't see any reason for backing down on my word.' In another variation, Frank attempted to get subjects to eat unsalted soda crackers. When they were told that the experiment required them to eat twelve crackers, the subjects all ate them without argument or protest.

However, in another condition, the situation was translated from one of social control to one of influence. Subjects were told, 'This is an experiment in persuasion. I am going to try to make you eat twelve crackers in the first row on the tray. Whether you eat them or not is entirely up to you and doesn't affect the experiment one way or the other. But if you resist, I shall try to make you eat them anyway.' Under such instructions, considerable resistance was produced and while verbal pressure from the experimenter succeeded in making several subjects eat a few more crackers, less than a third ate all twelve crackers. As an influence situation, the eating of crackers became a test of wills; as a social control situation, it simply involved the activation of the commitments involved in agreeing to be an experimental subject and no resistance was encountered.

At the point of refusal in the influence variation, the experimenter attempted to introduce legitimacy, by saying, 'The experiment requires that you eat one more cracker and that will be enough,' or 'If you eat just one more cracker, that will be enough.' These instructions were successful in getting two thirds of the recalcitrant subjects to take one more cracker. Eating the final cracker was seen as a way of terminating what had become an embarrassing and extremely awkward situation.[3]

Some other experiments show this form of social control even more dramatically. Pepitone and Wallace (1955) asked subjects to sort the contents of a waste basket which contained cigar butts, soiled paper, dirty rags, broken sticks, pieces of glass, damp kleenex tissue, sodden purina chow, and other disgusting debris. The results were essentially the same in a variety of experimental conditions – the subjects snickered and laughed, and then got down to work and sorted the garbage with no strong protestations.

Martin Orne and his associates (1962; 1965) stumbled onto similar results in pursuing research on hypnosis. Orne sought a task which an unhypnotized subject would break off but not because of pain or exhaustion; that is, the task needed to be so boring and meaningless that a normal subject would simply refuse to do it after a while. He found it extremely difficult to design such a task because of the powerful social control operating in face-to-face interaction with an experimenter who is accorded legitimacy. In one experiment, Orne gave the subjects a huge stack of 2000 sheets of simple additions, each sheet containing 224 such additions. The simple instruction of 'Continue to work; I will return eventually', was sufficient to get them to work for many hours with little decrement in performance. It was necessary for the weary experimenter to break off the task for the even wearier subject might have complied indefinitely. Even the addition of instructions to tear each sheet up into thirty-two pieces and to throw them away upon completion did not lead to significant resistance. When work stoppage occurred, the return of the experimenter to the room with instructions to continue was sufficient to ensure more work for additional hours.

Thwarted in this attempt to produce a breakdown of social control, Orne moved to more extreme tasks. Is the degree of control in hypnosis, Orne asked, actually any greater than the

3. For a discussion of the particular role of embarrassment in such experiments and an ingenious experimental demonstration and theoretical discussion of how it operates in social influence situations, see Modigliani (1966).

degree of control which an experimenter exercises over a normal waking subject when this subject accepts the legitimacy of the experimental situation? To test this, Orne and Evans (1965) used a series of tasks which were extremely disagreeable, and potentially harmful to either the subject himself or to others. The experiment called for a special apparatus – a box with a glass screen which could be slid into place and removed but which, because of the lighting and the type of glass, was impossible to see. Hypnotized subjects were compared with a group of un-hypnotized subjects who were instructed to pretend they were hypnotized and with other control groups of normal waking subjects.

Initially, subjects were asked to pick up a few harmless objects from the box – with the glass screen not in place, of course. Then, a harmless lizard was placed in the box and subjects were told to pick it up, followed by similar instructions for a fourteen-inch harmless green snake and a fourteen-inch venomous black snake, capable of inflicting a mortal wound. However, before the last task and unknown to the subject, the invisible glass screen was silently lowered into place so that subjects who attempted to comply would get only bruised knuckles instead of a snake bite.

At this point, the box was removed and the subject watched the experimenter pour concentrated nitric acid into a small shallow beaker. The experimenter dropped a coin into the acid and allowed the subject to watch it dissolve for approximately a minute. He then asked the subject to remove the coin with his bare hand and to plunge both coin and hand into a nearby basin of soapy, lukewarm water. If the subject complied (or if he did not comply, while he was diverted in some fashion), the beaker with acid was switched with one that appeared identical but contained a harmless solution. The experimenter then instructed the subject to throw the acid in the face of the lab assistant who had been helping with various aspects of the experiment. This completed the experiment proper and was followed by a fairly extensive postexperimental interview.

The results show a good deal of compliance with the experimenter's requests in all conditions. Of the six hypnotized subjects, five complied with all requests; the sixth, a young lady, became hysterical at the sight of the harmless lizard in the beginning and the other tasks were not used. All six of the subjects who were simulating hypnosis complied fully, carrying out all of the experimenter's requests although showing reluctance at a number of points. Of a group of six control subjects who were told that they were normal controls for a hypnosis experiment, five performed the acid tasks and three of the six attempted to pick up the venomous snake.

The latest and most significant work in this genre is that of Stanley Milgram (1963; 1964; 1965). Milgram focused his work on destructive obedience – obedience to demands which injure others. The basic experiment involves a naïve subject who administers what he believes are extremely severe electric shocks to another 'subject' who is in fact a confederate of the experimenter. The subject believes that he is participating in an experiment which involves the effect of punishment on learning. He is instructed to raise the shock level administered after each error which the victim makes in a learning task involving the pairing of words. The simulated generator which the subject uses is extremely convincing; it is marked with voltage designations from fifteen to 450 which are accompanied by verbal designations of slight shock, moderate shock, strong shock, very strong shock, intense shock, extreme intensity shock, Danger: severe shock, and two more positions ominously marked XXX. When the naïve subject pulls the generator switch, the generator lights and buzzes but, unknown to him, no shock is actually transmitted.

In Milgram's original experiment, the victim–confederate was in an adjacent room providing answers by pushing buttons. At the 300-volt level and again at the 315-volt level, he was instructed to pound on the wall and, thereafter, provide no more answers. Subjects typically turned to the experimenter at that point who advised them to treat no response as an incorrect response and to proceed with the shock schedule. If the subject asked about injury to the victim, the experimenter replied, 'Although the shocks can be extremely painful, they cause no permanent tissue damage.'

The results of this experiment are startling. Of the forty subjects, all proceed past the strong and very strong shock readings and none break off before reaching 300 volts. Even more startling, twenty-six of the forty reach the maximum level of 450 volts –

the XXX category. Such behavior is clearly not sadism. Subjects are under considerable stress and manifest it by sweating, stuttering, uncontrollable laughing fits, trembling, and other manifestations of extreme tension. Milgram quotes one observer:

I observed a mature and initially poised businessman enter the laboratory smiling and confident. Within twenty minutes, he was reduced to a twitching, stuttering wreck who was rapidly approaching a point of nervous collapse. He constantly pulled on his earlobe and twisted his hands. At one point, he pushed his fist into his forehead and muttered 'Oh, God. Let's stop it.' And yet he continued to respond to every word of the experimenter and obeyed to the end (Milgram, 1963, p. 377).

Why do subjects continue to honor a presumed obligation to an experimenter whom they do not know, to accomplish goals which are at best vague and obscure to them and which at the same time involve virtually gratuitous injury to another human being whom they have no reason to dislike? Variations of the experiment point to the fact that the strength of the obligation is heavily influenced by the physical presence of the experimenter. In one condition with forty fresh subjects, the experimenter leaves after presenting the initial instructions and gives subsequent orders over the telephone. Where twenty-six of forty were fully obedient when the experimenter was present, only nine of the forty subjects were fully obedient when the orders were conveyed over the phone. In a number of cases, the subject lied to the experimenter, saying that he was raising the shock level when he was in fact using the lowest level on the board. If the experimenter appeared in person after the subject refused over the telephone, he was sometimes able to reactivate compliance with the simple assertion, 'The experiment requires that you continue.'

Similarly, when the victim is brought into the same room with the subject, the number of obedient subjects goes down. The conflict becomes more intense for the subject with the experimenter looking at him and clearly expecting him to continue, while the victim very visibly indicates his pain and his desire to participate no longer. Such results suggest that the blindfolding of a condemned prisoner may have another meaning than the one usually attributed to it. It is not so much to protect the victim's feelings that a blindfold is needed but rather to protect the executioner from his surveillance.

The basic mechanism of control accounting for these results is the activation of commitments. By conveying the definition of the situation that the experimenter is a mere agent, carrying out the sometimes unpleasant demands of 'research' or 'science', he creates a situation where a refusal is an act of deviance. Well-socialized subjects who have volunteered their services find it difficult to commit such an act under the very eyes of the experimenter, but when they can do it without the embarrassment of a direct confrontation, it is much easier.

Perhaps the most powerful and common means of social control is simply the conveying of expectations with clarity and explicitness coupled with clear and direct accountability for the performance of such expectations. As long as legitimacy is accorded in such situations, individuals will regard their non-compliance as a failure and any interaction which makes such a personal failure salient is embarrassing, unpleasant and something to be avoided.

This point is no less true for complex, modern societies than for small communities. The activation of commitments still depends both on the acceptance of a general obligation and on reminders of what that duty is in specific situations. The connections between the top political leaders in a society and the members of a solidarity group may be remote and may pass through many links before they reach a person's boss or neighbor or colleague or whoever else happens to do the reminding. Nevertheless, at the last link in this chain between authorities and potential partisans, the desire to avoid the embarrassment of being derelict under surveillance is a powerful persuader. The possibility of losing such a potent means of control is a strong incentive for any set of authorities to achieve or maintain high trust on the part of potential partisans.

Participation and cooptation

One of the most interesting and complicated of control mechanisms is cooptation. Essentially, it involves the manipulation of access, but as a control technique it is double-edged. In his classic study of the Tennessee Valley Authority (TVA), Selznick

(1953) defined it as 'the process of absorbing new elements into the leadership or policy-determining structure of an organization as a means of averting threats to its stability of existence'. Earlier I argued that authorities normally will prefer to limit access to those elements most susceptible to control, but cooptation involves yielding access to the most difficult and threatening potential partisans. Why should any organization wish to deliberately create control problems for itself?

This mechanism arises in situations where control is already insufficient. It is a response to anticipated or actual pressure from partisans of such magnitude that it threatens the incumbent authorities and perhaps threatens the continuation of the system itself. Bringing such partisans 'inside' does not create control problems; it simply transfers the existing ones to a different arena. In particular, while cooptation removes some of the insulation between potential partisans and authorities, it makes the former subject to other control techniques which were previously not available. Representatives of the partisan group, once inside, are subject to the rewards and punishments that the organization bestows. They acquire a stake in the organization, having gained some control over resources whose continuation and expansion is dependent on the organization's maintenance and growth. New rewards lie ahead if they show themselves to be amenable to some degree of control; deprivation of rewards which they now enjoy becomes a new possibility if they remain unruly.

Besides these changes in the situation of the partisans, they are likely to enjoy some changes in orientation as well. First of all, their attitudes and commitments to the system may change. They may come to identify with the collectivity to such a degree that it will mute and subdue their original loyalty to a hostile outside partisan group which is trying to change the organization.

A desire to increase the potentialities for control lies behind the advocacy of admitting Communist China to the United Nations for many who hold such a position. UN membership is regarded less in terms of the access to influence it provides and more in terms of the control opportunities it offers. A hostile China is viewed as a greater threat outside the United Nations than inside. Once inside, it is argued, China would acquire interests which would make it a partner in maintaining the stability of the international system. It lacks such interests as an 'outlaw' with relatively little stake in maintaining peaceful and cooperative relations with other countries.

From the perspective of potential partisans, cooptation must be regarded as a risk. Representatives of coopted groups are likely to be charged with having 'sold out' at the least indication that they are pressing the group's demands with less vigor than previously. In fact, there is a tendency for such partisans to regard the entire opportunity for increased access as a form of manipulation. 'The more a ruling class is able to assimilate the most prominent men of the dominated classes the more stable and dangerous is its rule,' Marx argued. The very act of accepting access by a leader may be taken as evidence of desertion to the enemy either for selfish gain, i.e. as a 'fink', or through naïveté, i.e. as a 'dupe'.

What can a potential partisan group hope to gain by allowing itself and its leaders to be coopted? It can gain increased access to resources which will enhance its influence and bring about outcome modifications. In other words, cooptation does not operate simply as a control device – it is also likely to involve yielding ground. For this reason, there are likely to be parallel fears on the part of authorities. They may worry that the act of cooptation represents the 'nose of the camel' and be fearful of their ability to keep the rest of the camel out of the tent. Far from manipulation, some authorities may regard it as an act of undue yielding to pressure and the rewarding of 'irresponsible' behavior.

Both the partisan's and the authority's fears about coopta- tion are valid fears. Cooptation invariably involves some mixture of outcome modification and social control and the exact mix is difficult to determine in advance. The authority who opposes coopting the hostile element fears that outcome modification will dominate the mix; the partisan who opposes accepting it, fears that the social control element will dominate.

The TVA case described by Selznick (1953) is instructive in this regard. The newly founded organization was faced, in 1933, with a powerfully entrenched existing interest bloc in the Tennessee Valley. This bloc consisted of a complex headed by the Land

Grant Colleges, the more prosperous farmers represented by the American Farm Bureau Federation, and the Federal Agricultural Extension Service with its county agents. In some fashion, TVA had to confront this bloc whose territory the new organization was invading. Had TVA been firmly established with assured support of its own, it might have considered a strategy which would have challenged this bloc. In trying to become established, an alternative strategy recommended itself – to coopt the Farm Bureau complex into TVA. This policy was justified under the rubric of the 'grass roots policy' which emphasized partnership with local groups in the region. The most significant act of cooptation was the appointment of one of the leaders of the Farm Bureau complex to TVA's three-man board.

One of the consequences of the cooptation strategy was a considerable amount of influence by the Farm Bureau complex over TVA's agricultural policies. Decisions on fertilizer programs, on the degree of emphasis on rural cooperatives, on the place of Negro farmers in the TVA program, were apparently all heavily influenced by this partisan group in the valley. On the other hand, TVA was able to carry out successfully its public power program and a number of other important objectives which might have become the target of active opposition if the Farm Bureau complex had not been coopted. It is never easy to assess whether the 'price' in outcome modification was worth it or not, especially since one cannot know what would have happened if cooptation had not been used. The lesson to be drawn from the TVA example is not that it acted wisely or foolishly in coopting the Farm Bureau complex. Rather it is that *any* act of cooptation of potential partisans by authorities is likely to be a mixture of modification and social control and the balance of the mix is problematic and of concern to both parties.

Leeds's discussion (1964) of the absorption of nonconforming enclaves again illustrates the double-edged nature of this process. General Chennault and his followers in the period preceding the Second World War attempted to develop a group of trained fighter pilots (the 'Flying Tigers') to furnish air support for Chinese land forces opposing the Japanese. The military had yet to accept, at this time, the full significance of air warfare and tended to regard it as auxiliary to infantry and artillery. Consequently, the allocation of supplies and personnel to Chennault were limited and a variety of other means were used to control and isolate the Flying Tiger group. However, after the US entry into the war, this conflict proved too costly and a different control technique was used to deal with the rebellious group. In July 1942, the American Volunteer Group of Flying Tigers was transformed into China Air Task Force and inducted into the US Air Force under General Bissell. Later the group became the 14th Air Force under General Stillwell who was instructed to give Chennault full support. This ended the rebellion and removed the acute pressure from this partisan group. Along with the development of military technology and the experiences of the war, this absorption contributed to a major reorientation in the military toward the importance of air warfare. As in the TVA case, cooptation seems to have involved large amounts of influence for the coopted group.

Closely related to the issue of cooptation and protest-absorption is that of participation in decision making. A long line of social psychological experiments in laboratory and field settings has emphasized the importance of participation as a positive factor in the acceptance of decision outcomes. It is not always clear precisely what is meant by participation.

One may emphasize the influence aspects of participation. To increase the participation of a group of potential partisans may mean to increase its influence over decisions. If there is increased satisfaction in such situations, it is because the modified outcomes are closer to what the partisan group desires. It may have very little or nothing to do with the fact of participation itself. If the significance of participation stems from the attendant influence, then we should expect the same increase in satisfaction and commitment that we would get if outcomes were similarly modified without an increase in participation.

Participation has a social control aspect as well. Here it is claimed that the act of participating in a decision process increases commitment and acceptance of decisions even if outcomes are no more satisfactory. The classic case of such alleged 'participation' effects is the Hawthorne Study (Roethlisberger and Dickson, 1939) in which output increased following a variety of decisions made by a group of workers. These particular experiments are a weak reed on which to base any conclusion as Carey (1967) demonstrates in an appropriately harsh review. Carey argues that a 'detailed comparison between the Hawthorne conclusions and the Hawthorne evidence shows these conclusions to be almost wholly unsupported' (p. 403). But in a later, more careful study of 'participation' effects, Coch and French (1965) conclude that resistance to changing work methods can be overcome 'by the use of group meetings in which management effectively communicates the need for change and stimulates group participation in planning the changes. Such participation results in higher production, higher morale, and better labor–management relations' (p. 459).

Much of the small group work on 'democratic' methods of decision making has a strong social control emphasis. As Verba points out,

Participation is in most cases limited to member endorsement of decisions made by the leader who . . . is neither selected by the group nor responsible to the group for his actions. In group discussions, the leader does not present alternatives to the group from which the members choose. Rather, the group leader has a particular goal in mind and uses the group discussion as a means of inducing acceptance of the goal. . . . As used in much of the small group literature, participatory democratic leadership refers not to a technique of decision but to a technique of persuasion (Verba, 1961, p. 220).

Participation, like cooptation, is most likely to be some mixture of influence and social control. Many of the same issues arise. If the social control emphasis is paramount, partisans are likely to regard the process as pseudo participation and manipulation. But it is not easy to increase participation without also increasing influence. The increased access may be intended to lead to a greater feeling of participation and increased commitment of members, but those who are so admitted may not be very long satisfied with the trappings of influence. When conflicts arise, the new participants may be in an improved position to pursue their interests effectively.

By the use of *selective* participation, authorities may control some partisans by increasing the ability of others to influence. Hard-pressed authorities may welcome influence attempts by rival partisans for such influence may free rather than confine them. Under such circumstances, authorities may encourage increased participation by selected groups despite, or even because of, the increased influence that it will bring. The new pressures can then be pointed to as justification and defense for failure to take the actions desired by the first group; the second group in turn can be brought to appreciate the constraints which their rival places on the authorities.

The playing off of one partisan group against another as a technique of control is an ancient and familiar one. Machiavelli recommended it to his authorities and Simmel developed it in his discussion of the 'tertius gaudens', i.e. the third party who draws advantage from the quarrel of two others. It is captured in the admonition to authorities to 'divide and rule'. Simmel illustrates it by describing the Inca custom of dividing a 'newly conquered tribe in two approximately equal halves and [placing] a supervisor over each of them, but [giving] these two supervisors slightly different ranks. This was indeed the most suitable means for provoking rivalry between the two heads, which prevented any united action against the ruler on the part of the subjected territory' (Simmel, 1950, p. 165).

Such a control technique has certain dangers. First, while it may forestall the necessity of immediate outcome modification and increase the temporary maneuverability of authorities, it does not relieve the pressure in the long run and may even intensify it. For the moment, some of the resources of the partisan groups may be redirected into the conflict with each other but the authorities, by definition, control the choices which these groups are attempting to influence. Second, it is typically the case that rival partisan groups have some degree of common interest. If so, they may find it convenient to pool their resources in a temporary coalition. Thus, increased participation may lead to an enhancement of the influence it was intended to prevent.

Note that in the above discussion we are viewing organizational officials in their role as authorities. As partisans, these same individuals may desire increased influence for members of the same partisan group. The chairman of a state political party may argue for the widest possible citizen participation in the selection of delegates to the nominating convention because he believes that his own preferred candidate has a stronger following among the party rank and file than among the organizational regulars. In encouraging such rank and file participation, he is acting as a partisan attempting to influence the decision on selecting a candidate, not as an authority trying to minimize partisan influence on the decisions over which he personally exercises authority.

Summary

This chapter has emphasized the perspective of authorities on the possible attempts of partisans to influence the outcome of the decisions they make. The central problem from their standpoint is the containment of influence. Pressure from potential partisans can be relieved by yielding ground and modifying the outcome of decisions or by dealing with the source of pressure through some form of social control.

One form of control involves the insulation of decision makers from potential partisans. This can be done at the point of entry by selecting those who will not present problems or at the point of exit by expelling recalcitrant individuals or groups. Once in, potential partisans are subject to a wide variety of sanctions. Finally, the orientation of potential partisans can be controlled by manipulating information, idcology, imagc of authorities, friendship ties, norms, and values. If potential partisans are sufficiently socialized and have high political trust they can be controlled by the activation of commitments. Mechanisms like cooptation and participation seem to involve a mixture of outcome modification and social control as a way of dealing with particularly powerful or threatening partisan groups.

There is a major difference in the influence and social control perspectives on the meaning and significance of social conflict. The social control perspective leads to an emphasis on stability. Conflict, under this view, represents a failure of social control – the failure to contain influence.

This is not to suggest that stability, as used here, is a bad thing. The authorities in whose maintenance one is concerned may be a progressive administration, vigorously pursuing land reform and providing effective leadership in a wide variety of ways. Or, they may represent a totalitarian regime relying heavily on terror and repression as social control techniques. In any case the questions which arise from this perspective focus us on the manner in which authorities are left free to govern.

The influence perspective on the other hand leads to an emphasis on change. Conflict has a different meaning. Rather than a failure of social control, it is likely to be viewed as part of a social movement aimed at changing the content of decisions, the incumbent authorities, or the regime itself. Such potential partisans might be revolutionary or counterrevolutionary, progressive or reactionary. Again, no implication is intended about the desirability of change *per se*.

Perhaps the emphasis on stability in one perspective and change in the other is avoidable. Yet it seems to flow from the kinds of questions which arise naturally with each perspective. By taking both perspectives, one can avoid the characteristic blind spots of each one taken alone.

References

CAREY, A. (1967), 'The Hawthorne Studies: a radical criticism', *Amer. sociol. Rev.*, vol. 32, pp. 403–16.

COCH, L. and FRENCH, J. R. P., Jr (1965), 'Overcoming resistance to change', in Harold Proshansky and Bernard Seidenberg (eds.), *Basic Studies in Social Psychology*, Holt, Rinehart & Winston.

DAHL, R. A. (1961), *Who Governs?* Yale University Press.

EASTON, D. (1965), *A Systems Analysis of Political Life*, J. Wiley.

FRANK, J. (1944), 'Experimental studies of personal pressure and resistance', *J. Gen. Psychol.*, vol. 30, pp. 23–64.

GAMSON, Z. F. (1964), 'Social control and modification', Ph.D. Dissertation, Harvard University.

GAMSON, Z. F. (1966), 'Utilitarian and normative orientations toward education', *Sociology of Education*, vol. 39, pp. 46–73.

GOFFMAN, E. (1964), 'On cooling the mark out: some aspects of adaptation to failure', in W. G. Bennis, *et al.* (eds.) *Interpersonal Dynamics*, Dorsey Press, pp. 417–30.

LEEDS, R. (1964), 'The absorption of protest', in W. W. Cooper, H. J. Leavitt, and M. W. Shelly, II (eds.), *New Perspectives in Organization Research*, Wiley, pp. 115–35.

LERNER, D. (1958), *The Passing of Traditional Society*, Free Press.

MILGRAM, S. (1963), 'Behavioral study of obedience', *J. abnorm. Soc. Psychol.*, vol. 67, pp. 371–8.

MILGRAM, S. (1964), 'Group pressure and action against a person', *J. abnor. soc. Psychol.*, vol. 69, pp. 137–43.

MILGRAM, S. (1965), 'Some conditions of obedience and disobedience to authority', in *Current Studies in Social Psychology* (eds.) Ivan D. Steiner and Martin Fishbein), pp. 243–62. Holt, Rinehart, & Winston.

ORNE, M. T. (1962), 'On the social psychology of the psychological experiment', *Amer. Psychol.*, vol. 17, pp. 776–83.

ORNE, M. T. and EVANS, F. J. (1965), 'Social control in the psychological experiment', *J. Personal. Soc. Psychol.*, vol. 1 ,pp. 189–200.

PEPITONE, A. and WALLACE, W. (1955), 'Experimental studies on the dynamics of hostility', Paper read at Pennsylvania Psychological Association Meetings. (Described in Albert Pepitone, 'Attributions of causality, social attitudes, and cognitive matching processes', in Renato Tagiuri and Luigi Petrullo (eds.), *Person Perception and Interpersonal Behavior*, pp. 258–76. Stanford University Press.

ROETHLISBERGER, F. J. and DICKSON, W. J. (1939), *Management and the Worker*, Harvard University Press.

SCHLESINGER, A. M., Jr (1965), *A Thousand Days*, Houghton Mifflin.

SELZNICK, P. (1953), *TVA and the Grass Roots*, University of California Press.

SIMMEL, G. (1950), *The Sociology of Georg Simmel* (ed. Kurt H. Wolff), Free Press.

VERBA, S. (1961), *Small Groups and Political Behavior*, Princeton University Press.

18 R. E. Walton

Two Strategies of Social Change and their Dilemmas

R. E. Walton, 'Two strategies of social change and their dilemmas',
Journal of Applied and Behavioral Science, 1965, vol. 1, no. 2, pp. 167–79.

The type of intergroup setting which is of primary concern here is
described by the following assumptions. First, assume a desire on
the part of one group to change the allocation of scarce resources
between two groups – these could be status, political power,
economic advantage or opportunity, geographic occupancy, and
so on. Alternately, assume incompatible preferences regarding
social institutions – such as the Berlin Wall, racial segregation,
union shop. Second, assume that although the leaders of the
groups recognize these areas of conflict they also want to establish
a more cooperative set of attitudes between the groups. Third,
assume further that there is neither law nor a compulsory arbitration mechanism which can accomplish the desired change or
settle the conflict of interest.

Some of our most pressing problems of social change fit these
assumptions almost completely and others meet them to a lesser
degree. In international relations, for instance, the important
substantive conflicts between the United States and the Soviet
Union are accompanied by a general desire for more favorable
inter-nation attitudes. Moreover, in the present polarized world
where the stakes of change can be enormously high, no international legal machinery is available to settle the important issues.

In race relations, the civil rights movement of the last decade
has sought social change at times and in places where legal
machinery could not be brought to bear to establish and enforce
humane treatment for Negroes, to say nothing about equalizing
their right to vote, to use public accommodations, to find housing,
to apply for jobs, and so forth. At the same time, the majority of
Negro and white leaders have commented upon the necessity for
improved intergroup attitudes.

In labor–management relations, also, there are important substantive issues, such as hours, wages, and working conditions, which are neither specified by law nor amenable to resolution by appeal to a higher order of common values. Often these differences are accompanied by a genuine and mutual desire for harmonious intergroup relations.

How does the leadership of a group behave in these situations when they seek a change in the status quo? What actions are instrumental to the change effort?

Two groups of social scientists – viewing the same general situation – offer quite different explanations and advice. One change strategy is advanced by game theorists, diplomatic strategists, and students of revolutions. Their focus is on the building of a power base and the strategic manipulation of power. Another strategy is urged by many social psychologists and by many persons involved in human relations laboratory training. This approach involves overtures of love and trust and gestures of good will, all intended to result in attitude change and concomitant behavior change.

Tactics of the power strategy

In recent years there has been an attempt to explicate the rational tactics of power and strategic choice (Schelling, 1960; Rapoport, 1960; Boulding, 1962; Walton and McKersie, 1965). The work in this area suggests that the fixed sum games – those situations in which what one person gains the other loses – require the following tactical operations.

First, in order to establish a basis for negotiation with the other and improve the probable outcome for itself, a group must build its power *vis-à-vis* the other. Group A can increase its relative power by making group B more dependent upon it and by decreasing its own (A's) dependence upon B. Often the change is sought by groups with a relative power disadvantage. To command attention and establish a basis for a *quid pro quo*, they must threaten the other with harm, loss, inconvenience, or embarrassment. These threats in international relations range from nuclear war to unilateral cancellation of an official state visit. In civil rights they involve notoriety, demonstrations, consumer boycotts, and sit-ins, lie-ins, and the like. In labor relations they include wildcat strikes, authorized stoppages, unfavorable publicity campaigns. These tactics create a basis for negotiation only if the threats are credible. One important technique for increasing their credibility is to fulfil a given threat once or repeatedly, as required.

A second set of tactical operations is required in order for a group to make maximum use of its potential power. These include biasing the rival group's perceptions of the strength of the underlying preference functions. A leader of group A attempts to overstate his group's needs or preferences for various degrees of achievement of its stated objective. Also, leader A depreciates the importance to B of B's objectives. These operations require the skillful management of ambiguity and uncertainty. They involve manipulating communication opportunities such that B perceives A as being maximally (even if irrationally) committed to a course of action and that the leader of group B does not have a comparable opportunity to commit himself to a different set of actions.

An abundance of illustrative material from international relations is available for each of these tactical operations – for example, the Cuban missile episode, Berlin crises, and the crises over Suez, the Congo, and Vietnam. Leaders of various civil rights groups have behaved in similar ways. Illustrative encounters are those in Montgomery (school-bus boycotts over public accommodations); Pittsburgh (consumer boycotts over employment); Chicago (lie-ins and demonstrations over de facto segregation in schools); Birmingham (demonstrations over public accommodations); Mississippi ('invading' the state in the interest of voter registration and freedom schools). Analyses of the negotiations in any of the major trade union strikes – such as those in steel in 1959, in rails in 1963, and in autos in 1964 – would reveal labor–management behavior which conformed to the tactical operations of the power strategy.

Tactics of the attitude change strategy

Theoretical and empirical work in recent years has identified the conditions and actions which result in change in intergroup relationships (Naess, 1957; Janis and Katz, 1959; Osgood, 1959; Kelman, 1962; Berkowitz, 1962; Sherif, 1962; Deutsch, 1962; Gibb, 1964; Walton and McKersie, 1965). The areas of agreement in these writings may be summarized in terms of the tactics of attitude change.

Increasing the level of attraction and trust between persons or groups involves the following types of operations, considering the leader of group A as the acting party: minimizing the perceived differences between the groups' goals and between characteristics of members of the two groups; communications to B advocating peace; refraining from any actions which might harm members of the rival group (inconvenience, harass, embarrass, or violate them in any way); minimizing or eliminating B's perception of potential threats from A; emphasizing the degree of mutual dependence between the groups, accepting or enhancing the status of the representative of the rival group; ensuring that contacts between groups are on the basis of equal status; attempting to involve many members in intergroup contact; attempting to achieve a high degree of empathy with respect to the motives, expectations, and attitudes of members of group B; adopting a consistent posture of trust toward the other group; being open about A's own plans and intentions; creating a network of social relations involving many mutual associations with third parties.

There is tension between the ideas which underlie the two change strategies outlined above. However, the two groups of social scientists who are associated with these respective change strategies tend to handle this tension either by ignoring it or by depreciating the assumptions, ideas, and tactics of the other. It is true that both systems of ideas treat certain realities of the total social field; and, admittedly, it is possible for one to center one's attention on those particular situations where his ideas by themselves are appropriate and upon those particular aspects of a more complex situation where his ideas apply. The practitioner himself cannot do this. He must deal with the total reality. The leader of a group who is advocating and seeking change directly experiences the tension between these two persuasive systems of ideas.

Social scientists can become more relevant and therefore more helpful to the practitioner if they, too, confront these tensions between ideas, these dilemmas in action programs.

It is important to identify still a third distinct process of change, namely, problem solving. This process can be used whenever the basic nature of the issue is one where there is the potential that arrangements can be invented or created allowing both parties to gain or where one party can gain without the other's sacrificing anything of value to himself. In other words, integrative solutions are logically possible (Blake, 1959). However, this alternative of problem solving is not applicable in the specific intergroup situations assumed here: the substantive conflicts are ones which by the nature of the issues and the parties' basic preferences can be resolved only by dominance–submission or some compromise outcome.

Leadership dilemmas in pursuing both power and attitude change strategies

If – as we have assumed here – a leader of group A has the objective both of obtaining important concessions from B and of reducing inter-group hostility, he would prefer to pursue simultaneously both change strategies discussed above. But in many respects the strategies place contradictory tactical demands on a leader, forcing him to choose between these strategies or to find some basis on which to integrate the two in some broader strategy of change. Several of the contradictions, dilemmas, and choice points in the tactics of social change are discussed below.

Overstatement of objectives versus *De-emphasizing Differences*

On the one hand, it is often tactical to the power strategy to overstate one's ultimate goals or immediate objectives – in effect, exaggerating the differences between the two groups. The strategy of attitude change, on the other hand, would de-emphasize differences. Thus, the US references to the status of Berlin which overstate our pertinent preferences, needs, and requirements may improve our position in bargaining for new terms there; but these statements run the risk of convincing the Soviet Union that our differences run even deeper than they do and that there is less basis for conciliation and trust than they had believed.

Stereotyping: Internal cohesion versus *Accurate differentiation*

Stereotyping members of the rival group, focusing on their faults, impugning their motives, questioning their rationality, challenging their competence – these are often employed by leaders and members of the first group to build internal cohesion and willingness to make necessary sacrifices. For example, these tendencies occurred in a moderate form as the Mississippi Summer Project prepared their field staff and student volunteers for their work in 'hostile' Mississippi. The tendency to attribute negative attributes to members of the rival group may have aided in the implementation of the almost pure power strategy which characterized this particular project, but this tendency would have been a clear liability in another civil rights project where the objectives include achieving attitude change.

Emphasis on Power to coerce versus *trust*

If group A increases B's dependence upon A, this may enhance A's power to obtain substantive concessions, but it will not elicit more positive feelings. In fact, it can be argued that the trust-building process requires that A would communicate about *A*'s dependence upon B. A labor union may enhance its power position by making management more aware of the company's vulnerability to a strike. But the same union might elicit more trust if it were to indicate instead how much the union must count upon management.

Information: ambiguity versus *predictability*

Whereas ambiguity and uncertainty are often tactical to the power strategy, openness and predictability are essential to the attitude change strategy. Similarly, the first strategy is facilitated when there is limited and disciplined interaction; the second, when there is a more extensive and more open contact pattern. Thus, the power strategy dictates that we restrict the flow of information and people between the Soviet Union and the United States and that the limited contacts be formal and structured and that the agenda of these contacts be quite guarded. Attitude change strategy on the other hand, calls for freedom of travel, a variety of settings for international contact, and spontaneity and openness in these interchanges.

Threat versus *conciliation*

Review of the tactical operations of the two strategies reveals another important choice point in dual or mixed strategies, namely, What should be the role of threat or harm? When A is primarily pursuing an attitude change strategy, he communicates peaceful plans, he reduces perceived threat to B, and he refrains from actions that harm B. However, to pursue a power strategy in the interest of obtaining substantive gains, A engages in quite different tactics.

Even instances of uncontrolled aggression out of frustration can build bargaining power for the frustrated group and serve as an implicit threat of more aggression if substantive gains are not forthcoming. The Harlem riots in the summer of 1964 illustrate this point. Although it was generally said at the time that these outbursts hurt the civil rights movement, i.e. 'had set the movement back several years', many changes which accommodated the Negroes' demands and needs were soon made in the budgets, plans and organization of several commissions and departments of New York City. One column headline in the *New York Times*, July 1964, the week following the riots, read 'City Accelerates Fight on Poverty: $223,225 Grant Made Amid Reference to Racial Riots.' A casual content analysis of items in the news after the riots in Harlem, Rochester, Philadelphia, and elsewhere suggests that there were both substantive gains and attitudinal losses. Notwithstanding the fact that all responsible civil rights leaders deplored the wanton destruction of property and the indiscriminate defiance of legal authorities, their bargaining power was nevertheless strengthened in certain respects.

Hostility management: impact versus *catharsis*

This dilemma is related to the preceding one but can present a somewhat more subtle problem for group leadership. Both change strategies involve the purposeful management of hostile feelings. In the power strategy the expression of hostile feelings is managed in a way which creates optimal impact on the other group, communicating strength of interest in the issue or making a threat credible.

The attitude change strategy also involves the expression of hostile feelings, but in a way which creates an optimal impact on the expressing group. Hostility expression is managed in a way which allows catharsis and the re-evaluation of one's own group's feelings, but with minimum impact on the other group. Otherwise the hostility level will tend to be maintained or increased.

Coalition versus *inclusion*

One final dilemma relates to the question of whether A tries to involve third parties or publics in a coalition *against* B or in a social group *with* B. Building bargaining power in the interest of substantive change may require A to isolate B and attempt to generate disapproval of B. This has been an important aspect of the strategy of the civil rights movement in the last decade. The movement has tried to identify and isolate those officials and power groups in the South who oppose integration and those national officials in the Republican Party who are unsympathetic with certain legislative and enforcement objectives. This has created a forced choice situation for the moderates and for the uncertain.

However, a strategy of attitude change involves creating a network of social relations among A, B, and others. Applied to the civil rights movement, an emphasis on attitude change would actively encourage dialogue, understanding, and mutual influence among (a) groups in the movement, (b) the middle-of-the-roaders, and (c) the segregationists and other right-wing groups.

Coping with the dilemmas

How do those who seek both substantive changes opposed by another group and improvements in intergroup attitudes cope with these dilemmas?

If the group's leader sequences the emphasis placed upon these two objectives and their accompanying strategies, this does somewhat ameliorate the tension between the two sets of activities. In international negotiations between the East and the West, both sides have used a freeze-thaw approach. One may first engage in new initiatives intended to make substantive gains or to create a power base for the future, and then make peace overtures. As long as the cycle is not too short in duration and the initiatives and overtures are seen as genuine, a leader can engage in both sets of behaviors and still have them be credible. In race relations, a particular campaign may involve a street demonstration phase (powerbuilding) and a negotiation phase (a mixture of power bargaining and relationship building).

Another technique is to have the contradictory strategies implemented by different persons or subgroups. In international relations, power tactics occur in the confrontations between the United States and the Soviet Union in the United Nations General Assembly and Security Council, but their attitude change efforts are implemented by different groups involved in such activities as cultural exchange programs. In race relations, a similar distinction can be made between the programs of CORE and SNCC on the one hand and NAACP and the Urban League on the other. This technique makes it apparent that mixed or dual strategies can be pursued more readily by an organization than by a person, and more readily by a movement than by an organization.

Whether or not the activities are sequenced or assigned to different persons within a group, an important way of coping with these dilemmas is to choose actions which minimize them. Recognition of the tactical requirements of both strategies results in eliminating provocative acts which elicit negative attitudes and add nothing to the power strategy – for example, impeccable dress and demeanor in many civil rights demonstrations or the self-imposed norm of volunteers of the Mississippi Summer Project to avoid mixed racial couples' appearing in public even though eventual acceptance of such a pattern was one of the goals of the movement.

When the relationship between strategies is fully understood by the leader, he can select power tactics which have least negative impact on attitudes and choose attitudinal structuring activities which detract least from the power strategy.

Nonviolence is an attempt to meet the requirements of both strategies, but as a tactic it falls short of achieving an optimal integration. This is true in part because the distinction made between violence and nonviolence is more meaningful to the acting group than to the target group. The distinction usually refers to whether or not there is a physical violation of members of the rival group. In fact, other violations may be experienced by them as equally devastating – such as violation of their traditions and other social norms (integrating schools), assaults on their power base (voting drives). In short, in some situations the only maneuvers which effectively increase bargaining power really do hurt.

Overall strategy considerations

Although in many situations one must engage in the tactics of power only at some disadvantage in terms of achieving attitude change and vice versa, this is not always the case. Especially when one takes a longer-range viewpoint, one may discover that the substantive objectives of the power strategy are more likely to be realized at a later date if an improvement in intergroup attitudes is sought initially. The point is that attitude change may result in some lessening of the substantive conflict. If southern whites as a group were more accepting of Negroes, i.e. developed more favorable attitudes toward them for some independent reason, they would be less adamant on certain substantive issues – for example, segregated schools – and would, as a result, reduce the need for civil rights groups to utilize a power strategy. Moreover, in the case of many of the substantive gains which one may reach through the power strategy – an arms control agreement, a treaty on Berlin, an understanding reached regarding future employment practices affecting Negroes – the fulfillment of these arrangements is dependent upon the level of trust and confidence which exists in the relationship.

Similarly, a longer-range viewpoint may show that the objective of attitude change is more likely to be achieved at a later date if one engages in the power tactics initially. The substantive gains obtained by the power strategy almost always result in temporary setbacks in terms of the level of friendliness and trust between the groups; but in the somewhat longer run, the result may be better affective relations. Consider race relations. One reason why more positive attitudes may develop via the initial power strategy is that the commitment and self-respect which the Negroes usually demonstrate in pursuing the power strategy may engender respect on the part of the large white community – after the initial heat of conflict has subsided.

Another indirect and eventual way that the power strategy can lead to more favorable attitudinal bonds is through the mechanism of dissonance reduction. If as a result of substantive gains a group must be treated differently (more equal), there is a tendency to regard them differently (more equal) in order to make one's beliefs and attitudes congruent with one's behavior.

There is a third reason why a power strategy designed to obtain substantive concessions may achieve attitude change as well, particularly for a group which is currently less privileged and exercises less power. This refers to an important precondition for achieving a stable and healthy intergroup relationship – equal status and power between groups. This suggests that as long as group A remains at a power disadvantage and there is a potential for achieving power parity, A's mix of power and attitude change tactics will include relatively more power tactics. Thus, the power strategy for the civil rights groups during the last decade has dominated the attitude change strategy. This principle is also illustrated by the warlike actions of the Soviet Union during the period after the Second World War, when the United States alone possessed the atom bomb.

Whatever the existing balance of power, whenever B makes a move which would build his relative power, A will tend to act primarily in terms of the power strategy. This is illustrated by the United States' bargaining commitment moves when it discovered Soviet missiles in Cuba and when the Soviets attempted to make inroads in the Middle East and the Congo during the Suez and Congo crises respectively.

Implications

Recognition of these dilemmas is the first step toward developing a theory of social action which specifies the conditions under which one should conform to the tactical requirements of one strategy versus the other. But better theory is not enough. The agent of social change needs the behavioral skills required by simultaneously or sequentially mixed strategies. For example, international officials and civil rights leaders should be flexible enough to employ strategies of attitude change when a particular campaign reaches the negotiation phase.

What are the implications for training of leaders of groups

advocating major social change? Human relations training generally and laboratory learning in particular are geared to developing insights and skills central to the strategy of attitude change and are less relevant to the power strategy. I suggest that the conception of the problem of change should be broadened to incorporate – as necessary and legitimate – the power strategy.[1] We must understand what demands on leadership behavior are imposed by the power strategy of change both during the phase when power thinking necessarily dominates group leadership and the phase when preserving a power base is merely a consideration in designing an attitude change strategy. If these specialists deplore these power tactics simply because they violate their personal model of preferred social behavior, their advice which *is* appropriate and badly needed by the practitioner will be taken less seriously by him.

1. In the interest of sharpening the issues about our conception of the problem, I offer the following assertions regarding the role of bargaining, power, and violence in social change:

First, bargaining and bargaining tactics (including tactical deception, bluff, commitment, promises, threats, and threat fulfilment) are often necessary in social change situations where there are basic conflicts of interest. Moreover, many of these tactical operations are amoral in such situations.

Second, attempts to create cooperative relations between parties are more effective if there is some parity in their power. Power of a party derives from its capacity to influence some aspect of the fate of the other – either rewards or punishments. Often the only avenue open to a party with less relative power is to increase its capacity to harm (embarrass or inconvenience) the other. Moreover, it may be necessary for the party to engage in a series of maneuvers which are increasingly persuasive in communicating to the other party both a capacity and a willingness to use the power.

Third, where they are used, tactics of non-violence are effective at least in part because the other group perceives this method as an alternative to violence. The option of violence is indirectly suggested *by advocating non-violence*.

Fourth, there is experimental evidence that a cooperative bid by A is more effective in eliciting a cooperative response from B when it occurs against a series of non-cooperative moves by A. Maybe this paradox also operates in some social situations creating an incentive for initial non-cooperation.

References

BERKOWITZ, L. (1962), *Aggression: A Social Psychological Analysis*, McGraw-Hill.

BLAKE, R. R. (1959), 'Psychology and the crisis of statesmanship', *American Psychologist*, vol. 14, pp. 87–94.

BOULDING, K. (1962), *Conflict and Defense: A General Theory*, Harper & Row.

'City accelerates fight on poverty', *New York Times*, July 28, 1964, p. 15.

DEUTSCH, M. (1962), 'A psychological basis for peace', in Q. Wright, W. M. Evan and M. Deutsch (eds.), *Preventing World War III: Some Proposals*, Simon and Schuster.

GIBB, J. R. (1964), 'Climate for trust formation', in L. P. Bradford, J. R. Gibb and K. D. Benne (eds.), *T-Group Theory and Laboratory Method: Innovation in Re-education*, Wiley.

JANIS, I. L., and KATZ, D. (1959), 'The reduction of intergroup hostility: research problems and hypotheses', *Journal of conflict Resolution*, vol. 3, pp. 85–100.

KELMAN, H. C. (1962), 'Changing attitudes through international activities', *J. soc. Issues*, no. 18, pp. 68–87.

NAESS, A. (1957), 'A systematization of Gandhian ethics of conflict resolution', *J. conflict Resolution*, no. 1, pp. 140–55.

OSGOOD, C. E. (1959), 'Suggestions for winning the real war with Communism', *J. conflict Resolution*, no. 3, 295–325.

RAPOPORT, A. (1960), *Fights, Games and Debates*, University of Michigan Press.

SCHELLING, T. (1960), *The Strategy of Conflict*, Harvard University Press.

SHERIF, M. (ed.) (1962), *Intergroup Relations and Leadership*, Wiley.

WALTON, R. E., and MCKERSIE, R. B. (1965), *A Behavioral Theory of Labor Negotiations*, McGraw-Hill.

Acknowledgements

Permission to reproduce the readings in this volume is acknowledged to the following sources:

1 University of Oregon
2 American Psychological Association
3 *Journal of Applied Behavioral Science*
4 *Administrative Science Quarterly*
5 The Innovation Group
6 *Journal of Management Studies*
7 The MIT Press
8 Human Organization
9 University of Pittsburgh Press
10 Holt, Rinehart & Winston Inc.
12 John Wiley & Sons Inc.
13 *Administrative Science Quarterly*
14 *Journal of Social Sciences*
15 Harper & Row Inc.
16 John Wiley & Sons Inc.
17 Professor W. A. Gamson
18 *Journal of Applied Behavioural Science*

Author Index

Subject Index

Systemic change, 326–35, 353
Systems technology, 9

T-groups, 260, 445
Task structure, 223–4, 243, 245
Tavistock Institute, 307, 318, 324, 338, 352
Technetonic society, 9
Technocrats, 96
Technology, 45, 144, 157, 169, 180
Teleology, 14
Teleonomy, 14
Tennessee Valley Authority (TVA), 146, 469, 471–2
Tension, management of, 202–3
Theory-structures, 16–17
Therapeutic community, 231–3
Third parties, 390, 475
Threats, 384
Townsend Movement, 257, 260
Trade unions, 228–9, 234, 350, 371, 408, 411, 481
Training programs, 304

Transportation, 292–4
Trist studies *see* Coal mine studies
Turbulent environment, 145–7, 154–5, 221, 288–90, 295

Utilization process, 27
United States, 18–19, 55–6, 102–4, 411, 415–16
Universities, 102–4, 175, 203–5, 215–18, 221–3, 349, 350

Variables, 424
Vertical conflict, 348–51
Voluntary associations, 256–7, 258

Work values, 223

Xerox example, 172

YMCA example, 257, 258

Zeigarnik effect, 336–7

Penguin Modern Management

Readings

Business Strategy
Edited by H. Igor Ansoff

Collective Bargaining
Edited by Allan Flanders

Consumer Behaviour
Edited by A. S. C. Ehrenberg and F. G. Pyatt

Management and Motivation
Edited by Victor H. Vroom and Edward L. Deci

Management Decision Making
Edited by Lawrence A. Welsch and Richard M. Cyert

Management Information Systems
Edited by T. W. McRae

Management of Change and Conflict
Edited by John M. Thomas and Warren G. Bennis

Management of Production
Edited by M. K. Starr

Marketing Research
Edited by Joseph Seibert and Gordon Wills

Modern Financial Management
Edited by B. V. Carsberg and H. C. Edey

Modern Marketing Management
Edited by R. J. Lawrence and M. J. Thomas

Organization Theory
Edited by D. S. Pugh

Organizational Growth and Development
Edited by W. H. Starbuck

Personnel Management
Edited by D. E. McFarland

Programming for Optimal Decisions
Edited by P. G. Moore and S. D. Hodges

Systems Thinking
Edited by F. E. Emery

Trade Unions
Edited by W. E. J. McCarthy

Texts

Management and the Social Sciences
Tom Lupton

Writers on Organizations
D. S. Pugh, O. J. Hickson and C. R. Hinings